AMERICAN INFIDELITY

AMERICAN INFIDELITY

THE GILDED AGE BATTLE OVER FREETHOUGHT, FREE LOVE, AND FEMINISM

STEVEN K. GREEN

OXFORD

UNIVERSITY PRESS

OXFORD

UNIVERSITY PRESS

Oxford University Press is a department of the University of Oxford.
It furthers the University's objective of excellence in research, scholarship,
and education by publishing worldwide. Oxford is a registered trade mark of
Oxford University Press in the UK and certain other countries.

Published in the United States of America by Oxford University Press
198 Madison Avenue, New York, NY 10016, United States of America.

CIP data is on file at the Library of Congress

ISBN 978–0–19–782226–5

DOI: 10.1093/oso/9780197822265.001.0001

Printed by Sheridan Books, Inc., United States of America

The manufacturer's authorized representative in the EU for product safety is
Oxford University Press España S.A. of Parque Empresarial San Fernando de Henares,
Avenida de Castilla, 2 – 28830 Madrid (www.oup.es/en or product.safety@oup.com).
OUP España S.A. also acts as importer into Spain of products made by the manufacturer.

Contents

Introduction

In 1887, Charles B. Reynolds stood in the dock of the county court in Morristown, New Jersey, accused of blasphemy. The court documents described Reynolds as "a missionary, lecturer and writer on free-thought" who had been going from town to town "lecturing, preaching and distributing writings on his favorite topic." The charge of blasphemy arose from a pamphlet Reynolds had written, conveniently titled "Blasphemy and the Bible," which he had distributed on the streets of Morristown. The pamphlet ridiculed the god of the Old Testament for being intemperate, jealous, blundering, and afraid of people. Jesus fared no better in his depiction: he was a loud and annoying god-child who, like other children, "cried and screamed, squealed and kicked," and "was spanked when he was naughty." A Grand Jury indicted Reynolds under a blasphemy statute that dated back to colonial times. At the conclusion of a two-day trial in May, the jury returned a guilty verdict within an hour, and Reynolds was fined $25 plus court costs of $50.[1]

Reynolds's trial might otherwise have remained inconspicuous and forgotten had it not been for the fame of his defense counsel, Robert G. Ingersoll.[2] Ingersoll, known as the "Great Agnostic," was the nation's leading freethinker and arguably its most popular orator and lecturer, rivaling his friend Mark Twain. (Ironically, in his public lectures, Ingersoll's inflammatory rhetoric likely surpassed that of Reynolds.)[3] Ingersoll's presence guaranteed press coverage of the trial, and newspapers reported his impassioned closing statement, which was delivered over the course of two days. But Ingersoll's heroic efforts were ultimately for naught.[4]

The *New York Times* applauded the conviction, calling Ingersoll's arguments about freedom of speech "irrelevant" and a guise for permitting public indecency. Blasphemy—"speech on religious subjects as is calculated to disgust and revolt a large part of the community"—was legitimately a crime, the *Times* declared, and even if Reynolds's writings and remarks were not technically blasphemous, they were made in "bad taste," and the jury did "what every jury should do when the breach of taste amounts to a gross indecency." The *Times* regretted the "mouse [of] a fine of $25." But at least "the State of New Jersey has gone on record against blasphemy."[5]

Reynolds's trial was one skirmish in a larger battle pitting the dominant evangelical Protestant establishment against emerging forms of religious heterodoxy, especially "freethought." The establishment's goal was not necessarily to eradicate or marginalize religious skepticism—or not only that. They sought to advance Christian moral reform and to combat threats to Christian culture in the form of "vice." While the latter included activities such as gambling, alcohol consumption, and graft, the moral campaign against vice focused in large part on sex. Obscenity, prostitution, abortion, contraceptives, and "free love" were all targets. And they all, with the exception of prostitution, became identified with religious freethought. The connection was not tenuous. To push the boundaries of socially acceptable literature and art, to advocate for abortion and contraceptive use, to promote permissive sexual relations, and to urge gender equality within and without marital relationships—all presupposed a certain level of personal freedom from the control of the church or the government. Advocates of freethought understood the connection, as did their detractors. As the *New York Times* commented at the conclusion of Reynolds's trial, "[o]bscene literature and blasphemous literature stand upon the same footing. Both are to be suppressed, and the promoters of both to be punished for a violation of public decency."[6]

At the same time, some four hundred miles to the south in the Virginia Piedmont, a parallel case was underway. In a column adjoining its coverage of the Reynolds case, the freethought journal *The Truth Seeker* related the arrest of Elmina Drake Slenker, an occasional contributor to the journal who wrote pamphlets providing candid information on birth control, sexual relations, and sexual pathologies such as bestiality. Prosecutors charged Slenker with distributing obscene materials through the mail; the *New York Times* asserted that her "free thinking and infidel character" had led her for years to carry on "a wide 'free love' correspondence of the vilest character." After Slenker refused to swear on the Bible at her arraignment the *Times* ridiculed her "peculiar faith" and then applauded that the sixty-year-old "homely" woman was unable to make bail.[7]

The *New York Times* was hardly an outlier. Many in the nation's political and Protestant establishments believed that the moral order and stability of the nation were under siege. Vice and immorality were rampant, they claimed, particularly in the cesspools of America's cities. Prostitution was common, and its promoters preyed on poor immigrant children, turning them into child prostitutes. Saloons and gambling halls were abundant, serving as nests for all sorts of crimes. Pornography was readily available and as were nickel and dime pulp fictions that glorified crime and other immorality and threatened to ensnare and corrupt the innocent.[8] These maladies had led civic and religious leaders in New York City to organize the Society for the Suppression of Obscene Literature in 1872, which the following year became the Society for the Suppression of Vice.[9] For forty years, the organization was led by Anthony Comstock. Armed with criminal authority from the New York legislature, and as a special agent for the US Post Office Department, he prosecuted thousands of people for promoting and selling obscene materials. And because obscenity was ill-defined in the statute, it was left to Comstock, a conservative Christian, to determine what fell afoul of the law. Although Comstock detested all purveyors of vice and obscenity, he possessed a particular animus for freethinkers and nonbelievers like Elmina Slenker. A run-of-the-mill smut dealer might simply flaunt Christian morality for monetary gain. By contrast, freethinkers who advocated free inquiry, free love, and sexual equality—many of whom were members of the educated and professional classes—defiantly challenged the Christian foundations of morality. Comstock thus attacked freethinkers and their publications with a vengeance, conflating "[t]he infidel, the free-lover, [with] the smut-dealer." According to one historian, "[i]mpiety and indecency were synonymous to [Comstock] and he used epithets like 'infidel,' 'free luster,' and 'abortionist's pimp' interchangeably. Whatever Comstock deemed objectionable on religious or moral grounds became illegal."[10]

Although Comstock's forty-year obsession with combating vice and obscenity bordered on the pathological—and many people condemned his tactics—those within the Protestant and Catholic mainstream generally shared his belief about the threats presented by obscenity and his view that freethinkers were complicit in its promotion. Several leading freethinkers endured prosecution and jail time at the hands of Comstock. Freethinkers, or "Liberals," as they were frequently called, were the leading critics of his crusade and of the 1873 federal obscenity law that he eagerly enforced (the "Comstock Act" or "Comstock Law"). After Comstock secured the conviction of freethinker Ezra Heywood for mailing a copy of his critique of marriage, *Cupid's Yokes*, Liberals organized the National Defense Association, the forerunner to the American Civil Liberties Union. The Liberals' defense of free inquiry and the dissemination of information regarding birth control—and their broader defense of the secularization of society—opened them to widespread criticism. "Liberalism," wrote *Scribner's Monthly* magazine in 1881, "is another name for infidelity, and if infidelity naturally sympathizes with dirt, it is well that we know it. At any rate, 'liberals' are the only professed and open defenders of dirt, and it is represented by the men who are interested in pushing impure literature through the mails." The definitions of "infidel" and sexual "infidelity" had all but merged.[11]

This book examines the late nineteenth-century battle over freethought, free love, and feminism, a battle that in many ways was the most visible engagement in the cultural war between religious orthodoxy and religious heterodoxy. The term "free love" encompasses more than the advocacy of multiple sexual partners within or outside of marriage. Indeed, the number of "practicing" free lovers—meaning those who abjured marriage and had multiple sexual partners—was numerically insignificant, and many self-proclaimed proponents of free love disavowed accusations of promiscuity. In the nineteenth century, free love encompassed belief in promoting sexual equality, liberalizing divorce laws, reevaluating marital roles and authority, increasing reproductive freedoms, and, although rarely publicly stated, accepting same-sex relationships. It also celebrated the promotion of sexuality in art and literature.[12] The number of people who supported these causes was much larger, and they presented a challenge to Victorian Christian culture. Moral crusaders like Comstock understood that "free love," in this broader sense, was a significant threat to traditional Christian society, and they intentionally used the more sensational understanding of the term to undermine arguments about sexual freedom and equality and free inquiry.[13]

This book explores the motivations behind the establishment's late-nineteenth-century moral crusade against freethought, free love, and gender equality. This crusade occurred at a time when Protestantism was at the height of its power and influence—*the* dominant and seemingly unchallengeable force in the culture.[14] However, as many historians have noted, Protestants felt far from secure. They saw threats to their vision of a Christian America arising from within and without. From within, evangelical Protestantism faced challenges from Darwinism, biblical criticism, and the growth of pre-millennialist movements such as Adventism that disputed the dominant evangelical belief about creating God's kingdom on earth. While many moderate Protestants were able to reconcile aspects of evolution and biblical criticism with their theological framework, most conservatives could not shake the sense of theological compromise if not spiritual capitulation, producing what some called "modern doubt" and what others have termed the "spiritual crisis of the Gilded Age."[15] From without, Protestantism faced competition from immigration, socialism, Catholicism, and Mormonism, among other forces, as well as pressures arising from urbanization, industrialization, and labor unrest. In his 1885 bestselling book, *Our Country: Its Possible Future and Its Present Crisis*, Reverend Josiah Strong listed immigration, Catholicism, wealth disparities, Mormonism, socialism, the city, and conflicts over public education among the perils facing the nation. Conservative Protestants like Comstock vowed to fight back. As the *Presbyterian Quarterly* wrote in 1888, "[t]he new and strange perils that have come upon us—socialism, anarchism, Romanism, saloonism, political corruption, and kindred evils—can be relieved only by organized applied Christianity." The moral reform movement and campaign against vice were manifestations of this muscular, *applied* Christianity.[16]

Compared to the intractable challenges confronting Protestantism, the small freethought movement did not appear on first impression to represent a serious threat.[17] Why did conservative Protestants and moral crusaders like Anthony Comstock feel imperiled by freethinkers and include them among the "perils" listed above? Susan Jacoby has called the Gilded Age the "golden age" of American freethought, and she and other scholars have documented a resurgence of freethought during this period. Attendance at freethought rallies and events surged during the decades; thousands regularly attended lectures by Robert Ingersoll and Victoria Woodhull, though many people may have come for the novelty and entertainment value. Thousands also signed petitions on behalf of freethought causes, and *The Truth Seeker* magazine claimed over 50,000 subscribers by the 1890s.[18] While the appellation "golden age" is therefore deserving in a sense, the movement was fractured and never large (although admittedly, a greater number of Americans held heterodox beliefs than those who identified or affiliated with the freethought movement). Still, the movement punched above its weight; several leading freethinkers—Ralph Waldo Emerson, Robert Ingersoll, Octavius Brooks Frothingham, Francis E. Abbot, Elizabeth Cady Stanton, Victoria Woodhull, and D.M. Bennett—were quite prominent and had a significant impact on public attitudes about religious issues in the late nineteenth century. So, in a sense, Jacoby is correct that the Gilded Age represents "the high-watermark of freethought as an influential movement in American society."[19]

"Freethought," of course, is not self-defining. It included people holding a variety of beliefs, ranging from liberal Unitarians and Universalists, to spiritualists, to "New Thought" and "Mind Cure" (Christian Science) enthusiasts, to theistic and nontheistic "free religionists," to humanists, agnostics, and then atheists. Common among all of them was their rejection of orthodox Christian doctrine and the authority of the Bible and its purveyors, and their embrace of church–state separation. Freethinkers also advanced an epistemology based on reason and science. Many participants within the suffrage and women's rights movements, including Lucretia Mott, Susan B. Anthony, Matilda Joslyn Gage, and Elizabeth Cady Stanton, were also freethinkers.[20] In most instances, according to historian Leigh Schmidt, officials and clergy simply tolerated or ignored the local "village atheists." But that tolerance was frequently conditional and could quickly turn into intolerance if a local freethinker became too demonstrative. More than one freethinker served time in jail for their heterodoxy.[21]

If freethinkers shared another characteristic, it was their commitment to free inquiry and the freedom to broadcast their heterodox ideas. Freethinkers also generally believed that institutionalized religion, and Christian orthodoxy in particular, stifled free inquiry, scientific exploration, and human equality. As a result, many freethinkers were quite vocal about exposing the hypocrisy and "falsehoods" of Christianity. This made freethought a major threat to Protestant hegemony. Even though conservative Protestants preferred to call freethinkers "infidels," most were more accurately classified as "heretics" or "apostates," meaning they had renounced their previous orthodox beliefs. Indeed, many freethought leaders had previously trained as Christian ministers. Heresy and apostasy had always represented a greater threat to orthodox Christianity than heathenism. And while some freethinkers rejected the idea of religion outright, others, including many free religionists, sought to create an alternative nontheistic religion, what Ingersoll and Stanton called "the religion of Humanity." Finally, freethinkers were at the forefront of promoting women's rights—including marriage reform—and a true separation of church and state, one that would dismantle the quasi-legal privileges that Christianity enjoyed. As historian David Rabban has written, "freethought and free love [combined] interposed personal sovereignty and rationality in social, religious, and sexual spheres against the power of church and state." All these tendencies meant that freethought represented a significant if not an existential challenge to institutionalized, orthodox Christianity.[22]

Several previous works, both popular and scholarly, have explored aspects of this book's coverage. The leading figures discussed in this book—Robert Ingersoll, Anthony Comstock, Victoria Woodhull, Elizabeth Cady Stanton, D.M. Bennett, Octavius Brooks Frothingham, and Francis Abbot—have all received attention in earlier works.[23] Each of those studies has its own particular focus, whether it is on women's rights, nineteenth-century sexuality and its regulation, free expression and censorship, or the evolution of freethought. This book seeks to identify the overlapping and reinforcing aspects of these impulses and the way in which they impacted attitudes about the intersection of religion, culture, sexuality, and the law.[24] In so doing, this book seeks to answer three questions: Why did the freethought movement represent such a threat to orthodox Christianity, and how much of that threat was tied to its association with sexual reform? Why, despite its prominence, was freethought never able to attract and hold a sizable following sufficient to establish itself as a viable alternative to liberal Christianity and as an intellectual force in the culture? And why did Stanton's comprehensive vision of women's rights, which included gender reform, fail to gain traction, such that the movement had to accept more modest outcomes?

We begin by examining the conditions that gave rise to the freethought movement in the wake of the Civil War. Freethought emerged not as the only option in a lively market of ideas, but as the leading critic of Protestantism as the dominant cultural force in the United States.

NOTES

1. "The Trial of Charles B. Reynolds for Blasphemy, Morristown, New Jersey, 1887," in *American State Trials*, ed. John D. Lawson (St. Louis: Thomas Law Books, 1914–1936), 16:795–857; "Blasphemy," *The Truth Seeker*, Oct. 30, 1886, 696–697; "Convicted and Fined," ibid., May 28, 1887, 344–345; "Jersey Law Triumphant: Reynolds Found Guilty of Blasphemy," *New York Times*, May 21, 1887, 8; Leigh Eric Schmidt, *Village Atheists: How America's Unbelievers Made Their Way in a Godly Nation* (Princeton, NJ: Princeton University Press, 2016), 171–209.

2. "Mr. Ingersoll Will Defend Mr. Reynolds," *The Truth Seeker*, Aug. 21, 1886, 537; "On Trial for Blasphemy: Col. Ingersoll's Defense of Charles B. Reynolds," *New York Times*, May 20, 1887, 8.

3. Susan Jacoby, *The Great Agnostic: Robert Ingersoll and American Freethought* (New Haven, CT: Yale University Press, 2013), 1–15; see Robert G. Ingersoll, "The Gods" (1872), in Robert G. Ingersoll, *The Writings of Robert G. Ingersoll* (New York: Dresden, 1900), 1:7–90 (hereinafter *Works*).

4. "On Trial for Blasphemy: Col. Ingersoll's Defense of Charles B. Reynolds," *New York Times*, May 20, 1887, 8; "Jersey Law Triumphant," ibid., May 21, 1887, 8.

5. "The Conviction of Reynolds," *New York Times*, May 21, 1887, 4; "Jersey Law Triumphant: Reynolds Found Guilty of Blasphemy," ibid., May 21, 1887, 8.

6. "The Conviction of Reynolds," *New York Times*, May 21, 1887, 4.

7. "Mrs. Slenker's Arrest," *The Truth Seeker*, May 14, 1887, 312; "Violating Postal Laws," *New York Times*, April 29, 1887, 5; "Defiant Mrs. Slenker," ibid., April 30, 1887, 5; Schmidt, *Village Atheists*, 210–221.

8. Paul S. Boyer, *Purity in Print: The Vice-Society Movement and Book Censorship in America* (New York: Charles Scribner's Sons, 1968), 3–5; Timothy J. Gilfoyle, *City of Eros: New York City, Prostitution, and the Commercialization of Sex, 1790–1920* (New York: W.W. Norton, 1992), 58, 65, 181–195; Anthony Comstock, *Frauds Exposed; or, How People Are Deceived and Robbed, and Youth Corrupted* (New York: J.H. Brown, 1880).

9. "The Society for the Suppression of Obscene Literature," *New York Times*, May 9, 1872, 3.

10. Comstock, *Frauds Exposed*, 422; Anthony Comstock, *Traps for the Young*, ed. Robert Bremner (Cambridge, MA: Belknap Press of Harvard University Press, 1967), xvii.

11. Janice Wood, "The National Defense Association: Liberal Protector of Free Speech," in *An Indispensable Liberty: The Fight for Free Speech in the Nineteenth Century*, ed. C.C. Cronin (Carbondale: Southern Illinois Press, 2016), 228–249; "Mr. Comstock's Book," *Scribner's Monthly* (April 1881), 950.

12. Nicola Beisel, *Imperiled Innocents: Anthony Comstock and Family Reproduction in Victorian America* (Princeton, NJ: Princeton University Press, 1997), 164–167; Amy Werbel, *Lust on Trial: Censorship and the Rise of American Obscenity in the Age of Anthony Comstock* (New York: Columbia University Press, 2018), 261–279.

13. Taylor Stoehr, *Free Love in America: A Documentary History* (New York: AMS Press, 1979), 3–39.

14. See Kenneth Scott Latourette, *A History of the Expansion of Christianity: The Great Century* (New York: Harper & Bros., 1941), 4:457–461; Robert T. Handy, *Undermined Establishment: Church–State Relations in America, 1880–1920* (Princeton, NJ: Princeton University Press, 1991), 8–12.

15. See Paul Carter, *The Spiritual Crisis of the Gilded Age* (DeKalb: Northern Illinois University Press, 1971).

16. Steven K. Green, *The Second Disestablishment: Church and State in Nineteenth-Century America* (New York: Oxford University Press, 2010), 329–334; Josiah Strong, *Our Country: Its Possible Future and Its Present Crisis* (New York: Baker and Taylor, 1885, 1891), viii–x; "The Personal Liberty Movement," *Presbyterian Quarterly* (Jan. 1888), 544.

17. See Martin E. Marty, *The Infidel: Freethought and American Religion* (Cleveland: Meriden Books, 1961), 141 ("Native American freethought was feeble.").

18. Susan Jacoby, *Freethinkers: A History of American Secularism* (New York: Metropolitan/Owl Books, 2004), 149–185; Sidney Warren, *American Freethought, 1860–1914* (New York: Gordian Press, 1966, 1943), 15, 26–28; David C. Hoffman, *American Freethought* (Baltimore: The Johns Hopkins Press, 2025), ch. 4; "Freethinkers in Convention," *New York Times*, Sept. 23, 1879, 5 (reporting 5,000 attendees at a New York convention); "The Freethinkers Go Home," ibid., Sept. 3, 1883, 4 (reporting 2,000 attendees at a convention).

19. Jacoby, *Freethinkers*, 151; Roderick Bradford, *D.M. Bennett: The Truth Seeker* (Amherst, NY: Prometheus Books, 2006), 14–18.

20. Warren, *American Freethought*, 20, 42, 128–129; David Sehat, *The Myth of American Religious Freedom* (New York: Oxford University Press, 2016), 147–154.

21. Schmidt, *Village Atheists*, 202–204.

22. Leigh Eric Schmidt, *The Church of Saint Thomas Paine: A Religious History of American Secularism* (Princeton, NJ: Princeton University Press, 2022); Warren, *American Freethought*, 20; "The Gods," Ingersoll, *Works*, 1:89; David M. Rabban, "The Free Speech League, the ACLU, and Changing Conceptions of Free Speech in American History," *Stanford Law Review* 45 (1992): 47–114, 53.

23. Jacoby, *The Great Agnostic*; Frank Smith, *Robert G. Ingersoll, A Life* (Buffalo, NY: Prometheus Books, 1990); Amy Sohn, *The Man Who Hated Women: Sex, Censorship, and Civil Liberties in the Gilded Age* (New York: Farrar, Straus and Giroux, 2021); Werbel, *Lust on Trial*; Beisel, *Imperiled Innocents*; Anna Louise Bates, *Weeder in the Garden of the Lord: Anthony Comstock's Life and Career* (Lanham, MD: University Press of America, 1995); Boyer, *Purity in Print*; Heywood Broun and Margaret Leech, *Anthony Comstock, Roundsman of the Lord* (New York: Albert & Charles Boni, 1927); Amanda Frisken, *Victoria Woodhull's Sexual Revolution: Political Theatre and Popular Press in Nineteenth-Century America* (Philadelphia: University of Pennsylvania Press, 2011); Barbara Goldsmith, *Other Powers: The Age of Suffrage, Spiritualism, and the Scandalous Victoria Woodhull* (New York: Alfred A. Knopf, 1998); Mary Gabriel, *Notorious Victoria: The Life of Victoria Woodhull, Uncensored* (Chapel Hill, NC: Algonquin Books, 1998); J. Wade Caruthers, *Octavius Brooks Frothingham, Gentle Radical* (Tuscaloosa: University of Alabama Press, 1977); Sydney E. Ahlstrom and Robert Bruce Mullin, *The Scientific Theist: A Life of Francis Ellingwood Abbot* (Macon, GA: Mercer University Press, 1987); Jacoby, *Freethinkers*; Warren, *American Freethought*.

24. David Hoffman's recent book, *American Freethought*, addresses much of this book's material in its fourth chapter, though Hoffman's work extends from the 1790s to the mid-twentieth century. Geoffrey Stone's *Sex and the Constitution* (New York: Liveright, 2017), also addresses this intersection but dedicates only thirteen pages to discussing this material. Finally, David Sehat's excellent *Myth of American Religious Freedom* dedicates two chapters to discussing the intersection of these competing forces.

I

The Freethought Impulse

Between February and April 1876, the noted evangelists Dwight L. Moody and Ira Sankey held a much-anticipated revival, drawing overflow crowds to the New York City Hippodrome—a massive structure that had formerly been the home to P.T. Barnum's Circus. Thousands of New Yorkers in search of spiritual sustenance packed the prayer meetings to hear Moody's inspirational preaching and Sankey's captivating gospel music. The two evangelists were "American Geniuses" for their ability to relate Christianity to the masses, wrote a fawning *New York Times*. Although Moody preached a traditional form of Calvinism that emphasized human sinfulness, he also offered the promise of God's redemption for everyone. Moody, as the leading spokesperson for Protestant evangelicalism, "more than any other single individual determined the religious climate of the country in the immediate post-war decade."[1]

Six months later, similarly large audiences packed another New York City auditorium to hear a series of three lectures by Professor Thomas Huxley, the famous British anthropologist and expositor of the theory of evolution. The *New York Times* reported that a "large and cultured audience" attended the lectures, which indicated the broad interest in Huxley's remarks. Despite Huxley being an avowed agnostic (he had reputedly coined the term "agnosticism" in 1869), and the controversy surrounding what had come to be called "Darwinism," the *Times* pleasingly reported that Huxley's defense of evolutionary theory did "not run counter to the Biblical account of creation"; rather than being "subversive of religious faith," as some had charged, "this narrative offers no difficulties, and, on the contrary, strengthens faith."[2] A less flattering account in the *Christian Union*, however, took Huxley to task for failing to indicate "how far is the whole present order of nature" was explained by evolution or to clarify "that nature was originally called into being by a

Divine Creator." The *New York Evangelist*'s report on Huxley's lectures was even more critical, finding his claims wholly unconvincing. "Evolution may be true, but certainly he has not proved it," wrote the journal. "On the whole, we think we will stand awhile longer with our Bibles, and read the first chapter of Genesis with veneration." In many respects, the differing opinions about Huxley's presentations expressed by the *Times* and the two religious journals reflected the variety of views that Americans held about evolutionary theory and its relation to the biblical account of creation.[3]

Most likely, few New Yorkers attended both Moody's revivals and Huxley's lectures; the men were largely speaking to different audiences (although the *Times* listed the names of a handful of local clergy who were seen at Huxley's lectures).[4] The strong interest in both events, however, demonstrates the dynamic religious climate of the final third of the nineteenth century; despite the veneer of Protestant hegemony, attitudes about religious belief and its role in American society ran the gamut. Paradoxically, the Gilded Age was both one of the most religious eras in American history and the most skeptical, until our own.

The Dominance and Dilemma of Protestantism

By 1870, evangelical Protestantism—a belief in the authority if not inerrancy of the Bible and of its binding moral force—was the dominant form of American Christianity and was at the height of its broader cultural influence. Although the rise of American evangelicalism can be traced to the First Great Awakening of the late 1730s and 1740s, Gilded Age evangelicals traced their lineage to the Second Great Awakening, which took place around the turn of the nineteenth century. This series of camp meetings and revivals spawned new religious movements including the Disciples of Christ and Seventh Day Adventists and infiltrated orthodox denominations like the Presbyterians and Congregationalists, but it chiefly benefited groups with preexisting evangelical leanings: Methodists and Baptists. What connected all evangelicals was an emphasis on an experiential faith, of being "born again," and of receiving God's forgiveness of sin by accepting Jesus's redemptive mission. While the evangelical fervor of the camp meeting revivals would occasionally cool, new religious revivals sprung up in the 1830s and 1850s. These later revivals, led by evangelists like Charles G. Finney, were more likely to take place in urban areas and had deeper institutional ties.

Religious historians have long commented on how an informal "Protestant establishment" existed in nineteenth-century America, one in which a Protestant ethos held sway over the nation's culture and institutions.[5] Writing in 1873, Joseph P. Thompson, minister of New York's Broadway Tabernacle, estimated that membership in the seven major Protestant denominations exceeded 6.1 million people across 68,000 churches, but that "the number of persons who habitually attend the worship of these churches is probably 15,000,000." Thompson insisted that "[i]n reading the statistics of the American churches, it should be borne in mind that the term members by no means represents the total of worshippers in the several congregations, or of nominal adherents to a confession, but only those by their own act have united with the church proper."[6] Six years later, Philip Schaff of Union Theological Seminary offered a more generous, and possibly more accurate, estimate of church membership based on data from the 1870 US Census. Out of a total population of 38.5 million Americans, 21.6 million (including 73,000 Jews) attended religious worship, with the larger denominations being Methodists (6.5 million), Baptists (4 million), Presbyterians (2.2 million), and Catholics (2 million). Schaff's own data demonstrated that religious growth had recently slowed. The gain between 1860 and 1870 of 2.5 million adherents was only half of that of the previous decade, though he attributed that to the turmoil of the Civil War. Nevertheless, Schaff concluded that "[on] the whole we may venture to say that America, in proportion to her age and population, is better provided with churches, Sunday-schools, and religious institutions and agencies than any country in the world," save Great Britain.[7]

Church attendance was not the only measure of Protestantism's influence on the culture. Auxiliary religious organizations committed to the physical and moral betterment of humankind abounded: the Young Men's Christian Association (YMCA), the Salvation Army, the Woman's Christian Temperance Union (WCTU), the Student Volunteer Movement for Foreign Missions (SVM), and various Bible societies. Protestant norms informed daily customs, celebrations, and Sabbath observances, with all states imposing limitations on labor, business operations, and recreation on Sundays (enforcement was varied).[8] The most significant indicator of Protestantism's influence was the "nonsectarian" character of America's public schools, which advanced a form of pan-Protestantism through their curriculum, prayer, and

Bible reading. Even though many schools had dropped the more overtly devotional aspects of nonsectarian instruction by 1870—particularly in cities with growing Catholic and Jewish populations—the residual Protestant character of American public education was undeniable. And many of the nation's colleges, including public universities, operated under the sway of religious denominations or had administrators with religious backgrounds. For Protestants of the Gilded Age, education had become "symbolic of both our national unity and God's handiwork in history. As such, it was a sacred cause, worthy of religious devotion."[9] Thus, as religious historian Robert T. Handy once observed, "[i]n many ways, the middle third of the nineteenth century was more of a 'Protestant Age' than was the colonial period with its established churches."[10]

Yet Protestantism's influence over America's culture and institutions was tenuous. The most immediate challenge came from the dramatic rise in Catholicism, one of the forces that Josiah Strong had identified as threats to the nation. It was also intimately bound up with three others: immigration, education, and the city. The city had "become a serious menace to our civilization," Strong insisted, "because in it . . . each of the dangers we have discussed is enhanced, and all are focalized. . . . Because our cities are so largely foreign, Romanism finds in them its chief strength."[11] Starting in the 1830s, Protestants had reacted with growing distress to the upsurge in immigration from Ireland and the Catholic portions of Germany, which arose at a time when Protestants were consolidating their control over the culture and its institutions, including the schools. In the forty years between 1830 and 1870, the Catholic population had increased almost tenfold, to two million. A new influx of Catholic immigrants after the Civil War—now chiefly from central, southern, and eastern Europe—would boost the Catholic population to approximately twelve million by the end of the century.[12] As early as the 1840s, conflicts broke out across the country over Protestant religious exercises in the public schools and religious biases in the curriculum, a controversy that was only exacerbated by Catholic demands for a pro rata share of the public education funds to support its parochial schools. In urban areas, such as New York, Boston, Philadelphia, Baltimore, and Chicago, Catholic leaders began building political power and were able to extract patronage from city officials, including funding for their orphanages and other charitable operations. At the same time, Protestants alleged, Catholic leaders told their parishioners whom to vote for and disparaged essential republican principles such as self-governance, freedom of conscience, and the separation of church and state. As Strong summed it up, "[m]anifestly there is an irreconcilable difference between papal principles and the fundamental principles of our free institutions."[13]

The growth of Mormonism, with its theocratic blending of church and state and its practice of polygamy—anathema to Protestants—also threatened to undermine Protestant morality and fundamental American values. Even though polygamy garnered the greatest attention, critics acknowledged that it was practiced by only a small number of elites; as concerning for Protestant leaders was the near total dominance by LDS church officials over all aspects of Mormons' lives and the intense proselytizing fervor of Mormon missionaries. Protestants took solace in the fact that Mormonism was confined to the Great Basin in the West and was facing the legal wrath of the federal government which, through its campaign to eradicate polygamy, was also subduing the "ecclesiastical despotism" of the LDS church. Nonetheless, Strong warned, "the growth of this anti-republican power is such that, if not checked speedily, it will cause serious trouble in the near future. We fear that the nature and extent of this danger are not fully comprehended by the nation at large."[14]

That said, the most serious challenges to evangelical Protestantism—the ones that caused the greatest distress among religious leaders—were intellectual. Evangelicals' belief in a literal interpretation of the Bible—along with the story of creation, the great flood, and the miracles of the Old and New Testaments—faced broadsides from new scientific discoveries and theories like evolution, from biblical ("higher") criticism imported from Germany, and from newer philosophies such as Auguste Comte's Positivism, which disputed the possibility of metaphysical knowledge.[15] Darwinian evolution, with its doctrine of natural selection, represented the greatest threat because its underlying premise challenged accepted Christian views of creation and design. Some, like natural science professor James Woodrow, reconciled biblical creation with evolution by placing science and religion in separate categories. "[A] proper definition of Evolution excludes all reference to the origin of forces and laws by which it works," Woodrow insisted, such "that it does not and cannot affect belief in God or in religion . . . . [O]n these principles all alleged contradictions of natural science by the Bible disappears." Taking a different tack, liberal Congregational minister Henry Ward Beecher sought to harmonize the outlines of evolutionary theory and biblical criticism with the essentials of Christian doctrine. Beecher argued that '[i]f simple acts would evince design, how much more [would] a vast universe, that by inherent laws gradually builded itself . . . and steadily wrought toward more complex, ingenious, and beautiful results!" "Whatever theory may prevail of the origin of man will not prevent the fact that man has come upon the earth by a divine method," Beecher wrote in 1871. "There will not be ultimately any incongruity between true science and true religion."[16]

Beecher did not speak for a majority of Protestants, however, particularly those with more conservative perspectives. Many Protestants simply could not reconcile Darwinian ideas of natural selection with the biblical account of divine creation. A leading critic of evolution, Princeton Seminary theologian Charles Hodge, charged that Darwinism "is tantamount to atheism." The "denial of design in nature is virtually the denial of God. Mr. Darwin's theory does deny all design in nature, therefore, his theory is virtually atheistical." Another critic concurred that "the onward march of science is slowly but surely destroying faith in the Bible." And the fact that a significant number of Protestant intellectuals like Beecher and Lyman Abbott were willing to reconcile Darwinism with their faith troubled evangelical leaders who perceived it as sowing doubt among rank-and-file believers.[17]

The mid-century inroads of biblical higher criticism had less of an impact on the average Protestant layperson than Darwinism did, though it may have influenced the theological perspectives of their seminary-trained pastors. Higher criticism was a critique of a literal interpretation of the Bible. Throughout the history of Western Christianity, questions had arisen about how closely the Bible's message and authority were tied to a literal reading of the biblical text, in contrast to viewing certain passages as allegorical. By the early nineteenth century, however, the Bible's authority "had come to rest on a thoroughly literal reading of the text." According to historian James Turner, American "Protestants in general and Evangelicals in particular read the Bible with a flat-footed literalness unparalleled in the annals of Christianity." As Charles Hodge, that spokesperson for Protestant orthodoxy, asserted in 1873, "the Scriptures of the Old and New Testament are the Word of God, written under the inspiration of the Holy Spirit, and [are] therefore infallible, and of divine authority in all things pertaining to faith and practice, and consequently free from all error." The inspirational and infallible qualities were "not confined to moral and religious truths" alone but "extended to the statements of facts, whether scientific, historical, or geological." Thus, the instantaneous creation of humankind, the 6,000-year-old age of the earth, the Great Flood with Noah's Ark, and so forth, were all literally true.[18]

Higher criticism had arisen in German universities in the late eighteenth century even before evangelical biblical interpretation had "hardened into outright literalism." The movement took off in the 1830s with the publication of David Friedrich Strauss's *The Life of Jesus* (1835), translated into English a decade later, which challenged the accuracy of the Gospels' accounts of Jesus's life, declaring many of them to be myths. Strauss's explosive book was preceded by Charles Lyell's *Principles of Geology* (1833), which refuted the Bible's historical and geological timelines by arguing that the earth was millions of years old and had developed naturally and gradually.[19] From that point, it was impossible to prevent higher criticism from infecting theological study in Britain and the United States. British literary critic Matthew Arnold declared that "[t]o understand that the language of the Bible is fluid, passing, and literary, not rigid, fixed, and scientific, is the first step towards a right understanding of the Bible."[20]

Higher criticism made initial gains among American religious thinkers before the Civil War. The leader of liberal Unitarianism, Theodore Parker, proclaimed in an 1841 sermon that "modern criticism is fast breaking to pieces this idol which men have made out of the scriptures. It has shown that here are the most different works thrown together; that their authors . . . had only that inspiration that is common to other men equally pious and wise; that they were by no means infallible but were mistaken in facts or in reasoning." For Parker, the "current notions respecting the infallible inspiration of the Bible have no foundation in the Bible itself."[21] But the true impact of higher criticism was felt after the Civil War, when increasing numbers of American scholars undertook graduate or postgraduate studies in Germany, only to return to US universities and seminaries and pass on their knowledge to their students. The trend would facilitate the rise of Modernism within American Protestantism, liberalizing many previously evangelical churches and eventually leading to a backlash that produced Fundamentalism.[22]

These challenges to evangelical Protestant hegemony provided both the opportunity and the fuel for the rise of an active and visible freethought movement in the decades following the Civil War. However, the movement itself took root before that martial conflagration.

The Foundations of Gilded Age Freethought

Gilded Age freethought encompassed a broad range of perspectives about religion. On the rightward end of the spectrum were the liberal Unitarians, disciples of Theodore Parker, who rejected the denomination's continuing identification with Christianity and its essential doctrines. In the middle were Free Religionists, who disputed the idea of a Christian god and self-identified as rational theists but continued to insist on the importance of "religion." And on the left were agnostics and atheists, who doubted if not denied the existence of God and the value of religion. On the margins were spiritualists, who rejected the materialism of many freethinkers by believing in an active spirit world, but otherwise eschewed orthodox Christian doctrine and the authority of the Bible. What united them, in a broad sense, was their rejection of religious doctrine and authority and their embrace of church–state separation. As an unflattering article in *The Independent* described the larger movement, "[t]hey are spiritualists, free lovers, [and] loud-tongued infidels, who boast of the name infidel and curse with ribald jest the Church and all its works."

Depending on their perspective, freethinkers traced their origins to different sources.[23] The radical freethinkers on the left—skeptics, agnostics, and the handful of atheists—saw themselves as continuing in the tradition of eighteenth-century deism. They found inspiration in the writings of Voltaire, d'Holbach, Bolingbroke, and Hume, among others, but traced their intellectual origins to Thomas Paine, whom they embraced as a role model. Paine's writings, particularly his *Age of Reason*, with its blistering critique of clericalism, institutional Christianity, and biblical superstition, had set the tone for American deism during the 1790s and then for early nineteenth-century skepticism.[24] Gilded Age freethinkers embraced Paine as a true patriot and hero, not just for his stirring defense of independence and republicanism but also for his advocacy of freedom of thought. Paine's heroic status was only enhanced by the way he was vilified upon his return to America in 1802. In the eight years following the *Age of Reason*'s publication in 1794, reaction to the excesses of the French Revolution and the ascent of evangelicalism had all but discredited deistic thought. Paine's former friends—except Thomas Jefferson—abandoned him, and he died in poverty and obscurity in 1809. This enhanced his status as a martyr for later freethinkers.[25]

Gilded Age freethinkers, particularly those on the left, lionized Paine and promoted his legacy. Paine "believed in liberty and justice, and in the sacred quality of human equality," Robert Ingersoll boasted. But more significantly, Paine exposed the tyranny and hypocrisy of organized Christianity; he "examined the Scriptures for himself, and found then filled with cruelty, absurdity and immorality." Paine stood for "the right to think" and demonstrated that "[i]ntellectual liberty, as a matter of necessity . . . is wholly inconsistent with every creed in Christendom." He taught that "[i]nfidelity is liberty," Ingersoll insisted, and that "all religion is slavery." Understandably, Paine's concluding remark in *Age of Reason*—"when opinions are free, either in matters of government or religion, truth will finally and powerfully prevail"—became a rallying call for freethinkers.[26] Freethinkers regularly celebrated the anniversary of Paine's birth with rallies and public lectures. (To this day, the freethought journal, *The Truth Seeker*, founded in 1873, lists Paine as its inspirational founder.)[27]

While Paine never denied the existence of God, and was successfully marginalized by the religious establishment, he was a convenient boogeyman for critics of deism and "infidelity," like Timothy Dwight and Lyman Beecher. Writing in 1822, Dwight charged that with Paine's *Age of Reason*, "the whole mass of pollution was emptied on this country." Beecher, too, decried "the infidelity of the Tom Paine school." "I remember the time when there was no such thing as infidelity openly advocated in our land," he remarked. "The first public assault that was made upon the Bible was by Thomas Paine in his *Age of Reason* [which] went like an electric shock through the land, and, for a time unsettled the confidence of many." Fortunately, Beecher continued, "an era of prayer, and discussion, and revivals of religion, speedily followed, and the tide of infidelity ebbed."[28]

In the mid-1820s a new skeptical movement arose in the United States, and Paine was rediscovered. Nurtured by Jacksonian democratic ideals, workers' concerns, and the same voluntary impulse that fed the proliferation of evangelical groups, this "spiritual hothouse" fostered competitors to evangelicalism—Shakerism, Mesmerism, Mormonism, and then socialist utopian and radical reform communities, the latter often serving as breeding grounds for skepticism. These "free enquirers" who challenged Christian orthodoxy were reacting in part to the rise of moral reform societies created by evangelical/orthodox Protestants, which were designed to combat vice and institute order in a society experiencing rapid demographic shifts. The skeptics not only advanced heterodox ideas and challenged institutionalized religion but also embraced radical reforms such as women's and workers' rights. The most visible leaders of antebellum skepticism were the socialist reformer Robert Owen—the founder of the utopian New Harmony community—his son, Robert Dale Owen, and the scandalous Frances Wright, who bore various labels: the "Red Harlot of Infidelity," the "female Tom Paine," and the "female apostle of atheistic liberty," the last slur coming from Lyman Beecher. Wright was a popular lecturer—and a cultural phenomenon—who drew large crowds to her talks, which mixed attacks on religious orthodoxy with advocacy of sexual liberation and workers' rights. The skepticism of the 1820s–1830s, represented by Wright, Robert Dale Owen, Robert L. Jennings, Abner Kneeland, and Ernestine Rose, went beyond that of Paine, however, by disputing the existence of God and abandoning any goal of reforming Christianity. It also aligned freethought closely with abolition, universal education, and to a host of radical social reforms.[29] And, not surprisingly, "free enquirers" promoted the separation of church and state. People "would suffer no encroachment on religious freedom; no comixing of things spiritual and temporal," Robert Dale Owen wrote in the *Free Enquirer*. "The separation between things temporal and spiritual will be broadly marked out. Religion will stand by its own strength or weakness."[30]

Of all the social reforms that Wright and Owen advanced, two were particularly controversial and threatening to Christian social conventions. First, as noted, they advocated for women's social and sexual equality, for reforming marriage and divorce laws that kept women subjugated by their husbands. "Are not all women 'endowed with certain unalienable rights, among which are life, liberty and the pursuit of happiness,'" Owen asked rhetorically. "Do not marriages as well as governments 'derive their just powers from the consent' of the contracting parties? 'Whenever any marriage . . . becomes destructive of these ends, is it not right that it should be dissolved?'" Wright, using more damning language, criticized the "ignorant laws, ignorant prejudices, [and] ignorant codes of morals . . . [that] condemn one portion of the female sex to vicious excesses, and another to as vicious restraint . . . and generally the whole of the male sex to debasing licentiousness."[31] The two radicals also advocated, as the logical next step, for women's control over their reproductive functions. Owen published the first birth control manual written in the United States: *Moral Physiology, or a Brief and Plain Treatise on the Population Question*. Their advocacy of both issues established the initial connection between freethought, sexual equality, and free love that came to epitomize the freethought movement of the Gilded Age.[32]

Another leading skeptic of the period was Abner Kneeland, a former Universalist minister associated with Wright and Robert Dale Owen, who edited their newspaper, *The Free Enquirer*, during their travels. Wright's lectures in Boston in 1829 had spurred the organization of the city's First Society of Free Enquirers, and Kneeland moved to Boston to cultivate and lead the group. He founded the *Boston Investigator*, a long-running journal dedicated to freethought, which soon had two thousand subscribers, equaling that of Wright's and Owen's New York *Free Enquirer*. Kneeland, through his writings and popular public lectures, advocated not only freethought and workers' rights, but also equal rights for women—their equal standing in marriage and in the workforce, and a woman's right to separate ownership of property. Kneeland promoted the idea of "rational marriage," whether legally sanctioned or not, based solely on "sincere and mutual love," and dissolvable at will. Critics saw this as dangerously close to advocating free love. Finally, Kneeland advertised the sale of Owen's tract on birth control, *Moral Physiology*. Kneeland quickly became "a stench in the nostrils" of Boston society, dominated as it was by conservative Unitarians. Samuel Gridley Howe labeled Kneeland the "hoary-headed apostle of Satan" and charged that his journal "abound[ed] with blasphemy, ribaldry, and obscenity." Kneeland's proposals "[struck] at the very foundations of society," Howe insisted, by "[d]eriding the sacredness of the marriage compact, and describing it merely as an arrangement to be taken up and laid aside at pleasure."[33]

The activities of Wright, Owen, and Kneeland and the far-reaching agenda of antebellum skepticism alarmed orthodox Protestants and moral reformers. In addition to Boston's Society of Free Enquirers and New York's Moral Philanthropists, skeptical societies sprang up in other cities, including Philadelphia, Baltimore, Rochester, Pittsburgh, and St. Louis. Skepticism was making significant inroads in the West (the Mississippi Valley), critics feared, though both freethinkers and their clerical opponents exaggerated the gains. Howe claimed in 1834 that skepticism was "an extensive party, numbering perhaps fifty thousand, who openly and violently assail Christianity and attack our system of morals." Free thinkers encouraged the impression, asserting that "infidelity is spreading like wild-fire, and that in fifty years Christianity will be professed only by a miserable minority of male bigots and female fools."[34]

Not leaving anything to chance, orthodox Protestants attacked skepticism with a vengeance. Lyman Beecher delivered a series of lectures on "the epidemic of infidelity," later printed in pamphlet form. Infidelity, he charged, was "a conspiracy in our land, against the being of God, and our civil, and social, and religious institutions." One institution that Wright and other skeptics particularly threatened was marriage. Skeptics "contemplate[ed] nothing less than the abolition of marriage and the family state, separate property, civil government, and all sense of accountability," Beecher exclaimed. Their call for equality of the sexes—which was bad enough—was part of a larger agenda to achieve a leveling of the social classes where the "property of the world is to become common stock" for the sake of "blessed equanimity." Linus Smith Everett concurred that the inquirers' attack on the institution of marriage was "the most monstrous of all of the monstrous evils" that they promoted. "Individual property—Marriage—Religion—Customs; Sweep these away, and what would be left? They have denominated themselves *heretics in morals*, as well as in religion." And Samuel Gridley Howe agreed that the breadth of the infidel agenda extended beyond blaspheming God and undermining marriage to "question[ing] the rights of property" and "stir[ring] up the passions of the poor against the rich." Thus, for Beecher, Everett, and Howe, skepticism represented not simply a challenge to Christian belief but a sinister effort to undermine Christian society and its institutions.[35]

Joining Beecher's, Everett's, and Howe's polemics was a widely read insider's account, *The Cause and Cure of Infidelity* by David Nelson, who had succumbed to the snares of skepticism when serving in the militia during the War of 1812. Now a Presbyterian minister committed to combatting infidelity, Nelson characterized the lure of skepticism in almost cult-like terms as appealing to "man's depravity" and to "man's want of knowledge." Nelson naively believed that the cure for infidelity—or at least the preventative for those who were wavering in their faith—was to consider the "experimental evidence of Christianity," as if greater exposure to Christian doctrines would magically do the trick. Like Beecher and Howe, Nelson perpetuated the narrative of skepticism's looming threat to America's institutions: "Infidelity is now growing and spreading to an extent the blindness of the church does not expect." Skeptics were not some harmless "grey-headed professor" but were soldiers in "Satan's army" publishing "volumes of false statements, infidel manuals, [and] painted perversions of history" which were "spreading profusely" among the unsuspected public.[36]

The orthodox establishment fought back using measures beyond writings and lectures. Beecher led the drive to seek greater enforcement of laws prohibiting labor and commercial activity on Sundays by organizing another moral reform society, the General Union for the Promotion of the Christian Sabbath. Orthodox clergy and their allies also pressured owners of lecture halls to deny leases to freethought societies.[37] On a handful of occasions, the orthodox establishment resorted to more extreme measures, charging skeptics with blasphemy. Blasphemy was an offense under British common law, aspects of which American states had incorporated into their legal systems. Thus, in a leading 1811 decision, New York's Chief Justice James Kent declared blasphemy was not protected expression.[38] The number of blasphemy prosecutions in antebellum America is impossible to gauge, as most took place in misdemeanor or police courts with defendants not appealing the fines (leaving the cases unreported); many such offenses also did not involve committed skeptics publicly affirming their disbelief in Christian doctrine but defendants, often inebriated, engaging in profane swearing. But between 1821 and 1836, three notable blasphemy cases involved prosecutions of skeptics, with all three decisions identifying a connection between the religious and sexual forms of infidelity.[39]

The first, arising in Pittsburgh, was the prosecution of Abner Updegraph, a member of a liberal debating society, for asserting during a debate that "the Holy Scriptures were mere fable" that "constituted a great many lies." Updegraph appealed his conviction to the Pennsylvania Supreme Court, which brushed aside his free speech claim, maintaining that his statements were "a gross offense against public decency and public order, [and] tend[ed] to disturb the peace of the commonwealth." Christianity was "the law of our land," the justices declared, and "[n]o society can tolerate a wilful and despiteful attempt to subvert its religion." The fact that Updegraph's utterance had been made in a private meeting before a willing audience only made the offense worse; that there was "an association in which so serious a subject is treated with so much levity, indecency and scurrility," Justice Thomas Duncan wrote, would only serve as "a nursery of vice, a school of preparation to qualify young men for the gallows and young women for the brothel."[40]

A second blasphemy case arose in 1836 in Delaware, where the defendant, Thomas Jefferson Chandler, "not having the fear of God before his eyes, but being moved and seduced by the instigation of the devil," was convicted for uttering that "the virgin Mary was a whore and Jesus Christ was a bastard."

Despite the salacious nature of his words, Chandler claimed he was a skeptic and defended his statement based on the writings of his namesake, who had also disputed orthodox religious doctrine. His defense was for naught, with the Delaware Supreme Court affirming that blasphemy was a civil offense because Christianity lay at the foundation of the law, while highlighting Chandler's "flagrant violation of decorum" for comparing Mary to a prostitute. Chandler served a ten-day sentence in solitary confinement and paid a ten-dollar fine.[41]

The most famous antebellum blasphemy prosecution took place in Boston between 1834 and 1836 and involved Abner Kneeland, the publisher of the *Boston Investigator*. As noted, Kneeland, his newspaper, and his Society of Free Enquirers had been a bane to Boston's orthodox Unitarian establishment, which had opposed disestablishment in Massachusetts until the bitter end. Finally, after three years, its leaders had had enough of Kneeland's radical amalgam of skepticism, sexual liberation, and social leveling. In January 1834 they secured his indictment over three articles published in the *Investigator*. Two were reprints from the *Free Enquirer* that challenged the Virgin Birth and ridiculed prayer while comparing God to President Andrew Jackson, which greatly offended the Whig Unitarians. The third article, written by Kneeland, was a critique of his former denomination: "Universalists believe in a god which I do not; but believe that their god . . . is nothing more than a mere chimera of their own imagination." The article continued with other assertions that Universalists believed in Christ, in miracles, and in the resurrection of the dead and eternal life, "which I do not."[42] Kneeland was tried and convicted in municipal court for violating a 1782 statute that forbade the willful blasphemy of "the holy name of God, by denying, cursing, or contumeliously reproaching God, his creation, government, or final judging of the world." The judge sentenced the sixty-year-old Kneeland to three months in prison and a $500 surety bond to ensure good behavior, a significant sum for the time. Kneeland appealed his conviction to the Massachusetts Supreme Judicial Court, which conducted three additional trials, the first two resulting in mistrials, before finally reaching a guilty verdict in the third. The various trials, occurring over a two-year period, became a cause célèbre in Boston with Kneeland's supporters and detractors battling each other in newspapers and in rallies.[43]

The prosecutor in the first two trials was Samuel Parker, the son of an Episcopal bishop, who revealed his contempt for Kneeland's religious, political, and social beliefs in his arguments before the jury. Parker called Kneeland an atheist and infidel and a promoter "of the Fanny Wright system—atheism, community of property, unlimited lasciviousness, adultery and a thousand evils of infidelity." Parker asserted that Christianity served as the foundation for the constitution, the law, and for society itself. As a result, "[b]lasphemy is not only an offense against God and religion, but a crime against the laws, state, and government . . . [so] to reproach the Christian religion is to speak in subversion of the law." Kneeland's blasphemous writings were particularly subversive, Parker continued, because unlike "other infidels—Hume, Gibbon, Voltaire, Volney, etc.," whose works were read "only by men of literary habits," his cheap newspaper "is so widely circulated, so easily read" by the masses which presented a greater threat to social order.[44]

Kneeland's defense was inconsistent. He first denied any responsibility for the content of the two reprints from the *Free Enquirer* and claimed that the third article simply disputed the Universalist conception of God. He denied being an atheist—he claimed to be a pantheist—or that he had committed blasphemy. Kneeland then asserted that blasphemous language was protected speech under both the state declaration of rights and the US Constitution: "[t]he constitution and laws of the United States, so far from sustaining this statute against blasphemy actually destroys its validity." The judges, however, accepted the prosecutors' claims that Christianity was protected by law and that infidelity undermined the social order. In his charge to the jury in the first trial, Judge Peter Thacher went so far as to rewrite Kneeland's statement disavowing the Universalist conception of God by inserting a comma at a crucial place, such that it now read "Universalists believe in a god, which I do not." This, Thacher asserted, was proof of Kneeland's atheism and his blasphemy.[45]

After Kneeland's second conviction in 1835, he appealed the decision to the full Supreme Judicial Court, with Kneeland now representing himself. The court took two years to issue an opinion, ultimately affirming Kneeland's conviction. The majority opinion was written by Chief Justice Lemuel Shaw, a conservative Unitarian but also a well-respected jurist.[46] Shaw accepted the jury's finding that Kneeland had willfully denied the existence of God. The statute, however, was "not intended to prevent or restrain the formation of any opinions or the professions of any religious sentiments whatever, but to restrain and punish acts which have a tendency to disturb the public peace," Shaw wrote. Accordingly, the law was "not repugnant to, but entirely consistent with" the state declaration of rights.[47] Chief Justice Shaw steered clear of the prosecution's claims that the law incorporated Christian principles, but the court's only Democrat, Justice Marcus Morton, refuted the notion. Disestablishment in Massachusetts in 1833 had severed any such relationship, Morton maintained. Reading the declaration of rights broadly, Morton insisted that its language "clearly protects every citizen, not only in *adopting*, but in *professing*, whatever tenets he may think right; and necessarily included the right of *advocating* and *disseminating* them." And even though the constitution spoke of protecting *religious* sentiments, it must be interpreted to include "*irreligious*" sentiments and "extend to atheists." In a paean to the principle of freethought, Morton wrote:

> Any attempt, by legislation, to control or dictate the belief of individuals, is so impracticable, so perfectly futile, as to show at once, how entirely above all civil authority are the operations of the human mind, especially in the adoption of its religious faith.[48]

Kneeland, now sixty-four and emotionally and physically spent, served two months in jail, his sentence having been reduced by thirty days. He emerged in August 1838 to a crowd of three hundred supporters who gave him a hero's welcome. Even critics "deeply regretted the prosecution of Abner Kneeland for blasphemy," read an article in a Universalist journal. "Leave his character and his opinions to be settled by the tribunal of reason and free inquiry," another wrote, a sentiment that Kneeland had long advocated.[49] Even though he was now a living martyr for the freethought movement, the previously pugnacious Kneeland was exhausted and circumspect about advocating further for the cause. In 1839, he called it quits and moved with his wife to Iowa Territory to establish a village of freethinkers outside the glare of the public spotlight.[50]

Kneeland's conviction and departure from Boston signaled the decline of an active antebellum freethought movement. The economic Panic of 1837 took its toll on the membership in various skeptical societies and undercut hopes for a viable Workingman's Party that might ally with the freethinkers. The movement also suffered from a lack of prominent leadership; in 1831, Frances Wright married a French physician and traveled back and forth between Europe and the United States, which curtailed her activities. Although she attempted to resuscitate her lecture tours upon returning to America in mid-decade, Wright retired in 1839 beset by unrelenting criticism, illness, and marital difficulties. Robert Dale Owen turned to politics, serving in the Indiana Assembly and then in Congress from 1843 to 1847. And in the 1840s, some freethinkers drifted into Transcendentalism. Skeptical societies, like

New York's Moral Philanthropists, continued to operate into the 1840s but were less prominent than they had been a decade earlier.[51]

The Moderate Freethought Impulse

The second impetus for Gilded Age freethought—chiefly for more moderate freethinkers—was the Transcendentalism of the 1830s and 1840s. Transcendentalism arose out of liberal Unitarians' frustrations with Christian doctrines and with orthodox Unitarianism's conservative rationalism. Transcendentalists believed that God's presence transcended all aspects of the natural world and could be understood intuitively rather than through rational empiricism. Individual conscience in religious matters was essential, as was a belief in the divinity of human nature. Octavius B. Frothingham, later the leader of the Free Religionist movement, described himself in his early career as "a pure Transcendentalist, [and] a warm sympathizer with transcendental aspirations." He defined Transcendentalism as "an assertion of the inalienable worth of man; theoretically, it was an assertion of the immanence of divinity in instinct, the transference of supernatural attributes to the natural constitution of mankind." Transcendentalism, George Ripley added, "maintain[ed] that the truth of religion does not depend on tradition, nor historical facts, but had an unerring witness in the soul. There is a light . . . which enlighteneth every man that cometh into the world; there is a faculty in all . . . to perceive spiritual truth when distinctly presented."[52]

Transcendentalism commanded the allegiance of New England's intellectual elite: Ralph Waldo Emerson, Henry David Thoreau, George Ripley, Orestes A. Brownson, and Theodore Parker, among others.[53] Parker served as the intellectual inspiration for future Free Religionists for his willingness to discard archaic church doctrines, despite his remaining within Unitarianism. Parker called for distinguishing between the "transient" and "permanent" aspects of Christianity; the content of religion was not static—"nothing changes more from age to age than the doctrines taught as Christian." He insisted that "[f]rom the beginning of human history there has always been a continual progress of man's conception of God." Parker believed that the permanent or essential aspects of Christianity could be reduced to the "Idea of God," or sometimes simply the "Idea": "Infinite Perfection, Power, Wisdom,

Justice, Holiness, [and] Love." All other aspects of Christianity were transient and thus disposable.[54]

Parker's willingness to risk controversy by tearing down the pillars of Christian doctrine served as a model for later freethinkers. Parker was "the leader of a new 'departure'" in religion, Frothingham proclaimed. Under his influence, "[a]ll institutions and ideas went into the furnace of reason and were tried as by fire. Church and State were put to the proof." Moreover, Parker taught that faith had to be consistent with those laws of nature that were being uncovered through scientific discovery. "Science he counted his best friend; [he] relied on it for confirmation of his faith; and was only impatient because it did not move faster."[55] Despite being attacked as an infidel by the Unitarian establishment, Parker remained affiliated with the liberal wing of Unitarianism until his untimely death from tuberculosis in 1860, at the age of forty-nine. Yet Frothingham believed that his own Free Religion movement was the logical extension of Parker's theological work and that the latter would have led their movement had he lived into the 1870s.[56]

The warm light of Transcendentalism, at least as a distinct movement, was all but extinguished by the mid-1850s, though its influence remained strong among liberal Unitarians like Parker. Historian Perry Miller argued that one explanation "for the disappearance of the movement was simply that it won its point, or at any rate most of its points." Its legacy, nonetheless, set the stage for an even more radical questioning of Christian belief in the postwar era.[57]

Spiritualism

Coinciding with the mainstreaming of Transcendentalism in the 1850s was the rise of a third influence on the Gilded Age freethought movement: Spiritualism. Spiritualism was the belief in, and the practice of, communicating with deceased from the spirit world. Spiritualism, and the practice of holding seances, burst onto the American scene in the early fifties and quickly became a fad, attracting a following among the nation's upper and middle classes. "Scarcely another cultural phenomenon affected more people or excited more interest in the ten years before the Civil War" than did Spiritualism, writes historian Laurence Moore. "To qualify as a Spiritualist, one had only to believe in the individual soul's survival after death and the ability of the dead to communicate with the living."[58] Although many mediums were hucksters and frauds who deceived their attendees while pocketing their money, other spiritualist practitioners believed in the reality of their craft. Arising as it did in an era in which fantastical claims were widespread, Spiritualism seemed plausible, particularly to those who were willing to set aside skepticism to communicate with a departed loved one. Skeptic Robert Dale Owen attended numerous seances to examine their bona fides and came away convinced, arguing that Spiritualism revealed unexplainable phenomena that could not be easily dismissed. After describing his "vigilant precautions beforehand" to prevent any possible deception, Owen declared that he had "to admit that these marvelous phenomena were realities, or else to assume that the senses of sight, hearing, and touch are witnesses utterly unworthy to be trusted."[59]

At first glance, Spiritualism was an unlikely complement to freethought, considering the latter's emphasis on rationalism and materialism. But aside from its focus on an interactive spirit world, Spiritualism and its practitioners— distinct from casual participants in séances—shared much in common with freethought and especially with the direction in which the freethought movement was headed. First, spiritualists disputed the authority and authenticity of the Bible and Christian doctrine; communication with a spirit world was more immediate proof of a metaphysical realm, and more accurate. Most spiritualist leaders and practitioners repudiated basic Christian beliefs such as the Trinity, human depravity, original sin, substitutional atonement, and a final judgment after death. Spiritualists "either declared their independence from biblical authority or made the authenticity of Christian Scriptures dependent on the reality of modern spirit voices." They agreed with Transcendentalists that God was "eternally and everywhere in nature, [such] that special revelation was really unnecessary." As a result, Spiritualism was "antithetical to institutional religion because it asserted that truth came directly to the individual without mediation by minister, Bible, or church." Freethinkers shared these ideas.[60]

Second, spiritualists claimed that the practice had empirical and scientific bona fides, and (some) welcomed scrutiny of the séance. Spiritualist Alfred Cridge asserted that it was "highly probable, if not demonstratively certain, that spiritualism, in its large and broad sense, [denotes] a system of thought and science which recognizes the sovereignty of the interior, invisible, and permanent spirit or essence, over the external, visible, and transient form." And Robert Dale Owen insisted that the séance disclosed phenomena which "will ultimately be accepted by men of science and other skeptics as occurrences under [natural] law," such that "scientific materialists will gradually discover that, as part of the cosmical plan, there are intermundane, as well as mundane, phenomena." According to Laurence Moore, "Spiritualism became a self-conscious movement precisely by disassociating itself from any occult tradition and appealing not to the inward illumination of mystic experience but to the observable and verifiable objects of empirical science."[61]

And third, many spiritualist practitioners embraced women's rights and related social reforms, as did freethinkers. A significant proportion of spiritualist practitioners were women, and Spiritualism was frequently liberating for female mediums, providing them with a degree of financial and social independence from their husbands. And because spiritual knowledge depended on "the unhindered autonomy of female mediums," writes Ann Braude, "believers vigorously applied the principle of individualism to the role of women. As a result, [spiritualists] became ardent advocates of woman's rights." Braude continues that "[w]hile not all feminists were Spiritualists, all Spiritualists advocated woman's rights," such as marriage and divorce reforms. Most spiritualists did not endorse free love when it connoted infidelity or promiscuity; instead, they advocated freely expressed mutual desire unrestrained by conventional religious norms. Sexual intercourse should be restricted to expressions of mutual affection rather than based on a husband's sexual urgings, which would *limit* the frequency of sexual intercourse.[62] Still, critics of Spiritualism— and there were many—used its embrace of free love to charge that spiritualists advocated "spiritio-carnality" and the abolition of lawful marriage. As one critic warned, mediums "will receive revelations from high pretending spirits, cautiously instructing them that the sexual congenials will greatly sanctify them for the reception of angelic ministrations. Wives and husbands will be rendered miserable, alienated, parted, and their families broken up." The charge was summed up in an 1859 headline in the *New York Times*: "More of the Evils of Spiritualism—The Free-Love Element."[63]

According to Laurence Moore, a surprising number of liberal Unitarians, Universalists, Transcendentalists, and even freethinkers like Owen embraced Spiritualism "enthusiastically." In a sense, they all "demanded a simplification of faith. They either declared their independence from biblical authority or made the authenticity of Christian Scriptures dependent on the reality of modern spirit voices." Still, many religious liberals and freethinkers spurned Spiritualism, particularly when its practitioners engaged in dubious conduct. Theodore Parker and then Octavius B. Frothingham and Francis E. Abbot did not know what to make of spiritualists, whom they believed promoted superstition at the expense of materialism, despite their claims of scientific backing for séances. But they appreciated spiritualists' rejection of scriptural and creedal bondage. Robert Ingersoll also criticized Spiritualism for its "mingling of the supernatural and the natural" and its perpetuation of "the idea of immortality." "[M]aterializations of spirits . . . [were] only cunning frauds, the genuineness of which is established by the testimony of incompetent, honest witnesses." Over time, however, Ingersoll became more ambivalent about spiritualists: at least they were not bigoted, did "not believe in salvation by faith" or "preach the consolidation of hell." Although spiritualists relied on supernaturalism, they also believed in freedom of thought, Ingersoll remarked, which made them better than most Christians.[64] Spiritualism remained a popular movement and force into the 1880s, though it declined during the later Gilded Age. Throughout the period, however, Spiritualism continued to attract followers, particularly women, who were drawn to its reformist and gender-empowering positions.[65]

These three antebellum impulses—Jacksonian skepticism, Transcendentalism, and Spiritualism—thus served as the foundation for the rise of a vigorous freethought movement during the Gilded Age.

NOTES

1. "Moody and Sankey: The Hippodrome Meetings," *New York Times*, Feb. 10, 1876, 8; "The Hippodrome Services," ibid., Feb. 29, 1876, 8; "American Genius; Moody & Sankey," ibid., Nov. 23, 1875, 5; "Messrs. Moody and Sankey," *New York Evangelist*, Feb. 10, 1876, 8; James F. Findlay Jr., *Dwight L. Moody: American Evangelist, 1837–1899* (Chicago: University of Chicago Press, 1969), 200; Winthrop S. Hudson, *The Great Tradition of the American Churches* (New York: Harper & Row, 1963), 137–138.

2. "The Theory of Evolution: Prof. Huxley's First Lecture," *New York Times*, Sept. 19, 1876, 8; "The Theory of Evolution: Prof. Huxley's Second Lecture," ibid., Sept. 20, 1876, 10; "The Theory of Evolution: Prof. Huxley's Final Lecture," ibid., Sept. 21, 1876, 1; "Prof. Huxley and the Bible," ibid., Oct. 1, 1876, 6; Jacoby, *Freethinkers*, 134–136.

3. "Professor Huxley on Evolution," *Christian Union*, Sept. 27, 1876, 246; "Close of Professor Huxley, Lectures," *New York Evangelist*, Sept. 28, 1876, 4.

4. "The Theory of Evolution: Prof. Huxley's First Lecture," *New York Times*, Sept. 19, 1876, 8.

5. Robert T. Handy, *A Christian America*, 2nd ed. (New York: Oxford University Press, 1984), 24–81; Jon Butler, *Awash in a Sea of Faith: Christianizing the American People* (Cambridge, MA: Harvard University Press, 1990), 257–295;

William G. McLoughlin, *Revivals, Awakenings, and Reform* (Chicago: University of Chicago Press, 1978); Green, *Second Disestablishment*, 81–103, 173–203.

6. Joseph P. Thompson, *Church and State in the United States* (Boston: James R. Osgood & Co., 1873), 93–95.

7. Philip Schaff, "Progress of Christianity in the United States," *Princeton Review* (1879): 209–223.

8. Ibid., 224–227.

9. Ibid., 227–230; Handy, *Undermined Establishment*, 8–18; Steven K. Green, *The Bible, the School, and the Constitution: The Clash That Shaped Modern Church-State Doctrine* (New York: Oxford University Press, 2012), 11–44; George M. Marsden, *The Soul of the American University: From Protestant Establishment to Established Nonbelief* (New York: Oxford University Press, 1994); Robert Wood Lynn, *Protestant Strategies in Education* (New York: Associated Press, 1964), 22.

10. Robert T. Handy, "The Protestant Quest for a Christian America, 1830–1930," *Church History* 22 (1953): 8–20, 12

11. Strong, *Our Country*, 180, 181.

12. Edwin Scott Gaustad and Philip L. Barlow, *New Historical Atlas of Religion in America* (New York: Oxford University Press, 2001), 157–158; Handy, *Undermined Establishment*, 16–18.

13. Green, *The Bible, the School, and the Constitution*, 181–186; Strong, *Our Country*, 77.

14. Sarah Barringer Gordon, *The Mormon Question: Polygamy and Constitutional Conflict in Nineteenth-Century America* (Chapel Hill: University of North Carolina Press, 2002); Strong, *Our Country*, 112–120.

15. James Turner, *Without God, without Creed: The Origins of Unbelief in America* (Baltimore: Johns Hopkins University Press, 1985), 143–163; Schmidt, *The Church of Saint Thomas Paine*, 77–93.

16. James Woodrow, "Evolution" (1884), in *Critical Issues in American Religious History*, 2nd ed., ed. Robert R. Mathisen (Waco, TX: Baylor University Press, 2006), 383; Warren, *American Freethought*, 45–47, 70–71; Henry Ward Beecher, *Evolution and Religion* (New York: Fords, Howard & Hulbert, 1885), 115; Henry Ward Beecher, "Science and Religion Reconciled," *Scientific American*, Dec. 2, 1871, 352; "Mr. Beecher on Evolution," *Christian Union*, July 23, 1885, 16; S.R. Calthrop, "Religion and Evolution," *The Religious Magazine and Monthly Review* (Sept. 1873): 1–35.

17. Charles Hodge, *What Is Darwinism* (New York: Scribner, Armstrong, 1874), 177, 173; "Save the Bible," *Onida Circular*, Oct. 26, 1874, 1; Carter, *Spiritual Crisis*, 23–42.

18. Turner, *Without God, without Creed*, 143–144; Charles Hodge, *Systematic Theology* (New York: Scribner, 1873), 1:152, 163; Ira V. Brown, "Higher Criticism Comes to America," *Journal of the Presbyterian Historical Society* 38 (1960): 193–212.

19. Erik Linstrum, "Strauss's 'Life of Jesus': Publication and the Politics of the German Public Square," *Journal of the History of Ideas* 71 (2010): 593–616; Turner, *Without God, without Creed*, 144–147.

20. Matthew Arnold, *Literature and Dogma* (London: Smith, Elder, & Co., 1873), xv.

21. Theodore Parker, "The Transient and Permanent in Christianity," in Perry Miller, ed., *The Transcendentalists: An Anthology* (Cambridge, MA: Harvard University Press, 1950), 260–283; Brown, "Higher Criticism Comes to America," 197.

22. Brown, "Higher Criticism Comes to America," 198–207; William R. Hutchinson, *The Modernist Impulse in American Protestantism* (New York: Oxford University Press, 1976), 76–77, 91–94, 116–120, 197.

23. Warren, *American Freethought*, 20, 30, 75–116; "The New University," *The Independent*, Aug. 31, 1882, 16.

24. Christopher Grasso, *Skepticism and American Faith: From the Revolution to the Civil War* (New York: Oxford University Press, 2018), 99–100; Hoffman, *American Freethought*, chs. 1 and 2.

25. Thomas Paine, *The Age of Reason* (1794), in *The Life and Major Writings of Thomas Paine*, ed. Philip S. Foner (New York: Citadel Press, 1948, 1993), 463–604, xxxvi–xlvi; Eric R. Schlereth, *An Age of Infidels: The Politics of Religious Controversy in the Early United States* (Philadelphia: University of Pennsylvania Press, 2013), 194–195; Amanda Porterfield, *Conceived in Doubt: Religion and Politics in the New American Nation* (Chicago: University of Chicago Press, 2012); Schmidt, *Church of Saint Thomas Paine*, 28–31; Jacoby, *Freethinkers*, 63–65.

26. "Thomas Paine," Ingersoll, *Works*, 1:136, 138, 159; Paine, *Age of Reason*, 604.

27. George M. Macdonald, *Fifty Years of Freethought* (New York: Truth Seeker, 1929), 176; Schmidt, *Church of Saint Thomas Paine*, 1–2, 44; https://thetrut hseeker.net/.

28. Schlereth, *Age of Infidels*, 194–195; Foner, *Life and Major Writings of Thomas Paine*, xlv.; Timothy Dwight, *Travels in New-England and New-York* (New Haven, CT: Timothy Dwight, Pub., 1822), 4:269, 272–273; Charles Beecher, ed., *Autobiography of Lyman Beecher* (New York: Harper, 1864), 1:43; Lyman Beecher, "The Necessity of a Revelation from God to Man," in *Works* (Boston: Jewett & Co., 1852–1853), 1:159.

29. Frances Wright, "Miss Wright's Partin Address," *Free Enquirer*, June 19, 1830, 267; Grasso, *Skepticism and American Faith*, 6, 275–293; Schlereth, *Age of Infidels*, 188–190; Steven K. Green, *Separating Church and State: A History* (Ithaca, NY: Cornell University Press, 2022), 109–113; Lori D. Ginzberg, "'The Hearts of Your Readers Will Shudder,' Fanny Wright, Infidelity, and American Freethought," *American Quarterly* 46 (1994): 195–226; Celia Morris Eckhardt, *Fanny Wright: Rebel in America* (Cambridge, MA: Harvard University Press, 1984), 171–224.

30. Robert Dale Owen, "Things Temporal and Spiritual," *Free Enquirer*, June 19, 1830, 272.

31. Robert Dale Owen, "Editorial," *Free Enquirer*, Feb. 25, 1832, 141; Ginzberg, "'The Hearts of Your Readers Will Shudder," 212.

32. Robert Dale Owen, *Moral Physiology, or a Brief and Plain Treatise on the Population Question*, 2nd ed., ed. Ralph Glover (New York: R. Glover, 1846); Robert E. Riegel and Lawrence Eager, "The Birth Control Controversy," *Current History* 36 (Aug. 1932): 563–568; Ginzberg, "'The Hearts of Your Readers Will Shudder," 212; Arnita Ament Jones, "From Utopia to Reform," *History Today* 26 (1976): 393–401.

33. Henry Steele Commager, "The Blasphemy of Abner Kneeland," *New England Quarterly* 8 (1935): 29–41; Roderick S. French, "Liberation from Man and God in Boston: Abner Kneeland's Free-Thought Campaign, 1830–1839," *American Quarterly* 32 (1980): 202–221; Samuel Gridley Howe, "Atheism in New-England," *New England Magazine* 7 (Dec. 1834): 500–509; 8 (Jan. 1853): 53–62.

34. Albert Post, *Popular Freethought in America, 1825–1850* (New York: Octagon Books, 1974), 75–121; Howe, "Atheism in New-England," 501.

35. Lyman Beecher, *Lectures on Scepticism* (Cincinnati: Corey and Fairbank, 1835), 2:43, 3:58–51, 4:74; Beecher, *Works*, 1:13–139; L.S. Everett, *An Exposure to the Principles of the "Free Enquirers"* (Boston: B.B. Mussy, 1831), 30, 41; Howe, "Atheism in New-England," 55–59.

36. David Nelson, *The Cause and Cure of Infidelity* (New York: American Tract Society, 1837, 1841), 12–13; Grasso, *Skepticism and American Faith*, 215–226.

37. Green, *Second Disestablishment*, 94–95, 182–190; Post, *Popular Freethought*, 199–225.

38. People v. Ruggles, 8 Johns. 290 (N.Y. 1811); Green, *Second Disestablishment*, 162–165.

39. Green, *Second Disestablishment*, 160–169.

40. Updegraph v. Commonwealth, 11 Serg. & Rawl. 394, 398–399, 405, 408–409 (Pa. 1824).

41. State v. Chandler, 2 Har. 553, 570, 572 (Del. 1837).

42. Commonwealth v. Kneeland, 20 Pick. (34 Mass.), 206–207 (1838); Commager, "Blasphemy of Abner Kneeland," 31–32; Leonard W. Levy, *The Law of the Commonwealth and Chief Justice Shaw* (Cambridge, MA: Harvard University Press, 1957), 44–45.

43. Commonwealth v. Kneeland, 20 Pick, 213; Commager, "Blasphemy of Abner Kneeland," 29–41; Green, *Second Disestablishment*, 174–175; "Kneeland's Sentence," *Free Enquirer*, Feb. 23, 1834, 143; "Trial for Blasphemy," *Free Enquirer*, March 30, 1834, 181; "Atheism," *The Jesuit, or Catholic Sentinel*, March 8, 1834, 74; "Blasphemy—Atheism—Prosecution," *Evangelical Magazine and Gospel Advocate*, April 19, 1834, 125.

44. "The Trial of Abner Kneeland for Blasphemy," *American State Trials*, ed. John D. Lawson (St. Louis, MO: Thomas Law Book Co., 1921) 13:450–575, at 532,

459, 462. The quoted arguments are from the first trial, which Lawson maintains were repeated in the later trials.

45. Ibid., 507.

46. Levy, *Law of the Commonwealth and Chief Justice Shaw*, 51–56; Green, *Second Disestablishment*, 176–178.

47. Commonwealth v. Kneeland, 20 Pick, 220–221.

48. Ibid., 233–235 (Morton, J., dissenting).

49. "Abner Kneeland's Sentence," *The Trumpet*, June 30, 1838, 6; "Mr. Kneeland's Case," *Trumpet and Universalist Magazine*, April 21, 1838, 174; French, "Liberation from Man and God in Boston," 220.

50. French, "Liberation from Man and God in Boston," 220–221; Post, *Popular Freethought*, 106–107.

51. Post, *Popular Freethought*, 100–102; Eckhardt, *Fanny Wright*, 242–273; Grasso, *Skepticism and American Faith*, 259–273.

52. Miller, *The Transcendentalists*, 3–15; George Ripley, "Letter to the Church in Purchase Street" (1840), in ibid., 255; Grasso, *Skepticism and American Faith*, 259–273; Octavius B. Frothingham, *Transcendentalism in New England: A History* (New York: G. P, Putnam's Sons, 1876), 136.

53. Miller, *The Transcendentalists*, 3–15.

54. Parker, "The Transient and Permanent in Christianity," ibid., 259–283; Theodore Parker, "The Philosophical Idea of God," in *American Philosophical Addresses, 1700–1900*, ed. Joseph L. Blau (New York: Columbia University Press, 1946), 665, 670.

55. Octavius B. Frothingham, *Theodore Parker: A Biography* (Boston: James R. Osgood & Co., 1874), 125, 567.

56. Ibid.; Theodore Parker, "Theodore Parker's Experience as a Minister" (1859), in Miller, *The Transcendentalists*, 484–493; Stow Persons, *Free Religion: An American Faith* (New Haven, CT: Yale University Press, 1947), 66–67.

57. Miller, *The Transcendentalists*, 13; Warren, *American Freethought*, 97; David M. Robinson, "'The New Epoch of Belief'; The *Radical* and Religious Transformation in Nineteenth-Century New England," *New England Quarterly* 79 (2006): 557.

58. R. Laurence Moore, "Spiritualism and Science: Reflections on the First Decade of Spirit Rappings," *American Quarterly* 24 (1972), 475; R. Laurence Moore, "Spiritualism," in *The Rise of Adventism*, ed. Edwin S. Gaustad (New York: Harper & Row, 1974), 85.

59. Sally Morita, "Unseen (and Unappreciated) Matters: Understanding the Reformative Nature of 19th Century Spiritualism," *American Studies* 40 (1999): 99–125; Moore, "Spiritualism and Science," 476–479; Robert Dale Owen, "Some Results from My Spiritual Studies," *Atlantic Monthly* 34 (1874): 719–731, 722.

60. Moore, "Spiritualism," 83, 87; Ann Braude, *Radical Spirits: Spiritualism and Women's Rights in Nineteenth-Century America* (Boston: Beacon Press, 1989, 2001), 56–57.

61. Morita, "Unseen (and Unappreciated) Matters," 99; Owen, "Some Results from My Spiritual Studies," 724; Moore, "Spiritualism and Science," 477.

62. Braude, *Radical Spirits*, 56–58, 127–135; R. Laurence Moore, *In Search of White Crows: Spiritualism, Parapsychology, and American Culture* (New York: Oxford University Press, 1977).

63. "Rebuke of the Spiritualists," *New York Daily Times*, Sept. 29, 1854, 6; "More of the Evils of Spiritualism—The Free-Love Element," *New York Times*, Feb. 21, 1859, 8; "The Free-Love System: Origin, Progress, and Position of the Anti-Marriage Movement," *New York Daily Times*, Sept. 8, 1855, 2; Rev. William Ferris, "The Theology of Modern Spiritualism: Its Infidelity," *The Ladies Repository*, May 1856, 297–300.

64. "The Ghosts" (1877), Ingersoll, *Works*, 1:268, 270; "Superstition" (1898), ibid., 4:347; "Spiritualism," ibid., July 26, 1896, 8:557–558.

65. Moore, "Spiritualism," 97–98, 100–101; Braude, *Radical Spirits*, 192, 197–202.

2

The Emergence of Gilded Age Freethought

The freethought movement that emerged during the Gilded Age surpassed that of the 1830s. At no time in the nation's history were advocates of freethought more visible or vocal. Led by the widely popular orator Robert G. Ingersoll but supported by a large supporting chorus, Gilded Age freethinkers were less likely to keep their opinions about religion and related social issues to themselves. Freethought, and freethinkers, were at the center of many of the leading public debates of the day: over women's suffrage, marriage and divorce reform, access to abortion and birth control, censorship, labor reform, and more. The movement included several prominent figures such as Ralph Waldo Emerson, Wendell Phillips, Mark Twain, Walt Whitman, Oliver Wendell Holmes Jr., and Elizabeth Cady Stanton, none of whom hid their religious heterodoxy. Yet, to describe the Gilded Age as the "golden age" of freethought, as Susan Jacoby maintains, "is to suggest not that a majority of Americans were persuaded by rationalist or antireligious arguments but that those arguments reached a much broader public than they ever had in the past."[1]

Several factors arising after the Civil War nurtured religious skepticism and facilitated freethought's resurgence. Some factors have already been mentioned. Biblical "higher criticism" continued to make inroads into the curriculum of colleges and seminaries, with a new generation of Protestant ministers building on the earlier work of Theodore Parker by discarding central Christian tenets.[2] Following the Civil War, Darwinian evolution also impressed itself on the popular culture as it had already done on the field of natural science. Darwinism was but one part—albeit the most influential part—of the growing attraction of scientific exploration that sought to explain laws of nature without reference to the supernatural. Critics of Darwinism, like Harvard's Louis Agassiz, dismissed evolution as based on conjecture. A larger number of intellectuals, however, including philosopher John Fiske and botanist Asa Gray, endeavored to explain evolution as an empirical demonstration of God's existence embodied in design. But many clergy interpreted Darwinism as a repudiation of God as the First Cause. The publication of Darwin's *The Descent of Man* in 1871, which tied natural selection directly to human development, made it even more difficult to see God's hand in the process.[3] Robert Ingersoll praised Darwin, Huxley, and Spencer, writing that he "thank[ed] the inventors, the discoverers, the thinkers, the scientists, the explorers. These are the men who have broken, and are still breaking, the chains of Superstition."[4]

The postwar era also witnessed the demographic and political expansion of Catholicism in America. The American Catholic Church grew sixfold between 1865 and 1900, due chiefly to immigration. Beginning in the late-1860s, the "School Question"—the interrelated issues of Protestant prayer and Bible reading in the public schools and the public funding of Catholic parochial schools—thrust the nation into a decades-long acrimonious battle over the meaning of church–state separation. While Protestants and freethinkers split over the propriety of the former issue, they united—or at least shared common ground—in opposing the funding of Catholic education. Both groups also saw Catholic political power as a threat to American democratic institutions. Pope Pius IX's much publicized 1864 denunciation of liberalism, modernity, secular government, and church–state separation—directed chiefly at European audiences but felt in the United States—only reinforced long-standing suspicions about the Catholic Church's autocratic tendencies. Although Ingersoll regularly criticized the injustices perpetrated by both Catholicism and Calvinism, he heaped vilification on the Catholic Church, exclaiming that the pope "speaks against the liberty of man—against the progress of the human race. He speaks to calumniate thinkers, and to warn the faithful against the discoveries of science. He speaks for the destruction of civilization."[5]

Increased European immigration following the Civil War also fueled a growth in skepticism. Many European immigrants had battled the autocratic regimes of the Old World, rejecting religion while embracing socialism or communism. They brought their ideas about religion and political and economic reform to the United States and fueled the labor unrest of the late nineteenth century. One influential figure was Felix Adler, a Reform Jewish rabbi who came to the United States from Germany in 1873 to teach Hebrew at Cornell

University but shortly thereafter renounced his faith. Adler declared himself an atheist and went on to found the Ethical Culture Society in 1876 to advocate for a secular ethical alternative to religion and for social reform. Adler was a mainstay at freethought rallies. Prominent Reform Rabbi Isaac Wise also regularly associated with freethinkers, speaking occasionally at their meetings and events.[6]

Another element that helped fuel a postwar rise in freethought—discussed in greater detail in chapter 5—was the resurgent women's rights and suffrage movement. Many leading figures in the movement were either freethinkers or held unconventional religious views: Elizabeth Cady Stanton, Susan B. Anthony, Lucretia Mott, Ernestine Rose, Matilda Joslyn Gage, and Lucy Stone. Aside from the self-professed atheist Rose, Stanton was the most open about her religious heterodoxy. Stanton, along with Lucretia Mott, organized the Seneca Falls Convention for women's rights in 1848. Even at that early stage, she had tied the legal and societal subjugation of women to "a perverted application of the Scriptures" perpetuated by male clergy. Stanton declared that "the Gospel, rightly understood, pointed to a oneness of equality, not subordination . . . [and that she] could see no reason why marriage by false creeds should be made a degradation to woman."[7] As the years progressed, Stanton's religious beliefs radicalized and her attacks on Christianity and the clergy intensified. Though she was more outspoken than many radical feminists, she was not alone in seeing traditional Christianity as a root cause of women's oppression. Matilda Joslyn Gage, an agnostic and coauthor of *History of Woman Suffrage* with Stanton and Susan B. Anthony, wrote a pamphlet, "Women, Church, and State," that laid the subjugation of women squarely at the feet of institutional Christianity. Anthony shared many of her friends' agnostic views—"Miss Anthony is an agnostic," Stanton asserted in her 1898 autobiography—but she largely kept her religious views to herself, fearful that any outspoken attacks on religious norms would alienate more conservative allies, such as members of Frances Willard's Woman's Christian Temperance Union (WCTU). Anthony was correct, as Stanton's alignment of women's rights with freethought ideas ensured that her organization, the National Woman Suffrage Association (NWSA), would speak for only a small number of women and men in the greater suffrage and temperance movements.[8]

These various intersecting forces fostered the freethought movement during the Gilded Age. Scientific advances and higher criticism, and the challenges that both presented to religious belief, inspired a new generation of freethinkers. Additionally, many older freethinkers had supported abolition before the war—with some like Wendell Phillips taking active roles in the abolitionist movement—and they carried over their reformist tendencies to advocate for the social causes mentioned above: free scientific inquiry, suffrage and women's rights, labor reform, and universal secular education. What connected these various issues was a belief in human progress that turned on both personal and intellectual freedom. The masthead of *The Truth Seeker*, the nation's largest freethought journal (established in 1873), nicely summed up the interconnected nature of these causes by declaring its dedication to "science, morals, free thought, free discussion, liberalism, sexual equality, labor reform, progression, free education, and whatever tends to elevate and emancipate the human race." Although *The Truth Seeker* was the most successful freethought publication with a national readership, other local freethought journals appeared during the final third of the century, if only for brief periods. Abner Kneeland's *Boston Investigator* was still being published in the 1870s, while freethought journals arose in San Francisco, Buffalo, Kentucky, and Kansas, with at least three in Texas. *The Freethinkers' Magazine* (later renamed *Free Thought Magazine*), edited by Horace L. Green of Chicago, ran from 1882 to 1903 and represented a cerebral alternative to the more confrontational *Truth Seeker*.[9]

The Significance of Robert G. Ingersoll

During the last third of the nineteenth century, the public face of American freethought—and its most indefatigable advocate—was Robert G. Ingersoll, the "Great Agnostic." No other freethinker was more prominent or had a greater impact on public attitudes about secularism and freedom of thought. Between 1870 and 1899, Ingersoll traveled the country lecturing to large audiences in practically every state. One journal described Ingersoll as having a "magnetic personality," and he was renowned for his oratorical skills at a time when public lectures were a major form of entertainment; he rivaled his friend Mark Twain in popularity and notoriety. "Mr. Ingersoll is a very adroit, eloquent, witty and powerful speaker," wrote one reviewer. "However one may disagree with him, it is impossible for the moment to resist his evident sincerity and his stirring appeals." Although his lectures were frequently about current affairs, including advocating for women's suffrage, his most notable speeches critiqued Christianity, the Bible, and the clergy.[10] Ingersoll's lectures drew large audiences who were attracted by his oratorical wit but also by his topics. According to one scholar, his lectures "worked to empower ordinary Americans as participants in the radical changes shaping the world of thought in the final decades of the nineteenth century" and appealed not only to the religiously heterodox but also to those religious believers "willing to grapple with their beliefs and consider alternatives." His lectures also drew the ire of local clergy who knew that his popularity and political connections immunized him from anything harsher than condemnation from the pulpit. On one instance, he brushed off a threat from the head of the Pennsylvania Bible Society to have him prosecuted for blasphemy the next time he was in the state. "If all who take the name of God in vain were imprisoned there would not be room in jails to hold the ministers," he quipped. The threat of blasphemy merely showed "that my lectures are needed."[11]

Robert Green Ingersoll was the son of a Congregational minister who, despite his apparent orthodoxy, had fostered his son's inquisitive mind and love of reading. Having little formal education, Ingersoll read for the bar and became a successful lawyer in Peoria, Illinois, representing railroads and corporate interests. Appointed Attorney General of Illinois in 1867, Ingersoll had a bright political future within the Republican Party.[12] His conservative business and political outlook, though, stood in contrast to his progressive philosophical and social beliefs. In the late 1860s, he began giving lectures, many of which he published, that revealed not only his religious heterodoxy but also his utter disdain for the intellectual constraints imposed on people by organized religion. In 1869, Ingersoll gave his first controversial speech, commemorating the 100th anniversary of the birth of the great German naturalist Alexander von Humboldt. He commended Humboldt's commitment to reason and free inquiry, declaring that "[s]uperstition has always been a relentless enemy of science, faith has been a hater of demonstration, [and] all religions are inconsistent with mental freedom." Christianity, in turn, promoted a vengeful god and secured fealty through fear and ignorance. Ingersoll delivered his "Humboldt" lecture in Cincinnati two weeks later to an enthusiastic audience.[13] More talks followed, on "Tom Paine" (1870) and "The Gods" (1872), both of which continued his attacks on the stultifying nature of religion. Ingersoll painted Paine as a great patriot who was shunned for exposing the falsehoods of the Bible and for elevating reason and free inquiry over superstition. Paine was attacked for revealing "the Bible as childish, unimportant and foolish." Religion, Ingersoll charged, was "a hydra-headed monster, reaching in terrible coils from heaven, and thrusting its thousand fangs into the bleeding, quivering hearts of men." "Infidelity is liberty," Ingersoll concluded, while "all religion is slavery." "The Gods" picked up where "Tom Paine" had left off, arguing that every religion's god was selfish, uncompromising, and bloodthirsty. The Christian god was no exception: "The book, called the Bible, is filled with passages equally horrible, unjust and atrocious." The Bible, Ingersoll insisted, "is simply and purely of human invention—of barbarian invention." Reason and free inquiry represented the only hope for humanity.[14]

With the delivery and publication of "Tom Paine" and "The Gods," Ingersoll established himself as the nation's leading spokesperson for freethought, while the same lectures doomed any possible future political career. In his thirty years on the circuit, Ingersoll would repeat his more popular talks, such as "The Gods," while adding over two dozen additional lectures on related themes: "Ghosts," "God in the Constitution," "Heretics and Heresies," "Toleration," "What Must We Do to Be Saved," and "Why I Am an Agnostic." His wit and biting critique made him the most popular public lecturer of his time, and his ability to draw large audiences and his otherwise conventional politics kept him within the favor of Republican politicians, including James G. Blaine, Rutherford B. Hayes, and James Garfield.[15]

Although Ingersoll was by far the best-known advocate of freethought, he was not alone on the lecture circuit. Throughout the 1870s, '80s, and '90s, dozens of freethought "evangelists," including Benjamin Franklin Underwood, D.M. Bennett, Samuel Porter Putman, Edwin C. Walker, and Charles Reynolds, crisscrossed the nation's highways and backroads, speaking at local freethought societies and to general audiences in leased theaters or under tents. They met with varying degrees of success, though they commonly found both sympathetic and hostile audiences curious to hear their remarks. In the unregulated world of freethought, their theological and social perspectives frequently varied—a few speakers were atheists, more were agnostics, while still others were humanists. Speakers also had their own associated social causes, whether it was women's rights, labor reform, or economic equality and socialism. But what tied the lecturers together, and in a sense united them, was their attack on organized religion and the infallibility of scripture, and their devotion to reason and free inquiry. They also shared an unyielding commitment to achieving a complete separation of church and state.[16]

Moderate Freethought

Ingersoll saw little value in organized religion or a religious belief. God might exist—though Ingersoll doubted it—but humanity and human progress did not require religion, and society would be better off without it. This view was shared by freethinkers on the left.

In the late 1860s, a second, sometimes overlapping, strain of freethought emerged in the United States. This version differed from the more confrontational strain of freethought represented by Ingersoll and *The Truth Seeker* in that it sought to reform and redeem liberal theological thought rather than to reject religion all together. Instead of tracing its roots to Tom Paine and deism, this strain found its legacy in liberal Unitarianism and Transcendentalism as defined and promoted by Ralph Waldo Emerson and Theodore Parker.[17]

As discussed, by the 1850s Transcendentalism had declined as a separate intellectual movement having been absorbed into liberal Unitarianism and Universalism. That set up an eventual conflict between the liberal and conservative wings of Unitarianism. Conservative Unitarianism held sway in New England from 1820 to 1860, distinguishing itself from Calvinism by rejecting notions of predestination, human depravity, and Jesus's individual divinity. But otherwise, its adherents considered themselves fully Christian, accepting the divine inspiration of the Scriptures and the idea of an all-knowing and omnipotent God. In 1853, in reaction to the incursions from Transcendentalism, the American Unitarian Association had formally endorsed the divine origin of Jesus's ministry through the miraculous interposition of God and the authority of the Bible.[18] Then, at the conclusion of the Civil War in April 1865, Henry W. Bellows, leader of the conservatives and minister of New York's prestigious All Souls Church, called a conference to consolidate creedal consistency within Unitarianism. Bellows's successful move set off a rebellion among younger, liberal Unitarian ministers who had been influenced by Parker and Transcendentalism. These "Radicals," as they called themselves, founded the Free Religious Association (FRA) in 1867 "to promote the interests of pure religion, to encourage the scientific study of theology, and to increase the fellowship of the spirit." Leading the Free Religionists were two tireless advocates for free religious inquiry who would take the movement out of Christianity into the realm of rational theism: Octavius B. Frothingham and Francis E. Abbot.[19]

Frothingham is little known today, but in the 1870s he was one of the country's more prominent clergymen, rivaling the fame of his friend Henry Ward Beecher but having a reputation as the superior intellectual. Frothingham was the son of the influential pastor of Boston's First (Unitarian) Church, a graduate of Harvard, and a disciple of Theodore Parker. Frothingham embraced Transcendentalism in the 1850s. In 1859, at the invitation of Reverend Bellows, Frothingham became the founding minister of the Third Unitarian Church in New York City, but after the break with Bellows, his church dropped its denominational affiliation, becoming the Independent Liberal Church. Frothingham's learned sermons made him one of New York's more popular ministers, with Sunday attendance at his church averaging between eight hundred and a thousand people, most of them drawn from the city's liberal intellectual elite.[20] Frothingham maintained his pastorate through 1879, even as he moved increasingly away from any semblance of liberal Christianity. Instead, he began to advocate a "new theology" or "religion of humanity," which one biographer called "a synthesis of elements of Deism, transcendentalism, and Darwinism." Never rejecting theism, Frothingham sought to bring religion to terms with evolutionary theory and modern biblical criticism, believing the former held one key to understanding the intellectual development of humankind. "The supreme wisdom," wrote his biographer, "lay within the human mind rather than coming from some transcendent God. As a transcendentalist [Frothingham] believed God was within man and nature; as an evolutionist he was sure that all the forces of nature and society were working toward a progressive, humanistic end." Based on this humanistic theism, Frothingham and his coreligionists disavowed atheism and agnosticism, believing they could be freethinkers, committed to free inquiry, while remaining religious.[21]

Joining Frothingham in the leadership of the Free Religionist movement was Francis E. Abbot. Compared to Frothingham's privileged upbringing and standing among society's elites, Abbot had a more hard-scrabble career but was Frothingham's intellectual peer. More of a social philosopher and a pugilist, he saw Free Religion as a means of reforming society.[22] A graduate of Harvard College and Meadville Theological School, Abbot held his first pastorate at the Unitarian Society of Dover, New Hampshire, from 1864 to 1868. Already on the liberal extremes of unitarianism, Abbot shortly drifted away from any adherence to Christianity, adopting what he would later term "scientific theism." Scripture and Christianity—including Unitarianism—were in his view a perversion of true theism because they saw a conflict between science and a faith in God. The "being of God is a truth of knowledge, and knowledge is but a syndrome of Science." But religious authority "of every form," Abbot insisted, "opposes the principle of absolute Freedom, of unlimited free thought."[23] Like Frothingham, Abbot's commitment to unlimited freedom of thought did not lead to atheism, despite what some critics charged. "Outside of Christianity must my protest against error and sin henceforth be heard, but not outside religion, not, I trust, outside of spiritual fidelity—not, I believe in my soul, outside of God."[24]

Abbot's rejection of Unitarianism and the authority of the Bible caused a split within his congregation in 1868. Even though Abbot initially resigned as pastor, calling on supporters to help him create a new independent theistic society, the radical members prevailed on a vote within the congregation, taking control of the church away from the conservatives. The dispute set up a celebrated legal case before the New Hampshire Supreme Judicial Court, *Hale v. Everett*. In a controversial four-to-one decision, the justices awarded control over the church building and name to the conservative minority on the ground that "Deists, theists, free religionists, and other infidels, though they may be Unitarians in some sense, are not Unitarian Christians." In addition to the court's troubling foray into theological matters—no doubt assisted by Abbot's admission that he was no longer a Christian or a Unitarian—the majority engaged in an extended discussion about how New Hampshire's law, government, and society were founded on Christian principles. The justices asserted that even though they were unable to prohibit skepticism outright, they had no obligation to facilitate "doctrines subversive of the fundamental principles of Christianity."[25] The majority's holding elicited an impassioned dissent from Justice Charles Doe, who argued the majority had crossed a constitutional line by declaring which faction was authentically Unitarian and by perpetuating the false maxim that Christianity formed part of the law. The court, Justice Doe wrote, was "authorized to determine all the principles of the common law in force in this state; the court [was] not authorized to determine a single principle of Christianity."[26]

With the loss, the unemployed Abbot began tutoring at Harvard part-time, and eventually, in mid-1869, received a ministerial call from the Unitarian Society in Toledo, Ohio, whose leaders were impressed with Abbot's passion and intellect. Abbot accepted the pulpit on the condition that the church disaffiliate from the Unitarian fellowship, to which a majority of its members agreed. Abbot's tenure in Toledo was troubled and short-lived, however, as

Bellows's American Unitarian Association helped establish a new "First Unitarian Society" of Toledo, which sapped support from Abbot's society. By 1873 his Toledo Society was largely moribund and Abbot had moved back to Boston.[27]

A bright spot for Abbot's last years in Dover, one that continued during his time in Toledo, was the founding of the FRA in 1867. The year before, Abbot had attended the second national conference of the American Unitarian Association in Syracuse; there, he had petitioned the denomination to reconsider its creedal statement in favor of one supporting "perfect freedom of thought" and a "diversity of opinion," but he was voted down. While that rebuke contributed to Abbot's abandonment of Unitarianism, it also motivated him to form an organization to promote post-Christian theism. Needing a person of stature to head the new movement, Abbot and his allies solicited Frothingham, who agreed. In May 1867, the FRA held its inaugural meeting in Boston, drawing an overflowing and enthusiastic crowd, no doubt due to its list of notable speakers. In addition to Frothingham and Abbot, speakers included Ralph Waldo Emerson, skeptic-turned-spiritualist Robert Dale Owen, suffragist leader Lucretia Mott, Wendell Phillips, William Lloyd Garrison, Gerrit Smith—all leading abolitionists—and liberal rabbis Isaac M. Wise and Max Lilienthal. As the diversity of the list indicates, the FRA sought to appeal to a broad range of liberal religious opinion. The purpose of the Association was to provide a forum—through meetings, lectures, and publications—for discussing theological and philosophical matters without restriction and to follow those lines of inquiry wherever they led. The Association's bylaws made clear that it would "leave each individual responsible for his own opinions."[28]

Throughout its twenty-five-year existence, the FRA was never large—possibly five hundred members at its height—and its leaders were chiefly disaffected ex-Unitarians or former Transcendentalists. Moreover, its agenda was never overly ambitious. Its members were generally satisfied to engage in intellectual discussions. As one news article on the FRA's founding noted, "[t]hey do not seek to organize or control the radical religious movement in America—its very freedom precludes any such thought or effort—but contribute in their own way to the great work" of free religious inquiry.[29] A more critical analysis of the FRA, by the Methodist publication *Zion's Herald*, found even that limited agenda sufficiently troubling: Abbot, while being "a man of intellect," was "the most radical of radicals, proclaiming that the existence of a God and a hereafter can be ascertained only by science," while Frothingham, despite being "a man of remarkable culture," was "bold, revolutionary, and reckless, glorifying in the beliefs and unbeliefs of unbelievers." Both men were "fitting illustrations of the tendency of modern Free Religion to folly and ruin."[30]

Despite the FRA's commitment to full and free theological inquiry—and Frothingham's and Abbot's denouncement of Christianity—the Association's leadership had little interest in reaching out to the agnostics, atheists, and humanists on the left end of the freethought spectrum. Free religionists were reformers, seeking to identify the purest form of religion freed from the encumbrances of institutionalized Christianity. Radical freethinkers, such as Ingersoll, had no such interest. The casual and irreverent way in which Ingersoll and his ilk dismissed religion also annoyed Abbot and Frothingham, who took their intellectual project seriously. Although Frothingham commended Ingersoll's "aim to lift off the burden of superstition and priestcraft" and "to promote rational progress and goodness," he criticized Ingersoll's "cloudy sphere of agnosticism" and the dogmatism of both orthodoxy and infidelity.[31] Abbot's opinions were harsher, calling agnosticism "a pretended philosophy." He criticized the "crude, raw infidelism" promoted by Ingersoll. "Agnosticism declares that it is impossible 'to climb through Nature up to Nature's God'—that Nature is knowable and known, while God is both unknown and unknowable," Abbot wrote. "But Scientific Theology declares that it is impossible to know Nature in any degree without knowing God precisely in the same degree—that both are knowable, but neither is wholly known, by man." Abbot believed that "the progress of natural knowledge is itself the ever-progressive revelation of an Immanent God."[32] Summing up the differences between the two strains of freethought, Frothingham's contemporary and (fawning) biographer declared that "[m]odern infidelity is of two kinds: the old, destructive school of Paine and the French Revolutionaries; [and] the new, constructive religion which liberalists are professing."[33]

To consider Free Religion the "intellectual" side of Gilded Age freethought does a disservice to those freethinkers on the left who engaged in an active theological exchange with both orthodox evangelicals and liberal Protestants while criticizing the former's resistance to social reform. Unlike their radical freethinking allies, however, many leaders of moderate freethought had theological training and had previously served as ministers or on college faculties, so their primary focus was on the intellectual side of freethought. Most freethinkers in Ingersoll's camp had no such backgrounds. While Free Religionists also worried about the social implications of a dominant religious orthodoxy, whether that was imposed through evangelical Protestantism or Catholicism, they were chiefly concerned about orthodoxy's challenge to free and full theological inquiry, not to its practical applications. And the rank-and-file Free Religionist, as a member of the liberal elite, would have bristled if anyone had compared them to the likes of Charles Reynolds or—heaven forbid—Elmina Drake Slenker.[34]

The Liberal Agenda

Before long, Abbot became disillusioned with the limited agenda of the FRA, particularly with the apparent hesitancy of the organization's membership to address the deleterious societal effects of religious orthodoxy. This frustration inspired Abbot to establish a journal, *The Index*, in 1870, while he was toiling in Toledo. Abbot intended *The Index* to be the voice of Free Religion and ostensibly that of the FRA, although the journal remained independent of the Association until Abbot resigned as publisher in 1880. In its first issue, *The Index* declared its aim: "to increase pure and genuine religion in the world, . . . to increase freedom [of inquiry,] to destroy every species of spiritual slavery, to expose every form of superstition, [and] to encourage independence of thought and action in all matters that concern belief." It professed that it stood "squarely outside of Christianity [and] the authority of the Bible, the Church, or the Christ, but [would] rest solely on the authority of right reason and good conscience." *The Index* contrasted itself with the short-lived *Radical*, a journal that published chiefly theological essays by liberal Unitarians and Free Religionists, including Frothingham and Abbot. In his position as editor and chief compiler of content for *The Index*, Abbot reprinted news and articles that touched on the intersection of religion, politics, and social controversies alongside his own commentary on the various issues. (Abbot took pleasure in reprinting articles attacking *The Index* and Free Religion, no doubt as a means of self-validation.) "*The Index* is an agitator," Abbot proclaimed, "its work is agitation, the strenuous endeavor to apply the highest religious ideas of the time to a state of society" in distress. Abbot's commentary was usually thoughtful but at times caustic in its criticism of competing religious perspectives, whether that was Catholic, evangelical Protestant, liberal Protestant, or agnostic. As editor, Abbot walked a fine line, one that was not always clear to anyone but himself. For example, even though he fully embraced scientific evolution, he rejected Herbert Spencer's materialistic reductionism, which left no room for a deity. *The Index* quickly became a leading voice of theological liberalism, and it had a greater impact on public opinion than its audience of approximately 4,500 subscribers would otherwise suggest. Stow Persons, a historian of Free Religion, called *The Index* "easily the finest liberal journal in America."[35]

Abbot's *Index* appeared at a moment of conflagration among competing forces in American religion. Religious controversies abounded. In Utah, federal authorities and the larger American public expressed frustration at the seemingly intractable "Mormon Question" involving polygamy and the political power of the Mormon Church. As a correspondent to the *New York Times* opined in 1872, "[t]he Mormon problem is one of those rare social and religious phenomena demanding for its solution more real statesmanship than any political issue of the decade."[36] Of more immediate concern for most Americans, however, was the increasing conflict between Protestantism and Catholicism.[37]

As mentioned earlier, for approximately forty years controversy had surrounded the practice of Protestant religious exercises in the common schools and Catholic requests for a share of the public-school funds for their parochial schools. With the conclusion of the Civil War, the controversy—termed the "School Question"—grew more heated. In November 1869, the public school board for Cincinnati, Ohio, a city with approximately an equal number of Protestant and Catholic schoolchildren, voted to abandon its forty-year practice of daily religious exercises involving unmediated prayer and Bible reading. Almost immediately, a "Friends of the Bible" committee obtained a court injunction halting implementation of the board's resolution. The controversy garnered national attention, with emotions running high, particularly among evangelical Protestants, whose journals charged that there was a Catholic conspiracy to undermine America's public education system. "Shall the Bible or the Pope be Schoolmaster," screamed the Methodist's *Zion's Herald*. "Romanists" would not "rest until our whole system of common school education is utterly overthrown."[38] Liberal Protestants, however, including Henry Ward Beecher, Joseph Thompson of New York's Broadway Tabernacle, and Samuel T. Spear, editor of *The Independent*, supported the board's decision, as did several secular journals such as *Atlantic Monthly* and *Harper's Weekly*. After a heated trial involving several prominent lawyers, including future US Supreme Court justice Stanley Matthews, the Ohio Superior Court voted two-to-one to reinstate the religious exercises while affirming Ohio's status as a "Christian state." That victory for Protestant orthodoxy did not last, however, as three years later the Ohio Supreme Court reversed the Superior Court's ruling and reinstated the board's resolution. The unanimous court rejected the plaintiffs' argument that the state had a legal obligation to promote Christianity: "United with government, religion never rises above the merest superstition; united with religion, government never rises above the merest despotism; and all history shows us that the more widely and completely they are separated, the better it is for both."[39] Evangelical Protestants excoriated the decision as a much-feared harbinger of things to come. By mid-decade, several city school districts with high numbers of Catholic schoolchildren, including Chicago, St. Louis, Buffalo, and Rochester, had joined Cincinnati in dropping their Protestant religious exercises.[40]

While agitation grew over religious exercises in the public schools, Catholic leaders continued to push for public funding of their parochial schools. "We ask simply that the 'money raised by taxes' . . . shall be divided *pro rata*, and so, by dividing the difficulty, conquer it!" wrote the *Catholic World*. Although Catholic leaders were generally unsuccessful in securing funding from state legislatures—such funding was banned by laws or constitutional provisions in a majority of states, including New York and Massachusetts—they found greater success with local city governments, particularly in those cities with large Catholic immigrant populations.[41] In a July 1869 article titled "Our Established Church," *Putnam's Magazine* charged that the Catholic Church was the chief recipient of public political and financial largesse in New York City and in other eastern cities.[42] An 1872 report of the New York City Council of Political Reform corroborated the *Putnam's* story. The report included a section on "Sectarian Appropriations of Public Money" which alleged that hundreds of thousands of public dollars were paid by Tammany Hall not only to support religious charities but also to aid religious schools. Even though the report listed various religious denominations as recipients, over ninety percent of the funding, approximately $640,000 in 1871, went to Catholic institutions and schools. *Harper's Weekly* complained that at the same time as the Catholic Church was receiving funds for its schools and charities, the Catholic archdiocese had petitioned for the removal of the Protestant Bible from New York City Schools. Giving warning to its national readership, *Harper's* declared that such "crafty working, of which we have given sample, is going on all over the Union."[43]

Abbot's *Index* followed the School Question closely, reprinting articles and commentary offering a variety of perspectives. Abbot's opposition to both issues—religious exercises and funding—aligned him with liberal Protestants such as Beecher and *The Independent*'s Spear and those freethinkers on his left, including Ingersoll, who believed that public education should be completely secular with no form of religious instruction, and that no public funds from any source should pay for religious education or, for that matter, subsidize religious charities or houses of worship through tax exemptions. Abbot insisted that the ultimate goal was "the secularization of the public schools by discontinuing all religious exercises in them, and especially by redeeming the school system from its present sectarian Protestant character through the abolition of Bible reading as a school exercise." That goal required "the national ideal of a purely secular government" that can "intelligently defend the total separation of State and Church."[44]

As a critic of religious superstition and authoritarianism, Abbot eagerly denounced the Catholic Church. In a widely read article that appeared in *The Index* and other journals, "The Catholic Peril in America," Abbot warned about "the renewed aggressiveness of the Papal Imperialism" and how it would affect "the future of the United States." Abbot documented the phenomenal growth in Catholic church membership, institutions, and wealth. The "Roman Catholic Church is fast becoming the richest corporation in the land, with all its despotic money power in the hands of an episcopal 'Roman Ring,' who use it in making it greater and more efficient still for the overthrow of free institutions." While a real danger existed that the church might succeed "in its assault on the public schools, and (through them) all free institutions," the related danger was that "Catholic ambition is rousing Protestant Evangelical ambition to new and dangerous manifestations."

> This, then, is the Catholic peril in America—not alone that the Roman Catholic Church may become a ruling majority, or (what is worse) a ruling minority, with all the measureless miseries and mischiefs of such rule, but that, in order to strengthen the Republic against the possibility of such rulership, the great Protestant party may resort to measures involving the fundamental principle of the Republic itself . . . that the Church and State can be and ought to be wholly separate.[45]

By the time Abbot wrote "The Catholic Peril in America" in early 1876, he had a ready example of the second peril in mind: a movement among conservative Protestants to amend the US Constitution to include a recognition of

God and his sovereignty over the operations of government and unite church and state.

The "Christian Amendment Movement" had arisen during the darkest days of the Civil War when many religious conservatives believed that the war's travails were signs of God's disfavor. The nation's "calamities . . . result[ed] from our forgetfulness of God, and from slavery, so long as our nation's reproach," noted a report by the Northern Methodist Church, "and that it becomes us to humble ourselves and forsake our sins as a people, and hereafter, in our laws and acts, to honor God." Some believed that the nation had abandoned God by declining to formally recognize his authority and failing to enforce laws consistent with Christian standards. The solution—or at least one solution—was to amend the US Constitution to acknowledge his sovereignty over the nation and its institutions.[46]

Even though Protestants from various denominations, including Congregationalist theologian Horace Bushnell, believed in the need for a national rapprochement with God, the impetus for a constitutional amendment—and the leadership for the movement—came from members of an ultraconservative Protestant denomination: the Reformed Presbyterian Church, otherwise known as "Covenanters," who believed that governments, like individuals, were moral entities subject to God's laws. The only legitimate governments, they claimed, were those that acknowledged God's authority.[47] The Christian Amendment Movement initially secured the support of several prominent people, including Bushnell and Senators Charles Sumner and John Sherman, and even received an early endorsement from a mainstream Protestant journal, *The Independent*. That support enabled leaders of the movement to obtain two audiences with President Abraham Lincoln, who was noncommittal about the proposal. After an initial flurry of interest, wide support for the amendment evaporated, undermined by Union victories that, for Bushnell and others, now indicated God's approval of the nation.[48]

Following the war, the movement floundered for several years, only to be reborn as the National Reform Association (NRA) in 1868, now with an agenda broader than simply amending the Constitution—although that goal remained its centerpiece—that included "the preservation of the Christian Institutions of this country," to wit: "our civil Sabbath; the Bible in the public schools; [and] the securing of a uniform marriage and divorce law, conformed to the law of Christ." As its spokesman T.P. Stevenson declared in one address, "The Ends We Seek," "what we propose is nothing of a sectarian character. . . .

[A]ll our movement aims to preserve [are] the Christian institutions which have descended to us from our fathers." But those institutions—Bible reading, the oath, blasphemy laws, and "the Christian law of marriage"—were under attack by the forces of "infidelity and Romanism." After 1868, the NRA leaders worked assiduously to build support for its constitutional amendment by currying favor with conservative politicians and gathering petition signatures from sympathetic Protestants from across the nation. From 1868 until 1873, the honorary president of the NRA was US Supreme Court Justice William Strong, an old-school Presbyterian layman, who would figure proximately in future developments. Despite support from a handful of legislators, including Senators Sherman and Richard Yates, the petitions languished in the Senate Judiciary Committee.[49]

Most newspapers treated the NRA's activities and goals as a novelty, a "vain undertaking not likely to succeed," or "curious" but essentially harmless, according to the *New York Times*. Calling the NRA's motives "unquestionably good" and declaring the "sincerity and piety" of its leadership to be "above suspicion," the *New York Times* insisted that any such amendment "would be utterly ineffectual" in "strengthen[ing] the faith of the Christian [or] dispel[ling] the doubts of the unbeliever." "We think it best, therefore, to leave the Constitution as it is."[50]

Abbot documented the activities of the NRA with increasing alarm. Practically every week from 1871 through 1874, the pages of *The Index* issued a hue and cry about the threats to American democracy and secular government represented by the NRA and its proposed Christian Amendment. Enactment of the amendment, Abbot insisted, "will be the overthrow of the Free Republic and the erection of a Christian Theocracy in its stead. It will be the formal abolition of the great principle of the separation of Church and State. . . . It will be the return of the Dark Ages, or the persecution of science and free thought, of the frightful tyranny of ecclesiastical domination over the mind."[51] *The Independent*, which had changed its view on the NRA's proposed amendment in the late 1860s, also criticized the proposal. If the amendment were adopted, "it would fundamentally change the whole theory of the Constitution in regard to religion, and . . . establish a complete religious despotism." But unlike *The Index*, *The Independent* not only saw the proposal as likely to fail, but that Abbot's hyperbole was overblown. The "great majority of Americans," wrote Samuel Spear, have "too much sagacity to permit the establishment by law of any form of religion in this country, and too much common sense to suppose there is the slightest danger that such a thing will come to pass."[52]

Abbot disagreed. The goals of the NRA and its proposed Christian Amendment led Abbot to respond in four ways. The first came in January 1872, when Abbot sent out a call from the pages of *The Index* to all who opposed the amendment to sign their names to a giant counterpetition to be sent to Congress to "protest against such proposed amendments as an attempt to revolutionize the government of the United States, and to overthrow the great principles of complete religious liberty and the complete separation of Church and State on which it was established by its original founders." Abbot listed the counterpetition and the call for names on the front page of every issue of *The Index* for the next two years.[53] It proved to be his greatest success at *The Index*. On January 7, 1874, Charles Sumner—who also had a change of heart about the Christian Amendment—presented *The Index*'s mammoth counterpetition—containing some 35,179 names and measuring 953 feet in length—to the Senate. The staged event caught the attention of the regular press. "It is seldom that 35,000 people can be found to sign an appeal against a wise measure," wrote the *Boston Globe*, "and the 953 feet of the petition certainly go a great way in demonstrating the absurdity of the proposed constitutional plan of salvation."[54]

Abbot followed on his petition drive by issuing two new calls in the pages of *The Index* in early 1873. One was for the formation of local "Liberal Leagues" to gather signatures and to otherwise organize opposition to the activities of the NRA and similar efforts. The "Liberal Leagues" would "lay the foundations of a great national party of freedom, which shall demand the entire secularization of our municipal, state, and national government." In conjunction with his call for organizing, Abbot issued his most ambitious, and controversial, memorial: the "Nine Demands of Liberalism," a manifesto of freethought liberalism that left little in doubt. It called for the complete severance between religion and government through the abolition of tax exemptions for churches, courtroom oaths, Sunday laws, religious exercises in public schools, and chaplains for Congress and in the armed forces. The manifesto also called for prohibiting any public funding of "sectarian educational and charitable institutions." The final two demands insisted that all laws that enforced Christian morality be repealed and that "no privileges or advantage shall be conceded to Christianity or any other special religion; [and] that our entire political system shall be founded and administered on a purely secular basis." Abbot saw his Demands of Liberalism as constituting the platform of the Liberal Leagues, and he reprinted the Demands in every issue of *The Index* for the next several years.[55]

Abbot's Demands of Liberalism and call for organizing Liberal Leagues indicated that he and *The Index* had entered a new phase. For its first year or so, the journal had presented the case for post-Christian theism, or Free Religion, while highlighting the threats of religious authoritarianism, including from the NRA. O.B. Frothingham had been a contributing editor during this time, but his involvement with the journal now diminished. By issuing the Demands of Liberalism and calling for Liberal Leagues, Abbot had committed himself not simply to preserving separation of church and state but also to achieving the complete secularization of society, moving him closer to Robert Ingersoll. The "sole object of the Liberal League Movement is to secure the complete practical embodiment of the original national ideal of a purely Secular State," Abbot wrote, with the "aim to make the *total* separation of church and state the *fact*, as much as the *theory*, of our national existence." In organizing Liberal Leagues, rather than using the existing FRA, Abbot saw the need for activism, not just advocacy. It also indicated his willingness to ally with freethinkers on the left and liberal Jews. The threats from religious authoritarianism, he believed, necessitated that liberals of all ilk put aside their petty differences and unite.[56] Even though several of the Demands appealed to liberal Protestants like Samuel Spear and liberal Jews like Isaac Wise, the manifesto, with its "demands," went too far for some potential allies. Despite Abbot's hope that all liberals could unite around his manifesto, the Demands of Liberalism backfired. Religious conservatives, including the NRA, pointed to the Demands as evidence of the threat of "infidelity" and its assault on Christian institutions, which in turn necessitated a Christian Amendment.[57]

Abbot was still not finished. Borrowing from the NRA's playbook, Abbot proposed his own constitutional amendment. This strategy grew out of his counterpetition to the NRA's pending Christian Amendment in 1874. A month after Senator Charles Sumner had submitted Abbot's petition opposing the NRA's amendment, the House Judiciary Committee issued its report recommending that the proposed amendment be tabled indefinitely. Still, the House committee's report did not go as far as Abbot would have liked. It applauded the wisdom of "our Christian fathers," who ensured that nothing in the Constitution should refer "to any religious sect or doctrine," which was too much for Abbot.[58] He knew that notwithstanding the success of his counterpetition, the NRA had gathered 20,000 more signatures on its petitions to Congress, and that the organization pledged to try again in a future Congress. "The whole energies of the Association are devoted to collecting further signatures," warned *The Index*. "They intend to have 2,000,000 names to present to Congress in 1876, the national centennial year, in favor of their movement."[59]

In January 1874, around the same time that Charles Sumner submitted Abbot's counterpetition, *The Index* issued its first call for passage of a Religious Freedom Amendment to the Constitution. The first section of the proposed amendment essentially restated the language of the First Amendment, adding a prohibition on "favoring any particular form of religion." The second section made the same language applicable to the states, but then added language prohibiting any state religious test for officeholding or state action depriving any person of "his or her right, privileges or capacities" based on "any opinions he or she may hold on the subject of religion." A year earlier, in the *Slaughterhouse Cases*, the Supreme Court had ruled that the Privileges and Immunities and the Due Process clauses of the newly enacted Fourteenth Amendment did not apply the protections of the Bill of Rights to the states. That meant that state officials were bound only by their state laws when it came to respecting civil rights, including religious rights. At the time, eight state constitutions (out of thirty-seven) imposed a religious test for public officeholding, disqualifying non-Christians, while a majority required a belief in God to serve as a witness or to testify in court. And in previous decades, approximately a dozen state supreme courts had affirmed that Christianity lay at the foundation of the common law, such that public officials were obliged to apply the law consistent with Christian principles. "If the United States are one nation," Abbot wrote, "if all parts of every nation must, as a condition of healthy national life, be governed by one homogenous law and vivified by one common spirit—then the Freedom Amendment is in some shape absolutely essential to the future greatness and happiness of our country." Abbot would promote his Religious Freedom Amendment in the pages of *The Index* for the next three years.[60]

By 1875, the number of local Liberal Leagues had grown to thirty, emboldening Abbot to send out a call to form a National Liberal League, in part to unify the various local Leagues while broadening its base to include spiritualists, freethinkers, and other nontheistic secularists. Despite these efforts, Abbot's Liberal Leagues were increasingly in competition and at odds with Frothingham's FRA, in part over *The Index*'s militant tone and the decision to appeal to nontheists (Abbot, however, drew the line at atheists, arguing that one could be a freethinker, a rationalist, a non-Christian, but never an "infidel"). Nonetheless, Abbot asked all Liberals to put aside their theological differences and work toward securing "the complete practical embodiment of the original national ideal of a purely SECULAR STATE." "Liberals should now for a while resolutely ignore all side issues and work persistently for the absolute separation of Church and State," Abbot declared. This was to be the "sole object" of the coalition, hopefully to be achieved through the passage of the Religious Freedom Amendment.[61] In September 1875, Abbot called for a Centennial Congress of Liberals to meet in Philadelphia in early July 1876, to coincide with the Centennial Exposition being held in that city at the same time. Also, not by coincidence, Abbot planned his liberal congress to meet the day after the NRA's annual convention, also to be held in Philadelphia.[62]

Neither the National Reform Association's nor the National Liberal League's Philadelphia convention was heavily attended. Nonetheless, the secular and religious press reported on both conventions, noting the novelty of two competing organizations so diametrically opposed to each other meeting back to back. Many reports viewed the goals and proposed amendments of both groups as unnecessary and unachievable. Although siding with the position of the Liberal League, the *Boston Globe* opined that both organizations were "made up of earnest and well-meaning men, representing two opposing tendencies, both of which can by no means possibly prevail."[63] Henry Ward Beecher's *Christian Union* also questioned the goals of both organizations, though laying more criticism on the agenda of the Liberal League:

> To separate Church and State is one thing; to separate religion and politics is another. It is rather discouraging to find two conventions of eminent men that do not recognize the difference. It is not Christian features in the Government, but Christian spirit in the hearts of the people, we need to maintain; it is not religion in public life, but sectarian strifes and jealousies we need to abate.[64]

But the League's call for the "'immediate and absolute secularization of the State,' if it means anything," opined the *Christian Union*, "[m]eans the abolition of all recognition of religion from American institutions." This was a position that most liberal Protestants could not accept.[65]

At least publicly, and in the pages of *The Index*, Abbot was nonplussed by the low attendance at the Liberal Congress—approximately two hundred people. The participants gave impassioned speeches and passed resolutions consistent with the aims of the Demands of Liberalism. Abbot and his fellow Liberals believed they were at the forefront of a national movement and that time was on their side.[66] Abbot also believed that all liberals could unite under the banner of perfecting the separation of church and state. The official report of the Congress listed honorary vice presidents and officers of the League from across the freethought spectrum, ranging from O.B. Frothingham on one side to Robert Dale Owen and Rabbi Isaac Wise in the middle to Robert Ingersoll and D.M. Bennett, the editor of *The Truth Seeker*, on the other side. There is no indication that any of these figures attended the Congress, but apparently, they lent their names in support of the League's efforts. D.M. Bennett, for one, endorsed the Demands of Liberalism by reprinting it in several editions of *The Truth Seeker*. William Lloyd Garrison and Wendell Phillips also sent letters endorsing the aims of the organization. And the freethought lecturer B.F. Underwood, a frequent contributor to *The Truth Seeker*, not only attended but also presented a paper titled "The Practical Separation of Church and State." Abbot had reason to believe that they were witnessing the beginnings of a united, national freethought movement, one that would have a major impact on the secular character of the nation. Within two years, those hopes would be dashed.[67]

NOTES

1. Jacoby, *Freethinkers*, 152–153.
2. Turner, *Without God, without Creed*, 146–150.
3. Turner, *Without God, without Creed*, 171–187; Carter, *Spiritual Crisis*, 23–42; Warren, *American Freethought*, 45–72.
4. Ingersoll, "The Ghosts," 1:314–315.
5. Green, *The Bible, the School, and the Constitution*, 183–184; Robert G. Ingersoll, "Rome, or Reason?," *North American Review*, Nov. 1888, 503.
6. Benny Kraut, *From Reform Judaism to Ethical Culture: The Religious Evolution of Felix Adler* (Cincinnati, OH: Hebrew Union College Press, 1979); Daniel R. Langton, "Discourses of Doubt: The Place of Atheism, Skepticism, and Infidelity in Nineteenth Century North American Reform Jewish Thought," *Hebrew Union College Annual* 88 (2017): 203–253.
7. Ernestine Rose, "A Defense of Atheism," in *Mistress of Herself: Speeches and Letters of Ernestine L. Rose*, ed. Paula Doress-Worters (New York: Feminist Press,

2008), 295–300; Elizabeth Cady Stanton, Susan B. Anthony, and Matilda Joslyn Gage, *History of Woman Suffrage* (Rochester, NY: Charles Mann Printing, 1881), 1:79–80; Sehat, *Myth of American Religious Freedom*, 96–108.

8. Elizabeth Cady Stanton, *Eighty Years and More: Reminiscences, 1815–1897* (New York: European Pub., 1898; New York: Schocken Books, 1971), 161; Matilda Joslyn Gage, "Woman, Church, and State," in Stanton et al., *History of Woman Suffrage* 1:755–782; R. Laurence Moore and Isaac Kramnick, *Godless Citizens in a Godly Republic: Atheists in American Public Life* (New York: W.W. Norton, 2018), 60–61; Kathleen Barry, *Susan B. Anthony: A Biography of a Singular Feminist* (New York: NYU Press, 1988), 95–97; Elizabeth Griffith, *In Her Own Right: The Life of Elizabeth Cady Stanton* (New York: Oxford University Press, 1984), 45–46; Jeanne Stevenson-Moessner, "Elizabeth Cady Stanton, Reformer to Revolutionary: A Theological Trajectory," *Journal of the American Academy of Religion* 62 (1994): 673–697.

9. Jacoby, *Freethinkers*, 151–155, 187; Warren, *American Freethought*, 23–24, 36.

10. Jacoby, *Freethinkers*, 157–185; Jacoby, *The Great Agnostic*; Orvin Larson, *American Infidel: Robert G. Ingersoll* (New York: The Citadel Press, 1962); David D. Anderson, *Robert Ingersoll* (New York: Twayne, 1972); Thomas D. Schwartz, "Mark Twain and Robert Ingersoll: The Freethought Connection," *American Literature* 48 (1976): 183–193; "Current Topics," *Albany Law Review*, Jan. 25, 1890, 61; "Woman's Right to Divorce," Ingersoll, *Works*, 8:383–390.

11. Paul Stob, "Religious Conflict and Intellectual Agency: Robert Ingersoll's Contribution to American Thought and Culture," *Rhetoric and Public Affairs* 16 (2013): 719–752, 722; "Blasphemy," Ingersoll, *Works*, 8:202–204.

12. Herman E. Kittredge, "Ingersoll: A Biographical Appreciation," in Ingersoll, *Works*, 13:8–12; Smith, *Robert G. Ingersoll*, 58–79.

13. "Humboldt," Ingersoll, *Works*, 1:103–104; Larson, *American Infidel*, 100–101.

14. "Tom Paine," Ingersoll, *Works*, 1:121–165, 141, 158–159; "The Gods," ibid., 7–90, 14, 17.

15. Moore and Kramnick, *Godless Citizens in a Godly Republic*, 48–50; Larson, *American Infidel*, 98–115; Jacoby, *The Great Agnostic*, 57–64, 68.

16. Warren, *American Freethought*, 20, 27, 32–33, 40; A.L. Rawson, "The Conditions of Freethought in the United States," *The Truth Seeker*, June 25, 1881, 410–411.

17. Warren, *American Freethought*, 96–116.

18. Persons, *Free Religion*, 1–13 Robinson, "'The New Epoch of Belief.'"

19. Warren, *American Freethought*, 98–99; Caruthers, *Octavius Brooks Frothingham*, 100–101; Ahlstrom and Mullin, *The Scientific Theist*, 61–76; Octavius Brooks Frothingham, *Recollections and Impressions, 1822–1890* (New York: G.P. Putnam's Sons, 1891), 115–117; "Free Religion," *The Radical* (July 1867), 695–698.

20. Frothingham, *Recollections*, 74–76, 126–128.

21. Caruthers, *Octavius Brooks Frothingham*, 70–77, 108–112; Edmond C. Stedman, *Octavius Brooks Frothingham and the New Faith* (New York: G.P. Putnam's Sons, 1876).

22. Ahlstrom and Mullin, *The Scientific Theist*, 87, 90–91.

23. Francis Ellingwood Abbot, "A Radical's Theology," *The Radical* (June 1867), 585–598.

24. Ahlstrom and Mullin, *The Scientific Theist*, 51.

25. Ibid., 51–60; Hale v. Everett, 5 Shir. (N.H.), 9, 12, 133 (1868).

26. Hale v. Everett, 5 Shir., 202 (Doe, J., dissenting).

27. Ahlstrom and Mullin, *The Scientific Theist*, 58–60, 81–87.

28. Frothingham, *Recollections*, 119–123; "Free Religion," *The Radical*, 695–698; Ahlstrom and Mullin, *The Scientific Theist*, 66–69, 72–75; W. Creighton Peden, *The Philosopher of Free Religion: Francis Ellingwood Abbot, 1836–1903* (New York: Peter Lang, 1992), 38–41; Warren, *American Freethought*, 98–102; Persons, *Free Religion*, 45–54.

29. "Free Religion," *The Radical*, 698; "Meeting of the Free Religion Association in Boston," *New York Times*, May 29, 1869, 1.

30. Daniel Dorchester, "The Lives and Deaths of the Infidel Saints," *Zion's Herald*, March 9, 1871, 110.

31. Frothingham, *Recollections*, 254, 277.

32. Frances E. Abbot, "The Ground for All Liberal Religion," *The Open Court*, Dec. 26, 1889, 2012–2014; Francis E. Abbot, *The Way Out of Agnosticism; or, The Philosophy of Free Religion* (Boston: Little, Brown, and Co., 1890), 64; Ahlstrom and Mullin, *The Scientific Theist*, 96–97.

33. Stedman, *Octavius Brooks Frothingham*, 20; Edmond C. Stedman, "Octavius Brooks Frothingham: A Sketch," *The Galaxy* (October 1876), 478–489.

34. Persons, *Free Religion*, 76–80, 138–142; Warren, *American Freethought*, 96–112.

35. Caruthers, *Octavius Brooks Frothingham*, 123–124; Ahlstrom and Mullin, *The Scientific Theist*, 88–99; Persons, *Free Religion*, 85–90.

36. "The Mormon Question: Opposition to the Efforts in Congress for the Suppression of Polygamy," *New York Times*, Feb. 8, 1870, 1; "The Situation in Utah: The Struggle between the Federal and Mormon Officials—Legal Contests and Mutual Criminations," ibid., Sept. 24, 1871, 5; "The Mormons," ibid., May 11, 1872, 4.

37. Green, *The Bible, the School, and the Constitution*, 93–135.

38. Ibid., 93–102; "The Common School War," *Christian Advocate*, Dec. 3, 1869, 380; "Shall the Bible of the Pope Be Schoolmaster," *Zion's Herald*, Dec. 16, 1876, 590.

39. Green, *The Bible, the School, and the Constitution*, 96–135; Robert G. McCloskey, ed., *The Bible in the Public Schools: Arguments in the Case of John D. Minor, et al. versus The Board of Education of the City of Cincinnati, et al.* (Cincinnati,

OH: Robert Clarke & Co., 1870; New York: De Capo Press, 1964); Board of Education v. Minor, 23 Ohio St. 211, 248–254 (1873).

40. "Current Events," *Putnam's Magazine* (Jan. 1870), 134; "The Bible in the Schools," *New York Times*, June 12, 1872, 5; "Chicago Notes: The Bible in the Schools," ibid., Oct. 4, 1875, 5; "Schools in Chicago: A Non-Sectarian, Optional System. The Number and Usefulness of the Chicago Public Schools—How the Vexed Questions of the Day Have Been Settled—No Religious Exercises, No Corporal Punishment," ibid., Dec 19, 1875, 10; Green, *The Bible, the School, and the Constitution*, 117–119.

41. "Our Established Church," *Catholic World* 9 (August 1869): 577–587; John Webb Pratt, *Religion, Politics, and Diversity: The Church-State Theme in New York History* (Ithaca, NY: Cornell University Press, 1967), 212–218.

42. "Our Established Church," *Putnam's Magazine* (July 1869): 39–52; "The Unestablished Church," ibid. (Dec. 1869): 698–711; Green, *The Bible, the School, and the Constitution*, 181–183.

43. "Sectarian Schools," *New York Times*, February 16, 1872, 4–5; "Are Our Public Schools Free? *Catholic World* (October 1873), 1–9; *Harper's Weekly*, January 1, 1876, as reprinted in *The Index*, January 13, 1876, 16.

44. Samuel T. Spear, *Religion and the State, or The Bible and the Public Schools* (New York: Dodd, Mead, and Co., 1876); "Some Live Topics," Ingersoll, *Works*, 8:248–252; Francis E. Abbot, "The Catholic Peril in America," *The Eclectic Magazine* (May 1876), 553–567; *The Index*, Oct. 14, 1875, 486–487.

45. Abbot, "The Catholic Peril in America," *The Eclectic Magazine* (May 1876), 553–555, 561, 565; Abbot, "The Public School Question as Understood by the Liberal American Citizen: Two Lectures before the F. R. A. in Horticultural Hall, Boston, Feb. 13, and Feb. 20, 1876," in *The Collected Essays of Francis Ellingwood Abbot (1836–1903), American Philosopher and Free Religionist*, ed. W. Creighton Peden and Everett J. Tarbox Jr. (Lewiston, NY: Edwin Mellen Press, 1996); Ahlstrom and Mullin, *The Scientific Theist*, 91–92.

46. Report on the General Conference of the Methodist Episcopal Church," *The Christian Advocate and Journal*, June 2, 1864, 173.

47. *The Index*, October 28, 1871, 338; "Relation of the Church and State," *Presbyterian Quarterly and Princeton Review* 35 (October 1863): 689–690; Gary Scott Smith, *The Seeds of Secularization: Calvinism, Culture, and Pluralism in America 1870–1915* (Grand Rapids, MI: Christian University Press, 1985), 53–58.

48. *The Independent*, February 4, 1864, 4; Morton Borden, *Jews, Turks, and Infidels* (Chapel Hill: University of North Carolina Press, 1984), 68–69; Horace Bushnell, "Our Obligations to the Dead" (1865), and "Popular Government by Divine Right" (1864), in Horace Bushnell, *Building Eras in Religion* (New York: Charles Scribner's Sons, 1903), 286–340; Green, *The Bible, the School, and the Constitution*, 138–143.

49. David McAllister, *Christian Civil Government in America* (Pittsburgh, PA: National Reform Association, 1890, 1927), 23; T.P. Stevenson, "The Ends We Seek," *Proceedings of the National Convention to Secure the Religious Amendment of the Constitution of the United States* (Philadelphia: Christian Statesmen Assoc., 1874), 26–30; Green, *The Bible, the School, and the Constitution*, 146–150.

50. Frederick H. Hedge, "Shall the Nation, by a Change in Its Constitution, Proclaim Itself Christian," *Friend's Intelligencer*, May 18, 1872, 181; "Religion by Constitutional Amendment," *New York Times*, Jan. 10, 1871, 4; "Deity and the Constitution: Curious Proceedings in the Philadelphia Convention," ibid., Jan. 20, 1871, 5; Samuel T. Spear, "The Religious Amendment of the Constitution," *The Independent*, May 12, 1870, 2; "Christianizing the Constitution," *New York Observer*, Jan. 18, 1872, 18;

51. "The Religious Amendment to the Constitution," *The Index*, Feb. 4, 1871, 37; "The Proposed Christian Amendment to the United States Constitution," ibid., Jan. 2, 1872, 1–2.

52. "Religious Amendment to the Constitution," *The Independent*, May 18, 1876, 2; "An Unchristian Amendment," ibid., Feb. 27, 1873, 273; n.t., ibid., April 4, 1872, 6.

53. *The Index*, January 6, 1872, 5.

54. The Congressional Record, 43rd Congress, 1st Session, p. 432 (1874); *Boston Globe*, Jan. 8, 1974, l; "The Great 'Index' Petition Presented in Congress," *The Index*, Jan. 15, 1874, 30.

55. *The Index*, January 4, 1873, 1; "Nine Demands of Liberalism," in *Cornerstones of Religious Freedom in America*, ed. Joseph L. Blau (Boston: Beacon Press, 1950), 208–209.

56. "The Liberal League Movement," *The Index*, Oct. 14, 1875, 486; Ahlstrom and Mullin, *The Scientific Theist*, 101–104; Warren, *American Freethought*, 159–162.

57. "Religious Intelligence," *The Independent*, May 22, 1873, 649; Ahlstrom and Mullin, *The Scientific Theist*, 102–103; *Proceedings of the National Convention* (1874), 27–28.

58. House Miscellaneous Reports, Vol. 1623, No. 143, 43rd Congress, 1st Session, 1873–1874.

59. *The Index*, Feb. 19, 1874, 90; Green, *The Bible, the School, and the Constitution*, 159–161.

60. "Wanted: A Religious Freedom Amendment," *The Index*, Jan. 1, 1874, 6–7; Slaughterhouse Cases, 83 U.S. 36 (1873); Green, *Second Disestablishment*, 160–190; Green, *The Bible, the School, and the Constitution*, 160–169; Ahlstrom and Mullin, *The Scientific Theist*, 104.

61. *The Index*, Nov. 19, 1874, 555; "The Liberal League Convention," ibid., Sept. 20, 1875, 462; "The Liberal League Movement," ibid., Oct. 14, 1875, 486; Ahlstrom and Mullin, *The Scientific Theist*, 97, 128; Green, *The Bible, the School, and the Constitution*, 165–167.

62. "The Liberal League Movement," *The Index*, Oct. 14, 1875, 486; Green, *The Bible, the School, and the Constitution*, 167–169.
63. *Boston Daily Globe*, June 26, 1876, reprinted in *The Index*, July 27, 1876, 350.
64. "Two Centennial Conventions," *Christian Union*, June 28, 1876, 530.
65. Ibid.
66. *"Equal Rights in Religion," Report of the Centennial Congress of Liberals* (Boston: National Liberal League, 1876); "The Unfinished Window," *The Index*, Jan. 6, 1876, 6–7.
67. *"Equal Rights in Religion,"* 6, 19, 92–106; "Demands of Liberalism," *The Truth Seeker* (Jan. 1874), 1; "Demands of Liberalism," ibid. (Feb. 1874), 1.

3

The Battle over Free Love and Obscenity

Few ideas were more controversial or divisive during the Gilded Age than "free love." Free love was a capacious concept that was embraced by a diverse group of people. For some proponents, it meant that sexual relations should not be restricted to marriage. For a few, it meant the abolition of legal marriage. But for many, it meant freeing women from the constraints of a loveless marriage by liberalizing divorce and custody laws—which, in turn, would strengthen the institution of marriage by ensuring that unions were based only on love. This included re-evaluating the religious assumptions undergirding marriage, freeing it from its connections to traditional Christian doctrine while placing the wife and husband on an equal footing.[1]

Elizabeth Cady Stanton promoted this latter vision of free love, one that was directly tied to expanding women's rights. In an 1870 address, "On Marriage and Divorce," Stanton declared that reformers wanted "not merely suffrage and civil rights," or even "the social recognition of the equal rank of the sexes, though both of these must be had," but "freedom from all unnecessary entanglements and concessions." That meant "nothing short of unlimited freedom of divorce, freedom to institute at the option of the parties new amatory relationships, love put above marriage, and in a word, the obnoxious doctrine of Free Love." Free love did not presuppose any particular form of relationship, however. If one man and one woman, through mutual consent, chose "to live together through eternity," Stanton insisted, "that is just as much free love as the most unlimited variety in promiscuity. It is indeed of the essence of freedom that it does not attempt to prescribe what the result shall be." For Stanton, this notion of freedom also encompassed "freedom of conscience, free thinking, [and] freedom of intellectual speculation." Thus, the ultimate goal of free love was not to destroy but to "improve and perfect marriage."

The more radical Ezra Heywood agreed with Stanton in principle. Free love exposed the hypocrisy and cruelty of legally sanctioned marriage, which was not necessary for a consensual sexual relationship, Heywood insisted. "Free love, then, generates, but never annuls moral obligations."[2]

Despite Stanton's measured embrace of free love, she knew full well the danger of advancing "the obnoxious doctrine." Embracing the term immediately put one within the company of disreputable characters. Critics had accused Frances Wright and Robert Dale Owen of advocating—and practicing—free love. More accurate charges were laid on a handful of mid-century utopian, perfectionist communities. Members of John Humphrey Noyes's socialist Oneida Community practiced a form of free love where one could have sex with multiple partners (Noyes claimed to have coined the phrase "free love"). Even though Noyes justified the practice in religious terms as "Bible communism," free love remained highly controversial and open to criticism.[3] For detractors, the term was a shibboleth for sexual promiscuity and the destruction of marriage. The free love practiced by a community in Berlin Heights, Ohio—that "abode of wickedness"—was a "degrading and loathsome" affront to all virtuous people, wrote the *New York Times*. For critics, "'free love' became more than an easy label to post on any sexual unorthodoxy."[4]

While the salacious side of free love provided the largest amount of fodder for opponents, they feared the version of free love promoted by Stanton and other women's rights advocates even more. The greatest threat to Victorian society was the free lovers' challenge to the institution of Christian marriage and its various assumptions about gender roles. The Methodist *Christian Advocate* called free love a "monstrous doctrine" because it held that "Marriage is a mutual contract, to be terminated at the will of either party, in obedience to dictates of taste, profit, or fancy. This is the very essence, and the entire substance, of *free-lovism*; nothing worse has been uttered by the worst infidel clubs in the country." "Free-divorce is the corollary of free-love," added *Every Saturday* magazine. "Let a majority come to the free love standard of belief, and an abrogation of all law follows, and men and women will be on no higher plane than the beasts of the field."[5] *The Independent* insisted that the free love movement should more accurately be called the "Anti-Legal Marriage Movement." It would undermine the legal structures and protections of marriage that not only ensured a stable family but also secured property ownership, inheritance, and childrearing. If Christian marriage was the cornerstone of civilized society, then free love would take a sledgehammer to it.[6]

In the postwar years, one person came to personify the lurid side of free love: the "Notorious Victoria Woodhull." More than any other figure of the decade, Woodhull represented the threatening triumvirate of free love, freethought, and women's rights.[7]

The Notorious Victoria Woodhull

Victoria Woodhull was one of the more flamboyant and controversial public figures of the 1870s. Unabashedly self-promotional, Woodhull had a knack for being at the forefront of several cutting-edge social issues, including free love, marriage reform, Spiritualism, women's suffrage, and freedom of speech. She was the first woman to declare herself a candidate for president, and the first to testify before Congress. Woodhull would also be tied to what was arguably the greatest sexual scandal of the Gilded Age, that being the affair between the nation's leading pastor, Henry Ward Beecher, and one of his parishioners. Woodhull exposed the affair in her journal, only to find herself prosecuted by Anthony Comstock. Woodhull's public celebrity was matched by her infamy as a sex radical.[8]

The Victoria Woodhull of the 1860s was an unlikely celebrity. Born into a large family living a hard-scrabble existence in rural Ohio in 1838, she had little formal education. Her father was a disreputable con man and opportunist who, among other questionable ventures, promoted the teenage Victoria and her younger sister, Tennessee (Tennie), as mediums who would tell fortunes for a price. At fifteen, Victoria was married off to an alcoholic physician, Channing Woodhull, and the couple moved to California, where she supported the family as a seamstress, actress, and, reputedly, as a prostitute. After moving to Chicago, where she offered clairvoyant healing services to wounded Civil War veterans, Victoria divorced her husband, later marrying Colonel James Blood of St. Louis, who also practiced Spiritualism. Ambitious and surprisingly self-confident, Victoria—retaining the last name Woodhull—moved to New York City in 1868 with her husband, ex-husband, and twenty-two-year-old sister Tennie Claflin, all looking to make their mark. Through luck and gumption, Victoria and Tennie secured an introduction to Cornelius Vanderbilt, the railroad tycoon, who believed that they could help him contact the spirit of his recently deceased wife. Victoria impressed Vanderbilt with her skills as a medium while Tennie entranced the seventy-year-old philanderer with her sexuality, becoming his mistress. Vanderbilt financed the establishment of Woodhull, Claflin, and Co., the first Wall Street brokerage firm managed by women, and then their sensationalist journal, the *Woodhull & Claflin's Weekly*. Vanderbilt's wealth and connections ensured that Victoria's and Tennie's enterprises succeeded financially.[9]

Woodhull's activities shortly gained public attention. With the encouragement of her husband, Colonel Blood, and of Stephen Pearl Andrews—a freethinker, radical social reformer, and affiliate of the Modern Times commune—and with their editorial assistance, *Woodhull & Claflin's Weekly* advocated for women's suffrage, marriage reform, and the decriminalization of prostitution. The journal also served as a platform for promoting Woodhull as a leading reformer. Woodhull used her growing notoriety to lecture on a variety of issues ranging from women's suffrage to public finance. She advocated religious freethought, though she commonly referred to herself as a spiritualist.[10]

Woodhull also thrust herself into the political spotlight. By mid-summer 1870 she had become acquainted with Congressman Benjamin Butler, a Radical Republican and advocate for woman's rights. That relationship—social, political, and possibly sexual—served as the entrée for Woodhull to testify before the House Judiciary Committee in January 1871, on behalf of women's suffrage. A proposed Sixteenth Amendment to the Constitution to guarantee women's right to vote, sponsored by Elizabeth Cady Stanton, Susan B. Anthony, and their National Woman Suffrage Association (NSWA), had been languishing in Congress for several years. With Butler's assistance, Woodhull submitted the "Woodhull Memorial," which argued for recognizing a woman's right to vote pursuant to the citizenship clause of the Fourteenth Amendment, a legal theory previously advanced by Stanton. After considering Woodhull's proposal, a majority of the committee issued a report rejecting her argument, over the objection of Butler. Later, Woodhull threatened that if Congress did not grant full citizenship to women, she would mount a campaign for a new constitutional convention "to erect a new government, complete in all its parts." "We mean treason; we mean secession. . . . We are plotting revolution; we will overslough this bogus republic and plant a government of righteousness in its stead."[11]

Woodhull had not previously been involved with a suffrage organization, and her memorial caught Stanton and Anthony by surprise, with the *New York Times* noting they viewed her as an "interloper" in the movement.[12] But Anthony and Stanton shortly came to see the value of Woodhull's involvement and they invited her to address the NSWA convention in May 1871. Woodhull took the opportunity to press her militant position on sexual freedom. "Why do I war upon marriage?" she asked. Because it was "the most terrible curse from which humanity now suffers." She condemned the "thousands of rapes [which are] committed under cover of this accursed [marriage] license," and she called for the "abrogation of forced pregnancy" and for "the birth of love children only." "Sexual freedom means the abolition of prostitution both in and out of marriage, means the emancipation of woman from sexual slavery and her coming into ownership and control of her own body." The address established Woodhull as a leader of the radical wing of the woman's rights movement.[13] That same year, Woodhull announced that she intended to run for US president in 1872 under an independent Equal Rights Party. She also got herself elected president of the American Association of Spiritualists, even though she had not previously been involved with the organization and was no longer actively engaged as a medium.[14]

Woodhull's notoriety was running high, despite negative revelations about her lifestyle. A lawsuit revealed that she lived not only with her sister and husband, Colonel Blood, but also with her former husband, Dr. Woodhull, and rumors circulated about affairs with other men. Woodhull would later acknowledge an affair with Theodore Tilton, a prominent reformer and former editor of *The Independent*. In 1871 Tilton wrote a fawning biography of Woodhull that praised her as a visionary.[15] Her controversial stances caused a division within the women's suffrage movement, with members of the more conservative American Woman Suffrage Association (AWSA) seeing Woodhull as an obstacle to their ultimate success. Anthony also increasingly came to believe that Woodhull's penchant for notoriety detracted from the goals of the women's suffrage movement. On the other side, Harriett Beecher Stowe, an antisuffragist, ridiculed Woodhull's lifestyle and newfound commitment to women's rights in her novel *My Wife and I*, in which the Woodhull character had the name "Audacia Dangyereyes."[16]

Seeking to maintain her notoriety and make money to offset some bad investments, Woodhull stepped up the pace of her public speaking. On November 20, 1871, she delivered a memorable lecture, reputedly written by Stephen Pearl Andrews, to an overflow crowd of three thousand people at Steinway Hall. The title of the address, "The Principles of Social Freedom," did not reveal its substance (though the banners in the hall announcing "The Question of Free Love, Marriage, Divorce and Prostitution" gave it away), and for the first half of the talk she spoke in tedious generalities, according to one report.[17] Woodhull then segued to the heart of her lecture: social freedom meant sexual freedom and freedom from marriage. What she had intimated in her NWSA address, she now clarified by equating marriage with prostitution—only marriage was worse because wives had no choice whether to engage in sexual intercourse and then they lacked the financial independence of prostitutes. She also equated marriage with slavery. "[A]ll compelling laws of marriage and divorce are despotic, being remnants of the barbaric age in which they were originated," Woodhull declared. The only solution for (and way to reform) legal marriage was a system of free love. "And are you a Free Lover?" she asked her audience. "Yes, I am a Free Lover," she responded to her own question.

> I have an *inalienable, constitutional* and *natural* right to love whom I may, to love as *long* or as *short* a period as I can; to change that love *every day* if I please, and with *that right* neither *you* nor any *law* you can frame have *any* right to interfere. And I have the further right to demand a free and unrestrained exercise of that right.[18]

At other places in her speech, Woodhull denied that her version of free love led to promiscuity, which she called an "absurd proposition." The overall tenor of the address suggested otherwise, at least to many people. Woodhull's Steinway address caused an uproar and elicited denunciations from societal and religious leaders, with the Methodist *Zion's Herald* condemning Woodhull for "attempting to fasten the odium of Free-Loverism on the Woman's Suffrage movement." A Catholic priest reportedly warned his parishioners "against all doctrines so dangerous as those of Victoria Woodhull and the Free Lovers," while *Harper's Weekly* printed a Thomas Nast cartoon depicting Woodhull with dragon wings holding a sign saying "Be Saved by Free Love." It labeled her "Mrs. Satan." The fallout from the lecture reputedly caused Cornelius Vanderbilt to break with Woodhull and Claflin, withdrawing his financial support.[19] Although the lecture distressed Elizabeth Cady Stanton, she initially stuck by Woodhull, writing that "Victoria C. Woodhull stands before us today a grand brave woman, radical alike in political, religious and social principles." She was "the leader of the woman suffrage movement in this country."[20]

It would be easy to classify Woodhull as an opportunist and provocateur, one who sought to garner public attention and fame by taking sensational positions on social issues. Even her biographer Theodore Tilton noted that she had only recently embraced women's rights, though he claimed she was led to it by her spirit guide, Demosthenes.[21] While Woodhull's penchant for self-promotion is without doubt, the record suggests that she came to believe in the principles she espoused. Time and again, she reaffirmed her stance on woman's suffrage, women's rights, and marriage reform apart from her advocacy for free love and, as she liked to relate, she frequently suffered ridicule and abuse for her positions. She understood that her candidacy for president under the Equal Rights Party was a losing proposition, but the symbolism of how it related to the cause of women's rights was not lost on anyone. As much as she promoted herself, she apparently believed that her celebrity also brought needed attention to the various causes she embraced. Her penchant for sensationalism was too much for many in the women's rights movement, however, leading Susan B. Anthony to disassociate herself from Woodhull, writing in her diary that "[t]here never was such a foolish muddle" as "Mrs. S. consulting with and conceding to Woodhull." Anthony's disaffection with Woodhull caused a momentary rift in her relationship with Stanton.[22]

Woodhull's need to maintain herself as a public celebrity—for both status and financial reasons—led her to undertake her riskiest move by attacking a bastion of New York society. Henry Ward Beecher was the minister of the large Plymouth Congregational Church in Brooklyn, editor of the *Christian Union*, and lauded as America's best preacher. Beecher was the scion of a prominent family with one sister, Isabella Beecher Hooker, active in the women's rights movement and another, Harriett Beecher Stowe, the noted author. Henry, a liberal reformer himself, served as honorary president of Lucy Stone's AWSA, while Isabella was active in the more progressive NWSA and a devotee of Woodhull. Despite his public commitment to women's rights, Beecher was also a reputed philanderer. Rumors circulated in 1871 that Beecher was engaged in a long-standing affair with Elizabeth (Lib) Tilton, the wife of fellow reformer Theodore Tilton, who was a protégé of Beecher's. Despite Woodhull's past relationship with Theodore Tilton, her acquaintance with Isabella Hooker, and her admiration for Henry Ward Beecher's reform stances, she decided to expose the Beecher-Tilton affair, in part to retaliate for criticism she had received from Harriett Beecher Stowe and her sister Catherine Beecher.[23]

For several years, Woodhull had railed against the double standard that middle-class, married men maintained when it came to sexual affairs. In May 1871, in a response to her critics, Woodhull had written:

My judges preach against Free Love openly, practice it secretly. For example, I know of one man in a neighboring city, a public teacher of eminence, who lives

in concubinage with the wife of another public teacher of almost equal eminence. All three concur in denouncing offenses against morality. "Hypocrisy is
the tribute paid by vice to virtue." So be it.[24]

At the time, Woodhull's references to Beecher remained oblique, and she
still maintained a friendship with Theodore Tilton and Isabella Hooker. A
year later, hounded by unfavorable press and in need of money, Woodhull decided to expose the Beecher-Tilton affair, first discussing it during a speech
before the American Association of Spiritualists meeting in September 1872.
Then in November, she published an exposé in *Woodhull & Claflin's Weekly*.
The "Beecher-Tilton Scandal Case," as she titled the exposé, appeared in the
form of an imaginary interview between Woodhull and an unnamed reporter.
The purpose of the article, Woodhull claimed, was to expose the hypocrisy
of Beecher and other eminent men who claimed fidelity to marriage while
practicing free love. (Woodhull later denied allegations she had first attempted
to blackmail Beecher and Tilton.) Woodhull asserted that she did not condemn the sexual affair, which she believed all people had a right to engage in;
"[t]he fault with which I, therefore, charge him, is not infidelity to the old
ideas, but unfaithfulness to the new." While Beecher was "in heart, in conviction and in life, an ultra socialist reformer," he was a "upholder of the old
social slavery" of marriage. Woodhull felt it was her duty "to denounce him as
a poltroon, a coward and a sneak."[25]

The exposé "burst like a bombshell" on polite New York society, though
mainstream newspapers declined to republish its scandalous allegations.
Woodhull had reason to be satisfied with her exposé. Not only did the article
represent a culmination of her critiques about free love and marriage while
exposing the hypocrisy of one of the nation's most admired men; the printing
of over one hundred thousand copies of the article ensured that it reached a
wide audience and refilled the financial coffers of the *Weekly*. The wide distribution of the newspaper also guaranteed that the article found its way into the
hands of another person who was seeking to elevate his celebrity in New York
society: Anthony Comstock.[26]

Enter Anthony Comstock

If Victoria Woodhull was the most notorious woman in 1870s America,
Anthony Comstock was likely the most feared man. Comstock had moved

to New York City in 1868, the same year as Woodhull, though he took a very different path. Comstock was born into a deeply religious Congregationalist family in Connecticut in 1844. The key influences on his life were his austere upbringing, the death of his devout and adored mother when he was ten, and his utter conviction of human sinfulness instilled in him by his church. Serving in the Civil War, Comstock was reputedly repulsed by the lax behavior and immorality of his fellow Union soldiers, and he gained a reputation as a religious fanatic for preaching to his compatriots. Unable to find employment in Connecticut following the war, the poorly educated Comstock joined many young men in migrating to the city to find work. He obtained a job as a clerk in a New York City dry goods store, living in a boarding house while being exposed to the seamy side of urban life.[27]

New York City, like many large cities of the late nineteenth century, was a tale of contradictions: a powerful group of wealthy financiers and industrialists; a class of artists and intellectuals; a burgeoning group of middle-class clerks working for businesses; and an even larger number of poor laborers, many being recent immigrants, who sought to survive by whatever means were available. Crime, gambling, prostitution, and other forms of vice proliferated in parts of the city, with its offenders frequently preying on the newly arrived immigrants, particularly pressing children into prostitution. All sorts of lurid publications—dime novels, nickel magazines, and erotic postcards and photographs that survived on titillation and sensationalism—were readily available, facilitated by advances in printing. As the *New York Times* described the situation in January 1872:

> There is a certain dirty and dingy newspaper store, in the centre of one of our most thickly populated districts, which has been for many years, and is to this day, doing a handsome business of corrupting the youth of this City. . . . The attraction which draws [idle people] together is a number of vulgar and indecent photographs and stereoscopic views in a case by the door. . . . These licentious temptations are but a foretaste of the more filthy obscenities to be found inside the store, where a large collection of the foulest and most demoralizing literature and pictures is disposed of at good prices to the school-boys and youth of this City.[28]

The audience for such material and related temptations was huge: over one hundred thousand male clerks and even a greater number of laborers, many unmarried and living in boarding houses, roamed the streets after work hours, frequenting saloons, gambling dens, and brothels. Newspapers reported that

New York City had more than 20,000 prostitutes. Also commonly available were crude devices for enhancing sexual performance and "remedies" for preventing pregnancy and venereal disease—"rubber articles for Gents"— that were openly advertised in tabloids such as the *National Police Gazette*. According to one historian, by 1870, New York City "had become the carnal showcase of the Western world."[29]

Even before the Civil War, a variety of moral reform societies had sprung up in the larger cities to combat vice—chiefly gambling and prostitution—such as the New York Society of Public Morals and the New York Female Benevolent Society. These societies, having evangelical and Catholic connections, had met with limited success, due in part to indifference and corruption within city governments and police forces. In the 1850s, several wealthy businessmen founded the Young Men's Christian Association (YMCA) to address the vice problem from the perspective of the consumer by providing young men with a morally healthy alternative to the myriad immoral temptations readily available on the city's streets. The YMCA and its leadership espoused strong evangelical values, advancing Christian morality, Sunday observance, and temperance.[30] Following the war, with the influx of veterans and other young men into the city in search of employment, the YMCA shifted its approach to combatting the various vices that were enticing the naive men "to form habits of dissipation." In addition to decrying the temptations of gambling, drinking, and prostitution, the YMCA also condemned the availability of obscenity in the form of "vile weekly newspapers" and "licentious books." In 1866, the YMCA mounted a campaign for a stricter state obscenity law. Two years later it secured a law from the New York Assembly that not only prohibited "obscene" literature—otherwise undefined—but also the sale of "articles of indecent and immoral use," essentially sex toys, contraceptive devices, and abortifacients, as well as their advertisement.[31]

Settling in New York at that time, the highly moralistic twenty-four-year-old Comstock was aghast at what he encountered on the city's streets. Shortly after arriving, an acquaintance in Comstock's boarding house was "led astray" and became "corrupted and diseased" as a result of viewing obscenity, according to Comstock's later biographer. His friend's demise, apparently from venereal disease, led Comstock to have the purveyor of the obscene literature arrested.[32] From that point on, Comstock became a self-appointed, part-time crusader against obscenity. He would follow up on leads as to where obscene material could be bought, purchase it, and then return to the stores with police officers.[33] Before long, his crusade was consuming more of his time and resources, so in early 1872 he approached the secretary of the YMCA for support. That led to a meeting between Comstock and Morris K. Jesup, president of the association and a railroad magnate. Impressed with Comstock's passion and resourcefulness, Jesup and the other wealthy sponsors of the YMCA—J. Pierpont Morgan (finance), William E. Dodge (copper mining), and Samuel Colgate (soap)—agreed to financially support Comstock's activities. In March 1872, the YMCA formed a Committee on the Suppression of Obscene Literature, with Comstock as its secretary and agent in charge of enforcement, acting under a provision of the New York obscenity law that deputized private citizens to make arrests and gave them a percentage of the resulting fine.[34]

Comstock approached his role with zeal, based on his belief that he was doing God's work in "weeding out his garden." The *New York Times* reported that between March and August 1872, Comstock arrested more than forty sellers of obscenity. Although he concentrated on obscene literature and sexual devices, such as dildos, Comstock branched out by going after abortionists, brothels, and illegal gambling houses, as well.[35] Early on, Comstock established a reputation for obtaining incriminating material through questionable means, such as using aliases to obtain items through the mail and employing other forms of entrapment.[36] His benefactors and supporters in the press either ignored the charges or justified his tactics as necessary evils. *Literary World* called Comstock a "zealous and indefatigable agent" who does "occasionally, in his zeal, step very near, or indeed actually overstep, the dividing line between lawful and unwise interference." Yet, to the *New York Evangelist*, this "is legitimate warfare, and he is too plucky a man to be cowed from using the same effective instrument again." "Nothing, in our judgment, can be more legitimate than to catch a rogue in his own trap," echoed *Scribner's Monthly*. "The inequities that have been stopped by this means—the floods of fraud and impurity that have been turned back on their inventers through this machinery—are sufficiently notable to earn the gratitude of the public."[37] With the increase in arrests, Comstock's name began appearing regularly in newspapers as a leading enforcer against vice.[38]

Historians have long debated the motivations behind Comstock's crusade. Comstock frequently referred to the repulsive nature of the items and materials seized and the displeasure it brought him to undertake such activities. To accept Comstock's statements at face value, his crusade brought him no pleasure but he undertook the duty according to a call from God: "I humbly ascribe the glory for all of these grand results to His holy name."[39] Biographers and historians have proposed other explanations for his motivations. One is that Comstock was a misogynist—that he was *The Man Who Hated Women*, according to the title of a recent biography. Comstock had a narrow, Calvinist inspired view of the appropriate roles and attire of women, and of their proper sexual behavior. Women who engaged in prostitution, or who posed for titillating photographs, or who had abortions, not only flouted those roles but exercised power and independence from men.[40] A related analysis, proposed in a 1927 biography and since developed, was that Comstock was both afraid of sex and sexually repressed—Comstock wrote frequently about his struggle with temptation and sin: "This morning [I was] severely tempted by Satan and after some time in my own weakness I failed." (A possible reference to masturbation.) "Oh I deplore my sinful weak nature so much. If I could but live without sin I would be the happiest soul living." According to one scholar, people in such distress "play out their internal psychological conflicts on a very public stage" by seeking "to renounce their repressed impulses and desires through censorship campaigns."[41] A different line of analysis asserts that class, economic, and ethnic resentments explain Comstock's crusade and the support he received from his wealthy patrons at the YMCA. Comstock aspired to middle-class respectability and he sought the favor of his wealthy supporters, many of whom were businessmen and industrialists who needed a dependable and compliant working class. They agreed that the diversions of an urban nightlife—saloons, gambling halls, and brothels—and the corrosive effects of obscenity, undermined the reliability of a dependable workforce. This alternative lifestyle also threatened the Protestant, middle-class assumptions about the home and the family that buttressed class hierarchies.[42]

This last point raises still another possible explanation for Comstock's crusade: that, based on his own provincial Calvinist upbringing, he held a narrow if not antiquated view of the appropriate model of family and home life. The home and family were sacred institutions in which children learned to live godly lives and in which husbands and wives acted in their Christian-ordained roles while serving as moral guardians and examples. Parents were "divinely appointed artists to decorate the walls of memory's storehouse" with moral lessons and "God's Word," Comstock wrote. But the "first lewd thought is an entering wedge of Satan to corrupt taste for the divine and beautiful and checkmate parental training." This Victorian image of the home, and its security, was threatened by vice; husbands and sons would become corrupted by the lures of obscenity, prostitution, gambling, and drink, and the family social order would be undermined by the availability of abortion and contraceptive devices. The security of this ideal home was also threatened by free love—or "free-lust" as Comstock called it—which promoted promiscuity.[43]

All these explanations have merit, though one can debate whether Comstock's narrow view of appropriate roles for women rendered him a misogynist in the truest sense of the word. Central to all these explanations is Comstock's deeply abiding Calvinist faith and his strong belief in the ever-present temptation to engage in sinful conduct. As one historian described Comstock's religiosity:

> [Comstock] hated sin with a consuming passion. He loved and listened to God, saw and despised the devil's influence in the world. His conversations with God or sightings of Satan sometimes took a literal form that would place Comstock, in the minds of many, close to if not over the line into religious fanaticism. Other times, his religious faith seemed little different from that of most of other [orthodox] Christians.[44]

Also central to Comstock's motivation was his passion for shielding children from the snares of vice—protecting the youth was his constant theme, as is indicated by the title of his 1883 book, *Traps for the Young*. As Comstock wrote elsewhere, "we must preserve the moral purity of our youth. Their bodies must be developed, their minds cultivated, their systems preserved in health and purity, and kept free from the enervations of lust."[45] But, "[f]or more than half a century youthful minds have been debauched, cursed, and corrupted by obscene publications and pictures," Comstock insisted. Children were particularly susceptible to these evil influences. "Corrupt thoughts and perverted imagination set the wheels of evil habits in motion. Evil habits are like grooves in the brain, into which the wheels of a perverted nature continue to run, destroying all manly and womanly instincts, discounting future happiness, and mortgaging the soul to the spirit of evil." The future of American society was at stake: "Our hope for future prosperity is bound up in the preservation of the youth of to-day."[46]

One matter that did not appear to trouble Comstock was that there was no consensus definition of obscenity, legal or otherwise, at the time. According to a leading British legal decision, *Regina v. Hicklin*, obscenity could be any material that tended to corrupt the minds of people already open to immoral influences.[47] This played into Comstock's hands. For him, obscenity was "anything having a tendency to suggest impure and libidinous thoughts" or to corrupt morality, whether it was sexually explicit in and of itself. While he did not offer a substantive definition, Comstock provided examples: "criminal illustrated papers, blood and thunder stories, and dime and half-dime novels, infidel publications, licentious books and pictures, loose French art and publications, and the traffickers in articles of indecent and immoral use." As we will see, Comstock used the lack of agreement over obscenity to his advantage, allowing him to go after anything he believed to be immoral.[48]

In late 1872, Anthony Comstock was making a name for himself, though he had not acquired the fame he desired. The publication of Victoria Woodhull's exposé on the Beecher-Tilton affair provided him with the opportunity he had been looking for.[49] The issue of *Woodhull & Claflin's Weekly* hit the street on October 28; Comstock read the story shortly afterward and judged its contents to be obscene based on the story's reference to adultery, virginity, "terrible orgies" in the Tilton home, and Lib Tilton's possible miscarriage of Beecher's love-child.[50] On November 2, Comstock had Woodhull, her sister, and her husband arrested for violating an 1872 federal law that prohibited the mailing of obscene materials. The three were arraigned before a federal commissioner and committed to the Ludlow Street jail. At the same time, Tennie Claflin and Colonel Blood were also charged with criminally libeling a stockbroker, Luther Challis, by alleging he had raped an underage girl. Woodhull and Claflin languished in jail for a month before making bail, only to be rearrested in January 1873 on an additional obscenity charge. Throughout the drawn-out legal proceedings, Woodhull used her public platform to frame her prosecution as a travesty for freedom of speech, press, and religion, while she reaffirmed her belief in free love. Eventually, the judge dismissed the charges on a technicality that the 1872 law did not regulate the mailing of newspapers, only obscene materials.[51]

The charges against Woodhull secured Comstock the notoriety he sought, even if the ultimate resolution of the case did not give him satisfaction. Even before the judge had directed an acquittal, Comstock realized that deficiencies existed in the federal obscenity law. Supported by his benefactors at the Committee for the Suppression of Obscene Literature, Comstock traveled to Washington, DC, between December 1872 and March 1873, meeting with sympathetic legislators and other officials in hope of amending the federal obscenity statute (reportedly bringing with him a collection of seized photographs and dildos as exhibits). Two individuals in particular provided crucial assistance in drafting a new law—attorney Benjamin Abbott, brother of Beecher protégé Lyman Abbott, and Supreme Court Justice William Strong, the president of the National Reform Association, who introduced Comstock to influential senators and representatives. Congress was occupied with wrapping up the legislative session and certifying the Electoral College vote, but under the guidance of Speaker James G. Blaine, the House hurriedly approved the bill without debate at the last moment on March 3, 1873. The new law prohibited mailing anything of an "obscene, lewd, or lascivious" content or an "indecent character," while it expanded the category of types of publications covered. It also prohibited the mailing of any contraceptive device, abortifacients, or pamphlets with information about performing abortions or advertisements concerning securing one. The penalty for a conviction included a fine of up to a $5,000 and from one to ten years in prison at hard labor.[52] The new law received widespread public support. The *New York Journal of Commerce* commended Congress for strengthening the law "to punish these corrupters of youth, panderers of lust, and abortionists." Those "wretches who are debauching the youth of the country and murdering women and unborn babes, will soon be in the strong grip of the Government."[53]

With the passage of the "Comstock Act," Comstock was appointed Special Agent of the Post Office Department, authorized to interpret and enforce the law as he saw fit. Comstock claimed that the purpose of the federal law was "to prevent the United States mails from being used to poison the fountains of moral purity in the young." "My sympathy is with the children and youth, who are liable to be debauched for life" after viewing obscenity.[54] Two months after the law's enactment, the YMCA dissolved the Committee for the Suppression of Obscene Literature and its directors formed a new independent organization, the New York Society for the Suppression of Vice (NYSSV), with Comstock as its full-time paid agent. Comstock was now authorized and equipped to pursue smut-peddlers and abortionists under both federal and state law.[55]

In contrast to Comstock's newfound success, Victoria Woodhull and her sister Tennie experienced a decline in their fortunes, both real and figurative, following their arrests. The break with Cornelius Vanderbilt meant the loss of their financial backer, and their brokerage firm had to shutter after the financial crash in September 1873, while their *Weekly* continued publishing erratically. Woodhull faced constant public criticism for her outlandish statements. She had also become a pariah in the women's suffrage movement. All that remained was Woodhull's notoriety, and she went on a series of nationwide speaking tours to generate income. At least initially, she did not waver from her controversial positions. In one popular lecture, "Tried as by Fire; or The True and The False, Socially" (1874), she repeated her condemnation of marriage and support for free love and free inquiry: "I not only advocate sexual freedom, but also religious freedom." She warned of the hypocrisy of Christian moralists: "Let them beware lest the harlots get into the Kingdom before them." For the next three years, Woodhull capitalized on her notoriety, advertising herself as the "Queen of the American Rostrum."[56] Between tours, she became embroiled in the sensationalist lawsuit brought by Theodore Tilton against Henry Ward Beecher over her exposure of the latter's sordid affair with Lib Tilton.[57] Finally, in October 1876, Woodhull ended her lagging lecture tours and shuttered the *Weekly*. She and her sister Tennie left for England in 1877, allegedly after receiving a $100,000 payoff from Cornelius Vanderbilt's heirs. Shortly afterward, Victoria and Tennie met and married British nobles, and both settled down to comfortable lives while renouncing their previous sexual and social radicalism. Even though Woodhull was now gone, her legacy as a champion of free love and freethought remained.[58]

Comstock's War on Obscenity and Freethought

In the meantime, Comstock embraced his new vice-fighting authority with gusto, believing he was saving children and others from "the devil's seed-sowing of immorality, uncleanness, moral leprosy, and death."[59] The number of arrests and seizures during his first years as a federal agent—as recorded in his annual reports to the NYSSV and chronicled in the newspapers—was impressive. Less than four years into his crusade, Comstock reported that he and his deputies had seized and destroyed twenty-one tons of obscene materials, including 5,000 photographic negatives, suppressed the circulation of 160 publications, and secured the conviction of nearly 300 producers or sellers of obscenity.[60] Comstock relished his ability to trap willing purveyors of obscene materials; as he boasted after arresting one such publisher, "the devil's trapper was trapped."[61] Now equipped to make the arrests himself, he worked solo or with an entourage of deputies, often accompanied by newspaper reporters who filed flattering stories. On one occasion, Comstock attempted to rearrest the same purveyor who had sold obscenity to his boardinghouse friend who had subsequently died. A fight ensued and the seller sliced Comstock's face with a knife, resulting in a scar that he would cover with his trademark mutton-chop whiskers. It was but one of several physical attacks that Comstock enjoyed relating to his adoring public.[62]

As mentioned, Comstock's initial focus on obscenity soon expanded to include items and information related to contraceptives, abortifacients, and the performing of abortions. In some instances, he requested that information be sent to him through the mail; in other instances, he made the arrests directly using the authority of an 1840s New York law outlawing abortions after "quickening."[63] In one highly publicized—and tragic—case, Comstock pursued Ann Lohman, aka Madame Restell, a well-known abortionist and dispenser of contraceptives. Despite having once been imprisoned in the 1840s, Mme. Restell and her husband Charles Lohman, a freethinker, openly operated a family planning practice that served New York City's upper-class women. After several attempts to buy abortifacient powders from her, the undercover Comstock arrested Restell in February 1878, imprisoning her in the infamous Tombs Prison. Released on bail, the sixty-six-year-old Mme. Restell committed suicide on the eve of her trial by cutting her throat. The *New York Times* called her suicide "a fit ending to an odious career," but other newspapers, including the *New York Sun*, criticized Comstock's tactics as "doing evil [such] that good may come." Comstock reputedly justified her suicide as simply "[a] bloody ending to a bloody life." He bragged that Restell's suicide represented the fifteenth one among people he had prosecuted.[64]

For the first decade or so, secular and religious journals largely applauded Comstock's activities, though sometimes questioning his methods. As *Zion's Herald* reported in 1879:

> No one can hear Anthony Comstock relate the incidents of his work as a voluntary detective, in ferreting out the unmitigated rascals from their concealed dens, who are engaged in the frightful work of poisoning the minds of the youth of the land by issuing impure circulars, books and pictures, and in the manufacture of almost inconceivably vile instruments of vice, without being impressed with the conviction that God has called and commissioned this singularly shrewd, plucky, and devout man, every way adapted to his ungrateful task, for his persistent crusade.[65]

Literary World concurred that "nobody with the facts before him can be too thankful to the Society, and to its fearless agent, Anthony Comstock, for their vigorous measures in attempting to destroy this vile traffic." And writing in 1882, a fawning Methodist *Christian Advocate* declared that Comstock's "career presents a spectacle of heroism and vigorous and successful effort never surpassed by any single man in the history of moral reform."[66]

At least initially, Comstock's anti-vice crusade did not demonstrate any particular animus toward freethinkers, nor did he necessarily equate all freethought writings with obscenity. But the seeds of that conflation existed early on. At the 1873 annual convention of national YMCAs, which Comstock attended, one speaker made the connection by asserting that "[p]ernicious [obscene] literature includes scornful infidel literature, the more subtle and unobserved infidel literature through popular weekly and secular journals. . . . The devil has his colporteurs everywhere, pushing on his works, and so must the Christian." By then, Comstock appeared to agree.[67] Comstock's highly publicized arrest of Victoria Woodhull was likely motivated by several factors: his desire for the publicity of prosecuting a prominent celebrity and to curry the favor of the city's elite who admired Beecher. But Comstock was also repulsed by Woodhull's lifestyle, her affront to the Christian "ideal" of marriage and family, and to her religious heterodoxy, which she publicly flaunted. In her 1871 Steinway Hall lecture and elsewhere, Woodhall blamed Christian teachings for the oppression of marriage and called for free religious inquiry. Comstock did not pursue Woodhull *because* of her embrace of freethought; for Comstock, however, her heterodoxy was inseparable from her advocacy of immoral conduct. Her public disdain for orthodox Christian beliefs and mores made her promotion of obscenity that much worse.[68]

An early indication of Comstock's willingness to use an obscenity charge as a cover for prosecuting what he saw as religious heresy occurred in conjunction with Woodhull's prosecution. One of Woodhull's and Claflin's acquaintances and defenders was George Francis Train, an eccentric millionaire financier and women's rights supporter (and avowed racist).[69] Incensed over Woodhull's and Claflin's arrest, Train published a diatribe in December 1872 containing purportedly obscene passages from the Old Testament, adding his own sensational headlines, and daring Comstock to arrest him. Comstock obliged, charging Train in state court under the New York obscenity law, though newspapers reported that the arrest was for publishing "an obscene and *blasphemous* sheet." The erratic Train admitted that his paper "*was* obscene, and its object was the refutation and suppression to the Bible." In the unruly court hearings, Train made wild and vicious claims about the Bible, and several jurors were dismissed for stating that his "pagan" beliefs were evidence of his insanity. The legal proceedings deteriorated from there, with Train refusing to raise bail and languishing in the Tombs for five months while the court twice had him examined for insanity. The case was a debacle, with Comstock disassociating himself from it before the charges against Train were eventually dismissed. Train's goal of highlighting Comstock's religious biases was obscured by the disorderly proceedings.[70]

By mid-decade, Liberals were becoming increasingly aware of the potential risks associated with the overlap between free inquiry and "obscenity"—or at least of the strong connection between freethought and candid sexual expression. Still, many freethinkers believed they had the right to advocate for sexual liberation and gender equality. *The Truth Seeker* carried advertisements for R.T. Trall's controversial book, *Sexual Physiology*, a pamphlet titled "The Truth about Love," and Walt Whitman's *Leaves of Grass*, among others. In a July 1874 article, "Marriage," contributor B.F. Underwood—without advocating sexual promiscuity or free love (or even using that term)—called for equality of the sexes, the reform of marriage and divorce laws, and relationships based on "the gratification of their sexual passions."[71] Other articles and published letters criticized the inequities of Christian marriage: "Divest the marriage contract of its religious ideas brought down from the dark ages or civil and religious bondage," wrote another contributor, asserting that "this age of equal rights for all can ill afford its tyranny longer, in suppressing emotional and natural sympathy and love, and in authorizing in their place brutal lust and loathing."[72] Yet most articles, like Underwood's, avoided associating their pleas for sexual reform with "free love," because of the term's negative connotations. A letter from one subscriber related the concern:

> the masses have, through pulpit and press, been carefully educated to believe that the object of "Free-Lovers," is lust and sensuality. . . . [But] to Free-Lovers, ideas of sexual indulgence are of secondary consideration; they desire that all human beings should be joined together in the holy bonds of mutual love and affection. . . . None but the low and vulgar need the yoke of government; the noble govern themselves.[73]

Understanding the risks to the freethought movement—and demonstrating their own individual sensibilities—Francis Abbot, Octavius B. Frothingham, Robert Ingersoll, and D.M. Bennett of *The Truth Seeker* all denounced the availability of obscene literature and the radical understandings of free love, though they supported women's rights and marriage reform. In 1874, Bennett published an article in *The Truth Seeker*, "Free Love, What It Is and What It Is Not," that criticized the "Mrs. Woodhull" version of free love that promoted changing spouses, "whenever, and as often as [one] pleases," or committing adultery. Because *The Index* and *The Truth Seeker* did not see any connection between their advocacy of skepticism and obscenity, they did not cover Comstock's early activities or initially view them as directly threatening freedom of thought; however, they criticized Comstock's reliance on religious justifications for his crusade and his close affiliation with religious groups such as the YMCA.[74]

The threat became real when, in the spring of 1875, Comstock prosecuted John A. Lant, publisher of the freethought journal *Toledo Sun*, for reprinting a parody about the Beecher-Tilton case called "Beecher's Prayer" and a letter discussing physiological matters. (According to D.M. Bennett, Comstock had initially tried to prosecute Lant for publishing Robert Ingersoll's "Oration on the Gods.") Lant was convicted of obscenity and sentenced to eighteen months in prison at hard labor. Even though "the crime of blasphemy is but a relic of past credulity and superstition," opined a contributor to *The Truth Seeker* upon Lant's arrest, prosecutors like Comstock now sought "punish[ment] under a different aspect, and in place of 'blasphemy' the cry of 'obscenity' is raised." It was "unnecessary to endorse or uphold Mrs. Woodhull's personal theories of social reform . . . or the ultra views of Lant, in order to champion the cause of law, order, and justice, and to give these persons an equity of protection and justice."[75]

Comstock followed up on Lant's arrest with that of Edward B. Foote Sr., a freethinker, medical doctor, and author of several popular books that dispensed medical information about family planning. Although Dr. Foote had a conventional medical education, he practiced homeopathy and alternative medicine. His written work was geared toward dispelling misinformation about medical treatment and reproduction, in particular. His 1858 book, *Medical Common Sense*, named in honor of his hero Thomas Paine's treatise, and its expanded 1870 revision, *Plain Home Talk*, sold an estimated 500,000 copies. (*The Truth Seeker* regularly advertised Foote's *Plain Home Talk*.)[76] In January 1876, Comstock secured an indictment against him for mailing a copy of his pamphlet "Words in Pearl for the Married," which offered medical advice on avoiding pregnancy by using contraceptives, though it objected to inducing a miscarriage or procuring an abortion. Federal Judge Charles Benedict, who eagerly supported Comstock's crusade, refused to quash the indictment and ruled that the prosecution was not required to submit the allegedly obscene material to the jury for consideration because it would "pollute the record."

Foote was convicted and fined $3,500, with Judge Benedict suspending any prison time after receiving numerous letters and petitions from Foote's colleagues and supporters.[77]

As a result, when the National Liberal League convened in Philadelphia in July 1876 for its Centennial Congress, the issue of the Comstock Law's enforcement was on everyone's mind. Francis Abbot sought gallantly to have the delegates concentrate on church-state issues such as taxing church property, abolishing legislative and military chaplains, and, most importantly, defeating the NRA's Christian Amendment. But by the third day, delegates raised the matter of Comstock's prosecutions. Stephen Pearl Andrews offered a resolution calling for "the entire repeal or righteous modification of all such [obscenity] laws." He cited John Lant's imprisonment and Dr. Foote's conviction as evidence that the campaign was conducted "under the pretense of zeal for public morals, but really in behalf of religious and ecclesiastical despotism." Andrews's resolution divided the delegates over how best to respond to Comstock's crusade. Some did not want to be seen as siding with pornographers; James McArthur asserted that several "convictions have been made very properly for passing obscene materials through the mail." McArthur also believed the issue was distracting the delegates from their business: "We have come here to secure the separation of the Church from the State, to secure the absolute and total separation of the two." In contrast, B.F. Underwood supported Andrews's resolution as both relevant and appropriate. The resolution did not indicate approval of obscenity, he declared, but it "recognize[s] that there is an influence of an ecclesiastical character at work," exerted by the YMCA and subject "to the supervision of a special agent." William Potter concurred, arguing that under the pretext "of this general desire for the security of virtue, religious bigots [were] attempting to influence law-makers so as to secure entrance of their theology, and to strike at the circulation of the liberal literature which they must be opposed to." Sensing that support existed for taking some action, Abbot had the resolution referred to a committee. The next day, Underwood introduced a compromise resolution that "recognize[d] the great importance and absolute necessity of guarding by popular legislation against obscene and indecent publications." However, the League objected to all laws "which, by reason of indefiniteness or ambiguity," permitted the prosecution of "honest and conscientious" considerations on behalf of the public welfare. Adopting a middle position, the resolution demanded that "all laws against obscenity and indecency shall be so clear and explicit that none but actual offenders against the recognized principles of purity shall be liable to suffer therefrom." Abbot and the moderates hoped that with the resolution they had put the contentious issue behind them. But the controversy would only grow.[78]

Comstock versus Cupid

Ezra Heywood was similar to many people active in the greater freethought movement. A New Englander, Heywood had attended Brown University in the 1850s. He had planned on becoming a minister but had been inspired by radical abolitionists who embraced an array of social reforms, including women's rights. Also initially influenced by Theodore Parker's liberal unitarianism and John Humphrey Noyes's perfectionism, Heywood abandoned Christianity, becoming a skeptic, anarchist, and labor reformer, and working as an organizer for the National Labor Union after the Civil War. In 1865, Heywood married the equally radical Angela Tilton, with whom he shared a commitment to labor reform, women's rights and suffrage, free love, and eventually spiritualism. In 1872, the two established a newspaper, *The Word*, which promoted their various causes, and issued numerous booklets on economic and sexual reform. They opened a hotel in rural Massachusetts, Mountain Home Resort, which became a retreat for like-minded radicals. Heywood counted among his friends and supporters figures such as Wendell Phillips, Stephen Pearl Andrews, Elizabeth Cady Stanton, and Frederick Douglass.[79]

In 1876, Heywood wrote a pamphlet, *Cupid's Yokes, or The Binding Forces of Conjugal Life*, which was a searing critique of the legal institution of marriage and of other laws that regulated sexual conduct. In it, he argued that marriage promoted sexual depravity among men, with their wives and mistresses the victims. (Heywood also argued that capitalism was at fault by placing men and women "in unnatural antagonism" by making women financially dependent on their husbands, essentially turning a wife into "a 'prostitute' for life.") He advocated complete sexual freedom and the abolition of legal marriage; even though Heywood promoted free love, he and his wife were monogamous, a situation he believed most people would opt for even in the absence of traditional marriage. Despite using words like "sexual organs" and "sexual slavery," *Cupid's Yokes* contained no language or depictions that were sexually explicit or titillating. The pamphlet also spent considerable space criticizing Comstock and his righteous crusade against sexual freedom, with Heywood calling him a "religious monomaniac."[80]

Heywood's dual attack on the institution of marriage and on Comstock produced the expected result. In November 1877, an incensed Comstock obtained a warrant for Heywood's arrest for mailing *Cupid's Yokes* and R.T. Trall's pamphlet *Sexual Physiology*. Comstock called Heywood's work "a most obscene and loathsome book . . . [that] is too foul for description." As he later related in *Traps for the Young*, Comstock tracked down Heywood at a Free Love convention in Boston that Heywood and his wife Angela were addressing. Comstock purchased a ticket, entered the hall incognito, and joined the "mob of free-lusters." As Comstock continued, "I could see lust in every face." "After a little while the wife of [Heywood] took the stand, and delivered the foulest address I ever heard. It was too vile; I had to go out[side]." Unable to locate a policeman to assist in his arrest, Comstock then "sought light and help from above. I prayed for strength to do my duty, and that I might have success. I knew God was able to help me." Emboldened, Comstock returned to the hall and seized Heywood when he left the stage, secreting him away to the Charles Street Jail just ahead of an angry mob.[81]

Heywood's trial took place in US Circuit Court in January 1878. The indictment did not indicate which passages from *Cupid's Yokes* were obscene, and the judge ruled that the prosecutor was not required to enter the allegedly obscene portions into the record or argue it before the jury, thus denying Heywood's counsel the ability to present a defense of its content. Comstock simply testified that the works *were* obscene. After reviewing the materials en camera, the jury agreed. The judge later sentenced Heywood to two years in jail and fined him $1,000.[82]

In the same month that Comstock arrested Heywood, he set his sights on D.M. Bennett, the publisher of *The Truth Seeker*. In November 1877, Comstock appeared at *The Truth Seeker's* New York office with an arrest warrant charging Bennett with mailing two tracts, one titled "An Open Letter to Jesus Christ," and the other, "How Do Marsupials Propagate Their Kind?" The first, written by Bennett (which he acknowledged to be "pretty radical and outspoken") inquired as to why God would impregnate "a young Jewish maiden" while speculating whether the immaculate conception was "an example of free-love?" The second tract, by A.B. Bradford, had originally been written for *Popular Science Monthly*. Released on bail, Bennett took to the pages of *The Truth Seeker* to lambast Comstock as a "Torquemada" undertaking an

"American Inquisition," while soliciting contributions for his legal defense. Wasting few words, Bennett accused "St. Anthony" Comstock of being a "fanatic," "an over-vigilant zealot," and "a mercenary, false-hearted [and] unprincipled bigot." "Comstock is virtually a Ku Klux and his Christian clique (i.e., the YMCA) is a Ku Klux Klan."[83] Francis Abbot rallied to Bennett's defense in *The Index*, criticizing Comstock for seeking to prosecute "blasphemy," though reiterating that Liberals "emphatically and unqualifiedly approve of stringent legislation against the circulation of really obscene literature." Using his influence, Robert Ingersoll wrote the Postmaster General, David M. Key, to have the charges against Bennett withdrawn, or at least to embarrass the government—which apparently worked, as the charges were dismissed in January 1878. Comstock did not take the rebuke or character aspersions lightly, decrying Bennett's "poor-mouth cry" for making "himself a martyr to the cause of blaspheming obscenity (as his publication consisted of blasphemy and obscenity comingled)." Ominously, Comstock remarked that he would still "get the old Infidel into prison."[84]

The month before Heywood's and Bennett's arrests, the National Liberal League had held its second national congress, this time in Rochester, New York. Robert Ingersoll attended and was elected a vice president of the organization. Once again, Francis Abbot was able to prevent the "free love" issue from taking over the convention, keeping the proceedings focused on core church-state issues such as opposing the NRA's Christian Amendment, taxing church property, and securing "universal [secular] public education on the basis of universal suffrage" and the "total separation of church and state." None of the eleven resolutions adopted concerned obscenity or the enforcement of the Comstock Law.[85]

Now, with Heywood's and Bennett's arrests, and with the former's subsequent conviction and imprisonment, Abbot's vision of a unified, and moderate, coalition of freethinkers was unraveling. Abbot's efforts to distinguish between protecting free religious inquiry and supporting the prosecution of "real" obscenity—"libertinism versus liberalism," as he called it—were increasingly untenable. Abbot's seeming rigidity on the issue of free love only made matters worse. In addition to his qualified defense of Bennett, Abbot's support of Heywood had also been tepid. Writing in *The Index*, he said that Heywood's "'free love' theory of morals" was "false, one-sided, logically ridiculous, and morally mischievous in all its tendencies," though the anarchist had the "entire right to plead his case."[86] Relations between Abbot and the

radical freethinkers, led by Bennett, were becoming acrimonious. With the recent arrests, Bennett believed that reforming the Comstock Act and state obscenity statutes was foolhardy and that outright repeal was the only solution
that could protect free inquiry. *The Index*, Bennett wrote,

> proposes to amend these laws so as to remove the objectionable features. . . . It
> proposes to define obscene publications as those "designed expressly to demor-
> alize, pollute, and corrupt by ministering to lewd passions for the sake of profit
> to the publishers." This is worse by far than the law as it is. Comstock would be
> able to "drive a coach and four" through such a law at any time and judge and jury
> would make what they chose out of it.

"It is not enough to remove Comstock," Bennett insisted. "We must sweep the
ground from under his feet. We must kill, not scotch, the snake." Writing from
the Dedham jail, Ezra Heywood also called for repealing the Comstock Act.[87]

Popular sentiment among freethinkers was turning in Bennett's direction.
Even though his charges had been dismissed, Bennett mounted a petition in
favor of repealing the Comstock Act. By March 1878, supporters had gathered
between fifty thousand and seventy thousand signatures (news reports
varied).[88] Robert Ingersoll lent his name to the top of the petition, which was
introduced into Congress by Representative Benjamin Butler (who apparently had a change of heart after initially supporting Comstock). Ingersoll later
claimed that his name was added by mistake and that he had favored only modification rather than repeal of obscenity laws. "No one wishes the repeal of any
law for the suppression of obscene literature," Ingersoll wrote in response to
a false account in the *Boston Journal*. "For my part, I wish all such laws rigidly
enforced. The only objection I have to the [Comstock Act] is, that it has been
construed to include books and pamphlets written against the religion of the
day."[89] The petition was submitted to the House Committee on Revisions of
the Law, which held a hearing in March. Comstock rushed to Washington to
defend his law. His account of the hearing was a repeat of his melodramatic
telling of the Boston free-love meeting at which Heywood had been arrested.[90]
As Comstock entered the committee room, he saw "a copy of the vile paper
[*The Truth Seeker*], of which eight pages were devoted to a pretended account
of 'The Life and Crimes of Anthony Comstock.'"

> Everything looked black. I was alone. . . . I found [the committee room] crowded
> with the long-haired men and short-haired women, there to defend, obscene
> publications, abortion implements, and other incentives to crime, by repealing
> the laws. I heard their hiss and curse as I passed through them. I saw their sneers

and looks of derision and contempt. . . . It was not the blacking of my reputation that weighed me down, so much as the possibility that one of the most righteous laws ever enacted might be repealed or changed.[91]

As before, Comstock found strength and resolve from above. "The God they blasphemed I prayed to; the Sovereign they cursed I revered and sought to honor; the Almighty one they distrusted was the center of my hope, my trust, my all." Emboldened, Comstock gallantly defended the law before the committee, also charging that several of the signatures on the petition had been forged while other names "were of persons whom I had arrested." According to Comstock's account, it was his rousing defense that saved the law. "Then came the complete rout of the enemy; then came the answer to prayer; then came vindication; . . . then came positive proof that it is better to trust God, than to put confidence in men."[92] On May 1, the committee issued a report affirming the constitutionality of the postal law and recommending that it not be amended. The Post Office, it declared, was "not established to carry instruments of vice, or obscene writings, indecent pictures, or lewd books."[93]

The Liberals' effort at repealing the postal law merely confirmed Comstock's belief about the close connection between infidelity and obscenity. From that point forward, freethinkers became his chief nemesis. As he told a meeting of the Chautauqua Assembly in August 1878, "I have been covered over and over again with lies of the blackest, vilest kind, by a new element that has appeared against me. . . . The infidels, Spiritualists, Free-Lovers, and Liberals have joined hands in this city and elsewhere to protect and shield the dealers in obscene publications and articles of indecent and immoral use." Infidels, he declared, were "the worst men, dealing in the vilest matter," who "froth at the mouth when they speak of our blessed Savior" while "the most horrible blasphemies are indulged in against the Lord Jesus Christ."[94]

In a validation of the House Committee's decision, in June the US Supreme Court issued a decision upholding the constitutionality of the Comstock Act. The defendant in *Ex parte Jackson* had been convicted of mailing illegal lottery tickets, though everyone understood its implication for prosecutions involving obscene material. The Court affirmed Congress's authority to regulate "the entire postal system of the country," adding that the "right to designate what shall be carried necessarily involves the right to determine what shall be excluded." The justices also seemed to endorse Comstock's investigatory methods, writing that "[postal] officers can act upon their own inspection" (meaning their own instinct), and "must [frequently] act without other proof," particularly "where the object is exposed, and shows unmistakably that it is prohibited, as in the case of an obscene picture or print" which is "deemed injurious to the public morals." With that decision, all hope of repealing the Comstock Act vanished.[95]

The year 1878 continued to be a momentous one in the battle between censorship and freethought. In response to the arrests of Dr. Foote, Heywood, and Bennett, in the spring Foote's son, Edward Bond Foote (also a physician), helped establish the National Defense Association (NDA) to organize and finance the legal defense of people charged under the Comstock Act. (The National Defense Association would later evolve into the Free Speech League, which in turn served as the forerunner of the American Civil Liberties Union.)[96] While Heywood languished in jail, the NDA and his supporters held an Indignation Meeting on his behalf in Faneuil Hall, in Boston, on August 1. Organizers claimed that as many as six thousand "intelligent" and "enthusiastic" people attended the meeting to hear speakers condemn the Comstock Act and its namesake's tactics. "The Church is responsible for Comstock," asserted one speaker. "He is her agent. He does her bidding, and earns the salary which she pays."[97] The religious press panned the speakers' free speech claims, with the *Christian Union* calling it "absurd" to insist that "no man can be called to account for his words." If a publisher "uses his pen or his press to defile society and to disrupt the family, he is liable to answer to the society which he is endeavoring to destroy for his crimes against it." *Zion's Herald's* criticism was harsher, condemning the "blasphemies and immoralities" that were espoused at the meeting: "The freedom to think and to speak which we glory in, is a liberty restrained by Christian law and morals, and not a license to vicious and corrupting discourses."[98]

On the heels of the Indignation Meeting, D.M. Bennett and other freethinkers organized a freethought convention to be held upstate New York in late August. The organizers announced that several freethought luminaries, including Robert Ingersoll, O.B. Frothingham, Felix Adler, and Elizabeth Cady Stanton, would speak at the event, but newspapers later related that no person of significance addressed the convention.[99] Aside from adopting the predictable resolutions supporting church-state separation, defending Ezra Heywood, and condemning Comstock and his law, the only notable aspects of the Watkins Glenn Convention were the arrests of Josephine Tilton—Heywood's sister-in-law—and D.M. Bennett for selling copies of *Cupid's Yokes* in violation of the New York obscenity statute.

Tilton had, unwisely, decided to sell the pamphlet openly at the convention and, with Bennett's assistance, had sold a copy to an undercover associate of Comstock. Writing later in *The Truth Seeker*, an indignant Bennett claimed that Comstock had encouraged members of the local YMCA to entrap him. Bennett asserted that the Grand Jury had initially not been inclined to return an indictment, but eventually did so at the urging of a biased local judge who happened to be the brother of the YMCA member who had purchased the pamphlet. Bennett's arraignment and trial for violating the obscenity law were set for December.[100]

The Liberal League and Obscenity

While Bennett's new legal charges were pending, the National Liberal League held its third convention in Syracuse, New York, in October, 1878. Francis Abbot's hope of a convention unified around the goals of liberalism was about to be tested. As *Zion's Herald* wrote in advance of the meeting, "[o]ne of the leading questions to be discussed at the coming meeting . . . of the National Liberal (Infidel) League is how to secure 'the rights of free mail and free press,' and how to redress the wrongs of persons 'unjustly punished under the so-called Comstock laws.' Shall it demand the '*total repeal* of the existing law on this subject, and thereby practically protect and foster the circulation of obscene literature?'"[101]

Relations between Abbot and D.M. Bennett, as titular leaders of the moderate and radical wings of the freethought movement, had continued to deteriorate. During the spring, Abbot had used the pages of *The Index* to oppose Bennett's petition to rescind the Comstock Act. And as noted, Abbot had offered only qualified support for Heywood's and Bennett's legal problems. Bennett, in turn, had taken to sniping at Abbot, claiming that the latter's tempered criticism of Comstock's crusade was only facilitating it: "The *Index* is bending in the wrong direction." By failing to condemn Comstock outright, Abbot was guilty of "defending his champion of purity and respectability, Mr. Anthony Comstock."[102]

> Had the *Index* man worked as hard against Comstock and his laws as he has for them, had he co-operated with the body of Liberals of the country as zealously as he has opposed them, and had the true facts been generally placed before the people of the country, those laws would not to-day disgrace our statute books.[103]

Bennett also charged Abbot with feigning moral superiority over the radicals: "We cannot think that he will raise himself higher in the estimation of the Liberal public by pulling us down and insinuating that we are impure, untruthful, unjust, unkind, or immoral."[104] As the League's convention approached, Bennett openly challenged Abbot's bona fides as a freethought leader, writing that "a man who has been educated for the priesthood, and has officiated long in that capacity, is thereby necessarily rendered unfit for a leader in radical and reform movements." Repeal advocate Theron C. Leland also questioned Abbot's qualifications to lead freethinkers in their time of persecution. Abbot "dwells and insists on 'really obscene literature,'" Leland wrote in *The Truth Seeker*. "The Liberals of this country, before electing him again to the Presidency of the League, would like to have him define explicitly and accurately what is 'really obscene literature.'" Modifying the Comstock Act would not protect freethinkers' candid discussion of marriage reform or other "honest but unorthodox opinions," Leland insisted. Nor would it satisfy Comstock's supporters. "This Government is practically a Christian Government. The Government party are in power, and they want and will enforce Christian laws or none at all."[105]

The public feud distressed freethinkers who supported both journals. B.F. Underwood, an ally of Abbot and a contributor to *The Truth Seeker*, called on Liberals to put aside their differences and "unite in petitioning Congress to modify that 'obscenity act.'"

> Why should *The Truth Seeker* and the *Index* get into a dispute over this matter, especially where it is liable to degenerate into bad spirit and bitterness, and where it can do no good. Mr. Abbot is a hard worker in the cause of Liberalism, and has been years arousing Liberals to organize for the defense against every infringement on their rights by orthodoxy. . . . A more heroic or consistent defender of liberty for all, in the widest sense of the word, cannot be found in America.

Hoping to appease Bennett as well, Underwood added, "I know you, too, to be a warm-hearted lover and advocate of the same principles."[106]

Although the Liberal League convention attracted slightly more than one hundred attendees—significantly fewer than had been at the Watkins Glenn freethought meeting—the event received widespread coverage, chiefly for the free love and obscenity controversies. As the *New York Times* headline described the overarching issue: "Congress of the Liberal League: Free-Lovers and Conservatives Struggle for Supremacy." Acrimonious debate over whether to repeal or reform the Comstock Act broke out as soon as the convention had finished its official business, with delegates taunting each other with epithets while "recriminations were bandied about in terms the most vicious and unchaste." Even though the pro-repeal faction constituted the majority, they agreed to a compromise resolution to postpone ultimate judgment on the Comstock Act until the following year. But in a move that Abbot saw as a betrayal of that compromise, the repealers then nominated their own slate of officers for the League, and the delegates voted seventy-six to fifty-one to remove Abbot as president, replacing him with Elizur Wright, a respected former abolitionist leader and avowed atheist. Abbot and his supporters, including B.F. Underwood, promptly retired to a nearby hotel and organized a new, competing organization: the National Liberal League of America. Later efforts at reconciling the two factions failed, and both "Liberal Leagues" adjourned their meetings without taking any further actions.[107]

Francis Abbot reacted bitterly to being rejected by the organization he had founded. He charged that the repealers were insurgents who had forsaken the true cause of liberalism, with its focus on church-state separation, for libertinism. Still in control of *The Index*, Abbot nonetheless asserted that he had won a "moral victory" in Syracuse and that "only an empty shell of the [old] organization remains in the hands of the 'repeal' party; its life and soul are with the new 'National Liberal League of America.'"[108] At least initially, a handful of local Liberal League chapters, headed by "reformers," realigned with Abbot's new organization. Soon afterward, the organization changed its name to the "American Liberal Union" because the name "Liberal League" had become "so widely and injuriously associated in the public mind" with obscenity and free love. Within a year, however, the new organization ceased to exist except in the pages of *The Index*, succumbing to the reality that the freethought movement could not sustain more than one national organization. Abbot continued as editor of *The Index* for two more years, but now isolated from a base of support within both the Liberal League and the Free Religious Association, he grew increasingly embittered. In July 1880, he surrendered ownership of *The Index* back to the Free Religious Association, resigning as editor and turning his attention to teaching and advancing his theory of scientific theism.[109]

D.M. Bennett had traveled to Syracuse for the Liberal League convention, publishing an article in *The Truth Seeker*, the headline of which screamed "Repeal! Repeal! Repeal!" Not being a delegate and unable to participate in the convention's sessions, Bennett held court in a nearby hotel, where he sold copies of *Cupid's Yokes* and other pamphlets, barely escaping another arrest. (Although Bennett had not been directly involved in the Liberal League, evidence suggests he had helped orchestrate the coup in the League's leadership.) In reporting on the convention debacle later, Bennett could hardly restrain his pleasure over his rival's misfortune, comparing Abbot to an "unhappy boy" who, beaten in a game of marbles, gathers up his remaining ones and runs home.[110] Contributor Theron C. Leland was equally unkind, writing in *The Truth Seeker* that "Mr. Abbot now finds himself ousted from the cradle he has rocked, disowned by the child he has nourished into life. . . . May the rump League of pulpiteers, ex-judges, and reactionaries he carries with him, afford him all the consolations he hopes for him." But despite the victory for control of what Bennett now called "our League," he, Leland, and other repealers still chafed at "the insinuation that the repealer is 'the willing and conscientious abettor of obscenity and Freelove.'" They held Abbot responsible for the widespread adoption of that characterization by the press.[111]

The religious press did not need Abbot's help. "Is it not true," wrote the *Christian Union*, "that the majority of the Syracuse Congress unmistakably announced to the public, by the election of a new Board of Directors unanimously in favor of the repeal of [the Comstock] law, that they desire the same thing? Is it not true that the National Liberal League has thus put itself at the head of the vilest class of criminals in the community and made itself the mouthpiece of their hearts desire?" Using more colorful language, Reverend Joseph Cook, a popular lecturer (and Comstock and NRA supporter), declared that "the National Infidel League of Free Religionists" had "transformed themselves into a national lepers league of moral cancer planters."[112]

The chief victor to emerge from the schism within Liberalism was Anthony Comstock. He reveled in the infighting among "the infidels," whom he saw as his main opposition. Comstock allocated two chapters of his book, *Frauds Exposed*, written a year later, to describing the events surrounding the League's Syracuse convention, titling one of the chapters: "Infidelity Wedded to Obscenity: The Spouse of the National Liberal League."

> Is the National Liberal League the defender and sympathizer of those who deal in obscene matter and articles of indecent and immoral use? . . . Has the National Liberal League publicly endorsed the efforts to repeal these laws, or expressed sympathy with convicted dealers in obscene material? Do infidelity and obscenity occupy the same bed?[113]

Employing his flair for colorful language, Comstock panned the "groaning, howling, and fanatic raving of that convention at Syracuse, over this question" of repeal. "Let it be remembered," he continued, "that this pitting of the League in favor of obscenity, this hugging of the vile creature to their hearts, the rolling of this putrid mass under their tongues like a sweet morsal," has revealed the true face of infidelity.[114] Although Comstock called the Abbot faction "honest in their convictions," he still chastised them for their heterodoxy: when "death o'ertakes them," Comstock prophesied, "they may [finally] see how much wiser it would be, to be surer of being on the safe side of eternity, by that sincere repentance and faith, necessary for their soul's salvation." Compared to the repealers, though, Abbot and his followers "were neither base nor nasty enough."[115]

Comstock was riding high and gaining confidence in his crusade. He had beaten back the attempted repeal of his law, which had been upheld by the nation's highest court. His main opponents were divided and expending much of their energy on infighting. Newspapers continued to applaud his efforts, if not always his methods. Still, he faced a headwind of opposition from the radical freethinkers and their new National Defense League, who stood ready to defend authors and distributors of literary journals and medical books that were swept up in Comstock's unbounded definition of obscenity.[116]

There were setbacks as well. Following the Boston Indignation meeting, freethinkers organized a petition to President Rutherford Hayes seeking the pardon of Ezra Heywood, whose health was deteriorating in prison. Laura Kendrick, one of the organizers of the Boston meeting, spearheaded the petition, which by November had gathered six thousand signatures. She traveled from Boston to Washington, DC, to present it to the president. At the same time Elizur Wright, the new president of the Liberal League, intervened with President Hayes. On December 28, *The Truth Seeker* announced the petition's success—Heywood had been released after serving six months in prison. President Hayes had reputedly examined a copy of *Cupid's Yokes*, declaring it tasteless, but not obscene.[117] Comstock, who had also contacted Hayes upon hearing of the petition, was severely disappointed. He decried that "the petition Infidels and liberals, free lovers and Smutt dealers" had prevailed over the "solemn protest signed by the officers of our Society and an affidavit" by himself. Hayes had been misled about the true facts of Heywood's infamous crime, Comstock asserted: "Heywood never would have been pardoned, if the facts had not been suppressed and the President thereby deceived." Adding to Comstock's insult, Heywood was hailed as a martyr and hero at a second meeting in Faneuil Hall, on January 3, 1879.[118]

Having now fully conflated obscenity with infidelity and blasphemy, Comstock set his sights again on the "old infidel"—D.M. Bennett—likely because he was using the pages of *The Truth Seeker* to regularly criticize Comstock and, so far, had escaped his clutches. Bennett, Comstock wrote, was a "blatant infidel and blasphemer of all that is pure and holy." Bennett would soon become the next victim in Comstock's holy crusade.[119]

NOTES

1. Braude, *Radical Spirits*, 127–129; Stoehr, *Free Love in America*, 3–71.

2. Ellen DuBois and Elizabeth Cady Stanton, "On Labor and Free Love: Two Unpublished Speeches of Elizabeth Cady Stanton," *Signs* (Autumn 1975), 257–268; Ezra Heywood, *Cupid's Yokes, of the Binding Forces of Conjugal Life* (Princeton, MA: Co-operative Pub., 1878), 5; Kathy Peiss, ed., *Major Problems in the History of American Sexuality* (Boston: Houghton Mifflin, 2002), 249–252.

3. Eckhardt, *Fanny Wright*, 146–147; "The Free-Love System: Origin, Progress, and Position of the Anti-Marriage Movement," *New York Times*, Sept. 8, 1855, 2; Stoehr, *Free Love in America*, 29–39; "The Oneida Community: Free Love, Free Lovers, and Perfection," *Circular*, May 6, 1867, 67.

4. "The Berlin Free-Love Case: A Wife Rescued," *New York Times*, July 1, 1858, 2; "Radicals in Council: A Spicy Time on Free-Love—Very Broad Doctrines Freely Allowed," ibid., June 29, 1858, 1; Stoehr, *Free Love in America*, 5.

5. "'Free-Love' on the Rampage," *Christian Advocate*, Dec. 16, 1869, 396; "Free-Love and Free-Divorce," *Every Saturday*, July 22, 1871, 75.

6. "Fighting under Cover," *The Independent*, Oct. 19, 1871, 4.

7. "The Principle of Social Freedom, Involving Free Love, Marriage, Divorce, etc.— Lecture by Victoria C. Woodhull," *New York Times*, Nov. 21, 1871, 1.

8. Emanie Sachs, *"The Terrible Siren": Victoria Woodhull* (New York: Harper & Brothers, 1928); Mary Gabriel, *Notorious Victoria: The Life of Victoria Woodhull, Uncensored* (Chapel Hill: Algonquin Books, 1998); Barbara Goldsmith, *Other Powers: The Age of Suffrage, Spiritualism, and the Scandalous Victoria Woodhull* (New York: Alfred A. Knoff, 1998); Amanda Frisken, *Victoria Woodhull's Sexual Revolution: Political Theatre and Popular Press in Nineteenth-Century America* (Philadelphia: University of Pennsylvania Press, 2011); Myra MacPherson, *The Scarlet Sisters: Sex, Suffrage, and Scandal in the Gilded Age* (New York: Twelve Books, 2014).

9. Sachs, *"The Terrible Siren,"* 47–52; Frisken, *Victoria Woodhull's Sexual Revolution*, 6–9; Goldsmith, *Other Powers*, 156–162; MacPherson, *The Scarlet Sisters*, 3–13, 22–39; Helen Lefkowitz Horowitz, "Victoria Woodhull, Anthony Comstock, and the Conflict over Sex in the United States in the 1870s," *Journal*

of American History 87 (2000): 411–413; "Wall-Street Aroused: The Female Brokers—The First Day's Operations," *New York Times*, Feb. 6, 1870, 8.

10. *Woodhull and Claflin's Weekly*, ed. Arlene Kisner (Washington, NJ: Times Change Press, 1972); "Impartial Suffrage: Lecture of Mrs. Victoria C. Woodhull at Cooper Institute," *New York Times*, March 2, 1871, 8; "Principle of Finance: Lecture of Mrs. Victoria C. Woodhull Last Evening," ibid., Aug. 4, 1871, 8; "Mrs. Woodhull and Her Critics," ibid., May 22, 1871, 5; Frisken, *Victoria Woodhull's Sexual Revolution*, 25–27.

11. Sachs, *"The Terrible Siren,"* 56–59; MacPherson, *The Scarlet Sisters*, 61–65; "Women in Council: A Hearing by the Judiciary Committee of the House," *New York Times*, Jan. 12, 1871, 5; "Woman Suffrage," ibid., Feb. 2, 1871, 1; Victoria C. Woodhull, "The Right of Women to Vote and Protest," ibid., Nov. 8, 1871, 2; Woodhull, "The New Rebellion," in *Selected Writings of Victoria Woodhull*, ed. Cari M. Carpenter (Lincoln: University of Nebraska Press, 2010), 29–39; "The Great Political Issue of Equality," reprinted in *The Radical*, Sept. 1871, 145 (also announcing her nomination for president under the Equal Rights Party).

12. "Women in Council," *New York Times*, Jan. 12, 1871, 5; Goldsmith, *Other Powers*, 211–214.

13. Susan B. Anthony to Victoria Claflin Woodhull, Feb. 4, 1871, in *The Selected Papers of Elizabeth Cady Stanton and Susan B. Anthony*, ed. Ann D. Gordon (New Brunswick, NJ: Rutgers University Press, 2009), 2:415–416 (hereinafter *Selected Papers*); Elizabeth Cady Stanton to Victoria Claflin Woodhull, Dec. 29, 1871, ibid., 2:462–463; "The Anniversaries," *New York Times*, May 12, 1871, 8; "Woman Suffrage," ibid., May 13, 1871, 2; Goldsmith, *Other Powers*, 272–275.

14. Braude, *Radical Spirits*, 170–173; Woodhull, *Selected Writings*, 40–49.

15. "The Woodhull–Claflin Entanglement," *New York Times*, May 17, 1871, 2; Theodore Tilton, *Victoria C. Woodhull: A Biographical Sketch* (New York: Golden Age Books, 1871); Richard Wightman Fox, *Trials of Intimacy: Love and Loss in the Beecher–Tilton Scandal* (Chicago: University of Chicago Press, 1989), 123, 154; Altina L. Waller, *Reverend Beecher and Mrs. Tilton: Sex and Class in Victorian America* (Amherst: University of Massachusetts Press, 1982), 132–135.

16. Amanda Frisken, "Sex in Politics: Victoria Woodhull as an American Public Woman, 1870–1876," *Journal of Women's History* 12 (2000): 89–110; Margret Wyman, "Harriet Beecher Stowe's Topical Novel on Woman Suffrage," *New England Quarterly* 25 (Sept. 1952): 383–391.

17. Sachs, *"The Terrible Siren,"* 129–137; MacPherson, *The Scarlet Sisters*, 127–133; "The Doctrine of Free Love," *New York Tribune*, reprinted in *Maine Farmer*, Dec. 2, 1871, 2; "The Principle of Social Freedom, Involving Free Love, Marriage, Divorce, etc.," *New York Times*, Nov. 21, 1871, 1.

18. Victoria C. Woodhull, "The Principles of Social Freedom," in *The Victoria Woodhull Reader*, ed. Madeline B. Stern (Weston, MA: M&S Press, 1974), 23–24, 35; Goldsmith, *Other Powers*, 298–301.

19. "Physician, Heal Thyself," *Zion's Herald*, Nov. 9, 1871, 535; "Victoria Woodhull and Her Admirers: A Catholic Clergyman Denounces Them from the Altar," *New York Times*, Nov. 24, 1871, 8; *Harper's Weekly*, Feb. 17, 1872, 140, 143.

20. Elizabeth Cady Stanton, "Woman Suffrage Organizations," in *Woodhull & Claflin's Weekly*, Dec. 16, 1871, 34–36; Frisken, "Sex in Politics," 97–98.

21. Tilton, *Victoria C. Woodhull*, 28–29.

22. See Victoria C. Woodhull, "The Naked Truth, or the Situation Reviewed" (1873), in *Victoria Woodhull Reader*; "Notes," *The Radical*, Sept. 1871, 150–151; Susan B. Anthony to Elizabeth Cady Stanton and Isabella Beecher Hooker, March 13, 1872, in *Selected Papers*, 2:485–486; Diary, May 8, 1872, ibid., 2:492–494; Goldsmith, *Other Powers*, 310–323; Sehat, *The Myth of American Religious Freedom*, 148–150.

23. J.H. Paxton, *The Great Brooklyn Romance* (New York: J.H. Paxton, 1874); Horowitz, "Victoria Woodhull," 415–417; Waller, *Reverend Beecher and Mrs. Tilton*, 32–34, 116–118, Fox, *Trials of Intimacy*, 155, 194–195.

24. "Mrs. Woodhull and Her Critics," *New York Times*, May 22, 1871, 5. A different version is reprinted in *Woodhull & Claflin's Weekly*, June 2, 1871, 41; "Goldsmith, *Other Powers*, 286.

25. Fox, *Trials of Intimacy*, 155–157; "The Beecher-Tilton Scandal Case," *Woodhull & Claflin's Weekly*, Nov. 2, 1872, 9–13; "The Beecher-Tilton Scandal Case," in *Selected Writings*, 98–124; "The Beecher Scandal," *New York Times*, July 1, 1873, 2; Gabriel, *Notorious Victoria*, 183–184; Waller, *Reverend Beecher and Mrs. Tilton*, 1–4.

26. Goldsmith, *Other Powers*, 337–343; Horowitz, "Victoria Woodhull," 415–417.

27. Sohn, *The Man Who Hated Women*, 21–25; Anthony Comstock, "How I Came to Enter Upon My Work," *Christian Advocate*, May 17, 1888, 327.

28. "Obscene Literature—A Filthy Depot in the Heart of the City—How the Morals of Our Youth Are Corrupted," *New York Times*, Jan. 15, 1872, 2.

29. See "The Cry of the Children," *Christian Union*, April 16, 1873, 310; Gilfoyle, *City of Eros*, 29; Peiss, *Major Problems in the History of American Sexuality*, 239–241; Margret A. Blanchard and John E. Semonche, "Anthony Comstock and His Adversaries: The Mixed Legacy of This Battle for Free Speech," *Communications Law and Policy* 11 (2006): 320–322.

30. Gilfoyle, *City of Eros*, 181–185; Anna Louise Bates, *Weeder in the Garden of the Lord* (Lanham, MD: University Press of America, 1995), 51–53.

31. "The Young Men's Christian Association," *New York Times*, May 14, 1866, 5; "The Young Men of New York," ibid., Sept. 25, 1866, 8; Boyer, *Purity in Print*, 4–5; Bates, *Weeder in the Garden of the Lord*, 51–53; Werbel, *Lust on Trial*, 54–55.

32. Charles G. Trumbull, *Anthony Comstock, Fighter* (New York: Fleming H. Revell, 1913), 51–52.

33. "A Raid upon Dealers in Obscene Merchandise," *New York Times*, March 16, 1872, 3.

34. Trumbull, *Anthony Comstock, Fighter*, 63–64, 68–69; Comstock, "How I Came to Enter Upon My Work," 327; "The Society for the Suppression of Obscene Literature," *New York Times*, May 9, 1872, 3; "Measures for the Suppression of Obscene Literature," ibid., May 10, 1972, 8; Gilfoyle, *City of Eros*, 185–188.

35. Trumbull, *Anthony Comstock, Fighter*, 234; "Breaking Up the Trade in Obscene Literature—What Has Been Done Since March," *New York Times*, Aug. 28, 1872, 2; "A Vendor of Obscene Literature Sentenced," ibid., Oct. 4, 1872, 2; "Arrests for Malpractice," ibid., Aug, 31, 1872, 5.

36. "Conviction for Sending Obscene Literature through the Mail," *New York Times*, March 18, 1873, 2.

37. "The Obscene Literature Cases," *New York Times*, Aug. 29, 1872, 2; "A Case for Mr. Comstock," *The Literary World*, March 7, 1885, 78; "Exposure of Fraud and Crime," *New York Evangelist*, Jan. 13, 1881, 4, "The Comstock Laws," *Scribner's Monthly* (July 1881): 456–457.

38. "The Obscene Literature Cases," *New York Times*, Aug. 29, 1872, 2; Horowitz, "Victoria Woodhull," 425–426.

39. Trumbull, *Anthony Comstock, Fighter*, 22; Comstock, "How I Came to Enter Upon My Work," 327.

40. Sohn, *The Man Who Hated Women*.

41. Broun and Leech, *Anthony Comstock*, 56; Werbel, *Lust on Trial*, 15, 29–30; Mark I. West, "The Role of Sexual Repression in Anthony Comstock's Campaign to Censor Children's Dime Novels," *Journal of American Culture* 22 (1999): 45–49.

42. Bates, *Weeder in the Garden of the Lord*, 4–16.

43. Beisel, *Imperiled Innocents*, 8–10; Anthony Comstock, "How to Guard Our Youth against Bad Literature," *The Chautauquan*, (Aug. 1897): 520–524; Comstock, *Traps of the Young*, 158, 160.

44. Gaines M. Foster, *Moral Reconstruction: Christian Lobbyists and the Federal Legislation of Morality, 1864–1920* (Chapel Hill: University of North Carolina Press, 2002), 50.

45. Anthony Comstock, "The Extirpation of the Crime-Breeders of the Day a Public Necessity," *Belford's Magazine* (June 1890): 64–74.

46. Anthony Comstock, n.t., *The Independent*, March 14, 1889, 2–3; Comstock, "How to Guard Our Youth against Bad Literature," 523.

47. Regina v. Hicklin, L.R. 3 Q.B. 360, 371 (1868).

48. Broun and Leech, *Anthony Comstock*, 87; *The Independent*, March 14, 1889, 2.

49. Broun and Leech, *Anthony Comstock*, 93, 106–107; Horowitz, "Victoria Woodhull," 419–420.

50. "Victoria C. Woodhull's Complete and Detailed Version of the Beecher-Tilton Affair," 11, 13.

51. "The Claflin Family," *New York Times*, Nov. 3, 1872, 1; "Woodhull and Claflin," ibid., Nov. 5, 1872, 2; "In Jail Again," Jan. 10, 1873, 5; Victoria Woodhull, "The Naked Truth, or the Situation Reviewed!," *Woodhull & Claflin's Weekly*, Jan. 23, 1873, 3–7, 14–15; "Woodhull and Claflin Trial—Discharge of Defendants,"

ibid., June 28, 1873, 2; "An Act to Revise, Consolidate and Amend the Statutes Relating to the Post-Office Department," 17 Stat. 302 (1872); Broun and Leech, *Anthony Comstock*, 108–127; Horowitz, "Victoria Woodhull," 420, 431.

52. Comstock, *Frauds Exposed*, 389–392; Trumbull, *Anthony Comstock, Fighter*, 83–99; Broun and Leech, *Anthony Comstock*, 128–154; 17 Stat. 598–600 (1873); Wayne Edison Fuller, *Morality and the Mail in Nineteenth-Century America* (Urbana: University of Illinois Press, 2003), 105–108.

53. "Laws against Obscene Publications," *New York Times*, March 8, 1873, 7.

54. Anthony Comstock, "The Suppression of Vice Misrepresentations Corrected," *Christian Advocate*, June 20, 1878, 396; Anthony Comstock, *Frauds Exposed, or How the People Are Deceived and Robbed* (New York: J.H. Brown, 1880), 418.

55. Craig L. LaMay, "America's Censor: Anthony Comstock and Free Speech," *Communications and the Law* 19 (1997):1–59.

56. Victoria C. Woodhull, "Tried as by Fire; or the True and the False, Socially" (1874), 17, 20, in *Victoria Woodhull Reader*; Gabriel, *Notorious Victoria*, 219–236; Frisken, *Victoria Woodhull's Sexual Revolution*, 117–140.

57. Frisken, *Victoria Woodhull's Sexual Revolution*, 140–145; "The Beecher Scandal," *New York Times*, Oct. 4, 1874, 5; Waller, *Reverend Beecher and Mrs. Tilton*, 140–150; Fox, *Trials of Intimacy*.

58. Frisken, *Victoria Woodhull's Sexual Revolution*, 146–149; "The Vanderbilt Estate," *New York Times*, May 13, 1877, 12.

59. Anthony Comstock, "Historical and Modern Safeguards to Public Morality," *Christian Advocate*, Jan. 4, 1894, 4; Trumbull, *Anthony Comstock, Fighter*, 130–131.

60. "The Suppression of Vice," *New York Times*, Jan. 1, 1876, 2.

61. Comstock, *Traps for the Young*, 166.

62. Broun and Leech, *Anthony Comstock*, 145–154; "An Arrest by Mr. Comstock," *New York Times*, June 26, 1874, 2; "Arrested for Disseminating Obscene Literature," ibid., July 12, 1874, 1: "Mr. Comstock at Work," ibid., July 17, 1873, 8; "Suppressing Immoral Literature," ibid., Oct. 28, 1875, 2; "Comstock Still at Work," ibid., Nov. 20, 1878, 2; "The Assault on Mr. Comstock," ibid., Nov. 3, 1874, 5; Bates, *Weeder in the Garden of the Lord*, 105–106.

63. "Examination in the Malpractice Cases," *New York Times*, April 24, 1873, 2; "A Doubtful Doctor Arrested," ibid., June 10, 1879, 3. See U.S. v. Bott, and U.S. v. Whitehead, 24 Fed. Cas. 1204–1205 (1873).

64. "Miscellaneous News: Mme. Restell Arrested," *New York Times*, Feb. 12, 1878, 12; "The Case of Mme. Restell," ibid., Feb. 28, 1878, 5; "End of a Criminal Life: Mme. Restell Commits Suicide," ibid., April 2, 1878, 1; Broun and Leech, *Anthony Comstock*, 155–160; Sohn, *The Man Who Hated Women*, 113–131; D.M. Bennett, *Anthony Comstock: His Career of Cruelty and Crime* (New York: Liberal and Scientific Pub. House, 1878), 1068–1073.

65. *Zion's Herald*, April 3, 1879, 108.

66. "A Case for Mr. Comstock," *The Literary World*, March 7, 1885, 78; "Fighting with Beasts," *Christian Advocate*, April 6, 1882, 1.

67. "The Christian Convention," *New York Times*, July 11, 1873, 5.

68. Woodhull, "Principles of Social Freedom," 12, 23, 25, 32–33.

69. Ellen Carol DuBois, *Feminism and Suffrage* (Ithaca, NY: Cornell University Press, 1978), 93–101.

70. "G.F. Train in Prison," *New York Times*, Dec. 21, 1872, 12; "The Train Lunacy Investigation," ibid., April 23, 1873, 2; "Train's Sanity—A Jury Again Pronounces Him Sane," ibid., May 30, 1873, 2; Bennett, *Anthony Comstock*, 1023; Broun and Leech, *Anthony Comstock*, 108–114.

71. *The Truth Seeker*, Jan. 1874, 15; ibid., Jan. 15, 1875, 15; ibid., April 1, 1875, 15; B.F. Underwood, "Marriage," ibid., July 1873, 3.

72. L'incomu, "Individual Liberty," *The Truth Seeker*, Feb. 1874, 14; Elmina Slenker, "A Woman's Plea," ibid., June 1874, 7.

73. Letter from H. Weststein, *The Truth Seeker*, March 1874, 9.

74. Jacoby, *Freethinkers*, 164; "Free Love, What It Is and What It Is Not," *The Truth Seeker*, Sept. 1, 1874, 8.

75. "Sectarian Intolerance," *The Truth Seeker*, Aug. 15, 1875, 9; Bennett, *Anthony Comstock*, 1023–1024; "Have We a Free Press?," *The Truth Seeker*, Jan. 1874, 4; Bates, *Weeder in the Garden of the Lord*, 127–128; Bradford, *D.M. Bennett*, 110.

76. See *The Truth Seeker*, May 1874, 16; Aug. 1874, 16; and Sept. 1874, 15.

77. Janice Ruth Wood, *The Struggle for Free Speech in the United States, 1872–1915: Edward Bliss Foote, Edward Bond Foote, and Anti-Comstock Operations* (New York: Routledge, 2008), 34–36, 54–57; Bennett, *Anthony Comstock*, 1036–1042.

78. "Report of the Centennial Congress," 157–162, 170; Ahlstrom and Mullin, *The Scientific Theist*, 114–115.

79. E.H. Heywood, *Uncivil Liberty: An Essay to Show the Injustice and Impolicy of Ruling Woman without Her Consent* (Princeton, MA: Cooperative Pub. So. 1872); Martin Henry Blatt, *Free Love and Anarchism: The Biography of Ezra Heywood* (Urbana: University of Illinois Press, 1989), 15–63, 67.

80. Heywood, *Cupid's Yokes*, 9–12, 19–22; Blatt, *Free Love and Anarchism*, 103–105.

81. Comstock, *Traps for the Young*, 163–166; Blatt, *Free Love and Anarchism*, 113–114; Broun and Leech, *Anthony Comstock*, 172–173.

82. Bennett, *Anthony Comstock*, 1060–1061; "E.H. Heywood's Case," *The Truth Seeker*, Nov. 24, 1877, 374–375; "Conviction of E.H. Heywood," ibid., Jan. 26. 1878, 57; "Obscene Literature in the Mails," *New York Times*, June 26, 1878, 5; Blatt, *Free Love and Anarchism*, 115–118; Bates, *Weeder in the Garden of the Lord*, 135–137.

83. Bennett, *Anthony Comstock*, 1061–1066; "American Liberty: Is It a Sham?," *The Truth Seeker*, Nov. 24, 1877, 271–273; ibid., Dec. 1, 1877, 381; "No Examination Yet," ibid., Dec. 22, 1877, 404; Bradford, *D.M. Bennett*, 107–110, 116–117.

84. "The Voice of the Press," *The Truth Seeker*, Dec. 1, 1877, 384; "The Dismissal of Our Case," ibid., Jan 12, 1878, 24; Comstock, *Frauds Exposed*, 396; Bennett, *Anthony Comstock*, 1066; Bradford, *D.M. Bennett*, 118–121.

85. "National Liberal League," *New York Times*, Oct. 27, 1877, 1; "Liberal League Congress," ibid., Oct. 28, 1877, 1; "National Liberal League," ibid., Oct. 29, 1877, 1; *Christian Union*, Nov. 7, 1877, 397; Larson, *American Infidel*, 144.

86. *The Index*, Dec. 6, 1877, in Ahlstrom and Mullin, *The Scientific Theist*, 116–117, 120.

87. "The Main Question," *The Truth Seeker*, Dec. 29, 1877, 413; Bradford, *D.M. Bennett*, 147–148.

88. *The Truth Seeker*, Dec. 22, 1877, 404; Bradford, *D.M. Bennett*, 119.

89. *The Truth Seeker*, Dec. 29, 1877, 412; ibid., Jan 12, 1878, 24; "Obscene Literature," ibid., March 9, 1878, 152; ibid., June 8, 1878, 361 "Forty-Fifth Congress," *New York Times*, March 13, 1878, 2; "Freedom of the Mails," *Christian Union*, March 20, 1878, 239; Comstock, *Frauds Exposed*, 421; "The Circulation of Obscene Literature," Ingersoll, *Works*, 12:215–216.

90. Broun and Leech, *Anthony Comstock*, 177–179.

91. Comstock, *Frauds Exposed*, 424.

92. Ibid., 423–425, 429.

93. Ibid., 430.

94. "Suppression of Vice," *Christian Advocate*, Aug. 15, 1878, 524.

95. *Ex parte* Jackson, 96 U.S. 727, 732, 735–736 (1878); "Prohibited Mail Matter, *New York Times*, June 4, 1878, 4; *Central Law Journal*, June 14, 1878, 461; *The Truth Seeker*, June 15, 1878, 377.

96. David M. Rabban, *Free Speech in Its Forgotten Years* (New York: Cambridge University Press, 1997), 39–40, 44–76.

97. *Proceedings of the Indignation Meeting Held in Faneuil Hall, Thursday Evening August 1, 1878* (Boston: Benj. R. Tucker, 1878), 62; "Suppress Vice but Not Free Speech," *The Truth Seeker*, Aug. 17, 1878, 519.

98. "Free Speech," *Christian Union*, Aug. 7, 1878, 103; *Zion's Herald*, Aug. 8, 1878, 252.

99. "The Freethinkers' Convention," *The Truth Seeker*, June 22, 1878, 397; "The Watkins Convention," ibid., Aug. 17, 1878, 520; *Christian Union*, Sept. 4, 1878, 190.

100. "Another Arrest," *The Truth Seeker*, Aug. 31, 1878, 552–553; "Our Indictment," ibid., Sept. 7, 1878, 56; "Schuyler County Justice, ibid., Sept 12. 1878, 584–585; "The Watkins Arrests," ibid., Sept. 21, 1878, 600–601; Bradford, *D.M. Bennett*, 131–143.

101. *Zion's Herald*, Oct. 3, 1878, 316.

102. *The Truth Seeker*, Dec. 1, 1877, 384; "The Main Question," ibid., Dec. 29, 1877, 412–413.

103. "Misstatements Corrected," ibid., Oct. 12, 1878, 648.

104. "An Explanation," ibid., Jan. 26, 1878, 60.

105. "The Index Wet Blanket," ibid., Dec. 29, 1877, 413; "Indexes," ibid., Feb. 9, 1878, 88–89; Theron C. Leland, "Two Phases of Repeal," ibid., Oct. 12, 1878, 644; Ahlstrom and Mullin, *The Scientific Theist*, 117.

106. "Letter from B.F. Underwood," *The Truth Seeker*, Jan. 19, 1878, 46; "The True Position of F.E. Abbot," ibid., March 2, 1878, 136.

107. "Congress of the Liberal League: Free-Loves and Conservatives Struggle for Supremacy," *New York Times*, Oct. 27, 1878, 7; "A Liberal League Fight," ibid., Oct. 28, 1878, 5; "The National Liberal League Congress," *Christian Union*, Nov. 6, 1878, 378; "Second Meeting of the National Liberal League Congress," *The Truth Seeker*, Nov. 2, 1878, 696–697, 692–693; "Schisms among the Free Thinkers," *American Socialist*, Nov. 7, 1878, 356; Ahlstrom and Mullin, *The Scientific Theist*, 119–123.

108. "Churches and Ministers," *New York Times*, Nov. 3, 1878, 10; "The Index Shouts 'Victory,'" *The Truth Seeker*, Nov. 9, 1878, 712.

109. *The Independent*, Feb. 19, 1880, 17; *Christian Union*, July 7, 1880, 1; Ahlstrom and Mullin, *The Scientific Theist*, 123–135.

110. "A Bare Escape," *The Truth Seeker*, Nov. 2, 1878, 693; "The Index Shouts 'Victory,'" ibid., Nov. 9, 1878, 712.

111. "Notes on the Convention," ibid., Nov. 9, 1878, 708; "Continued Falsifications," ibid., Nov. 9, 1878, 712.

112. "A Liberal League Fight," *New York Times*, Oct. 28, 1878, 5; "Notes," *Christian Union*, Dec. 4, 1878, 473; Rev. Joseph Cook, "Rich and Poor in Factory Towns," *The Independent*, Nov. 28, 1878, 4.

113. Comstock, *Frauds Exposed*, 443.

114. Ibid., 454.

115. Ibid., 466, 450.

116. Rabban, *Free Speech in Its Forgotten Years*, 24–25.

117. "Heywood's Pardon: Will It Be Granted?," *The Truth Seeker*, Nov. 23, 1878, 745; "Pardon of Ezra Heywood," ibid., Dec. 28, 1878, 824–825; Blatt, *Free Love and Anarchism*, 131–132.

118. "Shall Vice Triumph?," *New York Evangelist*, Jan. 16, 1879, 1; Comstock, *Frauds Exposed*, 485–486; Blatt, *Free Love and Anarchism*, 132; Broun and Leech, *Anthony Comstock*, 174–175.

119. Comstock, *Frauds Exposed*, 419.

4

Freethought under Fire

After his arrest at the Watkins Glenn freethought meeting in August 1878, an indignant D.M. Bennett announced in *The Truth Seeker* that he would now sell *Cupid's Yokes* to subscribers. Bennett knew the risks—his trial for facilitating the sale of the pamphlet still awaited him in New York state court, so any subsequent sales might be evidence of willful disregard for the law. Additional sales were also likely to goad Comstock into action, something that Bennett seemingly welcomed. For Bennett, it was a matter of principle; he maintained that *Cupid's Yokes* was not obscene and that "we shall continue to maintain the right to sell it to whomever we please." Comstock, Bennett insisted, was using an unbounded definition of obscenity as a proxy for attacking "independent believers."[1]

> It should be borne in mind that the founders of our Government and the framers of our Constitution, in establishing that glorious instrument, recognized neither Jehovah, his son, nor his sacred Scriptures; and for that very reason the zealous devotees of the various sects in the land have felt sorely aggrieved. . . . It is true that within the last few years laws have been surreptitiously and unfortunately added to our statutes . . . for oppressing unbelievers not before possessed. . . . We feel confident that it was the design of the framers of our Constitution that no person should be oppressed on account of his religious opinions or for the want of religious opinions.[2]

Comstock, in turn, held a grudge against Bennett for sponsoring the recall petition and for having escaped his earlier prosecution, despite the fact he "[p]ublishes [the] most horrible and obscene blasphemy." Comstock therefore eagerly accepted Bennett's dare. In November 1878, as the pardon for Ezra Heywood was pending, Comstock wrote *The Truth Seeker* under an alias and ordered a copy of *Cupid's Yokes*, among other titles, to be sent through the mail. Bennett obliged and was promptly indicted. At the arraignment, in Bennett's account, Comstock entered the courtroom "looking as happy as a clam at high water" and whistling a "pious tune, 'The Sweet By and By.'" When one of Bennett's employees said something derogatory under his breath, Comstock whirled around, cursed him, and threatened "to kick [him] out into the hall." "This little incident," Bennett wrote, "shows the insolent, overbearing character of Comstock, who, while possessing immaculate purity himself, is capable of [displaying] impurity," as well.[3]

Bennett now faced two indictments for selling obscene material. He likely realized, however, that the greater threat to his freedom lay in the federal charge. In fact, out of deference to the federal prosecution, trial on the New York state charge from Watkins Glenn was delayed a second time, and then was ultimately dismissed. Comstock now had Bennett all to himself.[4]

Bennett's trial for violating the Comstock Act took place in the US Circuit Court in New York City from March 18 to 21, 1879. Presiding was Judge Charles Benedict, Comstock's favorite, who had overseen the trials of John A. Lant and Dr. E.B. Foote and who consistently sided with the crusader. Benedict revealed his bias from the beginning, ruling against every defense motion. He held that the prosecution could show the jury only the allegedly obscene passages from *Cupid's Yokes*, without allowing the jurors to consider the pamphlet in its entirety as a piece of social criticism. He also refused to allow Bennett's counsel to introduce titillating passages from the Bible to demonstrate the subjectivity and hypocrisy of the charges.[5]

Comstock was the chief witness for the prosecution, and he simply testified that he had received the "obscene" pamphlet from Bennett through the mail. The defense counsel attempted to call witnesses who would testify to the pamphlet's value as social commentary, including O.B. Frothingham, but Judge Benedict ruled that such testimony was "wholly immaterial"; the jury only had to determine "whether or not the marked passages are obscene, lewd, lascivious, or indecent, within the meaning of [his instructions]" regardless of their context. Whether Bennett intended to "corrupt youth" by selling *Cupid's Yokes* was also irrelevant; rather, it was only material that he intended to sell the pamphlet and it had the *tendency* to corrupt young minds.[6]

Bennett's other defense—aside from arguing *Cupid's Yokes* was not obscene—was that the prosecution was a pretext—that its "real object was to suppress an offensive heretical publisher." During cross-examination, Bennett's counsel elicited an admission from Comstock that after Bennett's arrest he had declared with satisfaction that "another class of publications, issued by Freelovers and Freethinkers, is in a fair way of being stamped out," suggesting that his prosecution was motivated by animus against freethought. Judge Benedict ruled that this statement also was "immaterial," and he later instructed the jury that the case had nothing to do with freedom of religion or of the press. "Freelovers and freethinkers have a right to their views," Benedict declared, "and they may express them, and they may publish them, but they cannot publish them in connection with obscene material." In so doing, Benedict undercut one of Bennett's main defenses. At the same time, however, Benedict allowed the prosecutor to prejudice the jury by asking defense witnesses whether they were aware of Bennett's previous arrest for publishing "An Open Letter to Jesus Christ," without adding that the charge had been dismissed. Then, in his closing argument, the prosecutor tied Bennett to the "slanderous" Victoria Woodhull while he referred derisively to the defense's chief expert and character witness as "Doctor Frothingham, or any other ham," who had the imprudence to think he could instruct the jury on whether the pamphlet was obscene.[7]

At the trial's conclusion, Judge Benedict instructed the jury that the test for obscenity, borrowed from a recent British case *Regina v. Hicklin,* was whether a book's content had the tendency "to deprave and corrupt the morals of those whose minds are open to such influences." But for a book to be obscene, Benedict added, it was not even necessary "that [obscene] words be found in it. The most obscene, lewd, and lascivious matter may be conveyed by words which in themselves are not of an obscene character." Such circular reasoning allowed almost any book to be found to be obscene, particularly if jurors were not required to consider the work in its entirety. Conscious of the allegations about Comstock's motives, Benedict again cautioned the jury that Bennett's "peculiar views on the subject of religion" had nothing to do with his prosecution, but then he proceeded to remind the jurors of them: "he may be an infidel; he may have peculiar and improper notions on the marriage relation; he may be a freethinker; he may be whatever he pleases." After highlighting Bennett's heterodoxy, he admonished the jurors that "that should have no effect upon your deliberations."[8]

The trial's outcome was never in doubt. After one juror's initial reticence, the judge required the jury to deliberate overnight, which resulted in a guilty verdict. Newspapers followed the trial closely. The Methodist *Christian Advocate* called the verdict "richly deserved," while *Zion's Herald* praised Comstock as a "singularly shrewd, plucky, and devout man" whom "God has called," and who was in "every way adapted to this ungrateful task." Both religious journals joined others in mounting a preemptive drive by soliciting President Hayes not to pardon Bennett as he had done in Heywood's case.[9] Bennett appealed his conviction to a three-judge panel of the US Circuit Court (which included Judge Benedict). The Court turned aside Bennett's complaints, including those alleging Comstock's religious animus, and affirmed his conviction. Judge Benedict then sentenced Bennett to thirteen months in prison at hard labor; a sentence of twelve months or less would have been served in a jail cell rather than in the harsher confines of Albany Penitentiary.[10]

A handful of secular journals condemned the prosecution for misapplying the obscenity laws. Despite calling *Cupid's Yokes* a "nasty book" and Bennett a "reprehensible man," the *Albany Law Journal* opined that a "more ill-advised, and more injudicious proceeding in the way of a prosecution was probably never brought into a court of justice." As anticipated, Bennett's supporters, led by Robert Ingersoll, mounted a petition drive for a presidential pardon, reputedly gathering 200,000 signatures (the number was likely exaggerated). Even though President Hayes had pardoned the author of *Cupid's Yokes*—Heywood—this time he declined to issue one for its distributor, succumbing to pressure from his devout wife and representatives from the religious community. Not leaving anything to chance, Comstock also traveled to Washington to lobby the president, supplying him with copies of indiscrete letters of the married Bennett to another woman, thus sealing the deal.[11]

Bennett's conviction hit a nerve among freethinkers who saw it as the most direct attack on their movement to date. It also became a rallying cry for greater organizing and resistance. Attendance at regional freethought conventions surged—likely in solidarity to the various prosecutions—with a September 1879 rally in Chautauqua Lake, New York, reputedly drawing five thousand attendees. Also, the once abstract idea of forming a separate political party, proposed at the 1878 National Liberal League convention, now gained greater support among freethinkers.[12]

An invigorated national League held its 1879 convention in Cincinnati in September. While the usual items were on the agenda, two matters preoccupied the attendees: opposing the persecution of freethinkers like Bennett and Heywood under the pretext of obscenity laws, and considering whether to organize a Liberal Party to nominate a presidential candidate for 1880.[13] The presumptive nominee was, of course, Robert Ingersoll, who took an active role in the convention. The politically savvy Ingersoll remained coy about his intentions, however, not wanting to be associated with the more radical (i.e., free love) elements at the convention or to jeopardize his standing within the Republican Party. In his address to the convention, Ingersoll spoke in flowing terms about the value of free inquiry and in favor of unity among freethinkers. He asserted he believed not only in "perfect civil and religious liberty" but also "in one man loving the one woman," clearly positioning himself among the moderates. He also denied any political ambitions, declaring "[t]here is no office I want in this world." As chair of the resolutions committee, Ingersoll orchestrated a moderate resolution that called for unimpaired use of the mail regardless of the material's "religious, irreligious, political, or content," but also condemned the mailing of obscenity. To the radicals' chagrin, the convention adjourned without taking a firm stance on repealing the Comstock Act.[14] Summing up the inconclusive meeting, the *Christian Union* reported that "a mixed collection of doctrinaires and Free Lovers" had "propounded a platform which is a curious mélange of political platitudes and communistic sentiments," one that would likely go nowhere. And the *New York Observer and Chronicle* mocked the proposal to organize a new political party with Robert Ingersoll as its presidential candidate. "What a noble platform for a party," the journal sneered. "'Free Circulation for Obscene Literature!' When Ingersoll becomes President, Bennett, of course, will become Post-master General."[15]

With his conviction and imprisonment, Bennett took on the status of a martyr and the leader of the movement. Throughout his imprisonment, Bennett retained the title of editor of *The Truth Seeker* and continued to write articles for the journal from his cell.[16] When Bennet was released in late April 1880, freethinkers hailed him as a hero. His supporters organized a large rally at Chickering Hall in New York City to celebrate his homecoming, a gathering that *Scribner's Monthly* labeled an "Apotheosis of Dirt." Seated on the stage with a weary Bennett were Elizur Wright, Samuel Porter Putnam, Stephen Pearl Andrews, Ezra Heywood, and other leading freethought radicals. Noticeably missing from the event, however, were the moderates. O.B. Frothingham, B.F. Underwood, Francis Abbot, the Drs. Foote, and other moderate freethought figures were absent, indicating that, despite the shared outrage over Bennett's prosecution, many freethinkers remained hesitant about any association with free love or obscenity. Robert Ingersoll was also absent, though he had worked for Bennett's pardon and then met with him privately upon his release.

The Chickering Hall rally indicated that despite Bennett's claim on leadership, the freethought movement was far from unified.[17]

That lack of unity was on display when the National Liberal League held its annual convention in Chicago in September 1880. Even though attendance was modest, convention organizers proclaimed the movement's health, asserting that 209 chapters existed across the nation with 82 represented at the Chicago meeting. The convention adopted the usual resolutions opposing Sabbath laws and military chaplaincies and supporting secular public schooling, the taxation of church property, and the "total separation of church and state."[18] But again, the chief issue was whether to call for a repeal of the Comstock law. (With the presidential election less than two months away, the idea of launching a National Liberal political party was tabled.) Robert Ingersoll, who had been elected vice president of the League, opposed any repeal resolution, proposing instead that they appoint a committee to work with the National Defense Association to defend people facing prosecution. "We are opposed to only a part of the [Comstock] law—opposed to it whenever they endeavor to trample Freethought under foot in the name of immorality." Ingersoll called the radicals' obsession with the obscenity laws a "stumbling block" that was sapping the movement's strength. "Had it not been for this [obscenity] business," Ingersoll declared, "the Liberal League of the United States would to-night hold in its hand the political destiny of the United States."[19]

Attorney Thaddeus B. Wakeman, who had organized Heywood's Indignation meeting in 1878 and had participated in Bennett's trial, responded that liberals could no longer rely on the fairness of the courts and that an outright repeal was necessary. Wakeman insisted that under Comstock's influence, the courts had become a "church inquisition." Freethinkers were "not equal before the laws as long as we have a semi-clerical aristocracy to punish whom they please." Wakeman and the radicals prevailed, with the convention adopting a repeal resolution. Ingersoll promptly resigned as vice president of the League and left the convention. Giving Ingersoll faint praise for his stance, the *New York Evangelist* reported with satisfaction that it was "very manifest that the great majority of the members of the League hold to the most abominable doctrines of free love." At least the "great orator" was not willing to join with those who insisted on "flooding the land with filth."[20]

Surprisingly, the person at the center of the controversy that was preoccupying the League, D.M. Bennett, was not at the Chicago convention, opting instead to attend a meeting of the Universal Federation of Freethinkers in Brussels, Belgium, that autumn. Once again, the League's willingness to become embroiled in the obscenity issue at the expense of conventional church-state matters limited the movement's broader appeal and provided conservative critics a handy argument with which to marginalize the overall movement. *The Presbyterian* was "glad to say [that] the League went to pieces on the question as to obscene pictures," while the *New York Evangelist* declared, "[t]he whole history of [the freethought] movement shows that infidelity and falsehood [are] the fitting supports of the grossest obscenity." Even Beecher's moderate *Christian Union* panned the meeting, writing "so grows this no longer honorable body by small degrees and beautifully less." The critics had a point. The League's leadership and Bennett's *Truth Seeker* seemed more interested in taking an absolutist stance against censorship than in appealing to a potentially broader, sympathetic audience. As a contemptuous *Boston Herald* opined, "[b]y driving Col. Ingersoll out of the League, Liberals have shown themselves false to their name."[21]

With Ingersoll's resignation, the organization was fully under the control of the radical faction led by Elizur Wright, Samuel Putnam, and Thaddeus Wakeman, with D.M. Bennett operating behind the curtain. Most Liberals were neither practitioners nor true advocates of free love, but they were willing to defend it out of their commitment to free speech and free inquiry. Bennett did not favor free love and criticized Ezra and Angela Heywood for candidly promoting the practice. Yet for Bennett, freethought meant little if it did not include the ability to advocate disagreeable ideas. Bennett's leadership of the freethought movement and unofficial control of the Liberal League did not last long, however. His prison stay had left him weakened, and after returning from Europe in November 1880, he unwisely embarked on an around-the-world tour the following July, which further taxed his health. After returning to the United States in May 1882, Bennett died in December of that year. Supporters attributed his untimely death to strain imposed by his "Christian persecutors"—"[t]here can be no doubt that the course pursued by the villain Comstock shortened his days," wrote one follower. Bennett's grave marker included the tribute: "The Defender of Liberty and its Martyr." In an unkind obituary, the *New York Times* sneered that Bennett, as an atheist and denier of eternal life, did not deserve a marker, but if it stated anything, it should note that he was a "blasphemer" and "addicted to obscenity as well as infidelity." Although Bennett had been a divisive figure, his death left the radical side of freethought without a leader, further weakening the movement.[22]

"My Special Enemies"

By the early 1880s, the freethought movement was tearing itself apart, and Anthony Comstock was riding high. Comstock's campaign against vice was expanding, with he and his minions going after prostitution and lotteries in addition to obscenity. His high-profile prosecutions of Woodhull, Heywood, and Bennett had made him famous, and he wielded considerable influence within religious and political circles. Popular and religious journals lauded his activities and praised his name. Writing in 1884, one journal bemoaned "the frightful increase in crime among our youth." The "real source of much of this mischief and the prolific feeders of crime were not so much well known or their danger half realized. They are to be discovered in the debasing and defiling publications that have been allowed a free reign and unrestricted course in our country." The person responsible for bringing this danger to light was Anthony Comstock, "the modern Saint Anthony," who displayed a "rare good sense in dealing with such matters."[23]

Comstock's campaign against vice was an indisputably religious crusade, which he did not deny. Under his Calvinist worldview, human susceptibility to vice, regardless of its form, demonstrated Satan's power and had to be resisted. He continually claimed to be doing God's will in protecting and perfecting a Christian society. The defiance of the freethought community—the only organized opposition he faced—confirmed for Comstock that his was a religious calling. Comstock saw the struggle in Manichaean terms, which justified his crusade against heterodoxy.[24]

In May 1880, Comstock spoke at a Sunday evening service in Portland, Maine, on the topic of "Evil Reading." He decried the availability of cheap "blood-and-thunder" publications that glorified crime and immorality. But his real enemy was elsewhere. "There is another class of publications that must be noticed," Comstock continued. "The Infidel publications are my special enemies." On one hand, they had "traduced my character, my work, myself," noted the thin-skinned crusader. But additionally, "[t]he Infidel publications and the Infidels deride the Bible, shake all faith, remove prayer, dry up the fountain filled with blood, attack even the spotless character of Christ. These publications are filled with blasphemy, and are yet are beyond the reach of the law." Even though the "Infidel publications" were the main defenders of obscenity in Comstock's mind, they were a threat to Christian society regardless of whether they were actually "obscene."[25]

Comstock's obsession with combatting religious heresy is evident in his 1880 book, *Frauds Exposed; or, How the People Are Deceived and Robbed, and Youth Corrupted.* Like his later book, *Traps for the Young,* Comstock wrote *Frauds Exposed* to publicize his activities and justify his methods, which were coming under scrutiny. Both books were part self-promotional memoirs and part diatribes about the evils confronting society. The frauds were many—lotteries, bank and investment frauds, medical quacks, even sewing machines. Out of the 500-plus pages of details—interspersed with accounts of Comstock's heroics—the book devoted over 150 pages to condemning freethinkers ("Liberals"). This focus was set out in the book's preface: "no part of this book can be of greater interest, than those chapters that expose . . . the infamous conspiracies entered into by the Liberals, to repeal the laws against obscene literature," Comstock wrote. "I have presented facts; I have drawn an indictment against this horde of blasphemers and revilers of the ever-living God, and I submit my evidence to sustain this indictment."[26]

In the book's discussion of obscenity, Comstock devoted little space to recounting his early prosecutions of book sellers, abortionists, and prostitutes. Rather, he quickly transitioned into an attack on Liberals and their organized opposition to the Comstock Act. It was "a *noted fact,*" Comstock wrote, "that *no sect nor class* . . . has ever publicly sided with the smut dealer, and defended his nefarious business, except the Infidels, the Liberals, and the Free-Lovers." "Under the thin guise of defending 'Freedom of Press,' 'Free Speech,' 'Free Thought,' and 'Personal Liberty,' they entered into the most diabolical conspiracy to repeal [the Comstock Act]." For Comstock, *his* Act represented more than his source of authority, power, and fame; the law validated his religious stance against immorality and provided him with the credibility he so desperately sought.[27] Although Comstock's vitriol against the freethinkers was based in part on their audacity to challenge his beloved law, it went much further. The "infidel of to-day," represented by the Liberal League, threatened to undermine the foundations of Christian society. Freethinkers were not only opposed to God, Jesus, and the Bible, but also to "laws and their proper enforcement," to "moral purity," to "the Christian sabbath," and to "principles that restrain corrupt appetites and passions." They favored "Blasphemy of the name of the Most High, and the ridiculing of the most sacred things." If allowed to expand, "this hydra-headed monster" would undermine the home and family upon which Christian culture was based.[28] Comstock's blistering critique of freethought all but invited its suppression if not eradication. But Comstock assured his readers that "there had been no arrest or conviction of any person . . . excepting such as was guilty of flagrant crimes against decency and morality."[29]

Comstock interspersed his critique of freethought with personal attacks on D.M. Bennett and Robert Ingersoll. *Frauds Exposed* repeated the story that Comstock had personally provided President Hayes with evidence about Bennett's alleged sexual affair, again demonstrating freethinkers' lack of morality. Calling Bennett a "would-be martyr and foul mouthed libertine," Comstock accused him of "professing devotion to his wife [while] he teaches free-love."[30] As for Ingersoll, he was a hypocrite for leading the repeal effort in 1878 but then claiming to oppose obscenity. Ingersoll was "a blatant infidel and scoffer" who sought "to be on both sides of a fence at one time," Comstock charged. He condemned Ingersoll for his "frantic efforts to outrage the most holy and sacred thoughts and feelings of the Christian community" and for seeking "to rob [it] of its beneficial results that come from the teaching of God's word." Ingersoll was "poisoning the moral atmosphere of the community" and would continue to do so "until the Nation shall be like Sodom and Gomorrah." Addressing Ingersoll directly, Comstock charged that "[y]our defense of obscenity mongers is infamous, and your practice damnable." Although there is little doubt that Ingersoll knew of Comstock's attack on his character, there is no record of him having responded publicly.[31]

Comstock had written *Frauds Exposed* to fend off criticism—not only from freethinkers but also from members of the mainstream press—that he was frequently overzealous, as with the prosecution of Bennett. How well the book was received is difficult to determine. The *New York Times* noted that it had a large subscription but panned that it was "written without particular evidences of ability" and with "a certain rude vigor" in its language. Conceding that the evils of vice needed "uprooting," the *Times* nonetheless questioned whether Comstock was "the right man to do it. Power is a dangerous thing to entrust a single man with, and Mr. Comstock may have exceeded the proper limits of his office without intending to do so."[32] The religious press was more receptive. The *New York Evangelist* praised *Frauds Exposed* and its "intrepid" author, writing that it "seems incredible to us that such diabolical sins as are here exposed could live and thrive in a Christian country." *Scribner's Monthly* was equally complementary, writing, "Mr. Comstock's book deserves wide notice from the press and a generous reception among the people." *Scribner's* also felt that the book's attack on freethought was justified, commenting that "Liberalism . . . is another name for infidelity, and if infidelity naturally sympathizes with dirt, it is well that we all know it." Even Beecher's *Christian Union* agreed that the book's "painful pages" clearly demonstrated that "infidelity is wedded to obscenity."[33]

Seeking further vindication, Comstock wrote *Traps for the Young* in 1883. Like his earlier book, *Traps for the Young* described a litany of traps employed by the devil to ensnare the nation's youth: dime and half-dime novels, gambling, obscenity, prostitution, and medical quackery (abortion). The book again provided embellished accounts of youth being corrupted and led astray and of Comstock's heroic efforts to combat the traps. *Traps for the Young* was a more ambitious work than its predecessor and tried to appeal to a wider audience, but "the style, subject, villains, and hero (Comstock) were the same."[34] And as before, Comstock dedicated the final third of the book to exposing the interrelated traps of free love, obscenity, and infidelity. Although it had been more than three years since D.M. Bennett's release from prison (and a year since his death) and the Liberal League's debacle over repealing the Comstock Act, Comstock wrote as if no time had passed. He again recounted the arrests and convictions of Heywood and Bennett, this time in greater detail. The book also allotted considerable space to the 1878 petition to repeal the law, which Comstock called "one of the basest conspiracies ever concocted against a holy cause." He criticized "[t]hese obscenity defenders" for "shout[ing] 'liberty' and 'freedom' on all occasions. It is chronic with many of them." Needing a villain of prominence, Comstock again overstated Robert Ingersoll's involvement in the repeal effort, claiming that "the entire movement centered in him." Even though five years had passed, Comstock had still not gotten over the Liberals' attempt to repeal his beloved "holy" law.[35]

But that was not Comstock's only complaint about Ingersoll. He again launched into a general broadside against Ingersoll for his "sneering, scoffing, and blasphemous lectures." Resorting to a personal attack, Comstock asserted that "Ingersoll's blasphemies and ridicule of holy things are only excelled by his egotism." Ingersoll was "the great American blasphemer" and "the Great Apostle of Infidelity."[36] In his attack on Ingersoll and freethought generally, Comstock again went far beyond a concern with obscenity.

> The Liberal leaders publish their works against religion, Christianity, divine and
> human laws. They loudly blaspheme the holy name of God. . . . They ridicule the

Savior of mankind, and scoff his teaching. The Bible they ridicule, and attempt to rob the peace of God. Sabbath laws, and all laws affecting morals of the community, they seek to abrogate, which unbridled scope is given to appetite and passion. While they thus tear down the pure and holy, they naturally favor the impure and base.[37]

Freethinkers' claims to religious freedom and free speech were, to Comstock, merely smokescreens. "The freedom sought by our forefathers to worship God did not mean to serve the devil," Comstock insisted. "Freedom to speak or print does not imply the right to say or print that which shocks decency, corrupts the morals of the young, or destroys all faith in God."[38] In the end, however, it was impossible to separate infidelity from its evil consequences. "Liberal publications and blasphemous rantings are the mortar that fills up the space between the stones of vice and crime." Infidelity "makes living in sin easier, the ruin of our youth surer."[39]

Frauds Exposed and *Traps for the Young* indicated that Comstock's anti-vice crusade was entering a new phase. After a decade of work, he had been relatively successful in shuttering erotic bookstores and driving many prostitutes and abortion providers underground. There was greater public consensus in favor of those activities, as well. His one resilient nemesis remained the Liberals: the educated freethinker and literary communities and medical practitioners. These so-called elites were far worse than the average smut-dealer because of their erudition and their tendency to defend immoral activities by referencing principles of freedom that might appeal to broader audiences.[40]

Through his books, Comstock sought not just professional validation, but personal validation as well. He valued his affiliation with the leaders of the NYSSV, who were prominent financers and businessmen, and was acutely conscious of his lower social status and lack of education. He sensed, no doubt accurately, that his patrons—Jessup, Colgate, Morgan, Dodge, and others—were more than willing for him to do the dirty work but that they would never accept him as an equal. The same elitism existed among many leading freethinkers—Frothingham, Abbot, Adler, Heywood, the Drs. Foote—who were highly educated and assumed an intellectual air that irked Comstock (the self-educated D.M. Bennett being the chief exception). Although Ingersoll also lacked a college education, he was a self-made attorney and intellectual force who circulated comfortably at the highest levels of society. The freethinkers' dismissal of Comstock infuriated the crusader. His enemies assumed "the wisdom and learning of scholars" while in truth, they were "arrogant, narrow-minded, and bigoted." In addition to being motivated by his strong religious beliefs, Comstock coveted respect and bristled at unflattering characterizations of his intelligence and abilities.[41]

In 1882, Comstock received some recognition when he was invited to participate in a symposium sponsored by the cerebral *North American Review* on the "The Suppression of Vice." Providing an alternative perspective was O.B. Frothingham. Appearing in print alongside the highly respected Frothingham should have supplied Comstock with the credibility he so desperately desired. It did not. Comstock's contribution was more subdued and less self-aggrandizing than his usual writing, but in seeking to appear measured and serious, his piece fell flat. Frothingham was polite and did not question Comstock's character. He and his supporters were "compelled by a sense of duty to fine moral considerations." But the rest of his piece was scathing. After acknowledging the societal challenges presented by vice, Frothingham offered "a few words of criticism" of people like Comstock who were engaged in "aggressive moral reform" through a "war of belligerency." He charged that the Society for the Suppression of Vice's operations were "uniformly sectarian in their character" and that they "represent the convictions of a peculiar party, a class, an order of men." "May they be trusted to declare what is 'objectionable' and what [is] not? Is their moral standard to be received without protest? Are we quite ready for their notions of blasphemy and infidelity?" Frothingham called for relying on persuasion and education, rather than resorting to persecution. Americans favor "laws that give voice to the enlightened conscience of the community," he insisted. "Statutes which embody the moral dogmatism of a sect are not popular." Compared to Frothingham's searing critique, Comstock's defense was tepid.[42]

Comstock continued to prosecute vice with vigor, most of it involving low-level obscenity and gambling. But as he sought to broaden his scope, some of his activities attracted greater criticism. After Comstock initiated a prosecution in 1882 over the sale of the bawdy medieval classic, *Heptameron*, sales of the book skyrocketed. "Mr. Anthony Comstock sometimes overdoes matters," commented the *Albany Law Review*. "It would be supposed that his experience in regard to former similar prosecutions would inoculate him with a grain of sense in such matters; but who ever knew a reformer with any discretion?"[43]

Between writing his two books, Comstock decided to go after Ezra Heywood a second time. In October 1882, Comstock appeared at Heywood's home in Princeton, Massachusetts, with an arrest warrant for mailing obscene material:

Cupid's Yokes (again), two poems by Walt Whitman—"To a Prostitute" and "A Woman Waits for Me"—and an issue of his newspaper, *The Word*, which contained an advertisement for a cervical syringe, which Heywood mockingly dubbed the "Comstock Syringe." Heywood spent two nights in jail before making bail, and his trial took place in Boston federal court in April 1883.[44]

To Comstock's chagrin, this trial turned out quite differently from Bennett's. Presiding was Judge T.L. Nelson, who, unlike Judge Benedict, expressed doubts about the charges. Also unlike that earlier trial, Judge Nelson dismissed the charge against *Cupid's Yokes* based on the indictment's failure to identify its obscene sections. He also dismissed the charge against Whitman's widely available poems, commenting that it was untrue that they were "too grossly obscene and lewd to be placed in the record of the court." Nelson then allowed Heywood to represent himself on the remaining charge about the syringe, which the prosecution insisted could be used to prevent conception in violation of the Comstock Act. Nelson gave Heywood considerable latitude to raise free speech and freedom of conscience arguments against the entire prosecution, not just this single count, which Heywood used to his full advantage. His rambling closing argument fluctuated between denying that his writings were obscene, maintaining that any definition of obscenity was too broad and indefinite, and arguing that he had a right to distribute his writings regardless of their content by virtue of "Freedom of Conscience and Liberty of the Press." He insisted that his was a religiously based prosecution arising from a church "whose every religious symbol originated in the sex organs of men and women." Heywood claimed that that the syringe was designed for hygienic purposes, though he acknowledged that it could be used to control conception. The advertisement had asserted at the top of the page that a "Woman's Natural Right to *Prevent* Conception is *unquestionable*," but that the syringe was "designed to prevent disease, promote personal purity and health." Still, Heywood jokingly remarked that "if Comstock's mother had had a syringe and used it judiciously the world would have been saved much trouble!" Despite those admissions, Judge Nelson instructed the jury that they would have to find that Heywood's chief purpose in advertising the syringe was for preventing conception. The jury returned a not guilty verdict in two hours. Heywood was vindicated, and Comstock would not pursue him again for *Cupid's Yokes*. "Mr. Heywood may be fanatical and rash, his methods may be disagreeably repugnant to sensitive people," wrote *The Truth Seeker*, "but no one can fail to admire him for his staunch advocacy of what he conceives to be the truth." People had said "that Heywood was foolish to thrust his head in the lion's mouth," the story continued, but "the outcome shows that he was wiser than his critics, for the nation is a little freer to-day than before the trial, and freedom of speech and press are in less danger from church interference."[45]

The outcome did not relieve Heywood from further prosecutions, however. Barely a month later, in May 1883, the New England Society for the Suppression of Vice, a Comstock affiliate, had Heywood arrested for violating Massachusetts's obscenity law. This time it was for publishing a pamphlet written by his wife, Angela, that advocated birth control and described sex organs in explicit terms. "[I]f the social relations of men and women can be discussed vulgarly," wrote *The Truth Seeker*, "Mrs. Heywood has found the way to do it." Still, the pamphlet was no less vulgar than "some of the trash found in the Bible." When the case finally came to trial a year later, Heywood's lawyer, H.L. Nelson, the son of Judge Nelson, had the indictment dismissed for failing to show Heywood's willful intention to corrupt the morals of youth.[46]

Heywood faced arrest for distributing obscene material two more times: once in 1887, which was dismissed, and once in 1890, which resulted in his second conviction. Comstock was reputedly behind both prosecutions but apparently not directly involved in the investigations. In the second case, Heywood was again charged with including obscene articles in his journal, *The Word*, which was then sent through the mail. The three articles, one written by Angela, all contained vulgar language and explicit references to sexual organs. The proceeding was reminiscent of Heywood's first trial in 1878, with federal Judge George M. Carpenter expressing open disdain for Heywood. Mailing obscenity, Carpenter instructed the jury, "may fairly be designated the foulest, meanest, lowest offense of which a human being can be guilty." While it was for the jury to decide whether the material was obscene, "I say the offense, so far as my imagination of guilt goes, is monstrous." The jury found Heywood guilty, and Judge Carpenter sentenced him to two years at hard labor in the Charleston State Prison. President Benjamin Harrison refused to grant a pardon, reputedly noting how Heywood was unrepentant for his crime. The sentence took a heavy toll on Heywood's health. He contracted tuberculous while in prison, which left him in a weakened condition. Heywood died a year after being released. As they had done following D.M. Bennett's death a decade earlier, freethinkers attributed Heywood's demise to his unjust imprisonment at the hands of Anthony Comstock: his death was "almost murder," asserted *The Truth Seeker*.[47]

The Great Agnostic

If Anthony Comstock was at the height of his power and influence in the 1880s, so too was his archenemy, Robert Ingersoll. Ingersoll's fame as a popular lecturer had taken off in the 1870s, and his resignation from leadership in the Liberal League in 1880 allowed him to concentrate on his public speaking. Although his agnostic beliefs and stinging criticism of religious doctrine were widely known, most of his lectures dealt with political and current events. But his lectures on religion were among his most popular, drawing large crowds at the price of fifty cents or a dollar a head, sometimes earning Ingersoll more in one night than the average person made in a year.[48] The announcement of an Ingersoll lecture usually drew the ire of local religious leaders, but his fame made it difficult to take action against him. An Iowa newspaper reported that the majority of attendees at one of Ingersoll's lectures "were strictly orthodox, and how they did roar" at his anecdotes; "there was a grand unison of orthodox cheers for the most unorthodox jokes." Ingersoll was also insulated by his political connections. Even though his Republican friends sought to disassociate themselves from his heterodox views, they valued his political commentary, which generally took a liberal Republican line but rarely challenged the policies that benefited the monied interests that financed the party.[49]

Some of Ingersoll's success lay in his ability to cast his freethought beliefs in the broadest terms. He promoted freedom of inquiry in its various applications: rationalism, science over superstition, women's rights, racial equality, the importance of humanistic values, an intuitive morality, and the betterment of the human condition writ large. He was thus able to appeal to people who might otherwise be put off by his agnostic beliefs. Historian Martin Marty insists, however, that Ingersoll's draw lay chiefly in the novelty of his remarks: "The audience[s], with nothing beyond emotional interest, ha[d] no ultimate attachments at stake [to his content,] . . . [and] were simply amused by the wit of good-natured infidels."[50] Contemporary critics drew harsher conclusions. Ingersoll, charged the *New York Evangelist*, "is always substituting rhetoric for logic, affirmations for argument, audacity for persuasion. He carries his point for the moment by ridicule, by satire, [and] by the most reckless perversions of evangelical truth." Hopefully, the *Evangelist* continued, attendees at Ingersoll's lectures would "wake up on the morrow morning to realize how wretchedly he has cajoled them." Ingersoll understood that entertainment value accounted for much of his appeal, but he also believed that he was encouraging his audiences to question their religious presuppositions, and perhaps validating some people's latent skepticism.[51]

In the 1880s, Ingersoll intensified his broadsides against religion and religious institutions. In 1880, he found time between his Liberal League activities and campaigning for James Garfield to write a new lecture, "What Must We Do to Be Saved," which ridiculed the esoteric doctrines that divided various Christian denominations. Ingersoll argued that the New Testament depicted a reasonable, humane, and forgiving God, but that later generations of Christian leaders—be they Catholics, Lutherans, or Calvinists—had invented doctrinal differences to justify privilege and persecution.[52] His critique set the stage for his next lecture, "The Great Infidels," which examined the historical and modern inquisitions designed to subdue heresy. Written in the wake of the Heywood and Bennett trials, the lecture was a vigorous defense of religious heterodoxy. Infidels—a term Ingersoll readily embraced despite Comstock's derogatory use of it—were the guardians of free inquiry, he claimed. "The history of intellectual progress has been written in the lives of Infidels." Just as "[p]olitical rights have been preserved by traitors, liberty of the mind [has] by heretics," Ingersoll insisted. "Infidels are intellectual discoverers. . . . and for that reason [they] excite the envy and hatred of the theological pauper" (i.e., Comstock).[53] A later lecture, "Liberty in Literature," offered a defense of Walt Whitman's *Leaves of Grass*, which Comstock had attempted to ban. Ingersoll praised Whitman's poetic description of true love while ridiculing Comstock, though not by name. "The provincial prudes, and others of like mold, pretend that love is a duty rather than a passion. . . . They have no idea of an honest, pure passion, glorifying in its strength," Ingersoll declared. "They do not walk the streets of the city of life—they stand in the gutters and cry 'Unclean!'"[54]

On more than one occasion local officials and ministers responded to Ingersoll's lectures with charges they were blasphemous. His lecture "What Must We Do to Be Saved," delivered in Wilmington, Delaware, in December 1880, produced an outcry among local clergy. When it was announced that Ingersoll planned to give his new lecture, "The Great Infidels," in Wilmington the following February, a judge urged a grand jury to indict him under a 1740 law against blasphemy. Although the grand jury declined to indict Ingersoll, it issued a report condemning his earlier lecture and threatening to enforce the blasphemy law in the future. *The Independent* applauded the move. Ingersoll "has a right, so far as the law is concerned, to be an infidel." But his "manner of talking about God and the Bible can hardly be regarded as anything less than an open and public insult to the religious faith of the great body of the American people," it insisted. He "ought to be punished for it." Facing the threat of an indictment, Ingersoll canceled his lecture.[55] Five years later, Ingersoll felt sufficiently secure about testing another threatened blasphemy charge for an upcoming lecture, this time in Brooklyn. Ingersoll goaded his accuser, the head of a Bible society, by delivering his newest lecture, "Blasphemy," to an enthusiastic audience. Asked by a reporter about the threatened charge, Ingersoll responded that he "did not suppose that anybody was idiotic enough to want me arrested for blasphemy." It seemed, Ingersoll continued, "that an infinite Being can take care of himself without the aid of any agent of a Bible society." "Let the Bible take its chances with other books." Despite periodic calls for his arrest, no further legal actions were initiated to silence the "Great American blasphemer."[56]

The dominant and unifying theme in Ingersoll's lectures on religion was the prevalence of superstition, irrationality, and intolerance within all religions, and particularly within Christianity. Religion, he argued, was the chief impediment to freedom of inquiry and the rights of conscience. "All the orthodox churches are obstructions on the highway of progress. Every orthodox creed is a chain, a dungeon."[57] Accordingly, Ingersoll frequently criticized the Catholic Church as "the enemy of intellectual liberty." The church, he said, had tried to stifle free inquiry at every turn: "It is the enemy of investigation. It is the enemy of free schools. That church always has been, and always will be, the enemy of freedom. It works in the dark." The pope "speaks against the liberty of man—against the progress of the human race." Catholic lay "members have no right to reason—no right to ask questions—they are called on simply to believe and pay their subscriptions." Fortunately, Ingersoll believed, the Catholic Church was in decline and would be laid low by the force of reason and the church's own overreaching and greed.[58]

Ingersoll also expressed disdain for orthodox Protestantism, and for Calvinism in particular. "Is Presbyterianism so narrow that it conceives of no excellence, no purity of intention, of no spiritual or moral grandeur outside of its barbaric creed?" The "best thing about the Pope," Ingersoll mocked, "was that he was not a Presbyterian."[59] He identified a specific threat from the

"God-in-the-Constitution Party," the National Reform Association, headed by Reformed Presbyterians. On one hand, he viewed the Association and its goal as "weak, fanatical, stupid, and absurd. What God are we to have in the Constitution? Whose God?" But on a practical level, he asked, suppose "we amend the Constitution and acknowledge the existence and supremacy of God—what becomes of the supremacy of the people, and how is this amendment to be enforced?" What would logically follow, Ingersoll surmised in a not-too-subtle reference to Comstock's efforts, "would be laws against blasphemy, laws against the publication of honest thoughts, laws against carrying books and papers in the mails in which this constitutional God should be attacked?" "To recognize a Deity in the organic law of our country would be the destruction of religious liberty" and would "place the country under the feet of priests." The framers "knew that to put God in the Constitution was to put man out. They knew that the recognition of a Deity would be seized upon by fanatics and zealots as a pretext for destroying the liberty of thought." But more fundamentally, the proposal went against the principle that the "Government of the United States is secular. It derives its power from the consent of man," not from some god.[60]

This disdain for orthodoxy, superstition, and intolerance led Ingersoll to comment on contemporary church-state controversies, though not as frequently as one might have expected from a lawyer. This infrequency is somewhat surprising, considering that three major church-state controversies were raging during Ingersoll's lecturing career: religious exercises (prayer and Bible reading) in the public schools, the public funding of private religious schooling, known jointly as the "School Question," and the LDS Church's practice of polygamy, known as the "Mormon Question."[61] Ingersoll's on-again, off-again affiliation with the Liberal League and other freethought groups, and his admiration for Tom Paine, left little doubt as to his position on various church-state issues, including Sunday laws, the taxation of church property, and chaplains in the military and in legislatures, in addition to the above issues. At the same time, however, his lectures rarely concentrated on immediate controversies—for instance, he never dedicated a lecture to defending the Nine Demands of Liberalism.[62]

Possibly Ingersoll felt that it was unnecessary to comment extensively on the contemporary challenges to church-state separation, that to do so would become tedious and that his positions on the issues were obvious to any attentive listener or reader. He may also have felt that freethought journals such as

The Investigator, *The Index*, *The Truth Seeker*, *Freethinkers' Magazine* (later, *Free Thought Magazine*), the *Blue-Grass Blade*, and *Lucifer, the Light Bearer* already offered sufficient commentary on specific controversies. The purpose of his lectures was to reaffirm the views of fellow freethinkers and to challenge those people who were open to reconsidering their religious preconceptions. His mission was to expose the irrationality of religious belief rather than its daily overreaching. Still, as the nation's most prominent freethinker, he had a unique platform for advancing the principles of church-state separation.[63]

When asked, however, Ingersoll did not shy away from discussing current church-state issues. Addressing a freethinker convention in Albany, New York, in September 1885, Ingersoll provided his audience with the specifics they liked to hear. "[C]ompel every church to pay taxes on its property as other people pay on theirs." Not only were exemptions unfair—the halls "in which Freethought and science are to be taught, pay taxes." By exempting church property "you increase the tax on other people owning the rest. To that extent, you united Church and State. You compel the Infidel to support the Catholic." He also condemned paid chaplains in the military and in legislatures: "It is useless to ask God to help the political party that happens to be in power." Equally wrong were religious proclamations from a public official who claimed to be "an agent of God."[64]

Ingersoll was also forthcoming in published interviews. He reaffirmed his opposition not only to tax exemptions for churches but also to the state's financial support for religious charities and asylums, going so far as to question their operation by churches in the first instance: "Charity belongs to humanity, not to any particular form of faith or religion." He opposed financial support for religious schooling and declared that "no religion should be taught in any school supported by public money." Secularism "is to be taught everywhere and practiced at all times. It is not a religion that is so dangerous that it must be kept out of the schools. . . . It belongs in the schools." As for Sunday laws, they simply promoted hypocrisy: "[n]othing ever did make a home more hateful than the strict observance of the Sabbath."[65] In the end, Ingersoll likely made few converts to freethought, though he went far to validate religious heterodoxy for the greater freethinking community. He also did more than any figure of the late nineteenth century to expose the larger public to ideas of free inquiry and secularism.[66]

Even though newspapers had reported Ingersoll's split with the Liberal League over whether to repeal the obscenity laws, he constantly fought back claims and rumors that he supported the legalization of obscene materials. Comstock was a prime promoter of this narrative, which forced Ingersoll to defend his positions on obscenity and the reform of marriage and divorce laws more than once.[67] On the former, Ingersoll insisted: "No one wishes the repeal of any law for the suppression of obscene literature. For my part, I wish all such laws rigidly enforced." However, he continued, "[c]ertain religious fanatics, taking advantage of the word 'immoral' in the law, have claimed that all writings against what they are pleased to call orthodox religion are immoral, and such books have been seized and their authors arrested. To this, and this only, I object."[68]

Ingersoll also strove to distance himself from being labeled a supporter of free love. The charge was ironic as Ingersoll was known to be a devoted husband and father and had a spotless reputation that distinguished him from his friend Henry Ward Beecher, to the chagrin of his critics.[69] He extolled the benefits of monogamy and marriage: "Marriage is the most sacred contract—the most important contract—that human beings can make." But marriages were "made by men and women. They are not made by the State, and they are not made by the gods." "As long as woman regards the Bible as the charter of her rights, she will be the slave of man." Although Ingersoll personally accepted many conventional attributes about men and women— "men are oaks, women vines"—he insisted on greater equality within marriages and on the right to a divorce. The "woman is the equal of the man. She has all the rights I have and one more, and that is the right to be protected." One thing he detested was "the man who thinks he is the head of a family." Because marriage was a mutual contract, then "the woman should be allowed a divorce for the asking." Ingersoll knew that his view that marriage was a civil contract which could be dissolved at will allied him with advocates of free love. At first, he criticized those who sensationalized the term as a way of marginalizing opposition to traditional patriarchal marriage. "The persons who make this cry are in all probability, incapable of the sentiment, of the feeling, known as love." But Ingersoll also wanted to assure his audiences that he did not endorse the concept. "My doctrine is the exact opposite of what is known as free love," he insisted. "I believe in the marriage of true minds and true hearts. . . . Where men and women truly love each other, that love, in my judgment, lasts as long as life." While this position placed Ingersoll at odds with the most extreme advocates of free love, it did not differ substantially from that of Elizabeth Cady Stanton, who embraced the term.[70]

Shortly before his death, Ingersoll returned to the subject of women's rights in a lecture titled "What Is Religion" (1899). The final section of the lecture, "Reform," was particularly dark for the usually upbeat Ingersoll. It addressed the social problems of poverty, overpopulation, and lack of birth control, and it revealed some radicalization of his thought late in life. "Why should men and women have children they cannot take care of, children that are burdens and curses," he asked. "Ignorance, poverty, and vice must stop populating the world," but "[t]his cannot be done by moral suasion . . . [or] by religion or by law." There was but one solution and that was the autonomy of women over birth control.[71]

> Science must make woman the owner, the mistress of herself. Science, the only possible savior of mankind, must be put in the power of woman to decide for herself whether she will or will not become a mother. This is the solution to the whole question. This frees woman. The babes that are born will be welcome.[72]

This was Ingersoll's most forceful statement on the independence of women. He did not specify what this autonomous decisional authority included, whether it extended beyond a refusal to have sexual relations to having access to contraceptive medications and devices or to include abortions. In his previous addresses concerning women's rights, he had never gone that far. But his appeal to science at least suggests that he was willing to consider it. This aligned him with those on the vanguard of the women's rights and free love movements.[73]

The "Golden Age"

As noted, Robert Ingersoll's popularity transcended his heterodox views. His appeal lay largely in the entertainment value of his witty oratory. Yet the popular appetite for Ingersoll's biting critique of religion suggests that freethought ideas continued to thrive despite the divisions within the National Liberal League and other setbacks freethinkers faced.

Even though the controversy over the obscenity laws had fractured the national organization between 1878 and 1880, local Liberal Leagues and freethought associations continued to be founded and flourish, at least temporarily. Freethinkers also regularly held local and national conventions, with a large gathering (five hundred to six hundred) meeting again in Watkins Glenn,

New York, in August 1882, and another the following year in Rochester attracting two thousand attendees.[74] The movement drew an expanding variety of people who were united by their religious heterodoxy but who otherwise supported related agendas: free love and marriage reform, women's suffrage, spiritualism, artistic freedom, prohibition, socialism and labor reform, and even political anarchy. Thaddeus B. Wakeman, now president of the League, advocated bringing labor organizations under the League's umbrella. Other members of the League wanted to revitalize the idea of a Liberal political party for the 1884 election, while still others advocated the public control of railroads and other large corporations. These calls led moderate Liberals, led by Samuel Porter Putnam, to argue that the cacophony of social causes was undermining the voice and mission of the League; they proposed that the organization return to its core goals, represented in the Demands of Liberalism. Putnam and the moderates prevailed at the September 1884 convention with the organization resolving to confine its energies to advancing freethought and the separation of church and state. The following year the League changed its name to the American Secular Union, under the leadership of Putnam as operating secretary and Robert Ingersoll as honorary president. The decision of the League/Union to finally put aside the fight against obscenity laws and other distracting issues was, in the end, a vindication for Francis Abbot. But by that point, Abbot—who was living in Boston in semiretirement while teaching and writing about scientific theism—had no interest in reengaging with the movement.[75]

Throughout the 1880s, dozens of freethought lecturers toured the country, preaching the virtues of free inquiry and helping to establish local organizations in such far-flung places as Kansas, Kentucky, Oregon, and Texas. B.F. Underwood was the most active lecturer, but he was joined by Samuel Putnam, Parker Pillsbury, Edwin Cox Walker, and Charles Reynolds, among others. No one, of course, was able to match the draw of Robert Ingersoll. New journals committed to freethought, marriage equality, and labor reform also sprung up, including *The Blue Grass Blade* (Lexington, Kentucky) and *Lucifer, the Light-Bearer* (Valley Falls, Kansas). The most notable addition was *The Freethinkers' Magazine* (later renamed *Free Thought Magazine*), established in Chicago in 1882 by Henry L. Green, a former ally of Francis Abbot. More cerebral and less sensationalist than *The Truth Seeker*, *Freethinkers'/Free Thought Magazine* listed Elizabeth Cady Stanton and B.F. Underwood as editorial contributors. *Freethinkers' Magazine* characterized its aim in this way:

> The mission of this Magazine is to establish, in one word, LIBERALISM, *pure and simple*! The emancipation of our people from all religious dogmas and superstitions. This great result can only be accomplished by cultivating and extending habits of free thought until, finally, the glorious motto and ideal, Universal Mental Liberty (U.M.L.), may be felt.[76]

These activities indicated that a core base of freethinkers existed across the country, one that the mainstream press rarely acknowledged. Still, freethinkers, their organizations, and their publications were a novelty for most observers, and a public nuisance for others. Every village "must have its infidel," wrote the *New York Times* sarcastically, "who is apt to be 'shrewd' of mind, far-seeing into the interior depts of millstones, argumentative, frank, [and] manly. . . . The true and typical village infidel never bothers his head over anything nicer in criticism than what he can gather from such valuable sources of information as the old 'Age of Reason' and the contemporary 'Gods' of the Peorian Colonel" (Ingersoll).[77]

Blasphemers

As discussed, Robert Ingersoll's popularity and political connections largely shielded him from legal efforts at censorship. Other outspoken advocates for freethought were not as fortunate. Between 1885 and 1905, a handful of blasphemy charges were brought against prominent freethinkers. The results were generally unfavorable for freethought.[78]

The most highly publicized blasphemy case of the period arose in Boonton, New Jersey, in 1886. Charles B. Reynolds was an active member of the Liberal League and peripatetic lecturer for freethought. He had come to his avocation only recently, having started out as an evangelist for the Seventh-day Adventist movement. That earlier career, which continued into the early 1880s, had prepared him for his later role as a traveling freethought lecturer. As Leigh Schmidt has observed, Adventists also existed outside the religious mainstream and, because of their persecution for refusing to follow Sunday laws, were fierce proponents of church-state separation despite their evangelical leanings. Although the reason Reynolds abandoned Christianity is unknown—he reputedly had attended a memorial for D.M. Bennett in late 1882 and been inspired—"Reynolds found it easy to recycle Adventist exegesis for secularist purposes." He joined the Liberal League and began contributing articles to

The Truth Seeker, quickly rising in the ranks of the freethought movement. Before long, he was sharing the stage with Robert Ingersoll at freethought meetings and, with his experience as evangelist, he embarked on a successful career as a freethought lecturer; as Schmidt notes, "Reynolds readily translated the Christian rhetoric of salvation into a religious dictation for secularism."[79]

In July 1886, Reynolds set up his revivalist tent in Boonton, New Jersey, a town of 2,500 people, at the request of a local Secular Union chapter. Prepared to do a weeklong "revival" there, the first evening's lecture was uneventful, but a large mob assembled on the second night, heckling Reynolds, hurling stones and then cutting the tent ropes. Reynolds complained to the town's mayor and marshal the next day, only to be arrested for committing blasphemy. Released after posting bail, Reynolds prepared to give his Wednesday night lecture but was confronted again by the mob, forcing him to flee and abandon his tent. Two days later, the ringleader of the mob swore out a complaint before a local grand jury alleging that Reynolds had violated a 1709 New Jersey law prohibiting "wilfully blasphem[ing] the name of God . . . or contumeliously reproaching Jesus Christ or by profane scoffing at or exposing them or either of them to contempt or ridicule."[80] While awaiting the decision of the grand jury, Reynolds went to Morristown, the nearby county seat, and handed out copies of a hastily prepared pamphlet, "Blasphemy and the Bible," which criticized the law. The pamphlet also made various sarcastic and derogatory comments about Christian doctrine, calling God a "stupid blunderer." That action resulted in the grand jury issuing a two-count indictment for blasphemy, one for the Boonton lecture and the second for the pamphlet. After several delays, Reynolds's trial was set for May 1887. Robert Ingersoll volunteered to defend Reynolds free of charge.[81]

When Reynolds's trial commenced on May 19, the courtroom and the gallery were "crowded to suffocation" with curious townsfolk, newspaper reporters, and a contingent of women from the local Secular Union. The prosecution had decided to proceed only with the second indictment for distributing "Blasphemy and the Bible" and called a handful of witnesses who testified to having received the pamphlet from Reynolds, the contents of which, the prosecutor simply argued, met the elements of the statute.[82] Ingersoll, in turn, called no witnesses and presented no evidence in his defense of Reynolds—there were no facts in dispute, only legal questions whether the pamphlet was "blasphemous" and whether the state could punish such expression. In his impassioned argument to the jury, Ingersoll did not challenge whether Reynolds's words and writings met the legal definition of blasphemy in the New Jersey statute. Rather, he attacked the doctrine itself, both as a legal concept and a religious one. "How has the church in every age, when in authority, defended itself?" Ingersoll asked. "Always by a statute against blasphemy, against argument, against free speech." Making a plea on behalf of freedom of inquiry, Ingersoll asserted that "by defining blasphemy, the church sought to prevent discussion—sought to prevent argument—sought to prevent a man from giving his honest opinion." Ingersoll's polemic on behalf of free inquiry possibly went too far, as he offered no limiting principle, stating that people "must have absolute freedom of speech."[83] His argument also likely went too long; he spent hours discussing various instances throughout Christian history of dominant sects persecuting smaller sects. Ingersoll also insisted that it was impossible to define blasphemy with any precision. "What is blasphemy in one country would be religious exhortation in another." And he argued that the old colonial law was inconsistent with the guarantees of freedom of speech and of religious belief found in the state constitution. Ingersoll's oratory had little to do with the facts of the case. Even he conceded that portions of Reynolds's pamphlet may have been offensive and off-putting to some people. But Ingersoll insisted on "defend[ing] [Reynolds's] right to speak, whether I believe in what he spoke or not, or in the propriety of saying what he said."[84]

Judge Francis Child, a lifelong resident of Morristown, felt obliged to make up for the prosecutor's lackluster performance by contradicting Ingersoll's presentation. He instructed the jury that the blasphemy law was "not obsolete, as Mr. Ingersoll would have you believe." Reynolds was charged with circulating a pamphlet "containing utterances which the law says constituted blasphemous libel, in as much as they deride and contumeliously reproach the holy word of Jesus Christ," Childs insisted. A person could hold whatever opinions they chose, "but if he uttered profane things against God or the Christian religion in a scoffing or railing manner," he was guilty of blasphemy. Childs declared that the statute was constitutional and the jury had to follow the law. Putting additional "spikes in the great pleader's guns," Judge Childs derided Ingersoll's argument, telling the jury that even "though Mr. Ingersoll defended freedom of speech by words so beautiful and fine of sentiment as to send a thrill through the veins of his hearers, he has not offset evidence with evidence." He closed by admonishing the jury that while they had the final say as to Reynolds's guilt or innocence, "[d]o not acquit him by violating the law yourself." The jury deliberated for about an hour and returned a verdict of guilty. Ingersoll paid the twenty-five-dollar fine and the fifty dollars in court costs for Reynolds and promptly left the courthouse.[85]

The *New York Times* applauded the verdict, sneering that Reynolds and the "greatest of infidel orators" had experienced "a sample of Jersey justice." Beecher's *Christian Union* was conflicted about the verdict, asserting that "[w]e demand for the infidel and atheist the political right to attack Christianity and even theism by argument, and without impediment." But that freedom did not include a "right to revile" another's faith, it continued; "free speech is not freedom to insult. And he who insults my religion insults me." *The Truth Seeker* portrayed the outcome as a travesty. At least Reynolds was "now free from the toils of New Jersey savagery, and [he can] resume his labors for intellectual liberty." Nonplussed, Reynolds returned to the lecture circuit, traveling to the more welcoming environs of the west coast, where he eventually settled.[86]

Reynolds's blasphemy prosecution was generally an anomaly. As Leigh Schmidt has documented, freethought lecturers like Reynolds, B.F. Underwood, and Samuel Putnam often faced resistance from local civic leaders and clergy but rarely any legal obstacles to their speaking. "In most instances," Schmidt writes, "freethinkers were given ample allowance to speak their mind," and "the sharp difference of religious opinion subsisting between infidels and Christians led not to a violent stand-off but to civil debate." This was due in part to a growing suspicion about the efficacy of holding someone accountable for publicly expressing their sincere but heretical religious beliefs. "Blasphemy is a fictitious offense," wrote one commentator following Reynolds's trial, "an imaginary crime for which the honest and best men have been subjected to imprisonment, torture, and death." The law of "blasphemy should be abolished altogether."[87]

Nonetheless, contemporary legal commentators Judge Thomas Cooley and Professor Christopher Tiedeman defended the constitutionality of blasphemy laws, provided they applied only to utterances intended to offend people's religious sensibilities, rather than to mere expressions of heterodoxy. "Legal blasphemy implies that the words were uttered in a wanton manner, with a wicked and malicious disposition, and not in a serious discussion upon any controverted point in religion," Cooley wrote. The wantonness element supposedly meant that "no opinion, however anti-Christian or even atheistic, can any longer be regarded from a legal point of view as blasphemous." While this represented a progression in the law, both commentators acknowledged it still was "open to grave objections" and potential abuses. (As if to prove that latter point, both writers justified applying the offense to words having "a direct tendency to undermine the moral support of the laws and corrupt the community.")[88] As previously discussed, Comstock's prosecutions of George Francis Train and D.M. Bennett were based chiefly on their blasphemous writings. Another example of abuse arose in May 1882, when Wolf Hirsh Rosentrauch was tried in Paterson, New Jersey, for reputedly declaring that "Jesus Christ was a bastard." On cross-examination, the complainant acknowledged that he had had a business dispute with the defendant and then proceeded to make antisemitic remarks from the witness stand. The jury found Rosentrauch not guilty, but it was still an ordeal.[89]

Ever since the Abner Kneeland case in 1836, freestanding prosecutions for blasphemy had all but vanished, merging into the related offense of profane swearing, to "contemptuously take the name of God in vain." Profane swearing generally required outrageous utterances, made in the presence of others, and designed to offend moral sensibilities, which was akin to Cooley's and Tiedeman's definitions for blasphemy. In the absence of those elements, a merely blasphemous statement was arguably legal. "There are many immoral acts and vicious conduct of persons which bring down the indignation of every virtuous person," wrote the North Carolina Supreme Court in 1845, but "they are left to the correction of the religious and moral influence of society itself."[90] Nonetheless, prosecutors continued to charge swearers for uttering or publishing "gross, scandalous, profane, and *blasphemous* language." Even though the "offense of using profane, obscene or blasphemous language is in its being a public or common nuisance," a court declared in 1882, the potential liability for plain blasphemous utterances remained a reality.[91] In 1880 in Philadelphia, Thomas Spratt was indicted for blasphemy and nuisance for uttering "with a loud voice and in the presence and hearing of diverse [citizens] . . . false, scandalous, malicious, wicked and blasphemous words" about Jesus Christ. The following year in Alabama, Joe Goree was convicted of making profane statements outside a church after services. Most profane swearing prosecutions likely did not involve freethinkers expressing their heterodox opinions but people who were either inebriated or mentally ill. Spratt possibly fit into one of the latter categories, as he was also charged with indecent exposure. But others—possibly Goree—were chiefly expressing their heretical beliefs. In reversing Goree's conviction for profane swearing, the Alabama Supreme Court noted that he had been talking in "a conversational tone" outside the church. The justices went out of their way to declare that *blasphemy* was no longer indictable, suggesting that Goree's conviction for swearing was a ruse for rebuking his blasphemous language. As another court revealingly acknowledged about how profane swearing could be a proxy for blasphemy: "Profane swearing is irreligious beyond doubt. And it may be admitted to be immoral."[92]

As a result, there is no way of knowing how frequently prosecutors in the late nineteenth century used profane swearing charges as a means of silencing the local "village atheist." Most prosecutions likely involved only common cursing that included using God's name in vain. Less than a dozen reported profane swearing decisions exist, those being in published appeals, and they likely represent only a small fraction of the cases in which a defendant simply paid a fine or never proceeded further than a trial. Most assuredly, however, lost in that indeterminate legal record were some freethinkers like Goree who were expressing their heterodox beliefs, just a little too enthusiastically.[93]

The *Reynolds* case was not the last attempt to silence a vocal freethinker through blasphemy or obscenity charges. In 1895, a Presbyterian minister in Hoboken, New Jersey, tried to have the local district attorney use the same blasphemy law as in *Reynolds* to prevent Robert Ingersoll from delivering his lecture "The Gods," but the prosecutor declined.[94] The year following Reynolds's case saw the first of several prosecutions of Moses Harman, publisher of the Kansas-based *Lucifer, the Light Bearer*, a self-described "Anarchist-Freethought Journal." Like many militant freethinkers, Harman had started out as a Protestant minister (Methodist) and had worked briefly as a schoolteacher. After participating in Liberal League events in the 1870s, Harman founded the *Kansas Liberal* in 1881, a newspaper that sought to "break the chains which have been riveted on the minds and souls of men and women by that religion of Fear and Hate, misnamed Christianity." For several years the *Liberal* followed the model of *The Truth Seeker*, ridiculing institutional religion and its purveyors. Harman changed the name of his paper to the provocative *Lucifer* in 1883 after he became associated with Edwin C. Walker, an occasional contributor to *The Truth Seeker* and the Boston anarchist paper *Liberty* and an active freethought lecturer. According to one biographer, Harman and the younger Walker "made a formidable combination" with Harman expanding his causes beyond freethought to include marriage reform, sexual equality, and individualist anarchy, and Walker promoting the same through his lectures across the Midwest. *Lucifer*, "devoted to the emancipation of women from sex-slavery," became widely read among freethinkers and sex radicals throughout the nation.[95]

Harman's increased willingness to publish articles and letters containing candid discussions of marriage reform and sexual relations subjected him to the scrutiny of a local affiliate of the Society for the Suppression of Vice and the wrath of the Comstock Act. In the spring of 1886, Harman announced in his newspaper that he would not censor the content of any correspondence he reprinted. Shortly afterward, he reprinted a letter from a Tennessee anarchist (the "Markland letter") that called nonconsensual marital sex "legal rape." "If a man stabs his wife to death with a knife, does not the law hold him for murder? [But] [i]f he murders her with his penis, what does the law do?" Other explicit correspondence followed. As was his practice, Harman regularly republished the letters with his own commentary on Christian morality's obsession with obscenity.[96]

In early 1888, Harman was arrested for violating the Comstock Act under an indictment that initially contained 270 counts of mailing obscene material. Following the indictment, a defiant Harman republished the Markland letter alongside passages from the Old Testament that detailed incest, prostitution, and fornication. His legal defense that the Bible contained similar "obscenity"—a favorite tactic of freethinkers—was unsuccessful, and the jury found Harman guilty. The judge sentenced him to five years in prison. His attorney had the sentence overturned on appeal after Harman served four months, and he was resentenced to an additional eight months. Harman was then rearrested for publishing another "obscene" letter while he had been awaiting the first trial: a letter from a physician that condemned, in graphic terms, the sexual abuse of female patients he had treated. Although the second trial was also for obscenity, the judge panned Harman's First Amendment defenses, writing that "it teems with homilies and essays on the liberty of individual conscience, and the liberty of speech and of the public press." Local newspapers also called for Harmon's conviction and for the shuttering of *Lucifer* for advocating free love and for "its rebellious, blasphemous, and corrupting utterances." Harman's conviction in that case resulted in an additional prison term of a year. After his release from prison in April 1896, Harman left Kansas to settle in Chicago.[97]

Also in the 1890s, Kentucky freethought publisher Charles C. Moore faced charges on multiple occasions involving the common combination of obscenity and blasphemy. Moore, too, was a former Protestant minister

(Disciples of Christ) who had lost his faith. After a stint as a journalist, he founded his own newspaper in Lexington in 1886, the *Blue Grass Blade*, which espoused freethought principles among other nonconformist ideas and regularly attacked the pretentions of the local Protestant establishment. Finally, in late 1893, Moore was arrested at the instigation of local clergy for making blasphemous remarks about a nearby church. After he spent several days in jail, the charge was dismissed. Then in 1894, Moore was again arrested for blasphemy for publishing an article that asserted the human parentage of Jesus while declaring that the idea of a union "between God and a Jew woman, I call that blasphemy."[98] After spending three months in jail awaiting trial on that charge, Moore fortuitously drew an "infidel judge" to hear his case (according to Moore's later recount) who, after affirming the "complete divorce between the church and the State," dismissed the charge. Blasphemy "must be considered a stranger to the laws of Kentucky," wrote the judge.[99]

In reporting on the 1894 charge, the *Albany Law Journal* criticized the prosecution, noting that the blasphemy statute was one hundred years old. "[I]n these United States, where freedom of speech and religion are guaranteed, there is no place for such a law, and never should it have been enacted." Asserting that Moore's beliefs were "shared in common with many other persons," the *Journal* proclaimed that "any man should be called to account before the courts of law for expressing any opinion on a matter of religion is preposterous and is repugnant to American free institutions." The *American Law Review*, published in St. Louis, expressed similar sentiments. "Every once in a while, an antiquated religious bigotry shows its hyena teeth in the form of an indictment against some respectable citizen, for what is called 'blasphemy.'" The *Review* noted the irony that such a charge could arise "in a State where [Thomas] Jefferson's statute of religious freedom is understood to be part of the fundamental law."[100]

That national legal journals called for an end to blasphemy prosecutions had only limited effect. In 1894, J.B. Wise, a Kansas freethinker, was arrested for mailing a postcard containing an obscene quotation from the book of Isaiah to a minister. Wise spent several weeks in jail, unable to make bail. His case dragged on for two years, and he was ultimately found guilty of violating the Comstock Act and fined fifty dollars.[101] Then, in 1898, Charles Moore was again charged with blasphemy, now along with obscenity, for sending copies of the *Blue Grass Blade* through the mail. This time the trial was in Cincinnati federal court, and the result was quite different. Rather than drawing a sympathetic judge as before, Moore faced a hostile prosecutor and judge, both intent on enforcing the Comstock Act. The accusation centered on an article in the *Blade* that stated that marriage was only "legalized sexuality." Though he was charged with mailing obscenity, the prosecution attacked Moore's infidelity while calling the *Blade* a "blasphemous" "Free Love" newspaper, seeking to prejudice the jury. Moore was convicted and sentenced to two years in the state penitentiary. For some reason, likely due to the putative obscenity charge, the public outcry over Moore's later prosecution was subdued. Moore was released after serving six months, his sentence commuted by President William McKinley. Nonplussed, Moore returned to publishing the *Blue Grass Blade*.[102]

The Harman, Wise, and Moore convictions possibly stand out because, by the turn of the century, prosecutions for blasphemy were increasingly rare. However, as stated, antireligious utterances could be charged as profane swearing or disturbing the peace, depending on the particular facts. As such, a larger number of convictions for blasphemy may have occurred under these alternative legal theories. The Harman and Moore cases are also notable because authorities went after freethought journals, apparently as much for their religious heterodoxy as for their allegedly obscene content. Moses Harman was convicted one last time in 1905 for publishing and mailing allegedly obscene articles that advocated birth control and sex education. He served a year in an Illinois prison at the age of seventy-five.[103] The last recorded convictions for blasphemy occurred during and immediately following the First World War and involved a Lithuanian immigrant, Michael X. Mockus, who was a Marxist and freethought lecturer. The anticommunist and xenophobic sentiments of the time likely explain Mockus's prosecutions—he allegedly declared that "Religion, capitalism, and government are all damned humbugs, liars, and thieves"—though he also disputed the authority of the Bible and church doctrines. Mockus was convicted in Connecticut and Maine courts, though acquitted by an Illinois jury. Apparently, he never served time in prison. At the dawn of the new century, blasphemy remained a handy cudgel for suppressing religious heterodoxy.[104]

Freethought on the Defensive

Robert Ingersoll did his best to put a positive, humanistic face on freethought. People had nothing to fear from agnostics and freethinkers, Ingersoll insisted, other than the challenge they presented to religious presuppositions and superstitions. Freethought promoted scientific inquiry and intellectual curiosity and sought to banish ignorance and prejudice. "The positive side of Freethought," Ingersoll wrote in 1890, "is to find out the truth—the facts of nature—to the end that we may take advantage of those truths, of those facts—for the purpose of feeding and clothing mankind." Freethought, he insisted, "is the mother of art and science, or morality and happiness."

> Instead of loving God, we love each other. Instead of religion of the sky—the religion of this world—the religion of the family—the love of husband for wife, of wife for husband—the love of all for children. . . . Let us live for each other; let us live for this world, without regard for the past and without fear for the future. Let us use our faculties and our powers for the benefit of ourselves and others.[105]

Despite Ingersoll's best efforts, the freethought movement could not escape charges that it promoted immorality and threatened the social order and stability of Christian society. These charges existed apart from allegations that freethought was in league with obscenity and free love. Some criticism was of a general nature, as with an article in the Catholic *Tablet* that bemoaned "the rapid progress of infidelity, materialism and indifference to religion," particularly among the working classes, which encouraged "sentiments of opposition to law and order." Freethought also promoted a false promise of discovering truth, noted the *Herald of Gospel Liberty*. Real "Truth is the Word of God"; so "[a]s is the difference between truth and falsehood, so is the difference between Christianity and infidelity. . . . while Christianity edifies, infidelity corrodes; while Christianity purifies, infidelity dissuades; while Christianity beautifies, infidelity disrobes of beauty."[106]

Other attacks were more specific. "The most serious result of skepticism in a land is to be seen in its affect on the morals of the people," opined the *Christian Advocate*. Beyond promoting a "want of faith . . . infidelity has a further and deeper reach. It goes to the very vitality of our daily life, and disjoins all of the firm articulations of the morals of society." Raising a more direct charge, the *New York Observer and Chronicle* declared that among the chief causes of crime were: "False opinions on religion and morals, which corrupt society. Infidelity, which rejects the Bible. . . . Atheism, which denies God—his existence, authority, and judgment."[107] The religious press rarely relented on its criticism of Ingersoll and other freethought lecturers, with the *Andover Review* charging Ingersoll with engaging in "aggressive infidelity" by attacking the authority of the Bible while "sneering" at Christian morality. Ingersoll was a "blatant infidel," a "moral incendiary," who "takes his place among the destroyers" of civilization, wrote the *New York Evangelist*. "Bitterly as Mr. Ingersoll hates Christianity," the *New York Times* added, "he must admit that its influence is on the side of morality and decency, and . . . however may be its particular religious delusions, is higher in the scale of morality than any pagan community."[108]

In April 1885, the *North American Review* published an article titled "Free Thought in America" which characterized Ingersoll and O.B. Frothingham as figurative bookends of the freethought movement. Neither man emerged unscathed. Ingersoll's unrelenting attack on religion, "its irrelevance, its recklessness, its impatience . . . can do no good; it may do no little harm," asserted the author. "[H]e is just the sort of person of whom America does not stand in need," particularly considering "the predominant vices [facing] America." In contrast, Frothingham's work was less threatening to society because it advanced "the fatal spirit of self-destructive latitudinarianism," which was essentially "empty air." To his credit, Frothingham does not "imitate Colonel Ingersoll in treating any[one's] gods with disrespect," noted the *Review*, "but he nevertheless measures them with his free-thought foot-rule, and finds them, at best, only a cubit high." The conclusion was that whatever its manifestation, freethought was at best a shallow and facile movement and at worst a destructive force.[109]

Another accusation facing the freethought movement was that it led to socialism and anarchism. Ingersoll and *The Truth Seeker* eschewed political radicalism and extremism, as did most freethinkers. "There is no place in this country for the Anarchist," Ingersoll wrote. "The source of power here is the people, and to attack the political power is to attack the people." Real differences separated the two ideologies. Conventional freethinkers regarded institutional religion and its defenders as being responsible for social inequalities, particularly the suppression of intellectual freedom. But while most anarchists and political extremists also rejected religion, they saw it as only one cause of the economic, social, and political inequalities that modern society faced. However, both shared a common belief that an alliance of church and state was inimical to human freedom.[110] Despite this tenuous overlap, any association with anarchism worried Ingersoll and Samuel Putnam of the American Secular Union. "Are Anarchists necessarily Atheists? Is the tendency of Anarchism toward Atheism?" asked the anarchist journal *Liberty*.

Although the answer to the first question was "not necessarily," the answer to the second was "unquestionably."[111]

It took only a handful of freethinkers who promoted sexual radicalism and political extremism—socialism, communism, or anarchism—to tarnish the larger movement. As discussed, Ezra Heywood supported labor reform and an individualistic form of anarchism in addition to free love and freethought.[112] Moses Harman also embraced the idea of individualist anarchism in which a person would be free from all legal and societal constraints on personal liberty, what he called "Autonomy-Self Law," which included those constraints governing marriage. In 1886, prior to his arrest for obscenity, Harman presided over the "autonomistic" marriage of his sixteen-year-old daughter to Edwin Walker where the newlyweds renounced all legal and clerical authority over their marriage. In his remarks, Harman announced that because marriage was, "strictly a personal matter, we deny the right of society . . . to regulate it, or to interfere with the individual man and woman in this relation." Harman's daughter and Walker were subsequently arrested and served six months in jail for unlawful cohabitation.[113] Harman also once wrote an article where he abstractly endorsed using dynamite to achieve social change. This confluence of freethought, free love, and anarchism, which Ezra Heywood espoused regularly in his journal *The Word*, was not uncommon.[114]

A seminal year in the annals of American anarchism was 1886, as on May 4 an explosive detonated during a peaceful labor rally in Chicago's Haymarket Square, resulting in the deaths of seven policemen and three civilians; an additional twenty-three officers suffered disabling injuries. Eight anarchists were arrested for the crime, and the trial became a national cause célèbre. The Chicago anarchist community was relatively prominent, split among various ethnic groups. A common factor shared by most members, aside from their anarchism, was a rejection of religion. "No God, No Master" was a frequent banner displayed at anarchist rallies.[115] During the trial of the Chicago Eight, Moses Harman defended the alleged anarchists. By contrast, Robert Ingersoll condemned anarchism and the deaths, understanding the public damage the event did to freethought. Ingersoll carefully criticized the trial judge for allowing the introduction of prejudicial material, but generally distanced himself from the matter. Privately, however, he offered his behind-the-scenes assistance to the defense counsel.[116]

Nonetheless, the association between anarchism and atheism was easily made. Observers noted the rampant irreligion among members of the various immigrant workers' unions. One of the convicted Haymarket anarchists, Samuel Fielden, had been a member of the Liberal League. Clergy railed about the threat of atheistic anarchism to Christian institutions; according to a contributor to *The Truth Seeker*, Chicago "ministers are howling that Anarchism is only the ripe fruit of Infidelity; that Anarchism and Infidelity are synonymous; that Infidelity will have to be suppressed before Anarchism can be stamped out, . . . [and] that the blame for the so-called Haymarket riot should be chargeable to Robert Ingersoll."[117] Religious journals echoed the same theme: "Infidelity and anarchy are closely allied," charged the *Christian Advocate*. "[A]ll publishers, preachers, and abettors of atheism, infidelity, and blasphemy against God and the Bible are morally guilty of the great crime for which these seven Anarchists have been tried and convicted," echoed the *Herald of Gospel Liberty*. The Haymarket trial "has served to set infidelity and Christianity over against each other in practical and striking contrast"; the whole episode was but the "fruit ripened upon the tree of rationalism planted by George Fredrick Hegel . . . . and watered and cultivated by Robert Ingersoll." As a Chicago anarchist journal summed up matters following the trial: "The Chicago *Evening Journal* calls attention to the fact that of all the condemned anarchists not one of them is a believer in God, or religion, or moral accountability. . . . They were infidels."[118]

The freethought movement suffered another blow to its reputation with the circumstances surrounding the untimely death of Samuel Putnam, leader of the American Secular Union, in 1896. Putnam's background was similar to that of other leading freethinkers: trained in the ministry (Congregationalist), he had drifted into Unitarianism, eventually rejecting it for skepticism. In the 1870s, Putnam had been inspired by Francis Abbot's *The Index*, later contributing articles to the journal and then to *The Truth Seeker*. In the late 1870s, Putnam decided to make a career as a freethinking lecturer in the mode of B.F. Underwood, if not Robert Ingersoll, but his failure forced him to return to the Unitarian pulpit briefly. Finally, in 1879 he permanently abandoned the ministry, moving to New York City, where he secured the patronage of prominent freethinkers, including D.M. Bennett, Edward Bliss Foote, and Thaddeus B. Wakeman. Before long, the tenacious Putnam had risen in the ranks of the Liberal League, becoming the operating secretary and then president of the American Secular Union. He built a reputation as "an indefatigable worker" who helped to revitalize the organization after it faced attacks in the 1880s and 1890s. In 1894, he published the massive *Four Hundred Years of Freethought*, which documented the evolution of skepticism since the Scientific Revolution.[119]

Even though Putnam had been instrumental in having the League/Union return to its core church-state mission and avoid involvement with free love and obscenity issues, he had a secret. Putnam had left his last ministry under a cloud: he had had an affair with a woman parishioner and then abandoned his wife and children. Despite hoping to keep the episode secret, Putnam had initially advocated a "new morality," what he termed "free marriage." Legal marriage, as currently practiced, he wrote in 1879, was "a relic of barbarism," a "coarse and degrading" system. "Even as religion must be free, even so must marriage be free." Francis Abbot had rebuffed Putnam in *The Index*, charging him with embracing "free love" by another name and demonstrating "a sad perversion of his private judgment." Chastened, Putnam had dropped his embrace of marital reform and his earlier advocacy had largely been forgotten.[120] In December 1896, however, tragedy struck. On December 11, Putnam was in Boston to deliver several freethought lectures. The next morning, his body was found along with that of a twenty-year-old unmarried woman named May L. Collins in her apartment. Both apparently had been drinking and succumbed to a gas leak in her room, and even though they were fully clothed, salacious rumors quickly circulated. *The Truth Seeker* defended Putnam's conduct as above-board—Collins was an aspiring freethought lecturer whom Putnam was mentoring—but others within the freethought movement saw it as an embarrassment if not a betrayal by a leader who had promoted the propriety of freethought. Horace L. Green of *Free Thought Magazine* wrote a scathing article criticizing Putnam's actions: "Mr. Putnam was a good man, but this damnable doctrine of free love first led him to intemperance, then to what is generally characterized as libertinism, and finally to his tragic death." He called on freethinkers to commit to "ridding our cause of this curse of free love and planting our moral standard so high it will command the respect of all good people." As Green feared, the episode reignited accusations about the connection between freethought and immorality, further damaging its image in the public mind.[121]

The freethought movement, and the American Secular Union, remained active into the twentieth century, but with the various headwinds it faced, the movement never fulfilled its promise as an alternative to religion. Historian Martin Marty insists that freethought never represented a serious challenge to Protestantism, particularly when moderates like Henry Ward Beecher and Lyman Abbott willingly conceded the irrationality of many traditional Christian doctrines and adapted their theology to scientific advances. Progressive Christian theology "will take [churches] away from superstition and credulity," Beecher maintained, "and plant them on grounds of reason." Never before, he insisted, "has religion been such an inspiration to whatever is humane, liberal, and generous." By contrast, organized infidelity was moribund and could never compete.[122] "Already we discern indications that the skepticism of our times is staggering and receding," chronicler Daniel Dorchester asserted in 1895. "Ingersollism has damned itself with its terrible blasphemies; and Free Religion is only a respectable annual spectacular parade of many-shaded inquirers, rapidly decreasing in number." With the death of Putnam in 1896, and then of Ingersoll in 1899, the "golden age" of American freethought had come to an end.[123]

NOTES

1. "Cupid's Yokes," *The Truth Seeker*, Sept. 7, 1878, 5; "Unjust Interference," ibid., Sept. 21, 1878, 601; *The Trial of D.M. Bennett in the Circuit Court* (New York: The Truth Seeker, 1879), v, 21–23.

2. "Schuyler County Justice," *The Truth Seeker*, Sept. 15, 1878, 584; "Principles and Personalities," ibid., Dec. 29, 1877, 412.

3. "Our Third Arrest," ibid., Dec. 21, 1878, 808; Broun and Leech, *Anthony Comstock*, 175; Bradford, *D.M. Bennett*, 151–153; *The Trial of D.M. Bennett*, v; United States v. Bennett, 24 F. Cas. 1093 (1879).

4. "Our Attendance at Watkins," *The Truth Seeker*, Dec. 28, 1878, 824; MacDonald, *Fifty Years of Freethought*, 230.

5. Macdonald, *Fifty Years of Freethought*, 244; *The Trial of D.M. Bennett*, vii; Bradford, *D.M. Bennett*, 165–168.

6. *The Trial of D.M. Bennett*, 44–50, 62–63, 65; Bennett, 24 Cas. at 1098; "D.M. Bennett's Trial," *New York Times*, March 19, 1879, 10.

7. *The Trial of D.M. Bennett*, vi, 19, 52–54, 122, 127–128, 139–141; Bennett, 24 Cas. at 1101; Bradford, *D.M. Bennett*, 172–177.

8. *The Trial of D.M. Bennett*, 153–154, 149–150; Bennett, 24 Cas. at 1101–1102; "Obscene Literature," *New York Times*, March 21, 1879, 3.

9. *The Trial of D.M. Bennett*, 171–174; "Home Secular News," *Christian Advocate*, March 27, 1879, 204; *Zion's Herald*, April 3, 1879, 108; "The Bennett Case Again," *Christian Advocate*, June 5, 1879, 364; "Reasons Why D.M. Bennett Should Not Be Pardoned by the President," ibid., July 3, 1879, 430; "The Bennett Case," *Christian Union*, April 2, 1879, 308; Bradford, *D.M. Bennett*, 177–180.

10. Bennett, 24 Cas. at 1101–1102, 1107; "The Case of D.M. Bennett," *American Socialist*, June 19, 1879, 196; Macdonald, *Fifty Years of Freethought*, 243–247.

11. "Current Topics," *Albany Law Journal*, May 17, 1879, 385–386; F.W. Evans, "Governmental Inquisition," *Shaker Manifesto*, August 1879, 181; Macdonald, *Fifty Years of Freethought*, 243–250, 269; Comstock, *Frauds Exposed*, 485–486; Broun and Leech, *Anthony Comstock*, 181–183; Bradford, *D.M. Bennett*, 227–230.

12. "The National Liberal League," *New York Times*, Aug. 9, 1879, 8; "Free-Thinkers in Convention," ibid., Sept. 29, 1879, 5.

13. *Christian Union*, Sept. 10, 1879, 201; "Fact and Rumor," ibid., Sept. 10, 1870, 212.

14. "Convention of the National Liberal League," Ingersoll, *Works*, 12:233–235; "The Circulation of Obscene Material," ibid., 12:218–220.

15. *Christian Union*, Sept. 24, 1879, 241; "Brevities," *New York Observer and Chronicle*, Aug. 28, 1879, 278.

16. See "Seventh Letter from Albany," *The Truth Seeker*, Feb. 14, 1880, 100–101.

17. "Greeting an Ex-Convict," *New York Times*, May 3, 1880, 2; "Home Again," *The Truth Seeker*, May 8, 1880, 290; "An Apotheosis of Dirt," *Scribner's Monthly*, July 1880, 463; Macdonald, *Fifty Years of Freethought*, 274–279; Bradford, *D.M. Bennett*, 233–243.

18. "The National Liberal League," *New York Times*, Sept. 19, 1880, 2.

19. "The Circulation of Obscene Material," Ingersoll, *Works*, 12:220–230.

20. "A Row in the National Liberal League," *New York Times*, Sept. 20, 1880, 5; "National Liberal League Congress," *The Truth Seeker*, Oct. 2, 1880, 637–640; "Letter from Chicago," *New York Evangelist*, Sept. 30, 1880, 1; Macdonald, *Fifty Years of Freethought*, 281–283.

21. Macdonald, *Fifty Years of Freethought*, 281; "Exposure of Fraud and Crime," *New York Evangelist*, Jan. 13, 1881, 4; *The Presbyterian*, reprinted in the *Christian Advocate*, Oct. 21, 1880, 681; *Christian Union*, Sept. 22, 1880, 222; *Boston Herald*, reprinted in *The Truth Seeker*, Oct. 9, 1880, 646.

22. Macdonald, *Fifty Years of Freethought*, 319–324; Bradford, *D.M. Bennett*, 249–262, 363–378; "Editor of the *Truth Seeker* Dead," *The Truth Seeker*, Dec. 23, 1882, 804–809; "In Memoriam," ibid., Jan. 6, 1883, 8; "On Picket Duty," *Liberty*, Jan. 20, 1883, 1; "A Proposed Monument," *New York Times*, Aug. 29, 1883, 4.

23. John Winthrop, "Our Boston Letter," *The Independent*, May 29, 1884, 5.

24. Bremner, ed., *Traps for the Young*, xv–xvi.

25. "Anthony Comstock in the Pulpit," *The Truth Seeker*, May 29, 1880, 345. See also "Suppression of Vice," *Christian Advocate*, Aug. 15, 1878, 524.

26. Comstock, *Frauds Exposed*, 7.

27. Ibid., 392–393,

28. Ibid., 443–445.

29. Ibid., 446.

30. Ibid., 496, 499.

31. Ibid., 513, 511, 514.

32. "New Books," *New York Times*, Jan. 16, 1881, 10.

33. "Mr. Comstock's Book," *Scribner's Monthly*, April 1881, 950; "Exposure of Fraud and Crime," *New York Evangelist*, Jan. 13, 1881, 4; *Christian Union*, Jan. 20, 1881, 11.

34. Robert Bremner, ed., in Comstock, *Traps for the Young*, xv.

35. Comstock, *Traps for the Young*, 158–187, 192.

36. Ibid., 187, 198, 200, 194; Broun and Leech, *Anthony Comstock*, 191–192.

37. Comstock, *Traps for the Young*, 197.

38. Ibid., 199.

39. Ibid., 202, 204.

40. Ibid., 197–198.

41. Ibid.

42. "The Suppression of Vice," *North American Review*, Nov. 1882, 484–510.

43. "Current Topics," *Albany Law Review*, March 4, 1882, 161.

44. "On Picket Duty," *Liberty*, Nov. 11, 1882, 1; "On Picket Duty," ibid., Nov. 25, 1882, 1; "Ezra H. Heywood Indicted," *New York Times*, Dec. 10, 1882, 14; *Free Speech: The Report of Ezra H. Heywood's Defense* (Princeton, MA: Co-Operative Pub., 1883).

45. *Free Speech*, 7, 17–18, 25, 37–38, 43–45; Blatt, *Free Love and Anarchism*, 142–147; "On Picket Duty," *Liberty*, April 14, 1883, 1; "The Value of the Heywood Victory," ibid., June 9, 1883, 3; "The Acquittal of Heywood," *The Truth Seeker*, April 21, 1883, 248.

46. *Free Speech*, 46–48; Blatt, *Free Love and Anarchism*, 147–148; "Notes," *The Truth Seeker*, June 2, 1883, 345.

47. "Mr. Heywood's Trial," *The Truth Seeker*, June 21, 1890, 388–389; "Judge Carpenter's Charge to Heywood's Jury," ibid., June 28, 1890, 405; "Death of E.H. Heywood," ibid., May 27, 1893, 325, 328; "Ezra Hoar Heywood," ibid., June 16, 1893, 358–359; Marshall Cushing, *Story of Our Post Office* (Boston: A.M. Thayer & Co., 1893), 613; Blatt, *Free Love and Anarchism*, 162–174.

48. "Col. Ingersoll at Booths," *New York Times*, May 24, 1880, 5.

49. Jacoby, *Freethinkers*, 169–170, 178–179; Jacoby, *The Great Agnostic*, 58–68.

50. Jacoby, *The Great Agnostic*, 77–128; Anderson, *Robert Ingersoll*, 80–83; Marty, *The Infidel*, 145, 147.

51. "The Recent Convention of Freethinkers," *New York Evangelist*, Oct. 1, 1885, 4.

52. "What Must We Do to Be Saved," Ingersoll, *Works*, 1:441–525; Anderson, *Robert Ingersoll*, 98–100; Larson, *American Infidel*, 158–161.

53. "The Great Infidels," Ingersoll, *Works*, 3:308–309.

54. "Liberty in Literature," ibid., 3:253–254.

55. "Severe on Ingersoll," *New York Times*, Feb. 8, 1881, 2; "Criminal Blasphemy," *The Independent*, Feb. 17, 1881, 16; "Official Recognition of Blasphemy:

Ingersoll-ism Denounced," *Christian Advocate*, Feb. 17, 1881, 108; *Zion's Herald*, Feb 10, 1881, 44; Larson, *American Infidel*, 161–163.

56. "Col. Ingersoll in Brooklyn," *New York Times*, Feb. 23, 1885, 2; "Blasphemy," Ingersoll, *Works*, 8:202–203; "Col. Ingersoll Not Stopped," *New York Times*, Feb. 25 1895, 1.

57. "Superstition" (1887), in Tim Page, ed., *What's God Got to Do with It? Robert Ingersoll on Free Thought, Honest Talk, and the Separation of Church and State* (Hanover, NH: Steelforth Press, 2005), 94.

58. "Liberals and Liberalism" (1888), Ingersoll, *Works*, 8:441; "Pope Leo XII" (1890), ibid., 8:442–444; "Some Live Topics," ibid., 8:255; "Rome, or Reason?," *North American Review* (Nov. 1888): 503–525.

59. "Heretics and Heresies" (1874), Ingersoll, *Works*, 1:233, 227. See also "Orthodoxy" (1884), ibid., 2:341–427.

60. "Liberals and Liberalism" (1888), Ingersoll, *Works*, 8:440–441; "God in the Constitution" (1890), ibid., 11:121–134; "Individuality" (1873), ibid., 1:201.

61. Green, *The Bible, the School, and the Constitution*; Green, *Separating Church and State*.

62. Jacoby, *The Great Agnostic*, 129–153.

63. See, generally, Page, *What's God Got to Do with It*.

64. "Convention of the American Secular Union," Ingersoll, *Works*, 8:239–244.

65. "Some Live Topics," Ingersoll, *Works*, 8: 248–255; "Secularism," ibid., 8:392.

66. Jacoby, *Freethinkers*, 184–185.

67. Comstock, "How I Came to Enter Upon My Work," 327; "Freedom of the Mails," *Christian Union*, March 20, 1878, 239; Joseph Waugh, "Morality of Freethinkers," *New York Evangelist*, Oct. 12, 1882, 1.

68. "The Circulation of Obscene Literature" (1878), Ingersoll, *Works*, 12:215–216.

69. Jacoby, *Freethinkers*, 164; "Ingersoll and Beecher" (1880), Ingersoll, *Works*, 8:40–42.

70. "The Liberty of Man, Woman, and Child," Ingersoll, *Works*, 1:329–398; "Woman's Right to Divorce," ibid., 8:383–390.

71. "What Is Religion?" (1899), Ingersoll, *Works*, 4:502–506.

72. Ibid., 505.

73. Jacoby, *The Great Agnostic*, 118–119, 127, 152.

74. "The Condition of Freethought in the United States," *The Truth Seeker*, June 25, 1881, 410; "The Free-Thinkers Go Home," *New York Times*, Sept. 3, 1883, 4; "Liberal Leagues Organizing," ibid., Sept. 9, 1883, 2; "Free Thinkers in Convention," *The Independent*, Aug. 31, 1882, 14; "The New University," ibid., Aug. 31, 1882, 16; "The Freethinkers' Convention," *New York Evangelist*, Sept. 13, 1883, 1; Macdonald, *Fifty Years of Freethought*, 314–317.

75. "The National Liberal League Congress," *The Truth Seeker*, Oct. 6, 1883, 628–629; "The Proposed Change in the League," ibid., May 31, 1884, 844; "The Convention," ibid., Sept. 13, 1884, 584–585; "The Eighth Annual Congress," ibid., Sept. 20, 1884, 596–597; Samuel P. Putnam, "To the Liberals of America,"

ibid., Sept. 20, 1884, 597; "The American Secular Union Congress," ibid., Oct. 24, 1885, 674; Ingersoll, "Convention of the American Secular Union," *Works*, 8:239–244; Warren, *American Freethought*, 166–169; Schmidt, *Village Atheists*, 51; Ahlstrom and Mullin, *The Scientific Theist*, 136–155.

76. Schmidt, *Village Atheists*, 40, 50; Jacoby, *Freethinkers*, 151–157; *The Freethinkers' Magazine*, 5 (Jan. 1887): 38.

77. "The Village Infidel," *New York Times*, June 28, 1885, 10.

78. "Col. Ingersoll Not Stopped," *New York Times*, Feb. 25, 1895, 1; "Blasphemy," *Columbia Law Review* 70 (1970): 694–733.

79. "Blasphemy," *The Truth Seeker*, Oct. 30, 1886, 696–697; Lawson, "The Trial of Charles B. Reynolds," 795–796; Schmidt, *Village Atheists*, 171–184.

80. "Reynolds Arrested for Blasphemy," *The Truth Seeker*, Aug. 7, 1886, 504–505; Schmidt, *Village Atheists*, 186–190;

81. Lawson, "The Trial of Charles B. Reynolds," 795–796; "Blasphemy," *The Truth Seeker*, Oct. 30, 1886, 696–697; Schmidt, *Village Atheists*, 190–195.

82. Lawson, "The Trial of Charles B. Reynolds," 798–799, 856; "Convicted and Fined," *The Truth Seeker*, May 28, 1887, 344.

83. "Trial of C.B. Reynolds for Blasphemy," Ingersoll, *Works*, 8:59–60; Leonard Levy, *Blasphemy* (New York: Alfred A. Knopf, 1993), 508–511; Schmidt, *Village Atheists*, 196–198.

84. "Trial of C.B. Reynolds for Blasphemy," Ingersoll, *Works*, 8:63, 66–68, 92–93.

85. Ibid., 856–857; "Convicted and Fined," *The Truth Seeker*, May 28, 1887, 344–345.

86. "Jersey Law Triumphant: Reynolds Found Guilty of Blasphemy," *New York Times.*, May 21, 1887, 8; *Christian Union*, May 26, 1887, 2; *New York Evangelist*, June 2, 1887, 3; "The Conviction of a Blasphemer," *The Independent*, May 26, 1887, 17; "Convicted and Fined," *The Truth Seeker*, May 28, 1887, 344–345; Schmidt, *Village Atheists*, 198–199.

87. Schmidt, *Village Atheists*, 201–202; "Blasphemy," *The Open Court*, May 26, 1887, 214–215.

88. Thomas M. Cooley, *A Treatise on the Constitutional Limitations*, 7th ed. (Boston: Little, Brown & Co., 1903), 671–673; Christopher Tiedeman, *A Treatise on the Limitations of Police Power in the United States* (St. Louis: F.H. Thomas Law Book Co., 1886), 167–171; "Blasphemy," *The Open Court*, May 26, 1887, 215.

89. "Tried for Blasphemy," *New York Times*, May 24, 1882, 3.

90. Bodenhamer v. State, 28 S.W. 507 (Ark. 1894); State v. Deberry, 27 N.C. 265–267 (1845); State v. Graham, 35 Tenn. 134–139 (1866); Green, *Second Disestablishment*, 239–242.

91. State v. Graham, 35 Tenn. at 135; State v. Chrisp, 85 N.S. 528–533 (1881); Young v. State, 78 Tenn. 165–167 (1882).

92. Commonwealth v. Spratt, 14 Phil. Rpts. 365–366 (1880); Goree v. State, 71 Ala. 7–10 (1881); State v. Powell, 70 N.C. 68–69 (1874).

93. Green, *Second Disestablishment*, 239–242.

94. "Col. Ingersoll Not Stopped," *New York Times*, Feb. 25, 1895, 1.

95. Hal D. Sears, *The Sex Radicals: Free Love in High Victorian America* (Lawrence: Regents Press of Kansas, 1977), 46–48, 53–64; Wendy McElroy, "The Life of a Grand Old Liberal," *The Freeman* (Feb. 1999): 47–51; Charles J. Reid Jr., "The Devil Comes to Kansas: A Story of Free Love, Sexual Privacy, and the Law," *Michigan Journal of Gender and the Law* 19 (2012): 71–148; Rabban, *Free Speech in Its Forgotten Years*, 41–43; *Lucifer, the Light Bearer*, Feb. 10, 1886, 1.

96. "Threatened with Prosecution," *Lucifer*, July 2, 1886, 2; Sears, *The Sex Radicals*, 74–78.

97. Sears, *The Sex Radicals*, 79–80, 98, 107, 109–112; "Home Again," *Liberty*, Sept. 13, 1890, 3; McElroy, "The Life of a Grand Old Liberal," 49–50; "Moses Harmon in the Penitentiary," *The Freethinkers' Magazine* (Feb. 1893): 108–110; United States v. Harman, 38 Fed. 827 (D. Kan. 1889); Harman v. United States, 50 Fed. 621 (C.C. Kan. 1892); United States v. Harman, 68 Fed. 472 (D. Kan. 1885); United States v. Harman, 45 Fed. 414 (D. Kan. 1891).

98. Charles C. Moore, *Behind the Bars* (Lexington, KY: Blue Grass Print Co., 1899), 9–11, 290.

99. Ibid., 290–294; "Judge Parker's Decision in the Moore Blasphemy Case," *The Truth Seeker*, July 21, 1894, 53; "Charles C. Moore," *Free Thought Magazine* (April 1895): 234–238.

100. "Current Topics," *Albany Law Journal*, April 28, 1894, 282; "Another Indictment for Blasphemy," *American Law Review* (July/August, 1894): 586; "Blasphemy as a Crime and Nuisance," *Liberty*, July 28, 1894, 7.

101. Macdonald, *Fifty Years of Freethought*, 82, 103–104, 124. The offending passage was from Isaiah 36:12: "hath he not sent me to the men that sit upon the wall, that they may eat their own dung, and drink their own piss with you?"

102. Moore, *Behind the Bars*, 221–243, 257–287.

103. McElroy, "The Life of a Grand Old Liberal," 50–51.

104. Related in Theodore Schroeder, *Constitutional Free Speech Defined and Defended* (New York: Free Speech League, 1919), 13–18, 451–456; State v. Mockus, 113 Atl. 39–45 (Me. 1921); Levy, *Blasphemy*, 512–515.

105. "Has Freethought a Constructive Side?," Ingersoll, *Works*, 11: 440–441.

106. "Growing Infidelity of the Times," *The Tablet*, reprinted in *New York Evangelist*, Aug. 18, 1881, 2; "Christianity and Infidelity Contrasted," *Herald of Gospel Liberty*, Nov. 27, 1890, 758.

107. "Infidelity and Bad Morals," *Christian Advocate*, Nov. 5, 1885, 713; "The Increase in Crime," *New York Observer and Chronicle*, Jan. 17, 1895, 68.

108. "Aggressive Infidelity Using Its Advantage," *Andover Review* (June 1888): 639–640; "A Sunday Night Performance," *New York Evangelist*, May 20, 1880, 4; "Mr. Ingersoll's Motive," *New York Times*, May 28, 1882, 24.

109. Robert Buchanan, "Free Thought in America," *North American Review* (April 1885): 316–327; Warren, *American Freethought*, 220–227.

110. "Trial of the Chicago Anarchists," Ingersoll, *Works*, 8:293; "The Truth Seeker and the Anarchists," *The Truth Seeker*, Sept. 25, 1886, 616–617; Jacoby, *Freethinkers*, 231–232.

111. "Is Anarchism Atheistic?" *Liberty*, June 30, 1894, 2.

112. Blatt, *Free Love and Anarchism*.

113. Sears, *The Sex Radicals*, 81–86, 89–96; Reid, "The Devil Comes to Kansas," 74–76; "Arrested!" *Lucifer*, Sept. 17, 1886, 1; "A Disgraceful Affair, Is It?," ibid., Sept. 21, 1886, 1–2; "Law and Love in Kansas, *The Truth Seeker*, Oct. 2, 1886, 633; "The Kansas Arrests," ibid., Oct. 30, 1886, 697; State v. Walker, 13 Pac. 279 (1887).

114. Reid, "The Devil Comes to Kansas," 73; Sears, *The Sex Radicals*, 104.

115. T. Messer-Kruse, *The Trial of the Haymarket Anarchists: Terrorism and Justice in the Gilded Age* (New York: Palgrave Macmillan, 2011), 1–4; Michael Fellman, *In the Name of God and Country: Reconsidering Terrorism in American History* (New Haven, CT: Yale University Press, 2010), 152, 167–168.

116. Sears, *The Sex Radicals*, 97; "Trial of the Chicago Anarchists," Ingersoll, *Works*, 8: 291–293; Jacoby, *Freethinkers*, 181–183.

117. Messer-Kruse, *The Trial of the Haymarket Anarchists*, 11; "The Chicago Troubles," *The Truth Seeker*, June 5, 1886, 359.

118. "Anarchy the Fruit of Infidelity," *Christian Advocate*, Feb. 2, 1888, 70; "In and about Chicago," *Christian Union*, May 20, 1886, 28; "The Effect of a Single Bomb," *New York Evangelist*, May 20, 1886, 4; "Infidelity and Anarchy," *Herald of Gospel Liberty*, Sept. 23, 1886, 8; Bruce C. Nelson, "Revival and Upheaval: Religion and Irreligion in Chicago's Working Class in 1886," *Journal of Social History* 25 (1991): 223–253.

119. Schmidt, *Village Atheists*, 25–59; Warren, *American Freethought*, 172–174.

120. "A Statement by S.P. Putnam," *The Index*, April 24, 1879, 201; "A Retrograde Ideal," ibid., April 24, 1879, 198.

121. Schmidt, *Village Atheists*, 59–72; "Dead from Asphyxiation," *New York Times*, Dec. 12, 1896, 17; Macdonald, *Fifty Years of Freethought*, 132–134; "Macdonald, the Truth-Shunner," *Liberty* (Jan. 1897), 4; Jacoby, *Freethinkers*, 163; "Samuel P. Putnam—May L. Collins—Obituary Notices—A Discordant Voice," *Free Thought Magazine* (Jan. 1896): 44–61.

122. Marty, *The Infidels*, 145–149; Henry Ward Beecher, "Progress of Thought in the Church," *North American Review* (Aug. 1882), 99, 100–102; Lyman Abbott, "Flaws in Ingersollism," ibid. (April 1890): 446–457.

123. Daniel Dorchester, *The Problem of Religious Progress* (New York: Eaton & Mains, 1895), 113–114.

5

Women's Rights and Religion

The decline of the freethought movement hardly meant the end of conflict over sex, gender, and religion. Conflict in these arenas also arose within the emerging women's rights movement, with reformers clashing over issues such as suffrage, marriage and divorce reform, temperance, and "home protection," the last reflected in part through the "purity" movement that paralleled Anthony Comstock's crusade against obscenity. The women involved in these causes were not overwhelmingly freethinkers or religiously heterodox. On the contrary, many activists were evangelical Protestants committed to putting their faith into action by reforming society. The largest and most influential women's organization was the Woman's Christian Temperance Union (WCTU), whose name clearly embodied a religious response to a social evil.[1] What united these various causes, however, was that the groups were largely headed by women and that they empowered women in increasingly public roles. This dynamic led some women to question other societal norms and conventions that prevented them from attaining greater freedom and independence. Although scholars have debated the extent to which these movements represented the rise of modern feminism, they undoubtedly served as feminism's forerunner, particularly when one considers the social and legal constraints that women faced in Victorian America. As one scholar has remarked, temperance "became the medium through which nineteenth-century women expressed their deeper, sometimes unconscious, feminist concerns."[2]

Several leading figures in the suffrage movement, however, were either freethinkers or held unconventional religious views: Elizabeth Cady Stanton, Susan B. Anthony, Lucretia Mott, Martha Coffin Wright, Lucy Stone, Ernestine Rose, and Matilda Joslyn Gage. Stanton, Rose, and Gage were the most open about their religious heterodoxy, although Anthony reputedly held agnostic views despite her Quaker upbringing. This chapter will focus on Christianity's complex role in the struggle for women's equality, particularly within the domestic sphere where marriage and divorce reform was at times associated with free love. On one end of the spectrum were Stanton, Rose, and Gage, who believed that women's subjugation was the result of their lack of political equality and their resulting inability to rectify oppressive domestic-relations laws, all of which were rooted in male-dominated religion. On the other end of the spectrum was Frances Willard, president of the WCTU, who perceived no conflict between her commitments to women's rights and evangelical Christianity. Anthony, no less committed to achieving equality than Stanton but more pragmatic, increasingly believed that Stanton's anticlericalism and condemnation of religion served as an impediment to achieving women's rights, including the right to vote, and she was willing to collaborate with the forces of religious orthodoxy to achieve the reformers' long-term goals. In a sense, the controversy within the women's rights movement over sexual equality and marriage reform paralleled that which divided the freethought community. Could women's rights advance only by defeating marital inequality and its chief facilitator, organized religion?[3]

The Antebellum Religious Origins of the Women's Rights Movement

The antebellum women's rights movement—which broadly encompassed the drive for improving a woman's conditions within the home, for greater independence from her husband, and for greater control over her children and personhood—arose from several sources. One was evangelical Protestantism, which attracted a disproportionate number of women. Even though male evangelists and preachers led the movement, its redemptive message of spiritual freedom appealed particularly to women. Antebellum evangelicals sought to reform American society as a way to usher in the second coming of Jesus Christ. The moral reform impulse nurtured various benevolent societies committed to spreading the Christian message and addressing immoral behavior: the American Bible Society, the American Tract Society, the American Sunday School Union, and the General Union for the Promotion of the Christian Sabbath, among others. Two causes in particular—abolitionism and temperance—attracted reformed-minded women, and they fueled the early women's rights movement.[4]

The abolition movement arose chiefly from commitments of evangelicals such as Arthur and Lewis Tappan, Theodore Weld, and Charles G. Finney, and then members of the liberal Hicksite Quaker community.[5] Devout women were attracted to abolitionism out of Christian benevolence but also out of a disdain for the slave-masters' "moral degradation" of enslaved women and the parallels that slavery presented to the subordination of women and wives, what some called "the slavery of sex." Also, unlike other moral reform causes, "abolition had an unavoidably political thrust and a tendency to outgrow its evangelical origins." The movement shortly divided between conservative and radical factions, the latter led by William Lloyd Garrison, who had strong anticlerical leanings and supported women's equality, including suffrage. Three early leaders in the suffrage movement, liberal Quakers Lucretia Mott and Lydia Maria Child and Unitarian Lucy Stone, were initially involved in Garrisonian abolitionism. "The actions of the early antislavery women in defending their right to speak out against slavery became the bridge between abolitionism and feminism," writes one scholar. "Though their primary commitment was to abolish slavery, [women] moved surely and inevitably to the realization that the enslavement of human beings took many forms."[6]

Elizabeth Cady Stanton's initial exposure to activism also came through abolitionism. Her close cousin, Gerrit Smith, was a leading abolitionist who radicalized over time, eventually becoming one of the financial backers of John Brown's Harpers' Ferry raid.[7] Her husband, Henry B. Stanton, was an abolitionist of the more conservative Finney school, and the two took their honeymoon by traveling to London in 1840 to attend the World's Anti-Slavery Convention. There, she met Lucretia Mott, who greatly influenced her views on various social issues. "When I first heard from the lips of Lucretia Mott that I had the same right to think for myself that Luther, Calvin, and John Knox had, and the same right to be guided by my own convictions, and would no doubt have a higher, happier life than if guided by theirs, I felt at once a new-born sense of dignity and freedom," Stanton later wrote. When it came to matters of religion, she continued, "[n]othing was too sacred for [Mott] to question, as to its righteousness in principle and practice."[8] Even though Mott and other women attendees had been credentialed by their local abolition societies, the convention leaders refused to recognize the women delegates or allow them to speak, which led William Lloyd Garrison and other radical abolitionists to sit in the balcony with the women in protest. That experience strongly impacted Stanton, who said that the exclusion served as the genesis of the decision to call a women's rights convention back in the United States. "The movement for women's suffrage, both in England and America, may be dated from this World's Anti-Slavery Convention," she wrote.[9]

Early temperance societies likewise arose out of the Protestant reform impulse and were similarly controlled by men. They excluded women from holding significant positions, seeing women's roles as limited to influencing their sons and reforming their husbands. Yet the temperance movement appealed to women not only for moral and religious reasons but also for the way in which men's alcoholism directly affected their families. Increasingly, women objected to the domestic abuse they experienced at the hands of drunken husbands, and then to the financial insecurity that frequently accompanied alcoholism. As moral reformer and senator Henry Blair said, temperance was "a maternal struggle."[10] The refusal of early temperance societies such as the United States Temperance Union and the Sons of Temperance to include women or recognize their unique perspective on the issue led to the formation of an auxiliary to the latter group, called the Daughters of Temperance, in the 1840s. Women's participation in the overall temperance movement, however, remained limited.[11]

Susan B. Anthony, who was also radicalized through abolitionism, became a temperance speaker in the late 1840s, traveling from town to town in upstate New York. Speaking to largely female audiences, Anthony condemned "the great evil of woman's entire dependency upon man for the necessary means to aid on any & every reform movement." In 1852, she helped organize New York's first women's temperance organization out of frustration with women's subservient role in the movement.[12] Elizabeth Cady Stanton became involved in the temperance movement at the same time, speaking at Anthony's Women's State Temperance Society convention that year. Stanton's address was notable because it tied temperance reform to the elevation of women generally: a "new era [was] dawning upon the world," she declared, "when woman, hitherto the mere dependent of man, . . . at length shakes off her lethargy . . . and stands upright in the dignity of a moral being." No woman, she declared, should marry an alcoholic, and further "let no woman remain in the relation of wife with the confirmed drunkard." This meant petitioning state legislatures "to modify the laws affecting marriage [i.e., property and divorce laws] and the custody of children." She concluded her address by criticizing churches and missionary societies for focusing on conversion rather than "devot[ing] [them]selves to the poor and suffering about us." Shortly thereafter, Stanton and Anthony collaborated for the first time by contributing articles to Amelia Bloomer's journal, *The Lily*, which focused on temperance issues and dress reform.[13]

Together, the causes of abolition and temperance, and the male dominance of both movements, served as catalysts for women to consider how each issue affected their status and rights overall. Already, Stanton and Anthony were moving beyond those specific issues to women's rights generally, with Stanton urging her new friend "to let the past be past, and to waste no [more] powder on the Women's State Temperance Society. We have other and bigger fish to fry." That mechanism would be women's suffrage.[14]

The Religious Evolution of Elizabeth Cady Stanton

Because Elizabeth Cady Stanton was the undisputed leader of the women's rights movement for fifty years, a proponent of sexual equality, and a prominent freethinker, her story deserves special attention. Her lifelong commitment to securing full and equal rights for women, including sexual freedom and the right to vote and participate in the political process, cannot be separated from her growing religious radicalism. Increasingly throughout her life, she viewed organized religion and the male-dominated clergy as leading causes of the ongoing subordination of women and impediments to their social, political, and personal freedom. Stanton, as much as any other figure, argued that these issues were intimately connected.[15]

Elizabeth Cady was born into a wealthy and prominent family in upstate New York in 1815. Her father, Daniel Cady, was a lawyer, judge, and strict Presbyterian. Though conservative in politics and conventional in domestic sentiments, Judge Cady recognized and nurtured the intellectual abilities of his third daughter, Elizabeth, ensuring she received instruction in literature, mathematics, languages, and the classics. Elizabeth recalled that her father once reacted to a display of her intellectual acumen by remarking, "Oh my daughter, I wish you were a boy!" In her autobiography, Elizabeth also recounted the rigidity of her religious upbringing, of attending "the cold hospitalities of the 'Lord's House,' there to be chilled to the very core by listening to sermons on 'predestination,' 'justification by faith,' and 'eternal damnation.'" Even at the time, Elizabeth wondered "why it was that everything we like to do is a sin, and everything we dislike is commanded by God or someone on earth." She related with pleasure that her childhood church was later converted into a mitten factory, now occupied by "the pleasant hum of machinery and the glad faces of men and women [who] have chased the [building's] evil spirits to their hiding places."[16]

Prevented from attending Union College with her brothers, Elizabeth enrolled in the Troy Female Seminary near Albany whose director, Emma Willard, nurtured the girls' intellectual abilities. While at Troy, Elizabeth attended a series of revivals conducted by Charles G. Finney, that "terrifier of human souls," whose "preaching worked incalculable harm to the very souls he sought to save," she later wrote. Nonetheless, due to her "gloomy Calvinist training" and her "vivid imagination," she fell under his spell, becoming "one of the first victims." So, a "most innocent girl believed herself a monster of iniquity and felt certain of eternal damnation," she recounted.[17] Elizabeth returned home in religious turmoil, often waking her father "to pray for me, lest I should be cast into the bottomless pit before morning." Alarmed, the family took her on a six-week trip to Niagara Falls, where she discussed rational philosophy with her brother-in-law, Edward Bayard. "Thus after many months of weary wandering in the intellectual labyrinth of 'The Fall of Man,' 'Original Sin,' 'Total Depravity,' 'God's Wrath,' 'Satan's Triumph,' 'The Crucifixion," 'The Atonement,' and 'Salvation by Faith,' I found my way out of the darkness into the clear sunlight of Truth. My religious superstitions gave place to rational ideas based on scientific facts."[18]

The story is a compelling account of Stanton's rejection of religious orthodoxy and embrace of heterodoxy and anticlericalism. It is also likely she embellished matters for effect, as historians have documented that Finney held his revival in Troy four years *before* her matriculation at the Female Seminary, although she apparently attended a later revival in Troy by a Finney acolyte. (Also, since they both lived in upstate New York, it is possible she may have heard Finney on some other occasion.) Whether Stanton invented the account of being rescued from religious fanaticism is less important than her retelling of the episode years hence to explain the genesis of her lifelong religious heterodoxy. The account may also have been a way for Stanton to distinguish and justify her secular vision of reform from the dominant evangelical strain of reform—represented by Finney—that she believed stood as an obstacle to women's equality.[19]

After they returned from the anti-slavery convention in London, the Stantons moved to Boston, where they lived for six years. At the time, Boston was the center of religious liberalism, including Transcendentalism, and Elizabeth became acquainted with the region's intellectuals and reformers: Ralph Waldo Emerson, John Greenleaf Whitter, John Pierpont, James Russell Lowell, Parker Pillsbury, Lydia Maria Child, Wendell Phillips, and Theodore Parker, among others. The intellectually curious Stanton thrived in this milieu, finding herself deeply influenced by "the soothing nature of Mr. Parker's theology." According to a biographer, "Parker's ideas freed Mrs. Stanton from the religious superstitions and fears of her youth. . . . Parker's liberal theology contributed to her self-esteem. Long before she acknowledged political rights or social equity, she had declared her religious independence." From that point Stanton borrowed Parker's practice of referring to God as the "Heavenly Father and Mother."[20]

Finally, in 1848, after moving to Seneca Falls, New York, and after giving birth to three sons, Stanton was able to renew her promise to hold a women's rights convention. Stanton organized the Seneca Falls Convention with Lucretia Mott, Martha Coffin Wright (Mott's younger sister), and Mary Ann McClintock. The other three women were liberal Quakers and, like Stanton, Garrisonian abolitionists. Although Mott remained a committed Hicksite Quaker throughout her life, she comfortably associated with more heterodox groups, attending Garrison's Anti-Sabbath Convention—designed to organize opposition to greater enforcement of Sunday laws—in 1848 and later actively participating in meetings of the Free Religious Association. Martha Wright later became an officer in Stanton and Anthony's National Woman Suffrage Association (NWSA), and, after being expelled from the Society of Friends for marrying a non-Quaker, she became a freethinker.[21]

In addition to planning and advertising the convention, the four women prepared a "Declaration of Rights and Sentiments" to be presented to the attendees for approval. Stanton was the driving force behind the document, which borrowed both language and natural rights theory from the Declaration of Independence. The Declaration of Rights asserted that it was a "self-evident truth" "that all men and women are created equal." Then, following the model of the Declaration of Independence, it set out various grievances: that men had denied women the "first right of a citizen, the elective franchise," had denied her "rights in property" including her own wages, had denied her "the facilities for obtaining a thorough education," had "framed the laws of divorce" to their total advantage, had perpetuated "a different code of morals for men and women," and had otherwise "made her, in the eyes of the law, civilly dead." Significantly, two of the grievances attacked male-dominated organized religion: that men had used religious authority to keep women in "a subordinate position," and that they had "usurped the prerogative of Jehovah himself, claiming it as his right to assign for her a sphere of action" in violation of her own rights of conscience.[22]

When the day of the convention arrived, Stanton read the Declaration to the one hundred-plus attendees. After lively discussion, sixty-eight women and thirty-two men signed the document. The following day, the convention debated a series of resolutions designed to address the grievances laid out in the Declaration. The most contentious resolution, and the only one not adopted unanimously, was the one promoted by Stanton calling for "the sacred right of elective franchise." Mott, being a Quaker and Garrisonian, abstained from participating in politics, so she opposed the suffrage resolution. Others apparently thought that a demand for voting rights would undermine sympathy for the other, less contentious resolutions. Importantly, though, the resolution passed, and suffrage soon became the central issue of women's rights. Surprisingly less contentious were those declarations that implied the church's complicity in subordinating women—asserting that gender equality was "dictated by God himself," and that men had "perverted [the] application of the Scriptures" to maintain their privileged position. Both Mott and Stanton supported these provisions.[23]

Two weeks later, a larger and more diverse group met in nearby Rochester to continue the earlier conversation. The leaders of the Seneca Falls Convention—Stanton, Mott, and McClintock—presented the Declaration of Sentiments and resolutions to the audience. Several men objected to the contents of the documents, declaring that "woman's sphere was the home." During the spirited debate, objectors raised religious arguments against the resolutions, namely, that the Bible "strictly enjoin[ed] obedience to husbands, and that man shall be head of the woman." Both Mott and Stanton responded, declaring that scripture was being misconstrued to benefit men. "[T]he Gospel, rightly understood, points to a oneness of equality, not subordination, and that property should be jointly held," Stanton asserted. "She could see no reason why marriage by false creeds should be made a degradation of women." Later, in summarizing events in the *History of Woman Suffrage*, Stanton noted with disdain how clergy had refuted early arguments for women's rights by "portraying in the darkest colors [in sermons] the fearful results to the Church, the State, and the home, in thus encouraging women to enter public life."[24]

At this stage in her life, Stanton's religious heterodoxy centered on revealing and reforming the corruptions of Christianity that had been perpetuated by male dominance. Neither pure Christianity nor scripture itself was to blame for women's subjugation; "the Bible is the great Charter of human rights, when it is taken in its true spiritual meaning," she declared following the Seneca Falls Convention. Rather, the Bible's "great, immortal, life-giving truths" had been "perverted by narrow, bigoted, sectarian teachers" who used "isolated passages of Scripture, to destroy the conscience and the sense of moral accountability in one half of the people of the earth." Nonetheless, Stanton had taken the initial step of disputing the prevailing Protestant view about the Bible's inerrancy and of its divinely ordained gender roles.[25]

From that point on, her growing religious radicalization paralleled her feminist radicalization. In 1851, Stanton and Anthony met for the first time when the latter was visiting Seneca Falls. The two women quickly connected, drawn to each other by their strong commitments to shared causes that advanced women's interests, but also by their different personalities, which complemented each other. Stanton was more philosophical and gregarious; Anthony more pragmatic and organized.[26] Stanton addressed Anthony's Women's State Temperance Society convention the following year, and then proceeded to make another notable address that same year to a women's rights convention held in Syracuse. That speech, read by Anthony on behalf of a pregnant, home-bound Stanton, urged that the only way that women would achieve social and political equality, and adequate educational opportunity, was through the right to vote. In order to achieve this goal, "[d]oes not the abuse of the religious element in woman demand our earnest attention and investigation?" She then launched into an attack on the clergy. "Priestcraft did not end with the beginning of the reign of Protestantism. Woman has always been the greatest dupe, because the sentiments act blindly, and they alone have been educated in her [by clergymen]. Her veneration, not guided by an enlightened intellect, leads her as readily to the worship of saints, pictures, holy days, and inspired men and books." Stanton maintained that this state of ignorance was perpetuated by "the most distorted views of God and the Bible and the laws of her being; and like the poor slave 'Uncle Tom,' her religion, instead of making her noble and free, [had] by the false lessons of her spiritual teachers . . . made her bondage but more certain and lasting, her degradation more helpless and complete."[27]

Two years later Stanton and Anthony helped organize a "Justice to Women" convention in Albany to coincide with the legislative session. The ostensible goal of the convention was to lobby the legislature for amendments to the women's property acts of 1848 and 1849 that had granted limited property ownership rights to women, but the attendees also petitioned the Assembly to grant a right of suffrage. The convention chose Stanton to testify before the legislature, and she advocated not only for a woman's right to vote, but also to serve on juries, to control her own wages and property, and for custody rights. (As she was to do in many of her early speeches, Stanton equated the legal and social status of married women with that of the enslaved, decrying that women were "classed with idiots, lunatics, and negroes" when it came to rights. A freed male slave, she argued, had more rights than a white woman.) Although she did not expressly call for liberalizing divorce laws, she criticized the religious assumptions underlying marriage, asserting that the institution was not "a Divine relation" but a civil contract which should "be subject to the same laws which control other contracts. Do not make it a kind of half-human, half-divine institution, which you may build up, but can not regulate."[28]

While Stanton never lost sight of the importance of securing women's suffrage, her attack on the religious institution of marriage only intensified in her mid-career. According to one scholar, during this time "she issued a thoroughgoing challenge to the concept of marriage that was based on Christian doctrine as well as on the common law tradition." As Lucy Stone's daughter caustically remarked years later: "Mrs. Stanton was really more interested in attacking orthodox religion than in promoting equal rights for women. In the early woman's rights conventions, she had loved to introduce some ultra-radical resolution that she knew could not pass."[29]

That passion was evident in her address to the 1860 women's rights convention. Several years earlier, the Indiana legislature had liberalized its divorce law, adding cruelty as a ground for divorce and reducing the residency requirement for obtaining one. This led to a celebrated 1860 debate on the issue of divorce reform between Robert Dale Owen, the liberal reformer and Indiana congressman, and Horace Greeley, the quixotic editor of the *New York Tribune*, with the latter calling Indiana a "paradise of free lovers."[30] With a divorce reform bill pending in the New York Assembly, Stanton used her entire address to attack the Christian assumptions of marriage and divorce. The "Divine institution of marriage" provided an excuse for the myriad agonies and indignities that many women suffered at the hands of drunken and abusive husbands. How could such marriages be called sacred, she asked, "where woman, the mother of the race—of a Jesus of Nazareth—unconscious of the true dignity of her nature, of her high and holy destiny, consents to live in legalized prostitution!" So "long as you insist on marriage as a divine institution, as an indissoluble tie, so long as you maintain your present laws against present divorce," Stanton continued, and "you make separation, even, so odious," you condemn women to "a life of concealed misery."[31] Elizabeth Blackwell and Wendell Phillips objected to interjecting the controversial issue of divorce reform into the convention, with Phillips insisting they should concentrate on abolition, temperance, and women's rights. Divorce reform was an "extraneous" issue, he remarked, "which admits so many theories, physiological and religious," and implies "what is technically called free-love."[32] Ernestine Rose came to Stanton's defense, criticizing the ease with which "the very advocacy of divorce will be called 'Free Love'" by those who insist on marriage's divine origins. Marriage was a "human institution," Rose insisted, and "I ask for a law of Divorce, so as to secure the real objects and blessings of married life, to prevent the crimes and immoralities now practiced [under the cover of marriage], [and] to prevent 'Free Love,' in its most hideous form."[33] Stanton and Rose lost the debate and the convention rejected the resolutions, likely due in part to Stanton's and Rose's insistence on tying the inequities of marriage to church doctrine.[34]

At this point in her career, Stanton had not rejected Christianity, nor would she ever fully do so. But her condemnation of the perversion of scripture to subordinate women, and of organized religion, would only become more intense in later years. "The life and teachings of Jesus, all pointing to the complete equality of the human family, were too far in advance of his age to mould public opinion," she would later write. "We must distinguish between the teaching attributed to Jesus and those of the Christian Church." Stanton's beliefs would retain an outward shell of Christian theism, but one that was filled with a growing agnosticism.[35]

The Postwar Controversy over Women's Rights and Marriage Reform

Following the Civil War, Stanton, Anthony, and other women's rights leaders lobbied Congress to include protections for women in the Fourteenth and Fifteenth Amendments, the latter of which secured the right to vote for

Black men. Their efforts failed. Women were excluded from the Fifteenth Amendment, and the language of the Fourteenth Amendment, while granting citizenship and legal protections to "all persons," protected the voting and representation of "male citizens" only, effectively reaffirming the subordinate status of women. Their former abolitionist allies—Wendell Phillips, Frederick Douglass, and even Gerrit Smith—objected to having the issue of woman's suffrage interfere with securing the "negro's hour" in the Constitution. The controversy split the newly formed Equal Rights Association, which had arisen at the end of the Civil War to advocate for greater racial and gender equality. Stanton and Anthony stubbornly refused to endorse the Fifteenth Amendment unless its language was expanded to include women, whereas Lucy Stone and Olympia Brown adopted a more measured approach. Following their defeat, Stanton and Anthony organized the NWSA in 1869 to push for a Sixteenth Amendment to the Constitution to guarantee women's suffrage.[36] For Stanton, at least, the NWSA always had broader goals, including marriage and divorce reform, the separate ownership of property, and fair and equal wages for women. Stanton's and Anthony's uncompromising approach precipitated a split in the women's rights movement, with Lucy Stone and her husband, Henry Blackwell, forming the competing American Woman Suffrage Association (AWSA) later that same year. In contrast to the NWSA, the AWSA included men, and Henry Ward Beecher, Frederick Douglass, and Stephen Foster were all members.[37]

This era saw Stanton radicalize further on religious issues. In the 1860s, she was drawn to Comtean Positivism, which rejected theology and taught that immutable laws governed not only science but also human affairs, with a final stage of development being a "religion of humanity" which promoted a nontheistic religious humanism. Later, Stanton dabbled in Theosophy, attracted to its teaching of essential truths that underlay religion, philosophy, and science. Chiefly, however, Stanton was increasingly drawn to the anticlericalism of religious skepticism. She admired Robert Ingersoll, corresponding and appearing with him occasionally, and she developed a close relationship with the freethinking lecturer B.F. Underwood and his spiritualist wife, Sara Underwood, who co-edited *The Index* following Francis Abbot's resignation. "But for [the Devil]," Stanton wrote jokingly to Benjamin Underwood in 1886, "what would become of our whole theological system[?] . . . 'Original sin,' 'salvation' through faith, the 'judgment seat,' 'everlasting punishment,' all these delightful mythologies, would have been lost without him." In addition to contributing occasional articles to *The Index* and *Freethinkers' Magazine*, Stanton also spoke before freethought groups.[38]

Her strong support for religious free inquiry and church-state separation—she opposed Sunday law enforcement and Bible reading in the public schools, writing that "no books in English literature [were] more unfit reading for young people than those of the Old Testament"—did not necessarily persuade freethought leaders to reciprocate with a strong endorsement of women's suffrage.[39] To be sure, many people within the freethought movement supported women's suffrage among other social reforms. Robert Ingersoll spoke eloquently on behalf of women's equality and suffrage, telling Stanton, "I am in favor of giving every right to women that I claim for myself, and I shall vote to do that if I ever have the chance." Ezra Heywood, D.M. Bennett, Samuel Putnam, and Frederick Douglass also supported women's suffrage, as did Parker Pillsbury, who wrote in Stanton's and Anthony's short-lived journal, *The Revolution*, that "[t]he question of [women's] suffrage is one of justice and right." "Government languishes to-day for the want of virtuous woman's influence and voice."[40] At times, however, freethought leaders expressed reservations about universal suffrage. In 1878, Francis Abbot advised the readers of *The Index* that freethinkers should resist women's suffrage because "the average woman is far more easily influenced by the clergy than the average man." (Abbot's admonition is curious, since in 1877 the National Liberal League had endorsed universal suffrage.) B.F. Underwood also worried initially that "the extension of suffrage to woman would strengthen the political power of Orthodoxy" and might lead to "a revival of restrictive and proscriptive legislation" that freethinkers opposed. These statements, written in 1878 and 1880, respectively, likely indicate both men's concern over the rising power of the WCTU, which had been founded several years earlier. Abbot and Underwood also did not want their freethinking supporters to be detracted from core church-state issues.[41]

Stanton responded by assuring "our liberal friends" that "the religious element of woman's nature [was] sufficiently broad to assure them that these women, armed with ballots, will not prove the dangerous element so many fear on the side of priestcraft and superstition." Although Stanton often asserted that women were naturally inclined to being duped by religious leaders, she also was optimistic that, when "at last emancipated[,] a rapidly increasing class of women" would lose "all fear and respect from such authorities." She also raised a counterargument for *The Index's* readers: "Woman's influence is not less dangerous because it is permitted no expression at the ballot box, but infinitely more so, for, by denying her all interest in politics, you intensify her enthusiasm for the Church." Stanton's persistence apparently brought Underwood and other dubious freethinkers around.[42]

It was during this period that Stanton embraced Victoria Woodhull, drawn to the latter's notoriety and her advocacy for women's rights, including sexual freedom. As discussed, in January 1871, Woodhull had single-handedly secured an invitation to address the House Judiciary Committee on women's suffrage (though the invitation and the substance of her address may have been supplied by Representative Benjamin Butler, an admirer). In her speech, Woodhull developed an argument made previously by Stanton and Virginia Minor that the citizenship clause of the Fourteenth Amendment could be interpreted to guarantee women's suffrage. Both Stanton and Anthony were initially impressed with Woodhull, leading them to invite her to address the NWSA in May 1871. The negative reaction to Woodhull's "Free Love" address in November of that year, however, led to a break between Anthony and Stanton over continued affiliation with Woodhull. By mid-1872, Anthony's position had prevailed, and the erratic Woodhull had moved on to exposing the picadilloes of Henry Ward Beecher.[43]

Stanton's momentary embrace of Woodhull reflected more than a mutual agreement on women's suffrage. She was drawn to—and perhaps deluded by—Woodhull's projection of herself as a capable and independent woman.[44] But Stanton also agreed on some level with Woodhull's promotion of marriage reform and her idea of free love. As discussed, in 1870, the year before they met, Stanton had announced her own version of "the obnoxious doctrine of Free Love," which revealed her increasingly radical ideas about marriage and divorce. In an address to a private audience, she insisted that a marriage founded on mutual respect and an equality of roles was still insufficient if the husband and wife had "abdicated their own individual sovereignty, sinking it in the vortex of marriage." What was needed, Stanton asserted, "is not merely suffrage and civil rights, and not merely in the second place the social recognition of the equal rank of the sexes, though both of these must be had, but Freedom." What this meant was "nothing short of unlimited freedom of divorce, freedom to institute at the option of the parties new amatory relationships, [and] love put above marriage." True freedom and equality thus required removing all legal and social constraints on relationships, she insisted. Although Stanton endorsed monogamy over more open relationships, both were equally valid in her view, for it was "the essence of freedom that it does not attempt to prescribe what the result shall be." Although her position was not as extreme as Woodhull's, Stanton's support for initiating "new amatory relationships" free from legal constraints was, essentially, free love.[45]

In giving the address, Stanton openly challenged "the more timid and conservative elements of female suffrage," most directly Lucy Stone and the members of the AWSA, but she also foretold the future cautious approach to women's rights that would be embodied by Frances Willard and the WCTU. The implications of true women's equality could not be constrained, she declared: "The men and women who are dabbling with the suffrage movement for women should be at once therefore and emphatically warned what they mean logically if not consciously in what they say." The "equality of the sexes" was merely "the first requisite, the first step on the road to social emancipation and social happiness." What was "next [is] social equality, and next Freedom, or in a word Free Love."[46] It is not known whether Anthony heard of Stanton's free love address, but if she did, she likely shuddered over her colleague's candid remarks. Lucy Stone apparently did hear about it, and she accused the latter of "holding free love doctrines," while alleging that the NWSA was infiltrated with "'loose women' and 'free lovers' who intended to make 'easy divorce' a part of their platform." Nonplussed, Stanton remained committed to tying the goal of women's suffrage to reforming the religiously grounded restraints on marriage, divorce, and sexuality.[47]

Stanton reached a national audience with her views in an 1884 article in the *North American Review* titled "The Need of Liberal Divorce Laws." She began by again asserting the inherent equality of men and women: "The normal condition of adult men and women is full independence, of freedom, and of equality." This situation was "the only true basis of a happy home, a united church, a peaceful state, [and] a well-organized society." She then addressed the common objections to liberalized divorce: that people would enter into marriage recklessly, knowing it could be easily dissolved; that it would "break up all family relations" which were sacred; that "unprincipled men" would abandon their wives; that it would cause greater harm to children than living under a broken marriage; and that "the Bible is against divorce." None of these arguments considered the standpoint of wives who existed in "a condition of slavery" at the hands of "tyrannical husbands," Stanton insisted. As for the scriptural argument against divorce, she retorted: "When those who are opposed to all reforms can find no other argument, their last resort is the

Bible." She chided men who quoted scripture to deny women their equality and independence: "[b]efore claiming that marriage is a divine institution, before binding women by further restrictive legislation, let the high-priests at the family altars purify themselves." Though pointed, the article was less explosive than her other writings and speeches in that it did not discuss sexual freedom or free love. But it was consistent with her other works in attributing women's subjugation within marriage to organized religion and the clergy. Both men and the church had perverted the "central truth, taught by that great founder of our religion," of "the sacredness of the individual."[48]

"Divorce Mania"

The growing division within the women's rights movement over marriage and divorce reform was but part of a larger controversy over the availability of divorce.[49] The liberalization of divorce laws by a handful of states, including Indiana and Connecticut, combined with an acceleration of the divorce rate following the Civil War, served as a wake-up call for religious and social conservatives.[50] According to one report, the divorce rate in Connecticut before the Civil War had been approximately one divorce for every thirty-five marriages; by 1878, it had increased to one in ten. Other states experienced similar increases. The report's author pointed to the growing incidences of fraud and collusion in many divorce proceedings, and attempted to find a correlation between the increase in divorces to a rise in illegitimate births and alcohol consumption. The report concluded that after "an extended and careful inquiry" there was "a strong probability that the period marked by the increase in divorces has witnessed a serious growth of many more dangerous forms of licentiousness." In essence, the availability of divorce fueled those same vices that Anthony Comstock battled. Comstock made the same connection, decrying "easy divorce" and "the disgusting revelations of marital infelicity" as contributing to the destruction of family life and to the rise in juvenile delinquency.[51]

The postwar rise in divorces alarmed clergy and religious commentators, with many conflating the threats of divorce, free love, freethought, and the destruction of the family. "At a time when skeptics, spiritualists, and free-lovers are inculcating the most licentious doctrines concerning marriage and divorce, it may be well for us to recur the teachings of God's word on this subject," wrote a contributor to *The Independent*. "We must not forget," the *Reformed Church Messenger* added, supplying the answer to *The Independent*'s query, "that marriage is a Divine institution—that it was ordained by the Almighty, and by Him alone." So "when the Legislature grants divorce contrary to the Divine law of marriage, and gives courts the power to do the same," they not only "destroy the whole conception of marriage," but "God is no longer the sovereign." "Marriage is not, then, as we too often hear, a civil contract," echoed *The Ladies' Repository*, "but a Divine ordinance, and 'what God has joined together, let no man put asunder.'"[52] Catholic journals also railed against the growing availability of divorce. The "frequency and facility with which divorces are obtained" was the "bane of the day," opined *Catholic World* in 1877, and "if not checked" will lead to "the ruin of the family" and the instigation of "socialism, communism, and free love." "[D]ivorce and free-love are not only incompatible with true morality," opined another Catholic journal, "but wherever they are, the atmosphere is far from pure."[53]

Religious figures also tied the upsurge in divorces to the threat of polygamy, that second "relic of barbarism" after slavery. "Scriptural marriage is at this time, and in this country, subject to severe strain," warned *Zion's Herald* in 1881. "Mormons practice polygamy and spiritualism flaunts its free love. Still more serious is the fact that civil courts decree divorces in large numbers and for slight causes." The *American Catholic Quarterly Review* concurred that "Divorce is, in reality, nothing but successive polygamy or polyandry, as the case may be.... It is a sheer mockery to talk about morality alongside of divorce; it is a mere play of words to acknowledge divorce, but to disown polygamy." Both practices destroyed the Christian ideal of marriage and undermined its sanctity. And the specter of free love stood in the shadows. Time and again, commentators used the bogeyman of polygamy to tarnish arguments for divorce reform.[54]

Legal commentators also began issuing warnings about the potential disruption to domestic relations, law, and family stability by expanding grounds for divorce and granting independent property rights to married women. The two most prominent commentators on this topic were James Schouler and Joel Prentis Bishop, both of whom wrote general treatises on domestic relations law that were published in the 1870s. Both authors criticized the liberalizing trend in granting divorces; the presumption in the law should be to uphold every marriage, Bishop insisted. Both writers also embraced the religious basis for marriage and prevailing Christian views about divorce. Schouler boldly asserted, "we may clearly trace in the New Testament writings an intent to bring into prominence the moral obligation of the marriage state, to discontinuance of lax and immoral unions, and to warn the legislator that those whom God hath joined many may not with impunity be put asunder." Bishop, more cautiously, declared that religious considerations could not govern civil divorce. Yet that fact did not mean people could not consider the effect of divorce on morality and social stability. He agreed that marriage was "intended to be for life, that only in the most extreme circumstances should it be dissolved"; it was "too sacred to be made a matter of temporary arrangement."[55]

Schouler also criticized the enactment of laws that "aim to secure to the wife the independent control of her own property, and the right to contract, to sue and be sued, without her husband." In addition to altering the long-standing common law rule of coverture, in which the legal identity of a husband and wife merged (the latter into the former), it portended a "sweeping reform . . . [of] conjugial duties" and social relationships. "The danger to be apprehended from all legislation of this sort is that it will weaken the ties of marriage by forcing both sexes into an unnatural antagonism; teaching them to be independent of one another, and to earn their own living apart; whereas God's law points to family and the mutual intercourse of man and woman as among the strongest safeguards of human happiness."[56] Bishop was less troubled by the new property laws, arguing that because they chiefly allowed women to retain ownership over property they brought into a marriage, they did not alter the marriage relationship or significantly affect coverture. Bishop also supported additional grounds for divorce beyond adultery: extreme cruelty, desertion, habitual drunkenness, and imprisonment; but "[b]eyond this line we come to grounds uncertain and shadowy." Even though Bishop conceded that those were legitimate grounds for divorce, he back-tracked by declaring that there was always a third-party interest in divorce proceedings: the public. He argued that the public had a stake in every divorce, not just to protect children and preserve the integrity of property interests, but to uphold morality and the institution of marriage per se, factors that judges should weigh against any additional grounds, even if the husband and wife agreed to a divorce. Schouler's and Bishop's exhaustive treatises reinforced the presumed dangers in liberalizing divorce laws and provided conservative judges ready arguments for narrowly interpreting any such laws.[57]

Another leading voice in the controversy over divorce was Timothy D. Woolsey, president of Yale College, who was trained in both the ministry and the law. Woolsey was a fierce opponent of expanding the grounds for divorce beyond adultery and "malicious desertion," and he effectively interwove statistics with legal and religious arguments to attack the liberalizing trend. Woolsey argued that out of all immoral and sexually related offenses—adultery, prostitution, and even rape, incest, and infanticide—divorce was the most deleterious to society because it was legal, prevalent, and increasingly accepted. It, more than any of the others, undermined the sanctity of marriage and threatened the security of Christian society.[58]

The re-evaluation of marriage relationships and liberalization of divorce grounds thus represented a major assault on the central institution of Christian society. Church leaders and religious commentators took up the issue with a vengeance; during the final third of the century, leading denominations—Episcopalians, Methodists, Presbyterians—reaffirmed their opposition to divorce by forbidding their clergy from officiating remarriages. Divorce also became both a proxy and a cudgel for opposing many aspects of the women's rights movement, particularly against reformers, like Stanton, who professed heterodox religious beliefs. Religious conservatives regularly conflated the various threats—women's suffrage, marriage and divorce reform, free love, and religious skepticism—in their battle for cultural hegemony.[59]

One notable commentator who emphasized the interrelated threats was Orestes A. Brownson, the former Transcendentalist turned conservative Catholic who edited the influential *Brownson's Quarterly Review*. At the time of the NWSA's founding, Brownson had declared, "We say frankly in the outset that we are decidedly opposed to female suffrage and eligibility."[60] In a later, more detailed commentary, titled "Women's Suffrage: The Reform against Nature," Brownson attacked Stanton and Anthony by name—even though Brownson had befriended Stanton during his Transcendentalist days in Boston—accusing the suffrage movement of a host of evils. The "woman's rights movement means the enfranchisement of the wife from subjection to her husband, and is therefore a revolt against the marriage relation itself, as instituted by the Creator," he insisted. "Indeed the whole movement is a movement for the abolition of Christian law, and of Christianity itself." Divorce, Brownson maintained, was a "Satanic doctrine" contrary to all Christian teaching. Brownson also denied that women were subordinated through marriage; the institution of marriage was neither oppressive nor "imposed by the male sex" but "expresse[d] the will and the reason of the Supreme Lawgiver," and therefore the "indissolubility of marriage" affected men and women equally. Mincing few words, Brownson declared that "[t]he advocates of woman's suffrage and eligibility are moved principally, whether men or women, by a desire to abolish Christian marriage and introduce in its place what is called FREE-LOVE. The whole movement, disguise it as we will, is a free-love movement." Suffrage, infidelity, divorce, and free love were all intertwined.[61]

Protestant commentators made similar connections to women's suffrage. Writing in the *Reformed Church Messenger* in 1883, the Reverend Cyrus Court declared that "the female suffrage movement is hostile in its very nature to the true idea of marriage." That "true idea" of marriage was, of course, divinely ordained, but "advocates of woman suffrage . . . throw contempt upon the Scriptural idea of man's headship in the family and in the Church, and upon the sanctity and inviolability of marriage, which is the basis and bond of society itself." The threat to Christian marriage was more than an indirect consequence of women's suffrage, however; the movement was led by "a large body of free-thinkers and humanitarian reformers, who heartily advocate woman suffrage as sort of a cure-all for the body politic." (On this point, Stanton likely agreed with Reverend Court.) Court also attacked Anthony directly for reputedly claiming "that the Bible and Church were opposed to all progress and reform." "All distinctions of sex may be ignored and removed from our statute books by radical visionaries who despise the teachings of history and the Bible, but the Almighty has made those distinctions for wise purposes," Court exclaimed. "If the divine arrangement is subverted, the foundations of society themselves will soon be out of joint." Absent from Court's critique was the common accusation that liberalized divorce would lead to free love, but he supplanted that by charging that suffrage would cause women to abandon their maternal duties, resulting in abortion and infanticide.[62]

The Reverend Joseph Cook expanded on Court's claims in one of his popular Boston Monday Lectures. The "evils of loose and frequent divorce" arose not only from women's rights advocates but from the "influx of half-educated, or illiterate immigrant populations (e.g., Catholics), who mistake American liberty for license," Cook charged in a March 1884 lecture. With immigrants having been exposed to the loose morality of Europe, "many of them become Infidels" upon settling in America, where they aligned with "obscure and infamous infidel organizations [that] favor loose divorce laws and advocate doctrines which undermine the permanence of the family and the sanctity of the home." Thus, for Cook, one leading cause for "loose divorce" beyond women's rights was "Infidelity, the poisonous doctrine of free love and liberal leagues and various propagandists of immorality."[63]

The campaign against divorce reform only intensified in the closing decades of the century. To combat laws that allowed people to find favorable venues for obtaining a divorce, opponents called for national legislation to impose uniform rules consistent with conservative Christian values. Presaging the growing problem in his 1870 treatise, James Schouler had proposed that "[s]o loose, indeed, and confusing is our local marriage and divorce legislation becoming, that it might be well to ask whether the cause of morality would not be promoted, if, by constitutional amendment, the whole subject were placed under the control of the national government."[64] In 1881, Theodore D. Woolsey joined with Vermont Congregational minister Samuel W. Dike in forming the New England Divorce Reform League to lobby for enacting legal restrictions on divorce. As president of the League, Dike took on the cause as a crusade; although he stopped short of seeking to abolish divorce entirely, he advocated limiting divorce to the sole scripturally sanctioned ground of adultery. Dike and his League experienced measured success in convincing several northeastern states to tighten their divorce laws. Four years later, the organization became the National Divorce Reform League. Its ultimate goal was securing either congressional legislation or a constitutional amendment to nationalize grounds for divorce. Joseph Cook, who boasted about his close friendship with Anthony Comstock, eagerly endorsed a constitutional amendment, but Samuel Dike realized that Southern legislators would oppose any legislation by citing states' rights (and out of a concern that any federal action might interfere with state anti-miscegenation laws).[65]

As an initial step, in 1884 Dike mounted a campaign for Congress to authorize a national study on divorce, believing it would strengthen his case for uniformity. Three years later, Congress directed the US Bureau of Labor to collect data on divorces and make recommendations regarding any possible uniformity in divorce laws. When released in 1889, the report revealed a rising divorce rate but, disappointingly for Dike, that interstate migration was not a significant factor in that rise, which undercut Dike's argument for the need for national uniformity in the laws. Because of the wide divergence among the states regarding eligibility for marriage and grounds for divorce, the report's findings were inconclusive.[66] Still, religious conservatives hailed the report as substantiating the growing threat to the Christian ideal of marriage and the family. Aside from the report's conclusions, wrote a columnist for *Bedford's*

Monthly, "a very strong argument is made that—even waiving the Divine sanction of marriage in which most people in this country still believe, and the Divine prohibition on divorce, except for one cause—the greatest good to our people, as a whole, is found in maintaining the strictest sanctity and indissolubility of the marriage relation."[67]

Significantly, religious opposition to liberalizing divorce laws—or at least a concern over the rising divorce rate—was not limited to conservatives. Belief in the centrality of marriage to family stability was widely shared. Lyman Abbott, a religious moderate and successor to Henry Ward Beecher at Brooklyn's Plymouth Congregational Church, fell back on the traditional argument that marriage was of "a divine order." Marriage, he asserted, was "the foundation of the State, or the Church, of society" and must be protected at all costs. Felix Adler of the Ethical Culture Society, an atheist, agreed that divorce menaced "the physical and spiritual existence of the human race." And in an 1889 symposium conducted in the *North American Review* following the Bureau of Labor's report, several female panelists blamed the increased divorce rate on women for being selfish and unrealistic about the requisites of matrimonial relationships. Because marriage involved the domestic sphere over which women exercised significant control, asserted one author, "[s]peaking broadly, women were to blame" for unsuccessful marriages. For many people, ingrained ideas about the sanctity of marriage and of appropriate gender roles transcended their possible religious origins. This made achieving divorce reform much more difficult.[68]

Elizabeth Cady Stanton responded to the Bureau of Labor's report in an 1890 article, "Divorce versus Domestic Warfare." The title succinctly stated Cady Stanton's view of the stark alternatives that women in dysfunctional marriages faced. She insisted that the question of divorce should be left to the states, to allow for greater experimentation. She lampooned the current "panic … [that] the foundations of our social life [will] be swamped in the quicksands of liberal divorce laws." On the contrary, she asserted, the "increasing number of divorces, so far from showing a lower state of morals, proves exactly the reverse. Woman is in a transition from slavery to freedom and she will not accept the conditions in married life that she has heretofore meekly endured." As she was apt to do, Stanton blamed organized Christianity for perpetuating women's subordination in marriage and for standing in the way of true divorce reform. "The Christian doctrine of marriage, as propounded by Paul in the seventh chapter of Corinthians, degrades alike the woman and the relation," she insisted. Regrettably, "[t]his influence still pervades our laws, corrupts our thoughts, and demoralizes our customs." As a result, she continued, it was "folly to talk of the sacredness of marriage, and maternity, where the wife is practically regarded as an inferior, a subject, a slave."[69]

Stanton never wavered in her belief in the interrelatedness of suffrage and liberalized divorce for achieving women's equality. Until the end of her life she remained the most prominent advocate of this confluence, even though she knew it divided the suffrage movement as well as the larger women's reform movement, which included the WCTU. Stanton summed up her unyielding position in her 1898 autobiography: "The question of divorce, like marriage, should be settled, as to its most sacred relations, by the parties themselves; neither the State nor the Church having any right to intermeddle therein. As to property and children, it must be viewed and regulated as a civil contract. Then the union should be dissolved with at least as much deliberation and publicity as it was formed." It was "folly to talk of the sacredness of marriage," she reiterated, while the wife was "regarded as an inferior." That situation could not "be called a holy relation."[70]

The Woman's Christian Temperance Union and the Limits to Reform

Elizabeth Cady Stanton's insistence on tying women's rights to marriage and divorce reform, and her harsh critique of institutional Christianity—ideas that Susan B. Anthony shared but did not actively promote—attracted only a small proportion of those women who chafed under the rigid gender roles of the Victorian era. While an increasing number of women desired greater freedom and security, most did not seek to challenge the institution of marriage or the assumptions about the appropriate roles of husbands and wives. Many of these chiefly middle-class, Protestant women found an outlet in the WCTU.[71]

Women had been attracted to the temperance cause for decades—Anthony had been involved during the 1850s—but the creation of a national, women's run temperance organization was spontaneous. Arising almost overnight in late 1873, women, fed up with the proliferation of saloons and the increase in male drunkenness following the Civil War, mounted a grassroots campaign in New York and Ohio to close saloons, using picketing and prayer. The movement, soon called the Women's Crusade, spread quickly throughout the

Midwest and met with measured, though temporary, success. The intensity of the Crusade could not be maintained for long, and while the militancy subsided within a year, the issue of temperance remained. In November 1874, veterans of the Crusade and other activists met in Cleveland and organized the WCTU.[72]

Initially, under the leadership of its first president, Annie Wittenmyer, the WCTU adopted a cautious approach, focusing on education and persuasion rather than political tactics. Wittenmyer also sought to centralize control over the movement and the WCTU's state and local affiliates. Disagreement among members over both restrictions led to the replacement of Wittenmyer by Frances E. Willard in 1879.[73] Willard, who served as president until her death in 1898, expanded the WCTU's membership and its agenda. Her broader vision tied temperance to other reforms that benefited women, starting modestly by advocating for a "Home Protection" ballot that would authorize women to vote on liquor-related issues that affected the home.[74] As president, she also promoted what she called the "Do-Everything Policy" to address the overall betterment of women and the family, an agenda that included labor and prison reform, health care, and child protection. Willard came to support women's suffrage in general, with the WCTU adopting a suffrage resolution in 1881 based on the rationale that it would give women greater control over their homelife. As Willard remarked on more than one occasion, a "Woman's vote is the highway to home protection and humanity's release," and "through equal suffrage women will help protect the both the external and internal interests of the home." Suppressing the liquor trade, however, remained the primary rationale for women's suffrage: "We want the ballot because the liquor traffic is entrenched in law, and the law grows out of the will of majorities." Under Willard's charismatic leadership, the WCTU attracted scores of conservative, Christian women, growing in membership from 27,000 in 1879 to some 200,000 by 1900, ten times larger than Stanton's and Anthony's NWSA.[75]

Despite the WCTU's proto-feminist agenda, the organization remained both conservative and *Christian* (though scholars have observed that Willard was likely more progressive than the membership).[76] Women needed the vote— at least as Willard explained it—not to advance women's rights overall, but to ensure home protection and enhance women's preeminent roles as moral exemplars. According to one scholar, "Willard recruited members with an ideology that invoked the Bible as its primary authority, defined motherhood as a qualification for political participation, and insisted upon political involvement as the fulfillment of women's God-given roles."[77] Additionally, under Willard's leadership, the WCTU aligned itself with various conservative Christian causes: it supported Sabbath observance through laws requiring closing of shops and preventing amusements, urged restrictions on Sunday railroad travel, and went so far as petitioning Congress to abolish Sunday mail. Most WCTU members also opposed liberalizing divorce standards, with the Union adhering to the traditional Christian view that adultery was the only valid ground for divorce. Willard, herself unmarried, expressed more openness to measured marriage reforms, endorsing raising the legal age of consent to eighteen years for women, and a greater ambivalence about strict divorce laws. With her support, the WCTU passed a cautious resolution in 1895 declaring that "the question of divorce is of equal importance to men and women" and calling for women to be included in any official commissions charged with revising such laws, so as "to ensure justice." Finally, Willard insisted that women exercise equal control over family income and have the right to refuse sexual relations with their husbands, drunken or not.[78]

The most significant religious cause adopted by the WCTU, however, was its "Social Purity" campaign. Begun in 1877, it initially concentrated on combatting prostitution. In 1883, Willard and the WCTU expanded the idea of "Home Protection" beyond addressing drunken and abusive husbands and fathers to embrace a larger concept of moral social purity. As described by one of its originators, social purity "work[ed] for the sanctity of the family—for the purity of the home—for the inviolability of marriage—for the honor of women—[and] for the innocence of children." "The same standard of morality must be uplifted for both sexes, since this is God's standard."[79] That year, the WCTU established the Department for the Suppression of Social Evil, changing its name two years later to Department of Social Purity to emphasize positive measures to address moral purity, in part encouraging men and boys to treat women with respect and maintain sexual purity, which included avoiding pornography as well as prostitution. The WCTU asked people to take what Willard called the "White Shield" pledge. According to Willard, its purpose was: "To maintain the law of purity as equally binding upon men and women"; "to discourage the association and marriage of pure young women with corrupt young men"; and "to educate and train all young people who are under my control or guardianship in these principles, and to use all possible means to promote the purity of our homes."[80]

One aim of the Department of Social Purity was to protect children from crime literature, but it expanded to include the suppression of other forms of immoral literature, art, and performances.[81] As a result, the WCTU generally supported Anthony Comstock's anti-obscenity crusade, including outlawing the advertising or mailing of contraceptives or abortifacients. Comstock, in turn, considered the WCTU to be a close ally—"[t]hey are the noblest women in the country," he effused—and he occasionally spoke at Union events. He saw a direct overlap between their corresponding agendas: "Wherever you find a brothel you find a bar," he proclaimed at the WCTU's 1885 convention. And "wherever you find an intemperate man you find an unclean one."[82] As he was inclined to do, Comstock overstated his influence on the Union's agenda. Speaking at a public meeting of the Department of Social Purity in 1894, Comstock bragged: "[a]s for this particular branch of the[ir] work, I feel it was taken up to a great extent through my efforts. I sent a very strong letter to Miss Willard . . . and since then they have been carrying on the campaign vigorously. I assist them in every way possible, and keep them posted on the details of the law referring to the different lines of work." Comstock's self-aggrandizing zealotry was apparently off-putting to some WCTU members, and despite some overlap, their agendas did not directly align. As one scholar has noted, the WCTU's program was broader than simple censorship—reporting obscene materials to legal authorities was not the primary goal of its purity in literature campaign; rather, it sought to educate men and boys and then to compete with immoral material by publishing its own "pure" magazines for children. Comstock's practical influence on the WCTU's agenda was limited. Still, the WCTU's campaign against immoral literature provided additional legitimacy for Comstock's moral crusade.[83]

Frances Willard's conservative social activism was also evident in her alignment of the WCTU with the Prohibition Party. Established in 1869 by Protestant clergy and attracting social reformers such as Justice Salmon Chase, Gerrit Smith, and John Russell, the party advocated for stricter alcohol restrictions and a prohibition amendment to the US Constitution. Aside from regularly nominating candidates for president and vice president under its banner, the party also endorsed a silver currency standard, the direct election of senators, and universal suffrage for men and women of all races.[84] Despite some shared causes, Willard initially kept the WCTU independent from any political party, but by 1882 she sought a merger between the Union's "home protection clubs" and the party, temporarily creating the Prohibition Home

Protection Party. Even though an official merger never transpired, Willard increasingly aligned the WCTU interests with the agenda of the Prohibitionists, speaking regularly at party gatherings.[85]

Aside from temperance and suffrage, the Prohibition Party also agreed with the WCTU on a host of Christian moral reform issues. Its platforms decried the "desecration of the Sabbath" and called for greater Sunday law enforcement, including enacting a national Sabbath law. The party also supported continuing prayer and Bible reading in the public schools and insisted on maintaining "the Christian law of marriage and divorce." And, revealingly, the party affirmed "Almighty God as the rightful sovereign . . . from whom the just powers of government are derived and to whose laws human enactments should conform as an absolute condition" (1884), and that "Almighty God [was] the supreme source of all government [and] that this republic was founded upon Christian principles" (1900), statements that aligned it, or many of its members, with the National Reform Association's efforts to secure an amendment to the Constitution recognizing the authority of God. Most of these positions received the support of Willard and the rank-and-file membership of the WCTU.[86]

The various causes that the WCTU advanced thus revealed a strong Christian orientation. Most WCTU members were evangelical women who had not previously taken part in reform movements. They opposed drinking because they considered it to be a sin, though a sizable number also opposed it because of the domestic problems it created for women because of their drunken, abusive, and neglectful husbands—thus, their attraction to the broader agenda of Home Protection. The Union's slogan, "For God, for Home, and Native Land," represented the interconnectedness of the issues that centered around God.[87] Willard, herself an evangelical Methodist, also viewed temperance through the lenses of sinfulness and home protection, and she regularly used religious terminology and justifications in her speeches. The "most sacred significance" of the Union's work, she declared, was to achieve the "tremendous evolution of the Christian ideal of home. Ours is a high and sacred calling."[88] At the same time, however, Willard apparently perceived little conflict between her devout faith and her purported lesbian relationships with other temperance activists. Overall, the Union's more measured and conservative version of reform appealed to a greater number of reform-oriented women and undercut support for the broader agenda of the NWSA.[89]

Collaboration and Compromise

Even before the WCTU endorsed women's suffrage in 1881, Susan B. Anthony had made overtures to Frances Willard, who was already on record in support. Anthony quickly recognized the advantages of working on suffrage with the larger WCTU, and her earlier work on temperance issues naturally drew her to their signature cause.[90] Willard's "Do Everything" program advocating labor reform, child protection, and dress reform also appealed to Anthony. Over the next two decades, Anthony spoke occasionally at Union conventions and rallies, though she generally limited her remarks to their shared interest in women's suffrage. A pragmatist as well as a strategist, Anthony was willing to look beyond the WCTU's religious agenda. On one instance, however, Anthony advised Willard against aligning with the Prohibition Party, despite their affirmative stance on women's suffrage, apparently concerned that the party's religious platform would appeal to the conservative membership of the Union and take the women's reform movement in the wrong direction. As Anthony remarked to a colleague, "some of our [NWSA] women oppose Prohibition and then hate that party because its leaders are, so many of them, working to put God in the Constitution."[91]

Stanton and other radical suffragettes like Joslyn Gage and Olympia Brown, an ordained Universalist minister, were less sanguine about working with the Union—or outwardly hostile to the idea. Gage declared the WCTU to be "[t]he great dangerous organization of the [women's] movement," and she called Frances Willard, with "her desire to introduce religious tests into the government, . . . the most dangerous person upon the American continent to-day."[92] Stanton also criticized the WCTU's religious agenda, telling Olympia Brown that "the church is the most powerful influence to-day in perpetuating the bondage of women. Those who advocate both temperance and woman suffrage should be consistent and carry out their principles just as fully into the religious sects as they do into the political parties."[93] Stanton bemoaned the conservatism of the younger generation of suffragettes, speculating with Gage about whether to create a new organization "that will be free to discuss religious and social questions. The suffrage movement languishes to-day because the new-comers and many of the old ones are afraid to take the advance step" but were content about "revising their Bibles, Prayer Books, catechisms, creeds and disciplines." "You cannot arouse enthusiasm any longer on the old lines," that is, progressive reform issues.[94]

Though they generally agreed on most issues, Stanton and Gage differed over the extent of the threat represented by the Prohibition Party's religious agenda. Despite the party's endorsement of universal suffrage, Gage could not get past the group's regressive religious platform. She criticized the party's support for uniform—and restrictive—Sabbath and divorce laws and its acknowledgment of God as the authority for all civil institutions. "With great inconsistency, while placing suffrage with the states, the Prohibitionists wish 'the Sabbath,' 'polygamy,' 'marriage and divorce,' to come under national law." "I could never work with the Prohibitionists," Gage declared, and she noted that several WCTU state chapters had adopted the party's platform as their own. One thing "which makes this party one of extreme danger is the W.C.T.U., upon which the Prohibition party depends its success."[95]

Surprisingly, Stanton took a more ambivalent view of the Prohibition Party than either Gage or Anthony. Initially, in 1884, Stanton had joined with Anthony in advising NWSA members against supporting the Prohibition Party. They suspected that the party supported women's suffrage merely as a means to secure prohibition: "Prohibition could not secure woman suffrage, but woman suffrage is the only power by which prohibition could be made possible." They also warned members that the party supported "the recognition of God in the constitution."[96] Four years later, however, in an article for the WCTU's journal, the *Union Signal*, Stanton gave the party a qualified endorsement. Unlike the two major political parties, the Prohibitionists alone were on record for women's suffrage, she wrote, and "[n]o women with proper self-respect can longer kneel at the feet of the Republican Party." (The latter statement was an oblique jab at Anthony, who openly supported the Republican Party.) For some reason, Stanton no longer believed that the Prohibitionists' religious agenda was practicable or represented a real threat. "The Prohibition platform foreshadows none of these dangers," she wrote. Only after "justice, liberty, and equality are secured to all the human family [via the vote], then, and not till then, will the essential elements of the Godhead be found in the Constitution." The article represented a rare instance in which Stanton was willing to place her goal of achieving women's suffrage above the larger issues affecting women's rights.[97]

Aside from an occasional article, however, Stanton generally avoided associating with the WCTU, though she did appear on the platform with

Willard at events such as the International Council of Women and the Woman's National Council.[98] Anthony's willingness to work with the WCTU caused tension between her and Stanton and Gage; writing to Olympia Brown in 1889, Anthony remarked, "I am not as intolerant of the 'so-called' Church women as are they . . . I do not approve of their system of fighting the religious dogmas of the people I am trying to convert to my doctrine of equal rights to women. But if they can afford to distrust my religious integrity, I can afford to let them." Anthony continued to speak at WCTU events throughout the 1890s, convinced that she could be a moderating influence on Union members while buttressing their support for women's suffrage. She was less than successful on either matter, as the overall women's rights movement, increasingly led by the WTCU, continued down a conservative path.[99]

Final Radicalization

The last two decades of the century witnessed the final transition in Stanton's religious views, which not only radicalized further, but took on a more prominent role in her overall perspective on reform.[100] In 1879, Stanton delivered a speech before a large audience at the Union Methodist Church in St. Louis, Missouri, titled "The Bible and Woman's Suffrage." Although conventional in many respects—the speech employed biblical passages to support suffrage rather than criticizing the Bible's misogynist shortcomings—the speech also revealed her growing frustration with the Bible. Clergy remained the primary problem, for sure; even though "the spirit and principle of the Bible teach justice, mercy and equality, narrow minds [i.e., clergy] uniformly dwell on the letter and misquote and misapply isolated texts of Scripture." She highlighted those parts of the Bible that promoted gender equality and praised those heroines—Deborah, Ruth, Naomi, Esther, and Vashti, among others—known for their independence and resilience. She urged the audience to reject "the puerile arguments of those who quote the Bible for woman's subjection." In other places, however, she invited her listeners to consider that the Bible itself might be the problem. The advancement "of civilization must outweigh the authority of parchments, however venerable and revered," she declared. "When Science [i.e., rational advancement] and Scripture stand opposed, the latter must suffer." Paraphrasing Frederick Douglass's statement, "Prove to me that the Bible sanctions slavery . . . I would, if possible, make a bonfire of every

Bible in the universe," Stanton remarked: "Prove that the Bible sanctions and teaches the universal subjection of woman to man as a principle of social order, and we should be compelled to repudiate its authority and do all in our power to weaken its hold on popular thought."[101]

Whether the Union Methodist address was the genesis of Stanton's most ambitious project—to undertake a revision of the Bible to reflect a woman's perspective—it coincided with two events that may have spurred her thinking in that direction. In 1871, religious historian Philip Schaff had assembled a group of conservative theologians to prepare a revision of the Old and New Testaments. The goal of the American Revising Committee was to address and rebut the threats to biblical authority presented by Darwinism, Higher Criticism, and Freethought, among other nemeses, by correcting perceived errors that existed within the King James Bible. When it was released in 1881, the Revised Bible caused a stir, with critics on the right and left finding fault with the revisions. Evangelicals such as Reverends Thomas DeWitt Talmage and W.C. Doane blasted the "needless changes" to the King James version, while Catholics criticized the entire idea of biblical revision.[102] Because the revisions did nothing to address the misogyny in scripture, Stanton believed that the entire effort was a missed opportunity to correct those errors. "There were hopes that in the last revision of the New Testament justice might at last be done woman and her equality with man clearly brought out," she commented upon its release, "but they did nothing, and still kept woman in a position that has taken away from her herself-respect." She was increasingly convinced that the Bible was problematic for women's rights, particularly when it was in the hands of men.[103]

Around the same time, in 1880, Stanton, Anthony, and Gage joined together to begin work on an arduous project—preparing a multivolume account of the women's rights movement, *History of Woman Suffrage*, containing the more important speeches, documents, and commentary going back to the Seneca Falls Convention. The collaboration would culminate in five volumes between 1881 and 1922, with Stanton dropping out as an editor after the third volume.[104] The first two volumes, both published in 1881, reproduced a handful of Stanton's addresses critical of religion, such as her 1852 letter to the Syracuse Convention. More importantly, the publication of the first two volumes coincided with a further turn in her religious beliefs, or at least an additional refinement in her opinion about the Bible, Christianity, and organized religion.[105]

Possibly influencing that turn, volume one of *History* included an essay by Gage titled "Woman, Church, and State," which offered a detailed account of the Christian Church's theological subjugation of women in collaboration with civil officials. For fifteen hundred years, Gage wrote, the Christian Church had promoted the doctrine of women's original sin, which "lies at the base of the religious and political disqualifications of woman" and "has been interpreted as sustaining man's rights alone." "The minds of people having been corrupted through centuries by Church doctrines regarding women, it was an easy step for the state to aid in her degradation." Gage tracked the integration of canon law into civil law to control marriage, divorce, inheritance, property ownership, and guardianships, culminating in the doctrine of coverture. The church and the state, acting in collusion, then used witchcraft persecutions to perpetuate the subordination of women. Gage concluded that nothing had changed over the centuries within church doctrine and little had improved within the law. "The Christianity of to-day thus continues to teach the existence of a superior and an inferior sex within the Church, possessing different rights, and held accountable to a different code of morals."[106] Gage's harsh critique held little back in its condemnation of both church and state. The essay was, in many respects, more damning of religion's subjugation of women than anything Stanton had written so far. Whether it influenced Stanton's attitudes about religion, it at least reinforced them; Stanton would rely on Gage's documentation and arguments in her future writings on religion. Gage, in turn, expanded her essay into a book, published by *The Truth Seeker* in 1893.[107]

Following the publication of the first two volumes of *History* in 1881, Stanton traveled to Europe, spending eighteen months with her daughter Harriot and son Theodore, who lived in England and France, respectively. While in England, she associated with religious radicals, including Reverend Moncure D. Conway; Stanton delivered a sermon at his freethinking church titled "What Has Christianity Done for Woman." She spent considerable time preparing the sermon, later concluding that the experience had been an epiphany in her religious development. She wrote in her autobiography that "I had been so long oppressed with the degradation of woman under canon law and church discipline, that I had a sense of relief in pouring out my indignation" in the sermon.[108]

Returning to the United States in the autumn of 1883, Stanton, with Anthony and Gage, began work on volume three of *History of Woman*

Suffrage, which was published in 1886. In the interim, Stanton dusted off her sermon, turning it into an article that was published in the *North American Review* in May 1885.[109] "Has Christianity Benefitted Woman?" was her most ambitious and damning critique of religion to date. In the article, which relied heavily on Joslyn Gage's work, Stanton moved beyond blaming the degradation of women on the misinterpretation of scripture by male clergy. The root cause of women's subjugation, she now saw it, was institutional religion. "All religions thus far have taught the headship and superiority of man, the inferiority and subordination of woman," Stanton asserted. "History shows, too, that the moral degradation of woman is due more to theological superstitions than to all other influences together." Also, the Bible itself, not its mere misinterpretation, was at fault. The "sacred Scriptures," she chided, made "woman an afterthought in the creation, the author of sin, in collusion with the devil, sex a crime, marriage a condition of slavery for woman and defilement for man, and maternity a curse to be attended with sorrow and suffering . . . [all as] a just punishment for having effected the downfall of man."[110] After she wrote the article, but before it was published, Stanton addressed the NWSA and offered many of the same condemnations. "You may go over the world, and you will find that every form of religion that has breached upon this earth, has degraded woman," she charged. "History shows one continual persecution of woman." When one of the attendees insisted that "we must not blame the Bible" for its misinterpretations, Stanton stuck to her claim that the Bible *was* part of the problem, responding "I want an expurgated edition of the Bible."[111]

Conservative clergy attacked Stanton's *North American Review* article as "intolerant, and startlingly free from the conventional limitations of delicacy." In response to the article, Congregationalist minister W.W. Patton delivered a sermon titled "Women and Skepticism," in which he charged that "the enlargement of woman's sphere tended to immorality." He was joined by Reverend Thomas DeWitt Talmadge, who condemned the suffrage movement as immoral. Stanton relished the controversy, writing Reverend Patton that "I have been trying for years to make the women understand that the very worst enemies they have are in the pulpit and you have illustrated the truth of my assertion." Responding to her critics in an article in *The Index*, she reiterated that "whatever spirit robs woman of her natural rights—to think, to know, to be all of which she is capable—and relegates the whole sex to certain limits of man's choosing, cannot be the spirit of a true religion." The episode convinced Stanton that it was time to undertake a revision of the Bible to reflect a woman's perspective. As she again remarked at a meeting of the NWSA that year, "what we demand is an expurgated edition of the Bible. Men have written it . . . revised it, and put in and taken out whatever suited their own ideas. Now what we want is to call a council of women for an expurgated edition of the Bible that shall place us in our true position as equals" to men.[112]

The Woman's Bible

Having convinced herself of the dire need for a revision of the Bible to reflect and celebrate a woman's perspective, Stanton undertook the project with gusto. As she wrote to the 1886 Convention of the NSWA, "[m]y convictions from year to year have been growing stronger that before we can secure woman's emancipation from slavery and superstitions of the past we have an important work to do in the church." After discussing the idea of Bible revision with British suffragette and skeptic Frances Lord, Stanton began soliciting leading women intellectuals to serve on a revising committee. Writing to Elizabeth Boynton Harbert in September 1886, Stanton insisted that the committee members "should all be liberal read & comment as they would on the letter & spirit of any book of human origin, [rejecting] the orthodox view in regard to woman . . . [as] man's inferior subject, subordinate slave." Stanton had grand plans for the project. If she could gather "twenty five intelligent well educated women [they] could make 'The Woman's Bible' a great feature of the general uprising, in this 19th century."[113] Many prominent women, including Julia Ward Howe and Reverend Olympia Brown, declined to participate in the project, thinking the venture was ill-advised, but Stanton eventually assembled a cohort of religious liberals: Unitarians and Universalists, followers of Theosophy and New Thought, and religious skeptics. The initial group included Frances Lord, Joslyn Gage, Clara Bewick Colby, Lucinda B. Chandler, Universalist minister Phebe A. Hanaford, Harriot Stanton Blanch (Stanton's daughter), Sarah Underwood, and Eva Ingersoll (Robert Ingersoll's wife).[114] Missing from the committee was Susan B. Anthony, who called the project "a work of supererogation." It was not as if Anthony disagreed with the substance of *The Woman's Bible* or even with Stanton's motivation. In an 1886 speech to the NSWA, at the time Stanton was organizing her revising committee, Anthony declared that "[i]t was men who had been inspired to write the Bible and men alone [who] had been allowed to . . . tell us what it meant.

Until the Bible had been translated by women and preached by women, . . . she would not believe it was against women." Rather, Anthony was concerned that the final product might divide the women's reform movement—particularly that it might alienate members of the WCTU—and distract from the goal of securing women's suffrage.[115]

Not all of the women remained on the committee until the end of what became a nine-year project. As Stanton described the undertaking: "We went through the whole Bible & marked all the passages referring to woman," which "occupied less than one-tenth of the whole Scriptures." "Then, we brought four cheap Bibles at 25 cents apiece, cut out th[o]se verses pasted them chapter by chapter at the top of a page in a black book, & wrote our commentaries thereon." In the end, Stanton did most of the writing.[116] The goal, she affirmed in *The Index* in August 1886, was "to free women from the bondage of the old theologies," as the Bible's "teachings are unfit for this stage of evolution in which the sexes occupy an equal place in the world of thought." For Stanton, the purpose of the *Woman's Bible* was not only to confront the misogynist interpretations perpetuated by male clergy and theologians but also to challenge the large number of Christian women who accepted traditional church doctrine. As one biographer put it, "[h]er campaign against the church, the clergy, and the Bible, she firmly believed, would provide the catalyst to women's emancipation."[117]

Finishing the project took longer than Stanton had hoped or anticipated. In October 1886, she departed on another trip to England and France, and did not return to the United States until March 1888. (While in England, she apparently met with Victoria Woodhull, who was living in London, having married the managing partner of one of England's oldest banks.)[118] Upon her return, Stanton helped organize the International Council of Women's meeting to celebrate the fortieth anniversary of the Seneca Falls Convention. Held in Washington, DC, in March 1888, the event attracted the leading women of the day, including Julia Ward Howe, Clara Barton, Lucy Stone, Susan B. Anthony, and Frances Willard. In her address to the Council, Stanton celebrated the modest advances in women's rights while calling for renewed commitment to the cause. Her speech steered clear of her usual criticisms of organized religion, though she commended "the secular nature of our government" and the importance of separation of church and state—both of which promoted "the rights of conscience . . . above all authority of church and State"—while she condemned efforts to "recognize the Christian theology in the Constitution."

Working behind the scenes at the Council, Stanton attempted to drum up support for her *Woman's Bible*, but it never materialized, and she later told a colleague that at that point "the project seemed so herculean that it was suspended."[119]

Other commitments continued to distract Stanton from returning to her *Bible*, including her ongoing advocacy of divorce reform and compiling the third volume of the *History of Woman Suffrage*. Also, in late 1887, Anthony began talks with Lucy Stone about merging the NWSA with the rival American Woman Suffrage Association, a process that took two years to complete. Anthony believed it made strategic sense to unite the two suffrage organizations, in the same way that it was logical to work with the WCTU to achieve the woman's vote. Stanton, who had maintained a grudge against Lucy Stone and resented Stone's criticism of her radical positions on religion and sexuality, was unenthusiastic about a merger.[120] Yet, on February 18, 1890, the seventy-four-year-old Stanton addressed the first meeting of the National American Woman Suffrage Association (NAWSA) as its honorary president. After commending the merger and the efforts of suffragettes going back fifty years, she turned to the "chief barriers" that stood in "the way of a more pronounced success in our movement." First noting the persistent "apathy and indifference" among some women and the constant challenges of organizing, she turned to a leading impediment to women's progress: organized religion, particularly its resistance to marriage and divorce reform. She challenged the audience that "time had fully come for women to demand of the church the same equal recognition she demands of the state," including removing the "masculine element" in religion and replacing it with "rational religion." She also called on Congress to reject the "narrow sectarian measures" being proposed, "such as more rigid Sunday laws . . . and to introduce the name of God into the constitution." She pleaded: "I hope this convention will declare that the Woman's Suffrage Association is opposed to all Union of church and State and pledges itself as far as possible to maintain the secular nature of our government." Because of these religious headwinds, however, she called for "no further legislation on the question of marriage and divorce until woman has a voice in the state and national governments." She urged her audience not to be lulled into complacency: "The enfranchisement of woman is not a question to be carried by political clap-trap" but through education and by "attacking in turn every stronghold of the enemy," the church included.[121]

After the convention, Stanton left for yet another trip to Europe to see her children and grandchildren. Upon her return the following year, she was further distressed at the conservative direction of the women's reform movement, not merely at the strength of the WCTU but with the cautiousness of many younger members of the NAWSA. Support for Stanton's religious agenda had been "waning in the last days of the NWSA," writes one scholar; "in the newly united movement, it virtually disappeared."[122] Finally, in 1895 at the age of eighty, Stanton found the motivation to return to her *Woman's Bible*. She reorganized her revising committee, soliciting commentators from a broad spectrum of women or, alternatively, seeking their endorsement of the project. Naively optimistic, she approached Frances Willard and the British temperance leader Lady Isabella Somerset, both of whom politely declined to be associated with her Bible.[123] In the end, the best she could muster was a similar group of liberal Protestants, New Thought practitioners, and freethinkers: Joslyn Gage, Clara Colby, Olympia Brown, Lucinda B. Chandler, Helen Gardner, Augusta J. Chapin, and Lillie Devereux Blake.[124] Again visibly absent from the committee was Susan B. Anthony, who sternly told Stanton, "No, I don't want my name on that Bible Committee. You fight that battle and leave me to fight the secular, the political fellows." As Anthony explained her reticence, "I simply don't want the enemy to be diverted from my practical ballot fight to that of scoring me for belief one way or another about the bible. The religious part has never been mine, you know. . . . So go ahead in your own way, and let me stick to my own."[125]

The *Woman's Bible*, published in two parts in 1895 and 1898, essentially amounted to extracted passages of the Bible mentioning women with accompanying commentary. The first volume contained the Pentateuch, the first five books of the Hebrew Bible/Old Testament.[126] The introduction, written by Stanton, set the tone for the book, denying at the outset that the Bible was divinely inspired: "the Scriptures, the creeds and codes and church discipline of the leading religions bear the impress of fallible man, and not of our ideal great first cause," God. "I do not believe that God inspired the Mosaic code, or told historians what they say he did about woman," she insisted. Because the Bible "taught that woman brought sin and death into the world, that she precipitated the fall of the race, [and] that she was arraigned before the judgment seat of Heaven, tried, condemned and sentenced," it could not be the true word of God.[127]

From there, Stanton's *Bible* turned to refuting the submissive portrayals of those "heroic" women figures commonly praised by the Bible's male authors—Sarah, Rachel, Rebekah—with the commentators emphasizing their "strength of character" and independent qualities, instead. The commentators also criticized the mistreatment of women and the prevalent practices of polygamy and concubinage in the Hebrew Bible, with Cara Colby remarking that "[t]he chief lesson taught by [this] history is the danger of violating physically, mentally, or spiritually, the personal integrity of woman."[128] Conversely, the commentators sought to rehabilitate those women the Bible's authors had traditionally spurned. Eve received particular attention and praise. Stanton declared the passage describing the simultaneous creation of Adam and Eve, rather than the later story of Eve being created out of Adam's rib, to be the correct account, which demonstrated woman's "true position, as an equal factor in human progress." The commentators also vigorously disputed the "masculine interpretation" of Eve's responsibility for introducing original sin into the world by eating the fruit of the tree of knowledge. Instead, the story demonstrated Eve's intellectual curiosity and desire for wisdom; Adam, who hid behind Eve when confronted by God for their mutual disobedience, was a coward and a whiner for blaming Eve. "Again we are amazed that upon such a story men have built up a theory of their superiority!" remarked Lucinda B. Chandler.[129]

The theme of women's self-sufficiency and empowerment continued into the second volume of the *Bible*. Ruth, Vashti, and Esther, rather than demonstrating traditional female virtues of self-sacrifice and submissiveness, were portrayed as strong and self-reliant women. "Self-development is a higher duty than self-sacrifice," wrote Stanton, and "should be woman's motto henceforth." Vashti, in particular, received praise for defying her husband, King Ahasuerus: "Vashti was the prototype of the higher unfoldment of woman beyond her time," and she stood "for the point in human development when womanliness asserts itself and begins to revolt and to throw off the yoke of sensualism and of tyranny."[130]

With respect to the Gospels, the commentators rejected the immaculate conception of Jesus, maintaining that the account was "a slur on all the natural motherhood of the world." They also disputed Jesus's divinity, the doctrine of the Trinity, and the miracles. "These Biblical mysteries and inconsistencies are a great strain on the credulity of the mind," Stanton remarked.[131] The commentators reserved their harshest criticism for the teachings of the Apostle

Paul, for his opposition to divorce and his misogynist commands that women be subservient to their husbands and that they remain silent in the church. "The doctrine of woman the original sin, and her subjection in consequence, planted in the early Christian Church by Paul, has been a poisonous stream in Church and State," Lucinda B. Chandler declared. "It has debased marriage and made both canon and civil law a monstrous oppression to women." The commentators noted the ongoing consequences of this "poisonous stream" on the social and legal status of women to that day. In the end, even though there was much in the Bible to commend—particularly its depictions of strong, independent women—much of that account had been overshadowed by the misinterpretations perpetuated by the Bible's male authors and later biblical commentators. *The Woman's Bible* sought to correct the record. Stopping short of condemning religion per se or the Bible in toto, *The Woman's Bible* was deliberately provocative.[132]

Reaction

Stanton's twin goals in publishing *The Woman's Bible* were to challenge the male religious establishment and to shake Christian women—and women in the suffrage movement—out of their lethargy. As she wrote in the conclusion to the first volume, "woman's strongest foes have been of her own sex; and because of her sense of duty and religious sentiment have been operative according to a false ideal, unintentionally women have and will continue to be bigoted . . . until they see with the eye of reason and logic, as well as with the sentiment which has so long kept them the dependent class."[133] Stanton felt that she and the other contributors had accomplished both goals. "The importance of this work cannot be over estimated," she wrote to Clara Colby. "Religious ideas are everywhere the strongest motive power of the race," and "the Bible is the Magna Charta of women's freedom when rightly interpreted." When their *Bible* is published, she predicted, "it will be the crowning achievement of the nineteenth century [leading to] the emancipation of women."[134]

As for the first goal, *The Woman's Bible*'s release in August 1895 did shake the male religious establishment. The reaction, overwhelmingly denunciatory, was not unexpected. The *New York Observer and Chronicle*, a Presbyterian journal, characterized the book as a "fantastic and inconsequential comment on God's word," one that "advance[d] no true 'cause' of woman, but only disgust[ed] all people of good taste and ordinary Christian piety." Employing more damning language, the *Christian Observer* called the project an "outrage," "accompanied by blasphemous comments" which will be "a handy weapon for every infidel enterprise." *Zion's Herald* (Methodist) was chiefly contemptuous, remarking that as men had struggled for centuries over biblical commentaries, it was difficult to accept that women possessed "the wide and accurate learning required to make a Bible revision." While *The Woman's Bible* "evinces the ingenuity, the inventive genius, of woman," *Zion's Herald* wrote sardonically, "we can hardly say so much for the wisdom of the undertaking." And as if to substantiate Stanton's claims, one clergyman declared: "It is the work of women, and of the devil." On the other side, a handful of liberal clergy, chiefly Unitarians and Universalists, praised *The Woman's Bible*, and *Free Thought Magazine* gave Stanton eleven pages to advertise the book. By contrast, *The Truth Seeker* gave it little coverage—the project was, after all, an attempt to salvage parts of the Bible. In noting Stanton's tendency to refer to "Our Father and Mother who art in heaven" when called upon to pray, *The Truth Seeker* sniped, "what use does a woman of Mrs. Stanton's freethinking tendencies have for prayer, whether to a uni-sexual or bi-sexual heavenly police commission?"[135]

Stanton relished the reaction from conservative clergymen. Responding to the accusation that her *Bible* was a work of the devil, she quipped: "His Satanic Majesty was not invited to join the Revising Committee, which consists of women alone." Anthony confirmed the distress that *The Woman's Bible* caused by congratulating Stanton for "making Rome Howl." Stanton more greatly valued the attention the mainstream press gave *The Woman's Bible*, noting that "it created a great sensation," with several New York dailies carrying excerpts from the commentaries. "Extracts from it, and criticisms of the commentators, were printed in the newspapers throughout America, Great Britain, and Europe," she recalled. The book quickly went into a third printing in the United States and a separate edition was published in England. Not all commentary from secular newspapers was complimentary, however, with the *St. Paul Daily Globe* calling the work "a handbook of infidelity," while the *Salt Lake Herald* panned it as "a cold-blooded proposition of literary butchery."[136]

When it came to accomplishing her second goal in publishing *The Woman's Bible*—to shake women out of their lethargy regarding church doctrine and biblical interpretation—Stanton fell short. The negative press coverage surrounding the book only reinforced the increasingly conservative perspectives of many women in the reform movement. Frances Willard, who at one point had considered participating on the revising committee before realizing its orientation, distanced herself from *The Woman's Bible*. In response to rumors that Willard had ever considered joining the project, the *Union Signal*—the WCTU's journal—editorialized in August 1895 that "we may as well reiterate that Miss Willard and Lady Henry Somerset had nothing whatever to do with 'The Woman's Bible.'"[137]

That the WCTU wanted nothing to do with *The Woman's Bible* was unsurprising. What distressed Stanton more was the reaction of several younger women who had assumed leadership positions in the NAWSA since her retirement from active involvement. Heading into the NAWSA convention in January 1896, Stanton got wind that the younger leadership intended to disassociate the Association from the *Bible*, or even worse, condemn the project. Rachel Foster Avery, the NAWSA's corresponding secretary, issued a report at the Association's executive committee meeting preceding the convention that strongly criticized *The Woman's Bible* and, by implication, Stanton. Since its release, Avery wrote, "the work of our Association has been in several directions much hindered by the general misconception of the relation of the organization to the so-called 'Woman's Bible.'" The NAWSA had been "held responsible for the action of an individual, an action which many of our members, far from sympathizing with, feel to be unwise." Avery's criticism did not stop with concerns about misattribution, however. She went on to dismiss the *Bible* as "a volume with a pretentious title, covering a jumble of comment[s] . . . without either scholarship or literary value, [and] set forth in a spirit which is neither that of reverence or inquiry." She recommended that the NAWSA adopt a resolution disassociating itself from the Bible and its lead author.[138] Even though Clara Colby had Avery's report tabled, Stanton was livid, telling Colby that it "was too bad [for Avery] to speak so slightly about all of the writers of the Bible [which included Colby], in order to belabor me." "Mrs. Avery knows nothing about style. . . . The Bible will live in spite of Mrs. Avery's opposition."[139]

The matter did not end there, however. Five days later, at the closing session of the NAWSA convention (which Stanton did not attend due to her poor health), Avery introduced a resolution distancing the Association from *The Woman's Bible*: "This Association is non-sectarian, being composed of persons of all shades of religious opinion, and that it has no official connection with the so-called 'Woman's Bible' or any theological publication."

The resolution, milder in its language than the report and omitting any reference to Stanton, was reputedly pushed by Carrie Chapman Catt and the Blackwells—Lucy Stone, her husband Henry Blackwell, and their daughter Alice Stone Blackwell—the leaders of the old AWSA. Nevertheless, the resolution led to a "long and animated" discussion that, according to newspaper reports, "provoked considerable debate and a little personal abuse" over the wisdom of the book.[140] Several delegates who favored the resolution related the difficulty they had encountered in "doing field-work and finding doors slammed in their faces" from people who objected to *The Woman's Bible.* "The 'Woman's Bible' has been seriously injurious to the work of organizing," Carrie Catt declared; "[e]very organizer has reported that they met the obstacle of the 'Woman's Bible' everywhere." Because of perceived association of the NAWSA with the *Bible*, "we shall be put back many years."[141] Other delegates countered that they had not encountered negative reactions and it was best to maintain "dignified silence" about the matter as they had done when critics had charged suffragists "were all free lovers." Stanton's defenders appeared to be in a minority, however.[142]

At the urging of her supporters, Anthony stepped off the dais from which she had been presiding and delivered an impassionate defense of her lifelong friend, despite her earlier reservations about the project. She reminded the delegates that the Association had long stood for "the right of individual opinion of every member." Anthony declared that "I was born a heretic" but the Association had "endorsed me," as it had stood by Ernestine Rose who was an unabashed atheist. Acknowledging that she had told Stanton that *The Woman's Bible* was "a great waste of time" for "descant[ing] on the barbarisms of 6,000 years ago," it was within her right to challenge prevailing religious presuppositions. Agreeing with the goal of writing the *Bible*, Anthony asserted that "I always distrust people who know so much about what God wants them to do to their fellows." She also disputed the idea that the *Bible* harmed the suffrage cause: "Neither you nor I can tell but Mrs. Stanton will come out triumphant and that this will be the greatest thing ever done in woman's cause." Anthony concluded her remarks with a passionate plea: "I pray you all, vote for religious liberty to each and all, without censorship, without inquisition. This resolution adopted will be a vote of censure. It cannot mean less."[143] Despite Anthony's moving defense, the delegates adopted the resolution by a vote of fifty-three to forty. Anthony, who was the only NAWSA officer to oppose the resolution, took the vote as a personal rebuke and considered resigning from the organization. Stanton was "thoroughly indignant" and blamed not only Carrie Catt and the Blackwells for orchestrating the censure but also, unfairly, Anthony for criticizing the *Bible* and for not resigning.[144]

Although the episode bruised Stanton's and Anthony's relationship and further alienated the former from the organization she had helped found, the two women later reconciled, though they continued to disagree over how much to connect women's rights to the issue of religion. "You say 'women must be emancipated from their superstitions before enfranchisement will be of any benefit,' and I say the reverse, that women must be enfranchised before they can be emancipated from their superstitions," Anthony wrote Stanton three months after the censure vote. "So you will have to keep pegging away, saying 'Get rid of religious bigotry, and then get political rights'; and I shall keep pegging away, saying, 'Get political rights first and religious bigotry will melt like dew before the morning sun.'" Stanton persisted in her belief that both reforms must at least occur together, telling Clara Colby that "[o]ne point I keep ever in view is to depreciate the Bible view of the Lord." But "Susan is so narrow that she sees nothing but suffrage."[145]

Despite being rebuffed by the censure vote, Stanton did not give up on her religious crusade. She defended *The Woman's Bible* in a December 1896 article in the *Boston Investigator*, the freethought newspaper founded by Abner Kneeland. "We have made a fetish of the Bible long enough," she insisted. "The time has come to read it as we do all other books, accepting the good, rejecting the evil, which it teaches."[146] In 1896, she reconvened members of her revising committee to finish their commentaries on volume two of *The Woman's Bible*—covering the books of Joshua through Revelation—which was published in 1898. In the Preface, Stanton defended the project against its critics, calling out some of them by name. "[I]n denying divine inspiration for such demoralizing ideas [as women's subordination] [*The Woman's Bible*] shows more worshipful reverence for the great Spirit of All Good than does the Church." Then, in the Appendix, inserted as a badge of honor, Stanton included the NAWSA's resolution condemning the first volume of the *Bible*, along with Anthony's remarks defending her friend.[147] Both volumes of *The Woman's Bible* would be bestsellers, vindicating the effort and cementing Stanton's reputation as a religious iconoclast. Even though the composition of the revising committee—including Joslyn Gage, Clara Colby, and Lucinda Chandler—indicated she that was not alone in her beliefs, her religious skepticism was not widely shared by women reformers. Her long-standing attempt to align the NWSA with freethought ideas ensured that the organization would speak for only a small number of women within the greater suffrage and temperance movements.[148]

For the final four years of her life, Stanton relentlessly defended her *Bible* and her views about organized religion being an impediment to the equality of women. Ironically, when her children Harriot and Theodore reissued her autobiography *Eighty Years and More* in 1922, they deleted the chapter on "Women and Theology," in which Stanton had traced the preparation of *The Woman's Bible*, as being too controversial. By then, Stanton's and Anthony's lifelong goal of achieving women's suffrage had finally been realized, but only after the movement had disassociated itself from the two women leaders' religious radicalism.[149]

NOTES

1. Ruth Bordin, *Woman and Temperance* (New Brunswick, NJ: Rutgers University Press, 1981, 1990), 3, 52.
2. Bordin, *Woman and Temperance*, 116, 162; Barbara Leslie Epstein, *The Politics of Domesticity: Women, Evangelism, and Temperance in Nineteenth-Century America* (Middleton, CT: Wesleyan University Press, 1986), 4; Alison M. Parker, *Purifying America: Women, Cultural Reform, and Pro-Censorship Activism, 1873–1933* (Urbana: University of Illinois Press, 1997), 5.
3. Sue Davis, *The Political Thought of Elizabeth Cady Stanton* (New York: New York University Press, 2008), 178–195; Stevenson-Moessner, "Elizabeth Cady Stanton, Reformer to Revolutionary," 673–697; Barry, *Susan B. Anthony*, 96–97; Christopher H. Evans, *"Do Everything": The Biography of Frances Willard* (New York: Oxford University Press, 2022); Ruth Bordin, *Frances Willard, A Biography* (Chapel Hill: University of North Carolina Press, 1986). This chapter draws from David Sehat's pathbreaking book, *The Myth of Religious Freedom*, which brilliantly discusses these overlapping themes. See especially 97–108, 133–154.
4. Green, *Second Disestablishment*, 91–103, 110–112.
5. James Brewer Stewart, *Holy Warriors: The Abolitionists and American Slavery* (New York: Hill and Wang, 1976), 20–23, 56–58.
6. Sehat, *Myth of Religious Freedom*, 84–96; Gerda Lerner, *The Grimke Sisters from South Carolina: Pioneers for Woman's Rights and Abolition* (New York: Schocken Books, 1967), 33–36; DuBois, *Feminism and Suffrage*, 31–36; Carol Faulkner, *Lucretia Mott's Heresy: Abolition and Women's Rights in Nineteenth-Century America* (Philadelphia: University of Pennsylvania Press, 2011); Blanche Glassman Hersh, "'Am I Not a Woman and a Sister,': Abolitionist Beginnings of Nineteenth-Century Feminism," in *Antislavery Reconsidered: New Perspectives*

on the Abolitionists, ed. Lewis Perry and Michael Fellman (Baton Rouge: Louisiana State University Press, 1979), 252–253.

7. Stanton, *Eighty Years and More*, 51, 60–63; Griffith, *In Her Own Right*, 24–26.

8. Stanton, Anthony, and Gage, *History of Woman Suffrage*, 1:422; Faulkner, *Lucretia Mott's Heresy*, 94.

9. Griffith, *In Her Own Right*, 32–39; Douglas H. Maynard, "The World's Anti-Slavery Convention of 1840," *Mississippi Valley Historical Review* 47 (1960): 452–471; Cady Stanton, *Eighty Years and More*, 71–84.

10. Epstein, *The Politics of Domesticity*, 92–93; Bordin, *Woman and Temperance*, 3–4; Henry William Blair, *The Temperance Movement: A Conflict between Men and Alcohol* (Boston: William E. Smythe Co., 1888), 504.

11. Epstein, *The Politics of Domesticity*, 92–93.

12. Barry, *Susan B. Anthony*, 60–63; Susan B. Anthony, "Speech to the Daughters of Temperance," March 2, 1849, in *Selected Papers*, 1:135–142; "Diary," Nov. 1853, ibid., 1:229–230.

13. Stanton, *Eighty Years and More*, 200–202; Barry, *Susan B. Anthony*, 63–68; Epstein, *Politics of Domesticity*, 93; Griffith, *In Her Own Right*, 76–77; Stanton et al., *History of Woman Suffrage*, 1:481–483; "Cady Stanton to Women's Temperance Meeting," Jan. 28, 1852, in *Selected Papers*, 1:191–193.

14. Reprinted in Alma Lutz, *Created Equal: A Biography of Elizabeth Cady Stanton, 1815–1902* (New York: John Day, 1940), 84; Griffith, *In Her Own Right*, 77.

15. Davis, *The Political Thought of Elizabeth Cady Stanton*, 1, 178–195; Sehat, *Myth of Religious Freedom*, 101–104.

16. Stanton, *Eighty Years and More*, 10, 20, 22–26; Griffith, *In Her Own Right*, 8–9, 15–17; Kathi Kern, *Mrs. Stanton's Bible* (Ithaca, NY: Cornell University Press, 2001), 40–41.

17. Stanton, *Eighty Years and More*, 35–37, 41–43; Kern, *Mrs. Stanton's Bible*, 41–42.

18. Stanton, *Eighty Years and More*, 43–44.

19. Kern, *Mrs. Stanton's Bible*, 42–44; Stevenson-Moessner, "Elizabeth Cady Stanton, Reformer to Revolutionary," 673–697.

20. Stanton, *Eighty Years and More*, 127–134; Griffith, *In Her Own Right*, 45–46; Elizabeth Cady Stanton, "Heavenly Father and Mother," *The Open Court*, Aug. 10, 1893, 3765.

21. Griffith, *In Her Own Right*, 50–52; Faulkner, *Lucretia Mott's Heresy*, 127–128, 201–202; Stanton et al., *History of Woman Suffrage*, 67–68.

22. Stanton et al., *History of Woman Suffrage*, 1:69–71; Davis, *Political Thought*, 50–56.

23. Stanton et al., *History of Woman Suffrage*, 1:71–73; Griffith, *In Her Own Right*, 54–57; DuBois, *Feminism and Suffrage*, 40–41; Faulkner, *Lucretia Mott's Heresy*, 140; Davis, *Political Thought*, 50–56.

24. Stanton et al., *History of Woman Suffrage*, 1:75–81; Davis, *Political Thought*, 58–61.

25. Elizabeth Cady Stanton and Elizabeth W. McClintock, "To the Editors, Seneca County Courier," July 23, 1848, in *Selected Papers*, 1:88–92.

26. Griffith, *In Her Own Right*, 72–74. See Elenore Kirk, "Two Women of the Present: Elizabeth Cady Stanton and Susan B. Anthony," *Phrenological Journal of Science and Health* (July 1870): 57–60.

27. Stanton et al., *History of Woman Suffrage*, 1:850–851; Sehat, *Myth of American Religious Freedom*, 96–108; Stevenson-Moessner, "Elizabeth Cady Stanton, Reformer to Revolutionary," 673–697.

28. "Address to NY Legislature," Feb. 14, 1854, in Stanton et al., *History of Woman Suffrage*, 1:591–605; Griffith, *In Her Own Right*, 81–83.

29. Stanton, "Divorce," April 1850, in *Selected Papers*, 1:162; Davis, *The Political Thought of Elizabeth Cady Stanton*, 82; Griffith, *In Her Own Right*, 101–105; Alice Stone Blackwell, *Lucy Stone: Pioneer of Women's Rights* (Boston: Little, Brown & Co., 1930), 230.

30. "Divorces at a Discount," *New York Times*, Aug. 20, 1859, 4; "New Discussion on Divorce," *Circular*, April 5, 1860, 38; Lynne Carol Halem, *Divorce Reform: Changing Legal and Social Perspectives* (New York: Free Press, 1980), 25.

31. Stanton et al., *History of Woman Suffrage*, 1:716–722.

32. Ibid., 733.

33. Ibid., 729–732.

34. Stanton, *Eighty Years and More*, 218–220; "Tenth National Woman's Rights Convention," May 11, 1860, in *Selected Papers*, 1:418–430.

35. Stevenson-Moessner, "Elizabeth Cady Stanton, Reformer to Revolutionary," 677–678; Kathi Kern, "'Free Woman Is a Divine Being, the Savior of Mankind': Stanton's Exploration of Religion and Gender," in *Elizabeth Cady Stanton, Feminist as Thinker*, ed. Ellen Carol DuBois and Richard Candida Smith (New York: New York University Press, 2007), 95–96.

36. Ellen Carol DuBois, "Outgrowing the Compact of the Fathers: Equal Rights, Woman Suffrage, and the United States Constitution, 1820–1878," *Journal of American History* 74 (Dec. 1987): 836–862.

37. Barry, *Susan B. Anthony*, 163–177, 187–194; Griffith, *In Her Own Right*, 121–141; DuBois, *Feminism and Suffrage*, 162–202; Robert E. Riegel, "The Split of Feminist Movement of 1869," *Mississippi Valley Historical Review* 49 (1962): 485–496.

38. Kern, "'Free Woman Is a Divine Being," 99–103; Kern, *Mrs. Stanton's Bible*, 53–68; Robert G. Ingersoll to Cady Stanton, Oct. 14, 1898, in *Selected Papers*, 6:248; Elizabeth Cady Stanton to Benjamin F. Underwood and Sarah Francis Underwood, April 5, 1887, ibid., 5:9–10; Cady Stanton to Sarah Francis Underwood, March 1889, ibid., 5:196; Elizabeth Cady Stanton to Benjamin F. Underwood, March 11, 1886, ibid., 4:494; Elizabeth Cady Stanton to Fredrick A. Hinckley, Oct. 26, 1879, ibid., 3:478–479.

39. Elizabeth Cady Stanton, "Let the Blue Laws Rest," *Omaha Bee*, March 17, 1889, in *Selected Papers*, 5:191–194; Elizabeth Cady Stanton, "Reading the Bible in the Public Schools," *Arena* (June 1897): 1033, 1037.

40. "Suffrage Address" (1880), Ingersoll, *Works*, 9:305–319; Ingersoll to Stanton, March 8, 1894, in Eva Ingersoll Wakefield, ed., *The Letters of Robert G. Ingersoll* (Westport, CT: Greenwood Press, 1973), 707; Warren, *American Freethought*, 128–130; Stacey M. Robertson, "'Aunt Nancy Men': Parker Pillsbury, Masculinity, and Women's Rights Activism in Nineteenth-Century United States," *American Studies* 37 (Fall 1996): 33–60.

41. See *The Index*, Aug. 1, 1878, and Sept. 23, 1880, reprinted in *Selected Papers*, 3:400 and 4:4; *New York Times*, Nov. 11, 1877, 10.

42. Elizabeth Cady Stanton to The Editor, *The Index*, July 22, 1878, in *Selected Papers*, 3:399–400; Elizabeth Cady Stanton, "The Politics of Reformers," *The Index*, Sept. 23, 1880, ibid., 4:1–4; Elizabeth Cady Stanton to Benjamin F. Underwood, Oct. 19, 1885, ibid., 4:442–443.

43. Griffith, *In Her Own Right*, 148–154; Du Bois, "Outgrowing the Compact of the Fathers," 852–856. In *Minor v. Happersett*, 88 U.S. 162 (1875), a unanimous Supreme Court rejected the argument that voting was an attribute of citizenship.

44. Banner, *Elizabeth Cady Stanton*, 126–129.

45. Elizabeth Cady Stanton, "On Marriage and Divorce," in "On Labor and Free Love: Two Unpublished Speeches of Elizabeth Cady Stanton," ed. Ellen DuBois, *Signs* 1 (Aut. 1975): 257–268

46. Ibid.

47. Davis, *Political Thought of Elizabeth Cady Stanton*, 166–167; Goldsmith, *Other Powers*, 206–207.

48. Elizabeth Cady Stanton, "The Need of Liberal Divorce Laws," *North American Review* (Sept. 1884): 234–245.

49. "The Divorce Mania," *Phrenological Journal and Science of Health* (June 1873), 398.

50. See "Divorces in Connecticut," *New York Evangelist*, June 15, 1871, 4.

51. Halem, *Divorce Reform*, 27–29; Samuel W. Dike, "Some Aspects of the Divorce Question," *Princeton Review* (Jan.–June 1884), 169, 171, 174; Anthony Comstock, *The Independent*, March 14, 1889, 2; William L. O'Neill, "Divorce in the Progressive Era," in *History of Women in the United States: Domestic Relations and the Law*, ed. Nancy F. Cott (Munich, Germany: Walter de Gruyter, 1992), 376–390.

52. R.M. Hatfield, "Marriage and Divorce," *The Independent*, Feb. 2, 1871, 8; "Marriage," *Reformed Church Messenger*, Feb. 2, 1870, 6; "The Religion of the Family: The Marriage Relation," *The Ladies' Repository* (Feb. 1871): 126–129.

53. "Divorce, and Divorce Laws," *Catholic World* (June 1877), 340; "Morality and Life," *American Catholic Quarterly Review* (July 1885), 444, 454.

54. Rev. A. Prince, "Desertion and Divorce," *Zion's Herald*, Jan. 6, 1881, 2; "Morality and Life," 454–456; Edward Stannwood, "National Jurisdiction over Marriage and Divorce as Affecting Polygamy in Utah," *Andover Review* (July 1884), A66.

55. James Schouler, *Treatise on the Law of the Domestic Relations* (Boston: Little, Brown, 1870), 295–302; Joel Prentis Bishop, *Commentaries on the Law of Marriage and Divorce* (Boston: Little, Brown, 1873, 1875), 1:2–12, 21–27.

56. Schouler, *Treatise on the Law of the Domestic Relations*, 16–18.
57. Bishop, *Commentaries on the Law of Marriage and Divorce*, 205–210; Sehat, *Myth of Religious Freedom*, 143–144; Michael Grossberg, *Governing the Hearth: Law and the Family in Nineteenth-Century America* (Chapel Hill: University of North Carolina Press, 1985), 21–24.
58. Theodore D. Woolsey, *Essay on Divorce and Divorce Legislation* (New York: Charles Scribner & Co. 1869); "Current Topics," *Albany Law Journal*, Jan. 29, 1870, 76; Theodore D. Woosley, "The Moral Statistics of the United States," *Journal of Social Science* (Nov. 1881): 129–135; Halem, *Divorce Reform*, 34.
59. Halem, *Divorce Reform*, 31–33.
60. Orestes A. Brownson, "The Woman Question," *Catholic World* (May 1869), 145.
61. Orestes A. Brownson, "Woman's Suffrage: The Reform against Nature," *Brownson's Quarterly Review*, Oct. 1, 1873, 508, 517–518, 526 (title taken from Horace Bushnell, *Woman's Suffrage: The Reform against Nature* [New York: Scribner & Co., 1869]).
62. Curtis Cort, "Woman Suffrage," *Reformed Quarterly Review* (July 1883), 343–364.
63. Joseph Cook, "Boston Monday Lectureship: New Proposals on the Divorce Question," *The Independent*, March 20, 1884, 5–6.
64. Stannwood, "National Jurisdiction over Marriage and Divorce"; Schouler, *Treatise on the Law of the Domestic Relations*, 298.
65. Halem, *Divorce Reform*, 34–36; Cook, "New Proposals on the Divorce Question," 5–6; Foster, *Moral Reconstruction*, 68–70.
66. "Easy Divorce: Its Causes and Evils," *New Englander* (Jan. 1884): 48–66; "One Thing or Another," *New York Evangelist*, Feb. 17, 1887, 3; Samuel W. Dike, "Sociological Notes: The Report on Marriage and Divorce," *Andover Review* (Nov. 1889), 528–536; Samuel W. Dike, "Statistics on Marriage and Divorce," *Political Science Quarterly* (Dec. 1889): 3–25; Carroll D. Wright, Commissioner of Labor, *A Report on Marriage and Divorce in the United States* (Washington, DC: Government Printing Office, 1889).
67. Walter Stowe Collins, "Our Divorce Statutes," *Bedford's Monthly* (May 1893), 599, 604.
68. Lyman Abbott, "Christ's Teaching on Moral Topics: Marriage and Divorce," *Outlook*, March 14, 1896, 477–479; O'Neill, "Divorce in the Progressive Era," 381–382; Amelia Barr et al., "Are Women to Blame?," *North American Review* (May 1889): 622, 638–642.
69. Elizabeth Cady Stanton, "Divorce versus Domestic Warfare," *Arena* (April 1890): 560–569.
70. Stanton, *Eighty Years and More*, 230–231.
71. Ian Tyrrell, "Temperance, Feminism, and the WCTU: New Interpretations and New Directions," *Australian Journal of American Studies* 5 (1986): 27–36.
72. Bordin, *Woman and Temperance*, 15–38; Epstein, *The Politics of Domesticity*, 95–107, 115–120; Jack S. Blocker, "Separate Paths: Suffragists and the Women's Temperance Crusade," *Signs* 10 (1985): 460–476.

73. Epstein, *The Politics of Domesticity*, 117–118; Bordin, *Woman and Temperance*, 38–51.

74. Frances E. Willard, "Home Protection: An Argument for Woman's Temperance Ballot," *The Independent*, July 10, 1879, 11; Frances E. Willard, "Home Protection," *Zion's Herald*, March 7, 1878, 78.

75. Epstein, *The Politics of Domesticity*, 118–121; Foster, *Moral Reconstruction*, 35–39; Suzanne M. Marilley, "Frances Willard and the Feminism of Fear," *Feminist Studies* 19 (1993): 123–146; Frances E. Willard, "The Woman's Cause Is Man's," *Arena* (May 1892): 712–725; Frances E. Willard, "The American Home," *Zion's Herald*, April 2, 1890, 110; Frances E. Willard, "Woman and the Temperance Question," *Forum* (Dec. 1887), 432, 439.

76. See Bordin, *Frances Willard*.

77. Marilley, "Frances Willard and the Feminism of Fear," 130.

78. "Temperance Notes," *Friend's Review*, Dec. 15, 1892, 329; Frances E. Willard, "How to Win," *The Chautauquan* (June 1885): 521–524; Bordin, *Woman and Temperance*, 108, 114; Epstein, *The Politics of Domesticity*, 133–135.

79. Mary A. Livermore, "Woman's Work in Moral Reform," *The Chautauquan* (Nov. 1886): 69–72; Bordin, *Woman and Temperance*, 110–112; Epstein, *The Politics of Domesticity*, 125–139.

80. *Friends' Review*, Nov. 29, 1888, 278–279; Parker, *Purifying America*, 6–7.

81. "Literature and Vice," *Friends' Intelligencer*, July 16, 1887, 460.

82. "Doing a Work of Vast Good," *New York Times*, Oct. 3, 1894, 3; "The Woman's Christian Temperance Union," *The Independent*, Nov. 19, 1885, 4; "Anthony Comstock Vindicated," *Christian Union*, Jan. 26, 1888, 116; "Stage Regulation Bill," *New York Times*, Feb. 25, 1897, 4; Parker, *Purifying America*, 9.

83. "Doing a Work of Vast Good," *New York Times*, Oct. 3, 1894, 3; "Comstock Not Wanted," ibid., May 26, 1896, 3; Parker, *Purifying America*, 25, 39–40.

84. See generally, D. Leigh Colvin, *Prohibition in the United States: A History of the Prohibition Party, and of the Prohibition Movement* (New York: George H. Doren, 1926).

85. Colvin, *Prohibition in the United States*, 276–291; Bordin, *Woman and Temperance*, 123–133; Epstein, *The Politics of Domesticity*, 120–123; "Temperance News: The Prohibition Convention," *Christian Union*, June 7, 1888, 728.

86. "The Prohibition Party and the Sabbath," *New York Evangelist*, Nov. 24, 1881, 2; "The Temperance Cause: The Prohibition Party," *Arthur's Home Magazine* (Oct. 1884): 593–594; R.B. Williams, "The Distinctive Features of the Prohibition Party," *American Journal of Politics* (July 1891): 64–71; Colvin, *Prohibition in the United States*, 110–111, 158, 190–191, 311; Lisa M.F. Andersen, *The Politics of Prohibition: American Governance and the Prohibition Party, 1869–1933* (New York: Cambridge University Press, 2013).

87. Foster, *Moral Reconstruction*, 36; Parker, *Purifying America*, 5; Marilley, "Frances Willard and the Feminism of Fear," 131.

88. Willard, "How to Win," 323.

89. Foster, *Moral Reconstruction*, 37; Tyrrell, "Temperance, Feminism, and the WCTU," 31–32; Evans, *"Do Everything,"* 49–50.

90. Susan B. Anthony to Frances E. Willard, Sept. 18, 1876, in *Selected Papers*, 3: 261–262; Susan B. Anthony to Elizabeth Boynton Harbert, Oct. 12, 1879, ibid., 3:473–475.

91. "Woman's Temperance Union," *New York Times*, Oct. 27, 1881, 2; Frances Willard, "Our Coming Politics," *The Independent*, March 24, 1887, 5; "Women's Historic Struggle," *New York Times*, Feb. 24, 1891, 3; "The Congress of White Ribboners," *Zion's Herald*, Oct. 25, 1893, 1–2; "American Temperance Women in Council," *Congregationalist*, Nov. 9, 1893, 652; Frances Willard to Susan B. Anthony, Aug. 15, 1888, in *Selected Papers*, 5:139–140; Susan B. Anthony to Elizabeth Boynton Harbert, Aug. 5, 1880, ibid., 3:556–557; Barry, *Susan B. Anthony*, 291–292.

92. Matilda Joslyn Gage to Elizabeth Cady Stanton, July 13, 1888, in *Selected Papers*, 5:126–129; Barry, *Susan B. Anthony*, 292.

93. Elizabeth Cady Stanton to Olympia Brown, Oct. 12, 1889, in *Selected Papers*, 5:211–213.

94. Elizabeth Cady Stanton to Matilda Joslyn Gage, Oct. 19, 1889, ibid., 5:214–215.

95. Matilda Joslyn Gage to Elizabeth Cady Stanton, July 13, 1888, ibid., 5:126–129.

96. Elizabeth Cady Stanton and Susan B. Anthony, "Appeal," July 30, 1884, ibid., 4:361–366.

97. Elizabeth Cady Stanton, "Parties or Platforms," *Union Signal*, Aug. 13, 1888, in *Selected Papers*, 5:135–138.

98. "International Council of Women," *Friends' Intelligencer*, April 14, 1888, 237; "Review of the National Council of Women," *Congregationalist*, March 14, 1895, 397–398.

99. Susan B. Anthony to Olympia Brown, March 11, 1889, in *Selected Papers*, 5:177–180; "The Women's National Council," *Friends' Review*, Feb. 21, 1889, 476; "American Temperance Women in Council," *Congregationalist*, Nov. 9, 1893, 652–653; Barry, *Susan B. Anthony*, 291–293.

100. Lisa S. Strange, "Elizabeth Cady Stanton's Woman's Bible and the Roots of Feminist Theology," *Gender Issues* (Fall 1999): 15–36.

101. Elizabeth Cady Stanton, "The Bible and Woman Suffrage," May 11, 1879, in *Selected Papers*, 3:446–465.

102. "Bible Revision," *New York Evangelist*, March 10, 1881, 4; "Objections to the Revision as a Substitute to the Authorized Version," *Christian Advocate*, June 23, 1881, 1; "The Clergy and the Revision," *New York Times*, May 22, 1881, 6; "The Revision Denounced: Strong Language from Rev. Mr. Talmage," ibid., June 6, 1881, 8; Kern, *Mrs. Stanton's Bible*, 71–76.

103. Kern, *Mrs. Stanton's Bible*, 76.

104. Stanton, *Eighty Years and More*, 326–327; Stanton et al., *History of Woman Suffrage*.

105. Appendix, in Stanton et al., *History of Woman Suffrage*, 1:848–851.

106. Gage, "Woman, Church, and State," in Stanton et al., *History of Woman Suffrage*, 1:755–782.

107. Mary E. Corey, *The Political Life and Times of Matilda Joslyn Gage* (Rochester, NY: Paramount Market, 2019), 151–169; Leila R. Brammer, *Excluded from Suffrage History: Matilda Joslyn Gage, Nineteenth Century American Feminist* (Westport, CT: Greenwood Press, 2000), 73–91.

108. Stanton, *Eighty Years and More*, 356–357; Stanton et al., *History of Woman Suffrage*, 3:928.

109. Stanton, *Eighty Years and More*, 378, 380.

110. "Has Christianity Benefitted Woman?," *North American Review* (May 1885): 389–400; Moore and Kramnick, *Godless Citizens in a Godly Republic*, 56–62.

111. Meeting of the National Woman Suffrage Association, Jan. 21–22, 1885, *Selected Papers*, 4:391–399.

112. J.R. Kendrick, "Letter," *North American Review* (June 1885): 572–573; "Woman Suffrage and the New York Assembly," Christian Advocate, March 5, 1885, 149; Kern, *Mrs. Stanton's Bible*, 97–98; "Has Christianity Benefitted Woman?," *The Index*, July 23, 1885, in *Selected Papers*, 4:433–436; ibid., 4:396.

113. Elizabeth Cady Stanton to Elizabeth Boynton Harbert, Sept. 13, 1886, in *Selected Papers*, 4:513–515.

114. Kern, *Mrs. Stanton's Bible*, 138–146.

115. Susan B. Anthony, "Remarks to the National Woman Suffrage Association," Feb. 19, 1886, in *Selected Papers*, 4:490–492.

116. Stanton, *Eighty Years and More*, 390–392; James H. Smylie, "'The Woman's Bible' and the Spiritual Crisis," *Soundings* 59 (Fall 1976): 305–328; Kern, *Mrs. Stanton's Bible*, 98–103.

117. Stanton, "The Woman's Bible," *The Index*, Aug. 19, 1886, in *Selected Papers*, 4:510–511; Kern, *Mrs. Stanton's Bible*, 99–100.

118. Stanton, *Eighty Years and More*, 393–411; Elizabeth Cady Stanton to Victoria Woodhull Martin, Nov. 12, 1886, in *Selected Papers*, 4:525–526;

119. Elizabeth Cady Stanton, "Address to the International Council of Women," March 26, 1888, in *Selected Papers*, 5:93–107; Elizabeth Cady Stanton to Clara Bewick Colby, Feb. 16, 1895, ibid., 677–678; "The International Council of Women," *Friends Intelligencer*, April 14, 1888, 247.

120. Lucy Stone to Susan B. Anthony, Nov. 7, 1887, in *Selected Papers*, 5:52–53; Minutes of Informal Conference between Lucy Stone and Anthony, Dec. 21, 1887, ibid., 5:59–67; Lucy Stone to Susan B. Anthony, Dec. 23, 1887, ibid., 5:68–69; Executive Sessions of the NWSA, Jan. 21–24, ibid., 5:166–170; Barry, *Susan B. Anthony*, 289, 296; Kern, *Mrs. Stanton's Bible*, 129–134.

121. Elizabeth Cady Stanton, Address to the National American Woman Suffrage Association, Feb. 18, 1890, in *Selected Papers* 5:249–263.

122. Stanton, *Eighty Years and More*, 412–431; Kern, *Mrs. Stanton's Bible*, 132.

123. Elizabeth Cady Stanton to Lady Isabella Somerset (and Francis Willard), June 5, 1895, in *Selected Papers*, 5:694–695; Lady Isabella Somerset to Elizabeth Cady

Stanton, June 5, 1895, ibid., 5:694; Frances E. Willard to Cady Stanton, Aug. 1, 1895, ibid., 5:703.

124. Elizabeth Cady Stanton to Clara Bewick Colby, April 16, 1895, in *Selected Papers*, 692–694; Elizabeth Cady Stanton to Augusta J. Chapin, June 6, 1895, ibid., 695–697; Kern, *Mrs. Stanton's Bible*, 138–150.

125. Susan B. Anthony to Elizabeth Cady Stanton, July 24, 1895, in *Selected Papers*, 699–701.

126. *The Woman's Bible*, Part I (New York: European Pub. Co., 1895).

127. Ibid., 1:13, 12, 7.

128. Ibid., 1:39–43, 49, 57; Kern, *Mrs. Stanton's Bible*, 163–165.

129. *The Woman's Bible*, 1:14–16, 102–103.

130. Ibid., 2:38–40, 88–92, 131, 85–88.

131. Ibid., 2:113–115, 121.

132. Ibid., 2:155–159, 163–164.

133. Ibid., 1:143–144.

134. Elizabeth Cady Stanton to Clara Colby, Feb. 23, 1895, quoted in Kern, *Mrs. Stanton's Bible*, 169.

135. "Notes," *New York Observer and Chronicle*, Jan. 23, 1896, 107–108; "Current Comment," *Christian Observer*, Jan. 29, 1896, 3; "The Woman's Bible," *Zion's Herald*, June 19, 1895, 392; Preface, *The Woman's Bible*, 2:7; Strange, "Elizabeth Cady Stanton's Woman's Bible," 28; Kern, *Mrs. Stanton's Bible*, 172–181; Elizabeth Cady Stanton, "The Woman's Bible—Revised by Woman," *Free Thought Magazine* (April 1895): 194–204; *The Truth Seeker*, July 27, 1895, 468. However, *The Truth Seeker* briefly advertised *The Woman's Bible* and Joslyn Gage's *Woman, Church, and the State*. See, ibid., Oct. 19, 1895, 669, ibid., Oct. 5, 1895, 637.

136. Preface, *The Woman's Bible*, 2:7; Susan B. Anthony to Elizabeth Cady Stanton, July 24, 1895, in *Selected Papers*, 5:699–700; Stanton, *Eighty Years and More*, 453; "The Bible Has Been Revised by Women," *Los Angeles Herald*, March 31, 1895, 16; "The Woman's Bible," *Washington Evening Star*, Feb. 6, 1896, 15; "Full of Ridicule," *St. Paul Daily Globe*, Nov. 26, 1895, 6; "Suffragists and the Woman's Bible," *Salt Lake Herald*, Jan. 30, 1896, 4.

137. Frances E. Willard to Elizabeth Cady Stanton, Aug. 1, 1895, in *Selected Papers*, 5:703–704.

138. Elizabeth Cady Stanton to Clara Bewick Colby, Jan. 24, 1896, ibid., 6:10–12; "The Woman's Bible," *Washington Evening Star*, Jan. 24, 1896, 8; Kern, *Mrs. Stanton's Bible*, 181–183.

139. Elizabeth Cady Stanton to Clara Bewick Colby, Jan. 24, 1896, in *Selected Papers*, 6:10–11.

140. Appendix, *Woman's Bible*, 2:215–217; "All in a Name," *Washington Evening Star*, Jan. 27, 1896, 12; Strange, "Elizabeth Cady Stanton's Woman's Bible," 28.

141. Debate of the NAWSA, Feb. 28, 1896, in *Selected Papers*, 6:14–16.

142. Ibid., 6:16–17.

143. Ibid., 6:17–18.

144. "It Is Now Over," *Washington Evening Star*, Jan. 29, 1896, 1; "Woman Suffrage Resolutions," *New York Times*, Jan. 29, 1896, 9; Elizabeth Cady Stanton to Clara Bewick Colby, Feb. 5, 1896, in *Selected Papers*, 41–43; Susan B. Anthony to Clara Bewick Colby, Feb. 10, 1896, ibid., 44–46; Susan B. Anthony to Elizabeth Cady Stanton, Feb. 10, 1896, ibid., 46–47; Elizabeth Cady Stanton to Clara Bewick Colby, Aug. 20, 1896, ibid., 90–91; Kern, *Mrs. Stanton's Bible*, 187–193.

145. Susan B. Anthony to Elizabeth Cady Stanton, April 1896, in *Selected Papers*, 6:61–62; Elizabeth Cady Stanton to Clara Bewick Colby, Aug. 20, 1896, ibid., 6:90–91.

146. "The Woman's Bible," *Boston Investigator*, Dec. 5, 1896, ibid., 6:113–114.

147. *The Woman's Bible* 2:6–8; Appendix, ibid., 2:215–217.

148. Moore and Kramnick, *Godless Citizens in a Godly Republic*, 60–61; Barry, *Susan B. Anthony*, 95–97; Griffith, *In Her Own Right*, 45–46.

149. Elizabeth Cady Stanton, "Woman's Position in the Bible," *Boston Investigator*, Sept. 10, 1898, in *Selected Papers*, 6:243–244; Elizabeth Cady Stanton to Lillie Devereux Blake, June 14, 1899, ibid., 6:296–297; Elizabeth Cady Stanton, "Are Homogenous Divorce Laws in All the States Desirable?," *North American Review* (March 1900): 405–409; Kern, *Mrs. Stanton's Bible*, 2–3; Strange, "Elizabeth Cady Stanton's Woman's Bible," 16.

6

"This Is a Christian Nation"

The previous chapters have considered only part of the religious complexity of Gilded Age America.[1] Protestantism—chiefly, the dominant evangelical strain—was at its height of power and influence. "The growth of Christianity in this country . . . has been the most marvelous ever known in any land or any age," exclaimed Daniel Dorchester in his 1890 history *Christianity in the United States*. "Our banners have uninterruptedly advanced, even more than in any previous period in the history of Christianity." Dorchester packed his massive study with statistics to demonstrate that the numerical growth of Protestant churches and in church membership had kept pace with the overall increase in population, even though much of the latter was due to immigration from non-Protestant countries. Despite immigrants bringing with them their permissive "European ideas of the Sabbath," and the lack of effective enforcement of Sunday laws, the "very general *voluntary* observance [of the Sabbath] by such large masses of people is clear evidence of a large amount of elevated moral sentiment which dominates the land." As for the challenge from the "'infidel,' 'deist,' and 'atheist,'" which included the "'Radical,' 'Liberal,' 'Free Religionist,' [and] 'Ingersolism,'" he insisted, "the Christian sentiment is now more dominant than ever before."[2] Substantiating Dorchester's conclusions, the British observer Lord James Bryce described the nation's religious character in similarly robust terms:

> The whole matter may, I think, be summed up by saying that Christianity is in fact understood to be, though not the legally established religion, yet the national religion. So far from thinking their commonwealth godless, the Americans conceive that the religious character of a government consists in nothing but the religious belief of the individual citizens, and the conformity of their conduct to that belief. They deem the general acceptance of Christianity to be one to the main sources of their national prosperity, and the nation a special object of Divine favour.[3]

Modern historians of American religion have generally confirmed this assessment. In his seven-volume study, *A History of the Expansion of Christianity*, Kenneth Scott Latourette reserved two volumes to what he called "The Great Century," concluding that the "nineteenth century was a time of unequaled expression of the vitality inherent in the Christian faith" in America. Fellow historian Martin E. Marty agreed that the Gilded Age "was clearly the hour of triumph for transformed evangelicalism."[4]

> Wherever one turned, signs of progress, growth, and success could be documented. . . . Protestantism had so molded the outlook, morals, mores, customs, and standards of the nation that the church and the world were almost indistinguishable. . . . Evangelicalism had shaped a culture and the culture had shaped evangelicalism. . . . All of these signs were impressive to partisans of Christianity and seemed oppressive and overpowering to its antagonists.[5]

Contemporary opinions about the true health of American Protestantism varied, however, depending on an author's perspective and how seriously one considered the external challenges. Protestant hegemony faced competition not only from freethought, feminism, Darwinism, biblical criticism, and Mormonism but also from unparalleled immigration that accelerated the growth of Catholicism, Eastern Orthodoxy, Orthodox Judaism, and Asian religions. Aside from these external threats, Protestant leaders feared that rank-and-file members had become quiescent about Protestantism's cultural dominance and that they presumed the invulnerability of Protestantism's interrelationship with republican government, an attitude that historian Henry F. May called "the summit of complacency."[6]

Writing in the *North American Review* in 1883, a self-described "Non-Church-Goer" offered an alternative to the rosy assessment of Protestantism's health, asserting that "only a small proportion, even of intelligent and eminently respectable people, are regular attendees upon religious services on Sunday." The main reason for this situation was that the church "so inadequately provides for [people]" by offering them only "a good deal of decayed theology." Indeed, "Non-Church-Goer" continued, the world has "been moving very rapidly during the last generation, and theology, which used to be in the van of human thought, and in some measure to lead in human progress, has fallen to the rear, and is in imminent danger of being left all together."[7] A contributor to *The Forum* grudgingly concurred, expressing concern about the "Present Outlook for Christianity" in the United States: "without controversy, Christianity appears to many of the wisest to be at the present day in deadlier peril than it has been at any time during the eighteen hundred years of its existence."[8] Rochester Bishop B.J. McQuaid, American Catholicism's leading pugilist, agreed with both assessments, but only in part. The Protestant Church was beset by "indifferentism, irreligion, infidelity, [and] atheism," McQuaid asserted, whereas the Catholic Church was vital and growing. "In all of its multitudinous forms Protestantism is decaying—is dying. . . . Protestantism has failed to do Christ's work, and will continue to dwindle away until nothing is left of it but remnants and a name."[9]

Other contemporaries, however, refused to accept that American Protestantism had become stagnant or was in decline. The "Non-Church-Goer's" obituary elicited considerable disagreement from respondents in the *North American Review*. Claims about the decline in church attendance were "palpably untrue," insisted Rev. William Hayes Ward. Current church affiliation, combining communicants with other attendees, was at its highest level in the nation's history, Ward declared, constituting thirty-five million people out of a total population of fifty million and representing "a rapidly increasing proportion of our population." He concluded that "[o]urs is a church-going people, a church-respecting, and a church-honoring people, and never more so than now."[10] Another respondent concurred that "public religious services of the Church have never been so numerously attended as now, nor by so large a proportion of intelligent and responsible people." A third, more circumspect respondent countered that attendance figures did not account for a noticeable indifference among some church-goers, something that he attributed to "preacher[s] waxing warm in defense of some fiction of theology" and to their "dreary, mechanical reading of the Scriptures." Still, to forecast the "speedy collapse" of "ecclesiastical institutions [was] simply silly."[11] Agreeing with this last perspective, Henry Ward Beecher wrote in 1882, "[t]he religious sentiment was never so intelligent, or so strong, in America as now." However, "if the American people are ever driven away from the Church, and from faith in the Christian religion," Beecher maintained, "it will be the fault of the Church and of the Pulpit" for not keeping Christianity relevant.[12]

Thus, despite Protestantism's putative health, the various internal and external challenges to its dominance remained a source of disagreement and a cause of concern. In his book *Our Country*, Reverend Josiah Strong warned about Protestant complacency in the face of its myriad challenges; it was increasingly evident, he wrote, "that church provision [alone] is becoming more and more inadequate to the needs" of the nation. Many Protestants blithely mouthed the mantra that America was a "Christian nation" without exploring the meaning of that statement, while other Protestants believed that America's status as a Christian (i.e., Protestant) nation could not be taken for granted. "Can Christianity effectually conserve the moral and religious interests of a State which is not merely organically separated from the Church, but which is without religious ideas in its constitution?" queried Daniel Dorchester. The question, he continued, was "whether these religious elements, which supplemented those omissions in the letter of the civil Constitution [will] gradually wear away, letting down the nation to the level of atheistical doctrines" and leading to "a moral deterioration" of the nation. Just as Christians had a duty to prevent that deterioration, the state, through its laws, policies, and public institutions, could not remain passive about the Christian character of the culture; to ensure that America remained a Christian nation, church and the state had to work in concert.[13]

Some activists aimed to ensure that this would happen. They renewed their efforts to enact and enforce morally based laws and policies. Some have already have been discussed: Comstock's anti-obscenity crusade, the effort of the National Reform Association (NRA) to secure a Christian Amendment to the US Constitution, the temperance campaign, and the Protestant and Catholic response to divorce law reform. Those reactionary measures continued throughout the 1880s and 1890s, supplemented by efforts to retain Protestant prayer and Bible reading in the public schools and to increase Sunday law enforcement, including a proposal to enact a national Sunday law. Even though freethinkers criticized such efforts—and Robert Ingersoll lampooned them as ineffective and as a sign of the fragility of religion—Liberal opposition was disorganized and did little to circumvent the momentum toward increased Christian involvement in government. Instead, Protestant efforts to perfect the nation's informal status as Christian were forestalled by a variety of social, demographic, and economic forces, as well as an internal dissidence over what it meant to be a "Christian nation."[14]

The School Question

The Ohio Supreme Court's 1873 decision in *Board of Education v. Minor*—upholding the banning of prayer and Bible reading in the Cincinnati schools—did little to abate the controversy over religious exercises in the public schools.

On the contrary, the decision convinced evangelical Protestants that the primary institution for perpetuating Christian morality in the culture, aside from the church, was under direct assault. Evangelicals had counted on common schools to pass on those Christian values necessary to perpetuate American culture. Now, that role had been called into question. Princeton theologian A.A. Hodge worried that "because the activities of the public schools are universal," the "perversion of the great educating agency cannot be corrected by the supplementing agencies of the Christian home, the Sabbath-school, or the church." The *Christian Statesman*, the journal of the NRA, expressed similar concerns. "With the expulsion of the Bible, come expurgated school books from which every trace of Christian thought has been carefully erased." The ultimate result would be that "the Christian people of the country will [be] robbed of their heritage in the public schools."[15] Even Catholic officials rejected the *Minor* decision, asserting that to "make the schools purely secular" was "worse than making them purely Protestant."[16]

Yet, for the first time since the founding of the nation's common schools, people were disputing the assumption that religious instruction was indispensable to education.[17] Freethinkers—led by Robert Ingersoll, Francis Abbot, and D.M. Bennett—endorsed the idea of secular public schooling. So did leaders of liberal Judaism such as Felix Adler and Rabbi Isaac Mayer Wise. Secularism was not "so dangerous that it must be kept out of the schools," Ingersoll insisted. "It belongs in the schools" rather than the Bible.[18] Elizabeth Cady Stanton, too, supported removing the Bible from the public schools. History "shows that the Bible has been the greatest block in the way of [human] progress," she declared. "Why then continue to read it in our public schools?"[19] And when Octavius B. Frothingham advocated retaining the Bible in the schools as a book on literature and ancient history, Francis Abbot excoriated him in the pages of *The Index*. To use the Bible as a text-book would satisfy no one while it would anger both Protestants and Catholics who considered the scriptures to be divine revelation, Abbot wrote, and it would become "the symbol of the political supremacy of religious rationalism." "[N]othing less than a total exclusion of the Bible is what the 'absolute secularization of the schools' must mean."[20]

Joining freethinkers and liberal Jews were an increasing number of liberal Protestants. During the Cincinnati controversy, Henry Ward Beecher had called for ending nonsectarian Bible reading. While Bible reading "would do a world of good and no harm" in most contexts, Beecher declared, to preserve the universality of public schooling, "I vote to exclude it." Beecher called on the common school to be a "civil and not religious institution," though he stopped short of demanding that it should be "secular." "Because the common school is not a religious institution, it is not therefore irreligious or unreligious."[21] Going a step further, Samuel Spear, editor of *The Independent*, called not only for suspending all religious exercises in the public schools but for a system of "secular education," a term that was a lightning rod for Protestants and Catholics alike. "If the state, as such, has no religion to propagate or establish, why should it undertake to have one in an educational system which it makes a common charge upon the people," Spear asked. He continued, "the State should not, by the use of the Bible or any other book . . . undertake the work of religious propagandism in the school which it creates and governs." Spear, a liberal Presbyterian minister, believed that instituting a secular education system was the only way to resolve complaints about the Protestant character of public schooling and to thwart Catholic demands for parochial school funding.[22]

Anticipating pushback, Spear acknowledged that public education "naturally and necessarily involves an element of *moral* education." But he called for schools to promote a "*secular* morality" of agreed-upon virtues—"good manners, self-control, truthfulness, honesty, and the like"—that could be taught apart from religion. These virtues "have existed in human thought and . . . in human practice" in multiple cultures for centuries. "They are not peculiar to Christendom or Christianity," he insisted.[23]

Another prominent voice in the debate over the religious character of public education was William Torrey Harris, superintendent for the St. Louis public schools from 1868 to 1880, and then US Commissioner of Education from 1880 to 1900. Harris agreed with Samuel Spear that American public education should be secular in orientation. People must preserve "the common school as a purely secular institution, without any religious instruction in it whatsoever," Harris insisted. This was mandated by the separation of church and state, he argued, but also to prevent "religious animus" and "the possibility of furnishing food for fanaticism and bigotry." Although Harris believed that schools should teach a universal morality, he agreed with Spear that it should be completely independent from religion. Religious instruction was inconsistent with attaining knowledge and hampered its development. "The secular branches of study—reading, writing, arithmetic, grammar and history—require a method of instruction different from that adapted to religious branches. In these secular branches the mind is to be trained to keep all its powers awake . . . [and] must be taught to be alert and critical." Once "the influence of the dogmatic tone of the religious lesson creeps into the secular recitations, [it] drives out critical acuteness and independent thinking."[24]

These arguments, though increasingly prominent, still represented a minority view. They went against the prevailing assumptions about the interdependence of morality and religion and were anathema to evangelical Protestants and Catholics alike. As Princeton's Hodge asserted, "[i]t cannot be questioned that morals rest upon a religious basis, and that a non-theistic ethics is equivalent to a positively antitheistic one." Agreeing with Hodge, a commentator in the *Reformed Quarterly Review* wrote that "there is no such thing as practical morality [in the public schools] unless it be rooted and grounded in the religious feeling of our human nature." That version of religion could not be left to chance, however; it must be "the *Christian* religion. . . . Any attempt, therefore, to exclude the Christian religion from any system devised for the instruction of the young, is a direct blow at Christianity itself."[25] Excluding religion from the schools also had ramifications for the nation writ-large. "The morality of the state is closely implicated with its duties in respect to the education of its youth," Princeton Theological Seminary's Lyman H. Atwater asserted. "[A]ll sound morality is rooted and grounded in religion, and not only so, the religion of the Bible," he continued. "A non-Christian, or non-biblical, morality is an infidel or atheistic morality. There is no neutrality here." Nonsectarian readings from the Bible were justified because "we are historically a Christian, and in a less degree Protestant, nation," a fact that was "disowned only by atheists and infidels."[26] Once again, Catholic commentators concurred with the Protestants' underlying premise, though not their solution of retaining *Protestant* prayer and Bible reading. Moral education could not be separated from Catholic doctrines, asserted *Catholic World*; a "secular morality," isolated from Catholic teachings and based on "nonsectarian" consensus values, would be little more than a "mongrel morality."[27]

Although the *Minor* case was a bellwether, it did not set a legal precedent, at least initially. Its greatest impact was to reinforce voluntary efforts to discontinue religious exercises. Following the *Minor* decision, public school districts in several cities with large Catholic populations either dropped prayer and Bible reading entirely or did so for schools located in non-Protestant neighborhoods. Chicago, Philadelphia, St. Louis, Buffalo, and Rochester boards of education canceled the practices despite criticism; when the New Haven school board took the same action, the board members were voted out in a special election.[28] More commonly, school districts conducted the exercises without comment or instruction by teachers and excused dissenting students from participating. This trend led one critic to condemn such "formal and perfunctory exercises" as "wholly inadequate as a means of moral instruction."[29] Also condemning this solution was Catholic Bishop B.J. McQuaid, who noted sarcastically that New York had made "great progress in the eliminating of every shade and semblance of religious instruction and usages from its common schools." Where the Bible was still read, it was only "in a very perfunctory way," but the "uselessness of the Bible as a mere reading-book was demonstrated long ago." McQuaid asked a question raised by Catholics and evangelicals alike: "Can a republic, of all forms of government, endure, whose children, for generations, are educated in schools without religion, without God?"[30]

While voluntary actions excluding Bible reading were becoming more common, legal challenges to ongoing religious exercises were generally unsuccessful. Following the *Minor* decision, courts in Illinois, Iowa, and Pennsylvania upheld readings from the King James Bible, delivered without note or comment by teachers, on the grounds the practices were nonsectarian and that objecting students were allowed to excuse themselves from participating.[31] The fact that Bible readings were accompanied by reciting the Lord's Prayer and the singing of "Gospel hymns" in two of the cases did not change the courts' view that the practices were nonsectarian, and judges in both cases expressed disdain for the plaintiffs' arguments. "Possibly," wrote the judge in the Iowa case, "the plaintiff is a propagandist and regards himself charged with a mission to destroy the influence of the Bible." Equally dismissive, the judge in the Pennsylvania case defended the value of Bible reading for nurturing morality and combatting vice. "The morality which the State deems it important thus to cultivate . . . is the morality of the Bible," he asserted. The judge also went to out his way to reaffirm earlier judicial declarations about the interdependence of the state with Christianity. The "notorious fact" was that "the prevailing religion in this Commonwealth is now and has always been Christianity," and any inspection of the state's law and institutions revealed that "the moral sentiment from which they spring and on which that are based, is generated by the Christian religion." The perpetuation of Christian society thus required retaining prayer and Bible reading in the schools.[32]

Then, in 1890, a second state supreme court struck down Bible reading in the schools, this time in Wisconsin. The holding in *Weiss v. District Board of*

School District was more sweeping than the *Minor* decision, which had essentially upheld the authority of school boards to abolish Bible reading (although the Ohio Supreme Court had strongly suggested Bible reading was inconsistent with constitutional principles). In *Weiss*, the Wisconsin high court took the next step by expressly holding that Bible reading was inherently sectarian and unconstitutional under its state bill of rights. Unlike the other decisions since *Minor*, the *Weiss* court scrutinized the way in which the Bible was used rather than deferring to school authorities that the practices were nonsectarian and inoffensive. "[W]e cannot doubt," Justice William Penn Lyon wrote for the court, "that the use of the Bible as a text-book in the public schools, and the stated reading thereof in such schools, without restriction, 'has a tendency to inculcate sectarian ideas.'" This, the court held, violated religious equality and the no-preference mandate contained in the state constitution; the religious practices "tend[ed] to destroy the equality of the pupils which the constitution seeks to establish and protect." At the same time, the justices rejected the school board attorney's arguments that the readings were justified on the basis that American government and law were based on Christian principles. Such claims were "entirely immaterial" for the operation of the public schools.[33]

Public reaction to the *Weiss* holding was mixed, with opposition being more muted than might otherwise be expected, possibly reflecting growing resignation among some Protestants. Evangelicals condemned the ruling, asserting that the Bible was not sectarian and accusing Catholics of orchestrating its removal.[34] But the *Christian Union* and *The Independent* defended the decision as consistent with the nation's growing religious diversity. The holding was "in harmony with the nature and structure of our political institutions," opined *The Independent*, "and is, moreover, just and equitable as between religious sects."[35] The *New York Times* also defended the Wisconsin holding, insisting that people had nothing to fear from a secular education system. "To say that a 'godless' instruction in those branches of knowledge, or in any other that are properly within the province of the public schools, is 'necessarily immoral,' is to make a perfectly meaningless assertion." The *Times* asserted that the decision represented the inevitable direction for public education, particularly if "the common school system [wishes to] maintain . . . its integrity." Increasingly, Americans were reconciling themselves with a system of *secular* public education.[36]

The *Weiss* decision provided additional ammunition for school boards that were abolishing or restricting religious instruction in their public schools. A survey conducted by the Woman's Christian Temperance Union (WCTU) in 1887 confirmed the trend, revealing that the Bible was not being read in schools in 175 counties out of 254 reporting. In those counties where the exercises persisted, Bible reading frequently was "not so generally read as formally." A contemporaneous report by the NRA substantiated those findings, noting that in Chicago, St. Louis, San Francisco, Rochester, Cincinnati, and "in a multitude of smaller places, the reading of the Bible and all religious exercises have been prohibited."[37] Education Commissioner William T. Harris also documented this phenomenon in a series of annual reports issued between 1884 and 1898. The reports indicated that not only was religious instruction in decline, but so too was the use of the Bible as textbook for teaching morals or literature. In his 1895 government report, Harris summarized that:

> There has been a change in public sentiment gradually growing toward complete secularization of the Government and its institutions. . . . Secularization of the schools is accepted or urged by many devout people who deem that safer than to trust others with the interpretation of the laws of conscience.[38]

As a longtime proponent of secular education, Harris may have been editorializing. His own reports, based on informal surveys of state education officials, indicated that many schools still used the Bible in some manner, although practices varied greatly by region. Where it remained, the true nature of its use was impossible to assess, as the responses invariably described the activities as nonsectarian and conducted for the purposes of instilling morals and character development. Devotional exercises were likely common in rural areas or in religiously homogeneous communities with small or politically powerless immigrant populations. Still, the reports indicated that a significant number of school districts had restricted religious exercises or discontinued them in their entirety. As one worried evangelical commented about the decline in Bible reading, it was "quite time to look after the floodgates, if it is not too late."[39]

Alarmed over the trend, religious conservatives approached their chief ally in Washington, DC, Senator Henry Blair, seeking federal action. Since assuming the chair of the Senate Committee on Education and Labor in 1881, Blair had introduced a series of bills that would have provided federal funding to states to encourage the operation of public schools where nonsectarian instruction would take place. The measures had passed the Senate on several occasions only to die in the House due to Southern opposition to federal intervention in the running of public schools, despite the bills' language accommodating segregation.⁴⁰ Blair never gave up on securing funding for public schooling through legislation, but in 1888, at the urging of the WCTU and the NRA, he proposed a constitutional amendment that borrowed from his funding bills. Like the latter, the measure prohibited state and federal funding of schools or institutions that were controlled by a denomination or instructed in the doctrines, tenets, or beliefs particular to any sect. This would have imposed an express prohibition on funding Catholic schooling, a position endorsed by Protestants and secularists alike. Blair's proposed amendment went further than his funding bills, however, by *requiring* each state to "establish and maintain a system of free public schools" where children between six and sixteen would be taught the "common branches of knowledge, and in virtue, morality, and the principles of the Christian religion." To placate critics of this last provision, Blair's proposal prohibited teaching "particular doctrines, tenets, belief[s], ceremonials, or observances" in any public school. Yet this provision, when read with the requirement that schools teach "virtue, morality, and the principles of the Christian religion," left no doubt that devotional religious instruction, not simply rote Bible reading, would be the national standard.⁴¹

In February 1889, Blair held hearings on his education amendment. They were dominated by religious conservatives who testified about the dire threats to public education from both infidels and Catholics. Witnesses condemned the *Minor* decision and the school boards that abolished Bible readings, arguing that these actions justified the amendment. Most witnesses refused to concede to Bible reading without note or comment, however. Rather, they urged that the exercises should be devotional in purpose and content. Not only should the Bible be read in the public schools, NRA's T.P. Stevenson urged, but Christian teachers "should inculcate the general [Christian] principles which have been regarded in the framework of our Government. If there is any sense in which we are a Christian nation, and which this is a Christian Government, in the same sense and to the same extent our schools ought to be Christian." Reverend James M. King of the Evangelical Alliance agreed that because "we are a Christian but not a sectarian nation," the "purely secular instruction of the youth" taking place in some schools placed the nation in "imminent peril." To blunt criticism, the witnesses insisted they were not seeking to turn back the clock but were only defending the practice of "nonsectarianism," which was under attack. The "Bible has been read and the general principles of morality and of the Christian religion have been inculcated in the American common school from the beginning of its history," Stevenson asserted. "In this respect we are seeking no change. We are resisting a change which amounts to a revolution." The witnesses claimed overwhelming public support for their position, but their statements revealed their desperation.[42]

Despite limited opposition to the measure at the hearings, Blair's education amendment suffered the same fate as his funding bills, dying in committee. Even though Blair and his supporters argued the amendment's provisions would simply preserve existing nonsectarian practices, proponents and observers alike understood the proposal for what it truly was: an effort not simply to forestall the secularization of public education but to reinvigorate its religious character. In a moment of candor, an NRA spokesman admitted in the *Christian Statesman* that the amendment "has its chief value in one phrase, 'the Christian religion'; but if it shall pass into our fundamental law, that one phrase will have all the potency of Almighty God, of Christ our Lord, of the Holy Bible, and of the Christian world, with it."[43] Catholics and Seventh-day Adventists lobbied against its adoption, though taking opposite positions on whether public schools should be secular. The Adventists' Alonzo T. Jones asserted that the "adoption of any such amendment . . . would be but the establishment of a national religion, and the enforcement of that religion upon all the States." *The Truth Seeker* also ran a series of articles opposing the amendment, characterizing it as "[if] not establishing a state church, it is establishing a state religion, and the church will not long be wanting. Our secular schools will soon be Sunday schools, and the 'principles of the Christian religion'—if anyone can define them—will be the abc's of the curriculum."[44]

The failure of Blair's amendment and school funding bills did nothing to resolve the School Question, which continued to embroil evangelicals, Catholics, secularists, and professional educators into the twentieth century. Unmediated Bible reading remained legal in most states, though increasingly based on the theory that the practices were conducted for nonreligious purposes. The Bible could be used to teach morality or for the purpose of "quieting" students, as one court held, but not to instill religious devotion or instruct in religious tenets, even where the latter were assumed to be universally held. In this way, unmediated Bible reading was consistent with a system of secular public schooling. But school boards were also free to dispose of the exercises altogether.[45]

Sunday Enforcement and the National Sabbath Law

A second concern for late-century evangelicals was the widespread neglect of Sunday observance and the lack of effective Sabbath-law enforcement by public officials. To a degree, this problem was not unique to the Gilded Age. Church observance and compliance with Sunday law restrictions on traveling, entertainment, working, and the opening of businesses had rarely been uniform or consistent during the early decades of the century. Practices and enforcement had varied widely in different regions and between urban and rural communities.[46] Still, despite the rise in church attendance during the final decades of the century, the period also saw increased defiance of both social and legal constraints on nonreligious activity on the Christian Sabbath. This shift in behavior and attitudes was due in part to market and commercial pressures that accompanied what Leigh Schmidt has called the "commercialization of the calendar."[47] Paralleling that shift, courts after mid-century transitioned from justifying Sunday-law enforcement on religious grounds to adopting secular health and welfare rationales for the laws or requiring that Sunday activity posed a "public nuisance" before it could be prohibited. As the California Supreme Court opined in 1881, "is has been held over and over again, in numerous States of the Union, that an act prohibiting the keeping open of certain places of business on Sunday is not a religious regulation . . . . It is purely a secular, sanitary, or police regulation." These changes in legal theory served only to further erode the idea of Sunday being a day meant for *religious* observance.[48]

By the Gilded Age, state Sunday laws were riddled with exceptions for "works of necessity or charity." The expanding number of legislatively and judicially created exceptions made Sunday laws appear arbitrary and ludicrous, as in 1880, when the Indiana Supreme Court ruled that the selling of cigars at a hotel stand on Sunday qualified as a "work of necessity" and was thus a permissible exception to the state Sabbath law. Other courts found that works of necessity included maple sugaring and picking ripe melons to prevent their spoilage. In contrast, traveling to visit a sick friend or to attend a funeral on a Sunday was not. In 1880, the *American Law Review* ridiculed the inconsistencies among state legal exemptions in an editorial appropriately titled "More Sunday-Law Absurdities."[49]

Sabbath laws that remained intact were often poorly enforced. Despite prohibitions on Sunday labor, entertainment, or playing sports, Sunday professional baseball flourished in many cities. In one example of the lax enforcement, police in Buffalo, New York, had turned a blind eye to Sunday baseball games for more than two years before they were finally forced to act by local religious leaders. Once in court, the judge chastised the Buffalo police commissioners for failing to enforce the law, but then noted that the local magistrate regularly dismissed all Sabbath citations, thus providing police little incentive to stop the games. In a rare instance of rigorous enforcement, the Nebraska Supreme Court in 1892 upheld a complaint against a Sunday baseball game, tracing the law to "the Ten Commandments [of] Moses" while affirming that all free governments were "based on divine law." As the national pastime grew in popularity, however, public officials acceded to permitting baseball games after 2:00 p.m. on Sundays.[50] Authorities also generally turned a blind eye to the publishing of newspapers on Sundays, more frequently going after the hawkers on the street. Newspapers regularly avoided the risk by printing Sunday papers on Saturday nights, letting the newsboys take their chances the next morning.[51]

Even when Sunday laws were enforced, many business found it more profitable to pay the small fines and continue operating on Sundays. One defendant charged with operating an opera house on the Sabbath admitted at trial that he made more money from theatrical performances on Sundays than from the other six days of the week combined. Baseball clubs made the same boast.[52] Robert Ingersoll regularly—and purposefully—delivered lectures on Sundays to packed auditoriums, daring authorities to enforce prohibitions on public entertainment. "The ministers have done their best to prevent all recreation on the Sabbath," Ingersoll chided. "They hate parks, they hate music, they hate anything that keeps a man away from church" and from "putting money in collection boxes, listening to sermons, [and] reading the cheerful histories of the Old Testament, imagining the joys of heaven and the torments of hell."[53] Commenting on a Sunday lecture by that "prince of infidels and blasphemers," the *Christian Advocate* lamented: "What a shame that professed Christians will, on the holy Sabbath, go to a theater, and pay $1 each to hear their religion ridiculed and their Christ blasphemed!" In another instance, the Pittsburgh police chief attempted to prevent an Ingersoll Sunday lecture by threatening to invoke a law that prohibited paid performances on Sundays.

A group of enterprising local freethinkers bought out the venue and opened the doors of the auditorium to the public for free.[54]

Evangelicals viewed the lax enforcement of Sunday laws and the changes in their legal rationales with alarm. Princeton theologian Lyman Atwater chastised legislators and judges for adopting secular justifications for Sunday laws—it was "incumbent on the State primarily and essentially [to enforce Sunday laws] because God commands it." Atwater acknowledged that refraining from labor and other activities was "expedient for man" because it "ensure[d] the physical and mental relaxation, as well as the spiritual and moral culture," but "irrespective of this, man is bound always and everywhere to observe it . . . because God commands it."[55] Monday Lecturer Joseph Cook agreed with Atwater, adding that it was a "vain endeavor to preserve Sunday as a day of rest, unless you preserve it as a day of worship. Unless Sabbath observance be *founded upon religious reasons*, you will not long maintain it at a high standard of the basis of economic and physiological and political considerations only."[56]

According to one scholar, considering the various pressures for relaxing and secularizing the Christian Sabbath, "what is astonishing and significant is the strength of the Sabbatarian movement in the Gilded Age and the extent to which it was able to preserve the American Sabbath both in custom and in law."[57] In May 1880, religious conservatives held a rally in Washington, DC, to draw attention to the issue of Sabbath observance. Leading citizens, including President Rutherford Hayes and members of Congress, listened as speakers called for increased enforcement and reaffirmed the religious purpose of Sunday laws. Presiding over the event, and delivering the opening address, was Supreme Court Justice and former NRA president William Strong, the same person who had assisted Anthony Comstock in securing the federal obscenity law. Strong acknowledged that on one level, Sunday laws were merely "a civil institution" that ensured "a rest day for all our people." But to "all believers in Divine revelation, it is a holy day instituted by God himself for all mankind." Strong bemoaned the "growing disregard of the Sabbath in this country." In particular, he pointed to immigrant neighborhoods in large cities, where "Sunday differs from no other day, except by an increase in vice and disorder." Such places, with their lax Sabbath observance, were "plague spots in the community, not only poisoning its morals, disturbing its good order, but depreciating its property. They are Sodoms." Strong closed his xenophobic remarks by calling on all "Christian men [and] patriotic men" to take steps "to restore the Sabbath to what it was intended to be by the framers of our laws and by our fathers." Other speakers, including Secretary of the Navy Richard W. Thompson, made similar appeals for stricter Sabbath-law enforcement based on religious grounds. Regardless of the legal justifications given for Sunday laws, Thompson insisted, we "must not forget . . . the important truth that it is absolutely necessary to our form of government that Christianity be preserved, and that the Sabbath be observed as one of the essential means of doing this." The rally, sponsored by the New York Sabbath Committee, helped to reawaken interest in stricter enforcement of Sabbath laws.[58]

At this time the NRA seized on Sabbath observance as one of its signature issues. The Association set its sights on obtaining stricter Sunday enforcement in the states—with the ultimate goal of securing a national Sunday-rest law. In 1879, the NRA convinced Pennsylvania legislators to enact a new Sunday law that stiffened Sabbath prohibitions and imposed a $1,000 fine on businesses that violated it. Shortly thereafter, Sabbatarians secured amendments strengthening Sunday laws in other states, including Arkansas, New Jersey, Ohio, and Tennessee. In 1884, the WCTU redoubled its efforts to secure greater Sabbath observance by creating a department "to Prevent Sabbath Desecration," with Frances Willard appointing Josephene C. Bateham, a former NRA employee, to head the effort. Joining the WCTU in 1888 was a new national organization, the American Sabbath Union (later, the Lord's Day Alliance), formed for the purpose of strengthening and enforcing Sabbath observance. Increasingly, noted one observer, the "Sunday question is coming to the front."[59]

The renewed attention on the Sabbath issue produced increased enforcement. During the 1880s and 1890s, Sabbath prosecutions accelerated in the South, particularly in Tennessee and Arkansas, with the latter state amending its Sunday law in 1885 to remove exemptions for Saturday observers while increasing the penalty from a fine to potential jail time. According to the newly formed Religious Liberty Association, an agency of the Seventh-day Adventist Church, approximately twenty-five people were indicted for Sabbath violations in Arkansas in 1885 and 1886. Most defendants were Seventh-day Baptists and Adventists who followed biblical dictates to observe Saturday but to work the remaining six days of the week. Officials prosecuted Saturday observers for such menial and nondisruptive activities as plowing, chopping wood, planting potatoes, and picking peaches. Many refused to pay the $25 or $50 fines and worked off their time on chain gangs with hardened criminals.[60] In 1886, the Arkansas Supreme Court upheld the conviction of a

Seventh-day Baptist for painting his church on Sunday. That same year, the Tennessee Supreme Court affirmed the conviction of a Seventh-day Adventist blacksmith for working on Sundays, ostensibly for serving non-Sabbatarian customers. In neither state did the law require prosecutors to prove that the Sunday activity caused a disturbance or was an annoyance to other people. According to the Tennessee court, it was "[un]necessary to a conviction that the proof should show that any person was disturbed" by the activity. Instead, it was sufficient that the acts were done "in such [a] public manner as to have been open to the observation of the public. Their tendency is to corrupt public morals, and the example is pernicious and contrary to law and the wellbeing and good order of society."[61]

One notable case involved R.M. King, an Adventist farmer from Obion, Tennessee, who was indicted in June 1889 for being a public nuisance after he was repeatedly fined for working his fields on Sundays. A jury convicted the elderly King after a particularly vituperative speech by the prosecutor charging Adventists with immorality for working on Sundays, equating their activities with the evils of polygamy. "I wish to God we had more Methodist Churches, and more Baptist churches, and more Presbyterian Churches . . . until every man was brought under the benign influences of these churches; but, in the name of God, I do not want any of these Advent[ist] Churches or Mormon Churches." The trial court fined King $75, an amount greater than provided under the statute, which he worked off in jail. After the Tennessee Supreme Court summarily affirmed King's conviction, his attorneys sought a writ of habeas corpus from a federal circuit court, arguing that Tennessee did not recognize a common law offense of nuisance.[62] In his opinion, Circuit Judge Eli S. Hammond initially chastised the prosecution for relying on religious "prejudices and passion" to justify the Sunday law. The Fourth Commandment was not a part of the common law, Hammond lectured, any more "than the doctrine of the Trinity or the Apostles' creed." But Hammond then upheld King's conviction, declaring that the court's purview was limited to considering the validity of the common law offense. By a "sort of factious advantage," Hammond wrote, "observers of Sunday have secured the aid of the civil law, and adhere to that advantage with great tenacity." Evincing frustration, Hammond stated that courts could not change "that which has been done, however done, by the civil law in favor of the Sunday observers." King, who had spent several months in jail, died before his attorneys could appeal Hammond's decision to the US Supreme Court.[63]

The resurgence in Sabbath prosecutions, spurred on by reaction to the secularization of Sundays, continued into the 1890s and produced holdings that had not been seen for decades. In 1894, the Maryland Court of Appeals upheld a conviction for husking corn on a Sunday. Relying on an antebellum case that had declared Maryland a "Christian community," the court held that the law's religious purpose meant that proving a nuisance or public disturbance was unnecessary. Acknowledging that the statute's ban on labor benefited certain Christian denominations, the court remarked:

> But it would scarcely be asked of a court, in what professes to be a Christian land, to declare a law unconstitutional because it requires rest from bodily labor on Sunday . . . and thereby promotes the cause of Christianity. If the Christian religion is, incidentally or otherwise, benefitted or fostered by having this day of rest (as it undoubtedly is) there is all the more reason for the enforcement of laws that help to preserve it.[64]

These and similar decisions indicated a renewed interest in stricter Sabbath enforcement and in the courts' role in ensuring public piety. Possibly, many judges and prosecutors had never actually abandoned their belief in the religious purpose of Sunday laws and had needed little encouragement to resurrect religious justifications for their enforcement. But whether public officials were already so inclined, the renewed attention given to Sabbath enforcement validated those leanings.[65]

Despite such holdings, the upsurge in enforcement did little to increase Sabbath observance, and it failed to initiate a wholesale revival of religious justifications in the law. Outside the South, courts continued to apply health and welfare and nuisance rationales. As the Minnesota Supreme Court wrote in a decision that repudiated its earlier reliance on religious justifications, "[i]t is unnecessary for us, at this time, to consider to what extent the legislature may, in harmony with the constitution, make laws recognizing the Christian Sabbath, and regulating its observance. All the authorities concur that the legislature may by law establish, as a civil and political institution, the first day of the week as a day of rest."[66]

Conservative Protestants were not satisfied with the increased Sabbath enforcement in a handful of states. Because states varied in their justifications and in legal exemptions for Sunday laws, and because of the growth of interstate commerce, conservatives argued that Sabbath observance was a *national* problem that required a *national* solution. Leading the charge to make Sabbath observance uniform was Wilber F. Crafts, a former Presbyterian minister and author of the popular 1884 book *The Sabbath for Man*. Crafts allied himself with Josephine C. Bateham of the WCTU, and together they petitioned Congress in April 1888 to enact laws prohibiting mail delivery, the running of trains, and all nonessential government activity on Sundays. The petition drive quickly evolved into a campaign joined by the NRA and the newly formed American Sabbath Union (ASU) to encourage Congress to enact a national Sunday law.[67]

Crafts and Bateham approached religious conservatives' favorite legislator, Senator Henry Blair, who held an informational hearing on the Sabbath issue in April. The following month, Blair introduced a bill designed to prohibit all interstate commerce and mail delivery and all business, labor, or recreation on federal property on Sundays. Although Blair sought to cast the bill's purpose as promoting a day of rest to benefit workers, the religious thrust of the measure was obvious from the preamble: "to secure to the people the enjoyment of the first day of the week, commonly known as the Lord's day, as a day of rest, and *to promote its observance as a day of religious worship.*" To build support for the bill, Blair had Crafts approach the Knights of Labor and other labor groups for their endorsement, which he secured. Crafts also solicited support from various Protestant denominations, and out of those discussions he helped organize the American Sabbath Union to coordinate efforts to lobby for the bill's passage.[68]

Senator Blair held a hearing on the bill on December 13, 1888, which coincided with a national Sabbath convention in Washington, thus providing a platform for religious conservatives to make their case. Crafts organized the testimony, and although several labor groups sent letters of endorsement, the hearing was dominated by witnesses from religious organizations, chiefly the NRA, the WCTU, and the ASU. In their testimony, Crafts, Bateham, and T.P. Stevenson of the NRA sought to strengthen their case by touting the health benefits of Sunday rest for workers. But the labor rationale was secondary to their overarching argument that the Sabbath should be observed for religious reasons. Crafts and Stevenson readily acknowledged their religious motives for the law, asserting the bill would strengthen the Christian features of the government and make federal law conform to God's laws. The Sabbath was "the law of God," which "binds nations and governments as well as individuals." Without stricter laws, Stevenson insisted, "[i]nfidelity and irreligion will sweep over the land; churches will be neglected; . . . children . . . will become infidels and worldlings; [and] our schools and colleges, perverted to secular education, will be seminaries of atheism."[69]

Despite such revealing statements, the Sabbath advocates walked a fine line. They believed that secular justifications for Sunday laws were a chief cause of the decline in observance; yet by emphasizing the religious basis for such laws they risked appearing sectarian and alienating labor groups. Opponents, led by Alonzo T. Jones of the Seventh-day Adventist Religious Liberty Association, seized on the inconsistency in the proponents' arguments. Jones charged that the bill was part of a larger effort by religious conservatives to create an unofficial theocracy. Any legislation imposing a religious doctrine would require the government to declare "just what are the principles of the Christian religion" and would be the first step to the "establishment of a national religion." Jones's testimony elicited a challenge from Senator Blair, resulting in an extended exchange which revealed Blair's disdain for immigrants and religious minorities, arguing that Mormon polygamists, too, claimed a religious exemption from the enforcement of salutary laws. Blair admitted his willingness to enact laws that favored the Protestant majority. He asked Jones, rhetorically: "You deny the right of the [religious] majority . . . to make a law in conformity with which the whole shall practice in society?" Opposition testimony was not sufficient to derail the bill, but it exposed the religious agenda behind it, which made many people uncomfortable. "When bills to enforce Sunday rest . . . are introduced into the United States senate," chided Elizabeth Cady Stanton, "it is time to rouse popular thought on these questions." Sabbath advocates continued to lobby for the bill into 1889, but Blair was unable to have it discharged from his own committee. The bill died when Congress adjourned in March of that year.[70]

In the end, Seventh-day observers and freethinkers were not responsible for the demise of Blair's Sunday Rest Bill or the resistance to widespread Sunday law enforcement.[71] Rather, the movement was forestalled chiefly by commercial and economic considerations. Efforts to restrict Sunday commerce—rail and ship transportation of goods—faced growing opposition from the business community. Judges grew increasingly sympathetic to arguments that the strict enforcement of bans on shipping and commercial transactions impeded economic development and that the law was generally unable to articulate when such transactions were of necessity. Allowing authorities to "arrest . . . embarrass, if not entirely stop, the great commercial interests and leading industries of the State," declared the Indiana Supreme Court, was "a result certainly not intended by the Legislature that enacted the law." Delays "in the running of trains, and in the transaction of its business [on Sundays] . . . would injuriously affect not only the company, but also the general public."[72] Similarly, in 1883 the Illinois Supreme Court interpreted the state's prohibition on Sunday *labor* not to extend to the conducting of *business* on that day. The Illinois court then extended its new exception to include contracts executed on a Sunday, surmising they too involved business transactions.[73] Judges also became annoyed at claims raised by offenders that Sunday laws shielded them from being accountable for fraudulent contracts or personal injuries that took place on Sundays.[74] "If the general rule of holding contracts, made upon Sunday, void, is, also, to shield the contracting parties from the consequences of their frauds, and to allow the dishonest and abandoned to retain whatever they may be able to get possession of under such contracts," opined one court, "then the rule itself will be productive of infinite mischief and should be discarded at once.[75]

Ruling against a similar defense to injuries sustained while traveling on Sundays, the Massachusetts Supreme Judicial Court wrote in 1880 that "[w]e must assume that the plaintiff was unlawfully travelling on the Lord's day. But this fact does not defeat his right to recover, unless this unlawful act was a contributory cause of the injury he sustained." Following that legal trend, the Maryland Court of Appeals permitted a plaintiff to sue for negligence even though the alleged injury occurred while he was working on a Sunday. That the injury was sustained "by reason of any neglect of [a] duty, or other wrongful act . . . on Sunday, can afford no excuse to the defendant, or exoneration from liability." These and other decisions, motivated chiefly by economic considerations and a desire for judicial efficiency, were instrumental in secularizing Sabbath laws.[76]

Chicago World's Fair

Concern about the desecration of the Sabbath was never far from religious conservatives' minds. The issue sprang to the fore in 1891 because of the upcoming Chicago World's Columbian Exposition. The Exposition, scheduled to open in late 1892 and run through 1893, was to be held in celebration of the four hundredth anniversary of Christopher Columbus's discovery of the Americas. In early 1891, reports emerged that the directors of the fair, backed by local political and business interests, intended to open the fair on Sundays to accommodate laborers who commonly worked six days a week (and hopefully to realize a financial boon from the large crowds expected on Sundays).[77]

When this became known, religious conservatives—the NRA, the ASU, and the WCTU, among others—raised a storm of protest. The Exposition was a "National Fair," asserted *The Chautauquan*, and the "Christian people of this country cannot afford to patronize a Sabbath-breaking fair. . . . We *must* protest against a national endorsement of Sabbath-breaking."[78] Wilber Crafts quickly organized the National Committee on Sunday Closing of the World's Fair to coordinate groups opposed to the opening and to pressure public officials. The objectors petitioned Congress to rescind a promised $5,000,000 federal loan to the Exposition unless its directors agreed to close the fair on Sundays. Various state legislatures followed suit, passing resolutions in support of a Sunday ban and directing their states' exhibits to close should the Exposition remain open on Sundays. Petitions and remonstrances purportedly containing two million signatures poured into Washington during the spring of 1892, forcing Congress to hold hearings on the issue.[79]

For four days in April, the House World's Fair Committee heard heated testimony from religious and civic organizations, the vast majority opposed to the Sunday openings. More than one witness asserted that the Exposition should be closed on Sunday because America was a "Christian nation." According to one newspaper report, Elliot F. Shepard, owner of the New York *Mail & Express* and president of the ASU, "made a plea for Sunday observance in general, and its enforcement at the World's Fair in particular, on the ground that this is a 'Christian Nation.'" As the *American Sentinel*, the journal for the Seventh-day Adventists, described the hearing, the "fervor upon the question [of closing the Exposition] rose almost to the height of a mania."[80]

The closing of the Chicago Exposition quickly became a political hot-potato in 1892, eclipsing more pressing matters. Senators and representatives, facing reelection in the fall, felt pressure from groups that made a vote for Sunday closing the litmus test for support. The ASU's Elliot Shepard told members of Congress that each one "who voted for Sunday closing would cover himself with glory in the eyes of the nation," while he threatened to print the names of noncompliant members in his newspaper to be "broadcast all over the country."[81] So "bold and dictatorial" were some of the overtures, wrote the *Boston Globe*, that one senator was constrained to rise in his seat, last week, and protest that they practically amounted to political blackmail. In many cases they are accompanied by the threat that any member of Congress who shall vote any aid or appropriation for the Columbian Exposition, except with the Sabbatarian proviso, will be systematically boycotted at the polls by the denominational constituencies cited in the memorials.[82]

Numerous senators and representatives endorsed a Sunday closing, with more than one agreeing the United States was "a Christian nation."[83] A bill conditioning the appropriation of Exposition funds to a Sunday closing was introduced in Congress in July. During debate on the measure, most congressmen sought to avoid the religious issue by offering secular rationales.[84] A handful, however, openly embraced the argument that a Sunday opening conflicted with America's Christian heritage. Senator Joseph R. Hawley of Connecticut, in declaring that the country was a "Christian nation," stated:

> The pervading sense of the Federal Constitution and the constitution of every solitary State and Territory is religious. They are founded on, and the common law is permeated with, the spirit of Christianity. Every statute book shows that it has been written by men who have a belief in the great universal doctrines of religion.[85]

Seventh-day Adventists opposed congressional efforts to close the Exposition, with its journal charging that supporters of the closing were not for "the separation of Church and State but [for] the concentration of the forces of a religion into a more complete union with the centralized power of the State." Freethinkers, coordinated by *The Truth Seeker*, sent thousands of letters to Congress against the closing, while Robert Ingersoll blasted the closing campaign as a grasp for political influence. Labor groups, too, led by the Knights of Labor, opposed Sunday closure. And Elizabeth Cady Stanton weighed in in a February 1892 article in the *North American Review*, asserting that the fair should remain open to serve the working classes. Christians "have the right to stay away from the exposition on Sunday" if they so desired, Stanton declared, "but they have no right to throw obstacles in the way of a majority by influencing popular sentiment or securing legislative enactments to prevent them from enjoying that day." She chided religious leaders for foolishly thinking that a Sunday closing of the Exposition "would drive the laboring masses to the churches, there to drop their dimes into the collection-boxes." Beyond voicing such criticisms, Stanton insisted that "it was a work of supererogation for Congress to do any legislating on this subject." It promoted "the Christian Sunday above all other sects" and would result in a "union in State and Church."[86]

Opponents of a congressionally mandated closing were outnumbered, however. Congress passed the conditional appropriation on August 4, and President Benjamin Harrison signed the bill into law the following day. At the same time Congress also authorized an outright gift of $2,500,000 to the Exposition with an identical Sunday-closing proviso. A later effort to rescind the closure resolution failed. As the *Washington Post* reported upon the passage of the appropriations, "[t]his disposes of one of the most stubbornly contested measures ever brought before Congress."[87]

Religious conservatives celebrated the vote as a major victory, with Wilber Crafts declaring the ban to be "the greatest moral victory since emancipation." Conservatives saw Congress's action as presenting an opportunity to revisit a national Sunday law and to renew efforts for uniform temperance and divorce laws.[88] However, their success was short-lived. The Exposition's directors accepted the appropriation and then declared their intention to open the fair on Sundays anyway. Financial considerations controlled the day, but Chicago Mayor Hempstead Washburn also insisted that to close the fair on Sunday "in order to recognize the Christian religion would clearly establish a religion by Federal law." The *Christian Advocate* complained that the directors were not only succumbing to pressures from local businesses, labor groups, and saloon owners but also playing into the hands of "atheists and anarchists [who] want the fair open."[89] After the first three weeks of operation, the fair remained open Sundays for the duration of the Exposition, to the chagrin of the religious groups. With most of the federal appropriations already spent, the Exposition directors felt little compulsion to close the fair on Sundays.[90] Religious figures organized a boycott of the fair and even urged US Attorney General Richard D. Olney to use troops to force the closing of the fair in accordance with the law. Olney did obtain a court injunction to enforce the closure in June 1893, but the Court of Appeals reversed the order the following month in an opinion by Chief Justice Melville W. Fuller (sitting as a Circuit Justice), which held that the fairgrounds were under the complete control of Exposition directors and operated at their discretion. As *The Independent* wrote with resignation, while the decision was probably legally correct, "[t]here is no court in Christendom that can make such a breach of contract seem honorable. . . . Morally it is wrong." *The Truth Seeker* celebrated: "*Jubilate! jubilate!*" A "great and a brilliant triumph has been won over bigotry." In the end, however, the financial boon the fair directors expected through the Sunday openings never materialized.[91]

Comstock and the Exposition

Controversy over the Columbian Exposition was not limited to its Sunday openings. The fair's exhibitions presented another target for Anthony Comstock's moral crusade. The Exposition was truly a world's fair, with exhibitions containing art, demonstrations, and performances representing the cultures of many nations. (Ironically, considering the Sunday closing controversy, the Exposition also contained an exhibition of the World's Parliament of Religions, which introduced attendees to the practices and traditions of non-Christian faiths.)[92] Among the more popular exhibitions on the fair's Midway Plaisance were the Persian, Turkish, Algerian, and Egyptian dance performances of the "hoochy-koochy," otherwise known as belly dancing or the *danse du ventre*. The belly dancers tested Victorian moral sensibilities in at least two respects: their revealing costumes, which showed the women's midriffs, and then their sensual body movements to the alluring music (the term *hoochy-koochy* was derived from the French word *hockequere*, which meant "to shake the tail.") To no one's surprise, the belly dance performance at the Streets of Cairo exhibit was "the hottest attraction" of the fair, at least among men and boys. As *Scientific American* reported sardonically, "farther down the Cairo Street is the theater which presents the national dances of Egypt. These dances are reprobated by ministers and moralists, but of course it is necessary for them to see them 'just once' before they can paint their sinfulness in lurid characters."[93]

Comstock was informed of the exotic dances on a visit to Wisconsin in July 1893, and he quickly traveled to Chicago to view the performances for himself. Comstock was "horrified" and "shocked" at what he saw, describing it as "the most shameless exhibition of depravity" he had witnessed in his twenty years of crusading work. He contacted the Exposition's Board of Lady Managers—a women's advisory group assigned to ensure the fair's propriety—whose members visited two performances and then called on the fair directors to shut down all belly dancing. The Exposition's director general ordered the shuttering of all such performances in August, and newspapers reported that officials raided several "Oriental dances" for the "good of public decency and morality" because they were not "in harmony with the tone of the exposition or the American code of morals." Despite an initial crackdown, the performance managers remained defiant and threatened lawsuits. The dances resumed, more popular than ever.[94]

Months later, Comstock was able to extract revenge. Following the Exposition's conclusion, three dancers from the Streets of Cairo exhibit toured New York City performing to packed houses. Comstock directed local police to arrest the women for their "obscene and indecent exhibition," with the officers obligingly doing so but only after sitting through two separate shows. Tried in police court, the women insisted on wearing their costumes during the hearing and testified that they had performed the dances throughout Europe to no objections. Comstock attended the trial, claiming that he was "defending womanhood in this city," but when he attempted to testify to what he had observed in Chicago he was shut down by the judge. Nonetheless, the dancers were convicted and fined fifty dollars each. Comstock's victory was a pyrrhic one, however, with newspapers panning the prosecution as misguided and overzealous. After the dancers paid their fines they continued their successful tour of the Northeast.[95]

While the dancers emerged relatively unscathed from Comstock's moral crusade, another person with a connection to the performances did not fare as well. Ida C. Craddock was an unmarried, eccentric, thirty-four-year-old writer who operated a sex counseling practice in Chicago. Prior to moving to Chicago from Philadelphia in 1892—chiefly to escape her domineering mother, who was a member of the WCTU—Craddock had worked for two years as the secretary for the American Secular Union and the corresponding secretary for *The Truth Seeker*. She broke with both entities in 1891 over their supposed support for free love—including their defense of Elmina Slenker—and because of her own growing attraction to Spiritualism. After moving to Chicago and setting up her sexology practice, Craddock "married" her spirit lover, and their "intimate relationship" became a central source of her advice on sexual relations.[96]

Craddock attended the *danse du ventre* performance at the Columbian Exposition and was struck by the erotic aspects of the dance, interpreting the movements as simulating intercourse. She quickly wrote an essay defending the dance, a portion of which was published in the *New York World*, which she then turned into a pamphlet, *The Dance du Ventre, as Performed in the Cairo Street Theatre*.[97] The pamphlet had less to do with the dance and more to do with

Craddock's views on sexual intercourse. She praised the *danse du ventre* as an ancient "moral . . . religious memorial related to Phallic or Sex Worship." Craddock advocated occasional sex for pleasure. In succeeding years, Craddock wrote additional sex manuals that provided similar advice and used graphic terminology, offering their sale through the mail. In her publications Craddock did not hide the fact that she obtained her knowledge about sex through her relations with her spirit husband. Her former employer at *The Truth Seeker*, editor George E. Macdonald, dismissed her as "derange[d]," questioning how "an unmarried lady" could "function [as] an instructor in conjugal amenities," and recommended that she exchange her spirit husband for a live one. At one point, Craddock's mother had her committed to an asylum for her "erotic hallucinations."[98]

After she moved back to Philadelphia in 1896, Craddock placed advertisements for her pamphlets in the newspapers, which caught the attention of the local postal inspector, who warned her against mailing sexually explicit material. Although she complied initially, Craddock resumed selling her pamphlets through the mail. Comstock had her arrested on federal obscenity charges in May 1898. Craddock, now back in Chicago, was defended by Clarence Darrow of the National Defense Association, who convinced her to take a plea deal in return for a suspended sentence.[99] Undeterred, in 1900 Craddock wrote a new, more explicit pamphlet, *The Wedding Night*, which also criticized Anthony Comstock's moral crusade, and again advertised it through the mail. State officials (Craddock was now living in New York City) prosecuted her in March 1902 under the state's "little Comstock" obscenity law, which resulted in a three-month imprisonment in the prison workhouse on Blackwell Island.[100]

The jail time devastated Craddock. Then, upon her release, Comstock had her arrested for violating the federal Comstock Act. The indictment, as in earlier obscenity prosecutions under the Act, declined to delineate the offending passages in *The Wedding Night*, declaring that a "more minute description of said obscene, lewd and lascivious language . . . would be offensive to the Court, and improper to be spread upon the records of the Court." In the October 12, 1902, trial in federal court, Comstock testified that the pamphlet was undoubtedly obscene and that Craddock had attempted to sell it to minors (a fabrication). The jury found Craddock guilty without even leaving the jury box, and the judge stated his intention to sentence her to prison. Fearing that she might receive the maximum sentence of five years imprisonment, on the morning of October 17, the day of her sentencing, Craddock committed suicide by slashing her wrist and turning on the gas in her apartment. Her suicide note, mailed to the *New York Sun*, condemned "Comstockism" while calling Comstock a "sex pervert" and a "sadist." Craddock stated that she was "taking my life because a judge, at the instigation of Anthony Comstock, has declared me guilty of a crime I did not commit—the circulation of obscene material." She warned the public about "the dreadful state of affairs which permits that unctuous sexual hypocrite, Anthony Comstock, to wax fat and arrogant, and to trample upon the liberties of people, invading, in my own case, both my right to freedom of religion and to the freedom of the press." Though Craddock was another victim of Comstock's crusade, she got the last word.[101]

Comstock's zealousness in pursuing Craddock did not escape criticism. In an editorial, Craddock's physician wrote that he had notified the prosecution that she suffered from "an insane delusion which completely dominated her entire life," a defense that should have been raised at her trial. But rather than allowing her counsel to pursue an insanity defense, Craddock had "an overpowering desire to have a legal adjudication upon her case." The physician nonetheless condemned the trial for going forward, charging that "Mr. Comstock's prosecution of this unfortunate was most indiscrete and unwise."[102] In a speech following Craddock's suicide, Comstock justified his prosecution as "only doing his duty" while he denied any responsibility for her death. His statement caused a "tumult" among the members of the audience, with one attendee calling Comstock a "menace to liberty-loving people." In another public rebuke, Reverend W.S. Rainsford, an Episcopal minister, chastised Comstock for "hounding" Craddock to her death. Rainsford called for Comstock's dismissal from his positions: "Mr. Comstock [is] unfitted for the place he occupies. He ought to be thrown out." Comstock brushed this off as a "mean, contemptable communication." But the public appetite for Comstock's moral crusade was growing thin. Following Craddock's death, contributions to an already financially struggling NYSSV dropped off sharply and the US Treasury Department informed the crusader that it would no longer pay his travel and witness fees.[103]

The "Christian Nation" Decision

In 1892, the US Supreme Court weighed in on the late-century controversy over the nation's religious character. On February 29, the Court handed down a decision in *Church of the Holy Trinity v. United States,* which concerned the 1885 Alien Contract Labor Law, which prohibited importing foreigners into the United States under contracts of employment. In 1887, New York City's prestigious Holy Trinity Episcopal Church had hired E. Walpole Warren, a well-known British pastor, to come to America to serve as its new rector. The employment contract, executed while Warren resided in England, violated the new immigration law, and the church was fined $1,000. After losing at trial, the church appealed the fine to the Supreme Court, arguing that the law had been misapplied.[104]

A unanimous Court reversed the lower court, holding that Congress had not intended the law to apply in that context. Authoring the opinion, Justice David J. Brewer wrote that both the statute's text and legislative history indicated that Congress had never envisioned the law would restrict the hiring of "ministers of the gospel, or, indeed any class whose toil is of the brain." Instead, wrote Brewer, Congress had intended the statute to apply "only to the work of the manual laborer, as distinguished from that of the professional man"; the purpose of the law "was simply to stay the influx of this cheap, unskilled labor."[105]

Justice Brewer could have ended his opinion there. But Brewer offered a second rationale for why the law did not apply to Reverend Warren. America was a "Christian nation," Brewer declared, one that had been founded by religious people who had formed a government based on religious principles. The nation's charters and laws acknowledged the importance of Christianity and accommodated its practice. Consequently, Congress would not—and could not—pass a law contrary to the pervasive Christian character of the nation. For this reason, a law effectively barring the hiring of a minister of the gospel could not apply in a Christian nation.[106]

In support of his argument, Brewer provided "a strange hodge-podge of religious pronouncements drawn from American history."[107] He quoted extensively from colonial charters and early state constitutions that acknowledged God's authority over human affairs and favored Protestantism. Brewer also cited several early judicial decisions that had declared Christianity to be part of the common law. Finally, Brewer pointed to "the multitude of [churches and] charitable organizations existing everywhere under Christian auspices," all of which announced the same truth:

> These, and many other matters which might be noticed, add a volume of unofficial declarations to the mass of organic utterances that *this is a Christian nation.*

> In the face of all these, shall it be believed that a congress of the United States intended to make it a misdemeanor for a church of this country to contract for the services of a Christian minister residing in another nation?[108]

The answer to Brewer's rhetorical question was a resounding "no."

What led Justice Brewer to add this second, and unnecessary, rationale for the holding is unclear. The church had made only a passing reference to the free exercise of religion in its brief; nor did Justice Brewer characterize the controversy as implicating such interests.[109] Equally unclear—at least from the opinion—was what Brewer meant. The phrase was not self-defining—American could be "Christian" in several senses of the word. Brewer's extensive reliance on historical data suggests, at a minimum, that he considered American to be Christian in a historical sense—that American culture had a significant religious tradition, one that had influenced the nation's "laws, its business, its customs, and its society." Brewer's failure to discuss the corresponding experience of religious exclusion and persecution indicates that he considered this history to be benign. Brewer's discussion of the prevalence of Christian institutions and influences, and his failure to note the nation's growing religious diversity, suggests that he also considered America to be Christian because most people practiced that faith. Beyond those points, however, Brewer did not make himself clear. He did not declare that America was specially chosen by God or that public officials had a duty to enforce Christian norms. Even though he cited Sabbath and behavioral laws as evidence for his argument, Brewer did not advocate their enforcement on religious grounds. Aside from the exceptional nature of Brewer's declaration, his discussion of America's Christian nationhood lacked a polemical quality; it was as if Brewer thought he was relating the consensus view of American church–state relations.[110]

That Brewer had included his Christian nation rationale for the holding was not a departure from his character, however. Only into his second term on the high court, Justice Brewer was already known for his religious devotion. The son of a missionary, Brewer was an active church-goer and a Sunday School teacher at First Congregational Church in Washington, DC. Off the Court, Brewer spoke and wrote extensively about religion and its role in society and public affairs. Raised in New England and a graduate of Yale, Brewer embraced values that were often associated with the late-Puritan ethic: honesty, civility, public piety, and civic responsibility. Unlike fellow New England Congregationalists Anthony Comstock and Joseph Cook, however, Brewer was a religious moderate, closer theologically to Henry Ward Beecher. Brewer eschewed doctrinaire Protestantism, declaring that "[t]here is ample room for theological differences." He personally questioned the "chronological accuracy" of many parts of the Bible, the Creation account, Jesus's virgin birth, and even whether Jesus was himself divine (rather, for Brewer, Jesus was "a *revelation* of the purpose and character of that divine being," God). While Brewer affirmed the "fundamental truths" of Christianity, he acknowledged that God could be called by different names or be revealed in different manifestations. "Many are the names by which He will be called." What was most important, Brewer insisted, employing language that parroted Beecher, was to embrace God's "infinite power, justice and love," which was the "one great truth which dominates time and eternity."[111]

Consistent with his moderate theological outlook, Brewer embraced various social reforms such as woman's suffrage and expanding educational and occupational opportunities for women. Though he personally decried the increase in divorces, he attributed the trend to greater freedoms and choices among women, declaring he "would not stay any progress in this direction."[112] Brewer also questioned the efficacy of enhanced Sabbath and temperance legislation. "Making men good by law has become a fad," he wrote in 1899.[113] In a possibly oblique reference to Anthony Comstock's crusade and the agendas of groups like the NRA, WCTU, and ASU, Brewer criticized reformers who believed that "[i]ntemperance, social impurity, gambling, and all sorts of vice are to be exterminated by statute and ordinance."

> But reforming men by statute is simply the old appeal to force. It is only the idea of the Inquisition softened and refined, and yet it has become very popular. Every new manifestation of vice had been followed not so much by more earnest efforts to reform the individual as by the enactment of new statutes, with more stringent provisions—an additional twist of the legislative screw.[114]

> * * * *

> You may, through the agency of the lawmaking power, remove temptations, take away opportunities and inducements to wrong, but you cannot legislate a man out of vice into virtue. No statute will write the ten commandments on the human heart or fill the soul with the gospel of love.[115]

Brewer's positions on social reform indicate that his view of what it meant to be a Christian nation differed from those of Anthony Comstock, Wilber Crafts, and the leadership of the NRA. But one is not left to speculate, since Brewer elaborated on his understanding in various writings, most notably in two books, *American Citizenship* (1902) and *The United States a Christian Nation* (1905).[116] In both books, Brewer initially reiterated themes contained in his *Holy Trinity* opinion: that American was Christian in a historical sense and in the way that Christian traditions and beliefs continued to influence customs and daily practices. The books then offered additional, nuanced understandings of the term. Brewer believed that Christian nations represented the highest form of civilization. A man of his era, Brewer assumed the superiority of Anglo-American culture—which was, by no accident, rooted in Protestantism. "The most thoroughly Christian nation is the most civilized," he asserted. Christian nations were the wealthiest, the most humanitarian, the most educated, and the most technologically advanced civilizations, and consequently, were superior to all other nations. Beyond these tangible manifestations, however, Christian nations were the most civilized because they were based on, and conducted their affairs according to, the highest moral standards.[117] While this reflected Brewer's belief in American exceptionalism, that superior status carried with it obligations to be moral examples to other nations of the world. A Christian nation, "in its dealings with other nations is bound to certain rules of conduct which it is universally conceded should be founded upon justice and righteousness." Brewer thus supported Christian foreign missionaries because "Christianity is so adapted to the most urgent needs of man," but he insisted that missionaries respect other cultures and practices and avoid exploiting other peoples. He decried the long history of abuse and exploitation of foreign peoples undertaken in the name of God.[118]

Finally, Brewer believed that a Christian nation should promote religious freedom and the separation of church and state. Religious liberty—the right to believe and practice the religion of one's choice—was at the heart of the freedoms promised by a Christian nation. "[E]ach [person] stands alone with his conscience," Brewer maintained. "No one is in duty bound as a citizen to attend a particular church service, or indeed any church service. The freedom of conscience, the liberty of the individual, gives to every individual the right to stay away" (although there was a corresponding "obligation not to unnecessarily interfere with or disturb those services.").[119] Brewer's support for church-state separation, on its own, indicates little, as even religious conservatives mouthed fealty to the concept. His view of the interrelationship of the two institutions was common among moderate Protestants.[120] On the one hand, he asserted, it was "universally recognized that religion lies at the basis of morality, and that for the purpose of securing the best and most thoroughly extended morality it is fitting that religion and the church be recognized." Still, "the settled rule in this country is of entire separation between state and church," Brewer wrote, "and yet that separation is not so complete that the state is indifferent to the welfare and prosperity of the church. . . . We believe that the best interests of both are promoted by enforcing entire separation between the state and the church."[121] As such, Brewer's overall understanding of separationism—he opposed financial support for religion but supported Sabbath observance and the limited use of the Bible in public school classrooms—is less important than the fact that he saw the principle of separation as characteristic of a Christian nation.[122] Not only was church-state separation consistent with those religious principles underlying a Christian nation; "the very fact that [America] has no Established Church makes one of its highest credentials to the title of a Christian nation. The great thought of the Master was that over the human soul there was no earthly sovereign." Brewer's belief in a strong religious influence in public life clearly differentiated his view of church-state separation from those of freethinkers, but his aversion to sumptuary laws distinguished him from Christian reformers like the NRA, the ASU, and even the WCTU.[123]

Little of Brewer's nuanced understanding of what it meant to be a Christian nation was to be found in his *Holy Trinity* opinion. *Holy Trinity* was an obscure case, and Brewer's Christian nation declaration had appeared as dicta to the holding. The secular press barely acknowledged the decision, summarily reporting the holding without noting Brewer's religious arguments. *The Independent* and the *Christian Advocate* also reported the holding without commenting on Brewer's dicta.[124] But a declaration of America's Christian nationhood from the nation's highest court could not remain unnoticed for long, especially by religious conservatives who were battling secularizing trends in the culture. *Pearl of Days*, the journal of the American Sabbath Union, cheerfully declared that the decision "establishes clearly the fact that our Government is Christian. . . . And this important decision rests upon the fundamental principle that religion is imbedded in the organic structure of the American Government—a religion that recognizes, and is bound to maintain, Sunday as a day of rest and worship." The ASU anticipated that the decision would lead to even greater enforcement of Sabbath regulations. "This decision is vital to the Sunday question in all its aspects, and places that question among the most important issues now before the American people." The NRA, in *The Christian Statesman*, also extolled the opinion, gleefully reprinting Brewer's words: "Christianity is the law of the land! This is a Christian nation!" Hailing the decision as affirming their long-sought goal, an NRA spokesman wrote that the nation should now "make a constitutional recognition of God as the Source of all authority, the Lord Jesus Christ as the divinely-appointed Ruler of nations, the Bible as the fountain of all law, and of the true Christian religion. This is our first and highest duty."[125] Public criticism of *Holy Trinity* came primarily from freethinkers, Jews, and the Seventh-day Adventists. Adventists blasted the declaration in a series of articles in the *American Sentinel*, declaring that it "culminates in the National Reform shibboleth" while it established a national religion "by fiat." "So the Supreme Court of the United States champions an establishment of religion," the *American Sentinel* continued. "What next?"[126]

"Next" was the Congressional hearing on the Sunday closing of the Columbia Exposition, which occurred only two months following the decision. Two nights before the hearing, Sunday closing proponents held a rally at Washington's First Congregational Church—Brewer's home church—where Reverend H.H. George of the NRA read from Brewer's opinion (there is no reference to Brewer having attended the rally). At the hearing, as discussed, fair-closing proponents testified that America was a "Christian nation" and several referred to Brewer's *Holy Trinity* opinion as supporting that proposition. In his remarks before the committee, the ASU's Elliot F. Shepard made "extensive citations" in support of his claims about America's Christian nationhood "from the opinion of Mr. Justice Brewer." But as previously noted, during the debates on the Exposition's Sunday closing, legislators generally steered clear of justifying the closing on religious grounds.[127]

The next fallout from the *Holy Trinity* declaration came in 1894. An emboldened NRA, feeling its political muscle after taking leading roles in Blair's Education and Sunday bills, and then in the Exposition closing, decided the time was ripe to pursue its constitutional amendment once more. The amendment was reintroduced in Congress in January 1894. The NRA organized a massive petition drive through its local chapters and those of the WCTU. By 1896, the number of petitions was so great that it forced Congress to hold hearings on the proposal.[128]

The House Judiciary Committee heard testimony on the proposed Christian Amendment on March 11, 1896. Religious conservatives dominated the hearing, citing the need to bring the Constitution in line with America's religious heritage. Testimony and memorials supporting the amendment came from the NRA, the ASU, the WCTU, the Christian Endeavor, and the

YMCA.[129] Unlike the earlier attempt in 1874, proponents were now able to point to the Supreme Court's declaration in *Holy Trinity* as support for the amendment. Reverend Stockton of the Presbyterian Synod of Pennsylvania testified that:

> The genius of our institutions, the trend of our national history, all law making and judicial interpretations of law, unite to proclaim that we are a Christian nation. And to settle it all, if you please, is the declaration of the Supreme Court, which, doubtless, is the mind of you all, where, in its judicial decision, it says that . . . we are a Christian nation.[130]

Justice Brewer's declaration became a double-edged sword, however, hurting the amendment's chances as much as it helped. Several congressmen argued that an amendment was unnecessary, noting that the nation was already Christian as Brewer's opinion demonstrated. Others voiced concern that the amendment would infringe on the rights of religious minorities and "conflict with the constitutional prohibition of the establishment of religion." Witnesses representing the American Secular Union, the Spiritualist Association, Seventh-day Baptists, and the Unitarian Church emphasized these concerns, with Samuel P. Putnam of the Secular Union warning that religious conservatives acknowledged that they intended to use an amendment as a springboard to greater legal enforcement of morals.[131] Religious moderates also raised concerns. Lyman Abbott declared that the Constitution was "[not] a proper place for the insertion of a system of theology or even an article of religious belief, however simple." *The Independent* also announced its opposition to the amendment, calling its proponents a misguided "band of agitators." "Putting the recognition of Christ into the Constitution would not make one citizen better, nor insure the better observance of one law." With support lacking in committee, the Christian Amendment was tabled indefinitely.[132]

Following the vote, Presbyterian scholar Sanford Cobb criticized the NRA for its efforts to amend the Constitution, calling them "idle and unnecessary" and appealing only to "superficial religious sentiment." Legal attempts to reverse the perceived secularizing trend were futile, Cobb wrote. "If the American people should insert the divine names in the constitution, that would not keep them from turning to infidelity, or make them a Christian nation after such perversion." The 1896 hearings were as close as the NRA would ever come to achieving its ultimate goal of amending the Constitution to reflect the kingship of Christ.[133]

Comstock's Final Crusades

By the late 1880s, Comstock's priorities had narrowed from pursuing vice writ large—gambling, lotteries, and "blood-and-thunder" publications—to concentrating on obscenity. But they had also expanded beyond pursuing smut-dealers to taking aim at literature and artistic representations of nudity. Although he disclaimed any intention to go after literature and fine art—acknowledging that museums displayed paintings and sculptures of nudes—Comstock lacked the ability to appreciate the nuances in art and was predisposed to see the evils lurking in any erotic depiction, visual or written.[134] As discussed earlier, Comstock faced a backlash after prosecuting the sale of *Heptameron* and *Leaves of Grass* in 1882; similar criticism arose three years later when he attempted to stop the sale of *Arabian Nights*.[135] But Comstock was unrepentant, writing in *Traps for the Young*: "So 'art' and 'classic' are made to gild some of the most obscene representations and foulest matters in literature. . . . 'Fine art' has lent its charms to pictures of lust, intensifying their power for evil, and finding an apology for them before the public." Aesthetics were of no concern to Comstock, "The same black stain appears, whether coarse and lewd or traced in lines of beauty." In his mind, "[t]he latter is the more insidious" because of its wider acceptance.[136] Comstock's targeting of art, as well as his questionable methods, drew increasing criticism. Even supporters advised him to concentrate on the more "flagrant offense[s] on common decency" rather than on literature and fine art.[137]

A turning point in the public's appetite for Comstock's far-reaching crusade against obscenity came in 1887, when Comstock raided the premises of Knoedler & Co., a prestigious New York City gallery of fine art that served the city's elite. Comstock seized thirty-seven photographic reproductions of nudes and semi-nudes of "the modern French school" that were displayed in the Paris Salon, including Alexandre Cabanel's "Birth of Venus." Three years earlier Comstock had successfully prosecuted August Muller, who ran a small shop in the Bowery, for selling a handful of similar photographs, which the court had described as "representing nude females in lewd, obscene, indecent, scandalous and lascivious attitudes and postures."[138] That conviction had not elicited a public outcry, but the prosecution of the prominent Knoedler gallery caused an uproar. Declaring that "nudity is not obscenity," the *New York Times* castigated Comstock as a "nuisance," a "virtuous dragon of morals," and a person of "a low grade of intelligence and a prurient turn of mind," who could not recognize art. The consensus among the secular press and the artistic community was that Comstock was out of his depth and out of control. Other criticism took the form of ridicule, with *Life* magazine speculating that "Mr. Comstock arrested Mr. Knoedler because he was informed that the picture-seller pronounced his name Nude-ler." *The Art Amateur* predicted that Comstock, "facetiously dubbed 'Saint Anthony'" by critics and admirers alike, "seems to be in a fair way to become a martyr also."[139] Following the arrests of Edmund Knoedler and his clerk George Pfeiffer, the New York *Evening Telegraph* published a scathing page-one article condemning Comstock, headlined "Our Art Censor: Anthony Comstock and the Harmless Objects of His Misguided Criticism," which included drawings of the thirty-seven seized photographs. Comstock urged the district attorney to have the *Evening Telegraph* indicted for printing the images, but his request was turned down.[140]

Newspapers closely followed the trial of Knoedler and Pfeiffer the following March, which took place in police court. Judge James T. Kilbreth considered the misdemeanor charges without impaneling a jury, concluding that thirty-five of the thirty-seven photographs were not obscene. Knoedler and Pfeiffer then pleaded guilty to the two remaining counts, and the judge imposed a minimal fine of $50.[141] Newspaper accounts reported the resolution as a pyrrhic victory for Comstock, at best. "Comstock was very far from congratulating himself on the victory," observed the *New York Sun*. The *New York Times* story was more brutal, noting that the Knoedler prosecution had yielded only a six percent success rate: "When [Comstock] goes the length of making seventeen mistakes out of every eighteen arrests a public necessity arises for either keeping him strictly in his place, or, if that cannot be done, of depriving him of the power which he abuses."[142]

Despite the blistering criticism of the prosecution, Comstock defended his actions, telling a meeting of the NYSSV that "[y]ear after year these laws against obscenity have been assailed by the so-called 'National Defense Association,' and so-called 'Liberals,' 'Free-Thinkers,' 'Free-Lovers,' and ex-convicts of this nation." As he had done throughout his career, Comstock raised the handy trope of conflating freethought and free love with obscenity. Digging in his heels, Comstock asserted that "Art is not above morals. Art is in conflict with the law when it assails morals, and when its charm is left to crime and vice." "Garbage smells none the less rank and offensive because [it is] deposited in a marble fount or a gold or silver urn." The leaders of the NYSSV stood by

Comstock, while acknowledging that "Mr. Comstock is fallible, and sometimes blunders."[143] Clearly bothered by the volume of criticism, Comstock wrote a booklet, *Morals versus Art*, that resorted to xenophobia, asserting that American youth were endangered by "lewd French art—a foreign foe." As in his earlier writings, Comstock described the threat in hyperbolic, if not graphic terms: obscenity was "like a parasite, fattening upon carrion. Its very presence poisons the moral atmosphere. Its breath is fetid, and its touch moral prostration and death." Comstock was unrepentant.[144]

Public rebuke of Comstock's overreaching continued. The same month as the Knoedler decision, a newspaper reported that Comstock, acting "through evasion of the truth—to put it mildly," had purchased photographs of nude females from a Philadelphia art supply store that discretely sold only to art students. On a motion by the prosecutor, the judge dismissed the charge of selling obscenity and rebuked Comstock for his actions. Later in the same month, Comstock addressed a YMCA assemblage at Princeton University. As the *New York Times* reported, before his arrival students mockingly draped red flannel pajamas over a nude campus statue, "The Gladiator," so as not "to offend his well-known ideas of art and morality."[145]

Comstock maintained his crusade against obscenity into the 1890s and the next century. At the same time, he persisted in associating freethought with obscenity. Writing in the *North American Review* in 1891, he criticized the secular press for "invading our homes with . . . the sickening details of loathsome and reeking crimes" which "blast the finer sensibilities and spread the pestilential seeds of crime and vice." Other influences were also to blame for moral decay, and he listed "infidel publications" between "dime and half-dime novels" and "licentious books" and "loose French art" pictures. "We are in the midst of a harvest of irreligion, skepticism and immorality," Comstock asserted. "The tendency to scoff at religion, to rail at moral reform, [and] the practice of emphasizing infidel and blasphemous lectures" were all to be deplored. Comstock then quoted favorably from Judge Benedict's jury charge in D.M. Bennett's trial, calling it "the most celebrated case ever tried . . . regarding the sending of obscene materials through the mail." He persisted in his belief that he was engaged in a mission ordained by God.[146]

Religious conservatives and the leaders of the NYSSV continued to support Comstock's crusade, though his audience was shrinking, and Comstock had apparently failed to learn the lessons of the "Knoedler fiasco." In 1894, a judge again rebuked him for threatening to prosecute publishers of literature—*Tom*

Jones, Decameron, A Thousand and One Nights, Aladdin—with the *New York Times* headline declaring, "Comstock Not Yet Enlightened." By the mid-1890s, Comstock was increasingly subjected to ridicule and derision by the press. "A good many good people have clung for a good many years to the belief that Mr. Anthony Comstock had his uses," panned a *New York Times* editorial in March 1895. "Faith in Comstock's inflexible opposition to vice and infallible scent for the lightest trail of indecency [had] caused people to [adopt] as favorable a sense as possible." Now, however, his "great lack of discrimination" in going after literary classics and art galleries had cost him popular support. "Mr. Comstock has sufficiently shown that if any man can be trusted to decide off-hand what is obscene literature and obscene art, he is not the man."[147]

Comstock's tattered reputation received another blow in 1905. In September, the New York Public Library removed a copy of George Bernard Shaw's *Man and Superman* from the shelves, which the author charged was done at the behest of Comstock. Shaw called "Comstockery . . . the world's standing joke," one that confirmed European opinion that the United States was "a provincial place, a second-rate country town civilization." Comstock denied being behind the move, remarking, "Who's Bernard Shaw?" but then applauded the censorship of such "contagious and vile" "obscenity." Comstock promised to investigate Shaw's work, later prosecuting the New York production of his play, *Mrs. Warren's Profession*, which delt with the "profession" of prostitution. The producer, Arnold Daly, had the charges dismissed. In the end, the ongoing dispute was great publicity for Shaw. Although Shaw did not coin the term "Comstockery," which had been used for a decade to describe overzealous prudishness, he made it famous.[148]

The following year, Comstock again went after a well-regarded art institution, the New York Art Students League, for images published in its magazine *The American Student of Art*. In August 1906 he raided the League's offices, seizing copies of the magazine, but he had to satisfy himself with arresting a young woman clerk who had nothing to do with the magazine's production.[149] Comstock had again overreached while underestimating the potential for backlash. New York's literary and art communities reacted with a torrent of indignation, calling Comstock's action "outrageous" and "unwarranted and absurd." One incensed artist declared Comstock to be "a human moral mothball!" League members drew on their talents by lampooning Comstock unmercifully in caricatures, some of which were hung on the outside of the

League's building. Comstock defended his actions, calling *The American Student of Art* a "lewd and libidinous publication."[150]

At the court hearing two months later, the press portrayed the clerk as a victim of Comstock's uninformed overzealousness while reporting on his courtroom antics, which drew the ire of the judge. In the end, Comstock agreed to drop the prosecution on condition that the League recall the offending magazine. Despite the additional damage to his reputation, Comstock emerged victorious, as the League decided to discontinue publishing the magazine out of concern for future legal liability. Censorship had won out. At the same time, however, Comstock had to dispel rumors that the Postmaster General was prepared to fire him as a postal inspector. The George Bernard Shaw and Art Students League fiascos were merely the more notable indications that Comstock's crusade against obscenity had become increasingly petty.[151]

Comstock's final crusade had him returning to the related issue of birth control—closely related to obscenity in Comstock's mind. The audience for information about and access to contraceptives and abortion had only grown since Comstock's initial prosecutions of Mme. Restell, Dr. Foote, and Ezra Heywood in the 1870s. By the 1910s, many outspoken leaders of the birth control movement were radicalized feminists, centered in New York's Greenwich Village. Anarchist and atheist Emma Goldman was the most visible advocate for tying reproductive freedom to sexual freedom and women's equality. Comstock was a target of Goldman's biting criticism; she called him "the autocrat of American morals" and equated him to Torquemada. Comstock was "the patron saint" of the WCTU, ASU, the Purity League, and the Prohibition Party, Goldman proclaimed, which together were "the grave diggers of American art and culture" and who kept women in subjugation. Goldman's radical newspaper, *Mother Earth*, took pleasure in ridiculing the misfortunes of "St. Anthony" while calling his sponsors at the NYSSV a "conspiracy of hypocrites, swine, and eunuchs, [who] dared not [to] bring this national nuisance to account."[152] In 1910, Goldman alleged that Comstock attempted to ban the mailing of *Mother Earth* for its advocacy of birth control, a charge Comstock denied. That led to a public confrontation between the two at a November event, where Comstock again justified his campaign against the evils of obscenity that was supported by "so-called liberals, free thinkers, and free lovers." Yet, despite her public advocacy of atheism and contraceptive use, Goldman was able to avoid Comstock's wrath. In 1916, however, the year following Comstock's death, Goldman was arrested at a public lecture on her new essay, "The Philosophy of Atheism," for statements promoting birth control. Convicted, Goldman refused to pay the $100 fine, preferring to serve fifteen days in a prison workhouse.[153]

While Comstock was unsuccessful in prosecuting Goldman, he found success with her protégée Margaret Sanger. Sanger and her husband, William, an artist, moved in 1910 to New York, where, as a nurse, she established a practice that focused on family planning for lower-income women. Already a socialist and freethinker, Sanger met Goldman and became radicalized under her tutelage. She came to see the issue of birth control—a phrase she may have coined—through the lenses of class and feminist struggles. Sanger promoted birth control in part so that poorer women would not have to resort to abortion; in a 1920 essay "Contraceptives or Abortion," Sanger maintained that abortion was "abnormal" and "dangerous," though at the same time insisting that a "woman who goes to the abortionist's table is not a criminal but a martyr—a martyr to the bitter, unthinkable conditions brought about by the blindness of society" to her status. Ironically, in her opposition to abortion, Sanger was not that far from her nemesis Comstock.[154]

In 1912, Sanger wrote a series in the *New York Call*, "What Every Girl Should Know," that discussed female reproduction and feminine hygiene, including how to prevent venereal disease. Comstock learned of the publication and reputedly had the local post office temporarily ban its mailing. That incident put Sanger on Comstock's watch-list. Two years later Sanger began publishing a new magazine, *The Woman Rebel*, dedicated to advancing the causes of working women, which included articles by Goldman and Sanger on sexual relations and contraception. Postal authorities declared *The Woman Rebel* to be unmailable, and after Sanger proceeded to mail copies, Comstock had her arrested in August for publishing "obscene, filthy, vile and indecent" articles sent through the mail. Facing a likely conviction with substantial prison time, Sanger fled to Europe before the trial.[155] Undeterred, Comstock went after Sanger's husband, sending a deputy to his studio to secure a copy of "Family Limitation," a pamphlet describing birth control methods that Sanger had written before her indictment (dedicated to "the emancipation of womankind and acknowledging 'No Gods or Masters.'"). Comstock then had William prosecuted for distributing his wife's pamphlet. William was tried in a highly charged proceeding that witnessed shouting matches between Comstock and supporters of the Sangers. William was convicted and chose to spend thirty days in jail rather than pay a $150 fine, elevating the Sangers' cause.[156]

The episode strained an already ailing Comstock, who died ten days later from pneumonia. In its obituary, the *New York Times* attributed his death to the "overwork and overexcitement" associated with the Sanger trial and his efforts to hold onto his position as postal inspector. Despite the *Times'* long running criticism of Comstock's activities, its obituary was surprisingly forgiving, downplaying his overzealousness and praising him as "a thoroughly honest man who through a long life, for the scantiest of material rewards, devoted his courage and energy, both remarkable, to the protection of society from a detestable and dangerous group of enemies." The *Times* did not indicate whether those enemies included the same ones Comstock had always listed: infidels and free-lovers.[157] Other obituaries were more critical, with the *Detroit Times* declaring that Comstock was "a complete, unqualified failure in his efforts to reform the morals of the American people." Substantially harsher, one editor who had been the subject of a Comstock prosecution wrote that "Comstock was a beast of such foulness that his carcass is not fit for fertilization even of the wind-swept fields of the open lands." The bulk of commentary fell somewhere in the middle, however, acknowledging Comstock's accomplishments while noting that his overreaching often put him out of touch with the nation's developing cultural tastes.[158] In some respects, Comstock's obsession with obscenity and freethought made him the final victim of his long crusade.

NOTES

1. The title of this chapter is taken from a declaration in Rector of Holy Trinity Church v. United States, 143 U.S. 457, 471 (1892).
2. Daniel Dorchester, *Christianity in the United States from the First Settlement down to the Present Time* (New York: Hunt and Eaton, 1890), 324, 575–576, 643, 732–742; Daniel Dorchester, *The Problem of Religious Progress* (New York: Philips and Hunt, 1881), 105–106.
3. Handy, *Undermined Establishment*, 7–29; James Bryce, *The American Commonwealth*, 2nd ed. (London: Macmillan Pub., 1891), 2:576–577.
4. Latourette, *A History of the Expansion of Christianity*, 4:457; Marty, *The Infidel*, 139.
5. Marty, *The Infidel*, 139.
6. "The Relation of Religion to Our Government," *Methodist Review* (Nov. 1899): 930–941; Handy, *A Christian America*, 62–69; Henry F. May, *Protestant Churches and Industrial America* (New York: Harper, 1949), part II.
7. A Non-Church-Goer, "Church Attendance," *North American Review* (July 1883), 76–77.

8. W.S. Lilly, "The Present Outlook for Christianity," *The Forum* (Dec. 1886), 318.

9. B.J. McQuaid, "The Decay of Protestantism," *North American Review* (Feb. 1883), 135–152.

10. Rev. Dr. Ward, *North American Review* (July 1883), 79–85.

11. Rev. Dr. Pullman, ibid., 85–91; Rev. Dr. Rylance, ibid., 92–97.

12. Henry Ward Beecher, "Progress of Thought in the Church," *North American Review* (Aug. 1882), 102, 99.

13. Strong, *Our Country*, 184–187; Green, *Separating Church and State*, 119–120; Handy, *A Christian America*, 62–69, 82–100; Dorchester, *Christianity in the United States*, 773–774. Richard T. Hughes and Christina Littlefield's new book, *Christian America and the Kingdom of God* (Urbana: University of Illinois Press, 2025), examines a related manifestation of the Christian nation impulse through the Social Gospel movement.

14. Handy, *A Christian America*, 62–69; Handy, *Undermined Establishment*, 11–25.

15. A.A. Hodge, "Religion in the Public Schools," *New Princeton Review* (Jan. 1887), 28, 31; *The Christian Statesman*, Feb. 28, 1874, 35. See also "The Public School Problem," *New York Evangelist*, Jan. 1, 1874, 2.

16. "The School Question," *Catholic World* 11 (April 1870), 94.

17. Thomas Jefferson represents one of the few figures who had earlier rejected that assumption. See Steven K. Green, *The Grand Collaboration: Thomas Jefferson, James Madison, and the Invention of American Religious Freedom* (Charlottesville: University of Virginia Press, 2024), 228–229.

18. "Secularism," Ingersoll, *Works*, 8:392; Green, *The Bible, the School and the Constitution*, 99–100.

19. Stanton, "Reading the Bible in the Public Schools," *Arena* (June 1897), 1034.

20. *The Index*, June 24, 1875, 294.

21. Henry Ward Beecher, "The Common School," in *The Bible in the Public Schools: Opinions of Individuals and of the Press, and Judicial Decisions* (New York: J.W. Schermerhorn & Co., 1870), 8–9, 12; Beecher, "Has the State a Right to Establish Common Schools?," ibid., 22–24; Beecher, "The School Question," ibid., 17–18; "Henry Ward Beecher on the School Question," *New York Tribune*, December 3, 1869, 5.

22. Samuel T. Spear, "The Bible and the Public School," *Princeton Review* (March 1878), 361, 387.

23. Spear, *Religion and the State*, 58–60.

24. William T. Harris, "The Division of School Funds for Religious Purposes," *Atlantic Monthly* (Aug. 1876), 171–184; W.T. Harris, "Some General Principles of Religious Instruction in the Schools," *The Independent*, Sept. 4, 1890, 1–2.

25. Hodge, "Religion in the Public Schools," 31; "George F. Mull, "Morality in the Public Schools," *Reformed Quarterly Review* 30 (Oct. 1883), 467–488.

26. Lyman H. Atwater, "Morality, Religion and Education in the State," *Princeton Review* (March 1878), 410, 411, 420; Lyman H. Atwater, "Civil Government and Religion," *Presbyterian Quarterly and Princeton Review* 18 (April 1876), 226–227.

27. "Morality in the Public Schools, *Catholic World* (Aug. 1883), 709–718; Thomas McMillan, "How Shall We Teach Morality?," ibid. (Feb. 1889), 592–599.

28. "Chicago Notes: The Bible in the Schools," *New York Times*, Oct. 4, 1875, 5; "The Bible in the Public Schools," ibid., Dec. 30, 1875, 5; "Bible Reading in the Schools," ibid., Sept. 8, 1880, 4; "Rochester Resolve," *New York Observer and Chronicle*, July 1, 1875, 2; "The Public School Problem," *New York Evangelist*, Jan. 1, 1874, 2; "Public Schools in New Haven," *Christion Union*, Oct. 2, 1878, 266; "The New Haven Victory," *New York Observer and Chronicle*, Sept. 26, 1878, 1; R. Laurence Moore, "Bible Reading and Nonsectarian Schooling: The Failure of Religious Instruction in Nineteenth Century Public Education," *Journal of American History* 86 (March 2000): 1581–1599.

29. "The Bible in the Schools," *New York Times*, June 12, 1872, 5; "The Bible in New Jersey," Oct. 31, 1875, 12; "The Bible in the Schools," ibid., April 6, 1880, 2; "Morality in the Public Schools," *Atlantic Monthly* (June 1883), 748, 749; Green, *The Bible, the School, and the Constitution*, 117–118.

30. B.J. McQuaid, "Religion in Schools," *North American Review* (April 1881), 332–344.

31. McCormick v. Burt, 95 Ill. 263 (1880); Moore v. Monroe, 20 N.W. 475 (Iowa 1884); Hart v. School District of Sharpsville, 2 Lanc. 346 (Pa. Comm. 1885); Green, *The Bible, the School and the Constitution*, 239–240.

32. Moore, 20 N.W. at 476; Hart, 2 Lanc. at 349–352.

33. State ex rel. Weiss v. District Board of School Dist. No. 8, 44 N.W. 967, 975, 973 (Wis. 1890).

34. "The Bible Is Not Sectarian," *Christian Advocate*, April 3, 1890, 209–210; J.P. Barrett, "Beware!," *Herald of Gospel Liberty*, April 17, 1890, 244; J.W. Bashford, "Is Christianity Outlawed in Wisconsin?," *Zion's Herald*, May 21, 1890, 1.

35. "The Outlook," *Christian Union*, March 27, 1890, 435; "The Bible and Public Schools," *The Independent*, June 19, 1890, 11; "Current Topics," *Albany Law Journal*, Dec. 20, 1890, 489–491;

36. "A Report on Schools: The Conference Opposes the Secular Idea," *New York Times*, April 8, 1890, 8; "The Bible in Schools," ibid., March 19, 1890, 1, March 20, 1890, 4.

37. "Respecting Establishments of Religion and Free Public Schools," *In Defense of the Public Schools* (Philadelphia: Aldine Press Co., 1888), 95.

38. William T. Harris, *Report of the Commissioner of Education for the Year 1894–1895* (Washington, DC: Government Printing Office, 1896), 2:1656; Moore, "Bible Reading and Nonsectarian Schooling," 1585–1586.

39. Harris, *Report of the Commissioner* (1897–1898), 1539–1563; ibid. (1896–1897), 2189–2191; ibid. (1888–1889), 622–634; "The Decline of Bible Reading," *Christian Observer*, Dec. 8, 1897, 4; Moore, "Bible Reading and Nonsectarian Schooling," 1586, 1597–1598.

40. Congressional Record, 47th Cong., 1st Sess., XIII (Dec. 12, 1881), 227 (authorizing funding for "public schools not sectarian in character"); Gordon

B. McKinney, *Henry W. Blair's Campaign to Reform America* (Lexington: University Press of Kentucky, 2013), 86–87, 113–114, 121–130: Alan J. Going, "The South and the Blair Education Bill," *Mississippi Valley Historical Review* 44 (Sept. 1957): 267–290.

41. "Religion and Schools," Notes of Hearings before the Committee on Education and Labor, United States Senate, on Joint Resolution S.R. 86, February 15, 1889, 3.

42. Ibid., 10–13, 23, and passim.

43. *Christian Statesman*, July 26, 1888, reprinted in Alonzo T. Jones, *Civil Government and Religion, or Christianity and the American Constitution* (Chicago: American Sentinel, 1889), 49.

44. "Religion and Schools," Notes of Hearings, 105–110 (testimony of Prof. Alonzo T. Jones); Jones, *Civil Government and Religion*, 44; John Whitney Evans, "Catholics and the Blair Education Bill," *Catholic Historical Review* 46 (October 1960): 273–298; "Conspiracy against the Republic," *The Truth Seeker*, Feb. 23, 1889, 114; "The War on Senator Blair's Bill," ibid., Feb. 16, 1889, 104.

45. Green, *The Bible, the School and the Constitution*, 239–241; Billard v. Board of Education, 76 P. 422, 433 (Kan. 1904).

46. See Green, *Second Disestablishment*, 182–190, 227–247; Andrew J. King, "Sunday Law in the Nineteenth Century," *Albany Law Review* 64 (2000): 675–772.

47. Leigh Eric Schmidt, "The Commercialization of the Calendar: American Holidays and the Culture of Consumption, 1870–1930," *Journal of American History* 78 (Dec. 1991): 887–916. See also Alan Raucher, "Sunday Business and the Decline of Sunday Closing Laws: A Historical Overview," *Journal of Church and State* (Winter 1994): 13–33.

48. Green, *Second Disestablishment*, 231–247; King, "Sunday Law in the Nineteenth Century," 678, 681; Sparhawk v. Union Passenger Railway Co., 54 Pa. St. 401 (1867) (requiring evidence that running trains of Sunday created a public nuisance); *Ex parte* Burke, 59 Cal. 6, 13 (1881).

49. *New York Times*, May 17, 1880, 4; Whitcomb v. Gilman, 35 Vt. 297 (1862); Wilkerson v. State, 59 Ind. 416 (1877); "Sunday—Settlement in Nature of Will—Necessity or Charity," *Central Law Journal*, April 29, 1892, 371; Sunday Law—Police Regulation," ibid., Jan. 20, 1899, 57; State v. Petit (Mn. 1898); "More Sunday-Law Absurdities," *American Law Review* (Aug. 1880): 585–586.

50. "Sunday Base-Ball Games," *The Independent*, Aug. 29, 1889, 13; "Sunday—'Sporting'—Playing Baseball," *Albany Law Journal*, Dec. 31, 1892, 531; "Sunday Baseball," *New York Observer and Chronicle*, April 21, 1898, 528; In re Rupp, 33 App. Div. 468, 470–472 (N.Y. 1898); State v. O'Rourk, 35 Neb. 614, 592 (1892); Warren L. Johns, *Dateline Sunday, USA* (Omaha, NE: Pacific Press., 1967), 59–64.

51. "The Secular Sunday Newspaper," *New York Evangelist*, Feb. 4, 1897, 4; "Law: Sunday Newspapers," *Christian Advocate*, Nov. 21, 1889, 765; "Victims of the

Sunday Law: Many Violators Arrested, but Most of Them Are Discharged," *New York Times*, Dec. 4, 1882, 1.

52. Lindenmuller v. The People, 33 Barb. 548, 550 (N.Y. Sup. 1861); "Sunday Baseball," *New York Observer and Chronicle*, April 21, 1898, 528.

53. "Col. Ingersoll's Lecture," *New York Times*, May 17, 1880, 8; "Some Live Topics," Ingersoll, *Works*, 8:253–255; "Colonel Ingersoll on Sunday Tyranny," *The Truth Seeker*, July 29, 1893, 47–473; Manfred Jonas, "The American Sabbath in the Gilded Age," *Journal for American Studies* 6 (1961): 89–114, 102.

54. "The So-Called Freethinkers' Convention," *Christian Advocate*, Oct. 1, 1885, 632; "Pittsburg Is a Pious Town," *New York Times*, May 16, 1891, 1.

55. Lyman H. Atwater, "Civil Government and Religion," *Presbyterian Quarterly and Princeton Review* 18 (April 1876), 195, 201.

56. Statement of Joseph Cook reprinted in Jones, *Civil Government and Religion*, 73.

57. Jonas, "The American Sabbath in the Gilded Age," 94.

58. *The Right of the People to the Sunday Rest* (New York: New York Sabbath Committee, 1880), 5–7, 19; "Observance of the Sabbath," *New York Times*, May 17, 1880, 5.

59. Gaines M. Foster, *Moral Reconstruction: Christian Lobbyists and the Federal Legislation of Morality, 1862–1920* (Chapel Hill: University of North Carolina Press, 2002), 93, 96; "Women's Temperance Union," *New York Times*, Oct. 24, 1886, 10; Eric Syme, *A History of SDA Church–State Relations in the United States* (Mountain View, CA: Pacific Press, 1973), 24–31; A.H. Lewis, *A Critical History of Sunday Legislation from 321 to 1888 A.D.* (New York: D. Appleton & Co., 1888), 1; "Religious News: National Sabbath Association," *Christian Union*, Dec. 20, 1888, 733; "A Timely Movement," *Christian Advocate*, Dec. 20, 1888, 833; King, "Sunday Law in the Nineteenth Century," 706–708; Handy, *Undermined Establishment*, 72.

60. See *The American Sentinel*, March, 1886, 24; ibid., July, 1886, 56; Alonzo T. Jones, *The Two Republics, or Rome and the United States of America* (Battle Creek, MI: Review and Herald Pub. Co., 1891), 786–798, 877–895; William Addison Blakely, *American State Papers Bearing on Sunday Legislation*, rev. ed. (Washington, DC: Religious Liberty Association, 1911), 654–664, 668–675.

61. Scoles v. State, 47 Ark. 476 (1886); Parker v. State, 16 Lea. 476, 480 (Tenn. 1886).

62. In re King, 46 Fed. 905, 906 (W.D. Tenn. 1891); *The American Sentinel*, March 27, 1890, 102–103; ibid., July 10, 1890, 214; ibid., August 14, 1890, 254. The procedural history and excerpts of the case are reprinted in Alonzo T. Jones, *"Due Process of Law" and Divine Right of Dissent* (Battle Creek, MI: The National Religious Liberty Assoc., 1892), 2–8.

63. In re King, 46 Fed. at 912–915.

64. Judefind v. State, 28 At. 405, 406–407 (Md. 1894).

65. Mayor v. Linck, 12 Lea. 499, 518 (Tenn. 1883); Salter v. Smith, 55 Ga. 244 (1875); Jones, *The Two Republics*, 786–798.

66. State v. Ludwig, 21 Minn. 202, 205 (1875); Brimhall v. Van Campen, 8 Minn. 13 (1862). See also People v. Dennin, 35 Hun. 327 (N.Y. App. Div. 1885); People v. Bellet, 57 N.W. 1094 (Mich. 1894); Eden v. The People, 161 Ill. 296 (1896); State v. Powell, 50 N.E. 900 (Ohio 1898).

67. Gaines Foster, "Conservative Social Christianity, the Law, and Personal Morality: Wilber F. Crafts in Washington," *Church History* 71 (Dec. 2002): 799–819; Jonas, "The American Sabbath in the Gilded Age," 104; *New York Times*, December 6, 1888, 2; Jones, *The Two Republics*, 820–826; Alonzo T. Jones, *Civil Government and Religion, or Christianity and the American Constitution* (Chicago: American Sentinel, 1889), 65–77; Syme, *History of S.D.A. Church–State Relations*, 29–31.

68. "Senate Rest Bill," Notes of a Hearing before the Committee on Education and Labor, United States Senate, Thursday, December 13, 1888, 50th Cong., 2nd Sess., Mis. Doc. No. 43, 1, 95–96; Foster, *Moral Reconstruction*, 97–98; Foster, "Conservative Social Christianity," 803–804.

69. "Senate Rest Bill," 31, 35; Foster, *Moral Reconstruction*, 96–101.

70. "Senate Rest Bill," 73–101; *The National Sunday Law: Argument of Alonzo T. Jones before the United States Senate Committee on Education and Labor, Dec. 13, 1888* (Oakland, CA: Pacific Press Pub. Co., 1889); Jones, *Civil Government and Religion*, 43–77; Jones, *Due Process of Law*, 59–63; Elizabeth Cady Stanton, "Let the Blue Laws Rest," *Omaha Bee*, March 17, 1889, in *Selected Papers*, 5:191–194; Foster, *Moral Reconstruction*, 96–101.

71. "The Blair Sunday Bill," *American Sentinel*, April 24, 1890, 133; "The War on Senator Blair's Bill," *Truth Seeker*, Feb. 16, 1889, 104 (criticizing proponents of Sunday bill, including the Knights of Labor); "Religion in Government," ibid., March 9, 1889, 152 (on Blair Sunday bill).

72. King, "Sunday Law in the Nineteenth Century," 734–737; Edgerton v. State, 67 Ind. 588, 593 (1879); Yonoski v. State, 79 Ind. 393, 395–396 (1881).

73. Richmond v. Moore, 107 Ill. 429 (1883).

74. See Norfolk & W.R. Co. v. Commonwealth, 24 S.E. 837, 841 (Va. 1896); Read v. Boston & A.R. Co., 4 N.E. 227 (Ma. 1885); White v. Lang, 128 Mass. 598 (1880).

75. Adams v. Gay, 19 Vt. 358, 369 (1847).

76. White v. Lang, 128 Mass. 598, 599 (1880); P.W. & B.R.R. Co. v. Lehman, 56 Md. 197, 228 (1881).

77. Foster, *Moral Reconstruction*, 100–101; W.J.R. Taylor, "The Sunday Opening Question at the World's Fair," *The Independent*, Sept. 24, 1891, 13; William H. Armstrong, "Sunday at the World's Fair," *Arena* (Nov. 1891), 730.

78. "Close the Columbian Exposition on Sunday," *The Chautauquan* (Nov. 1891), 222. Other opposition came from the Epworth League (Methodist), Christian Endeavor Society, YMCA, the Good Templars, and Sons of Temperance. *The American Sentinel*, April 14, 1892, 119.

79. "The Secular Union Wakes Up," *The Truth Seeker*, March 12, 1892, 166; "The Battle Thickens over Sunday Opening," ibid., May 20, 1893, 309, 312;

Washington Post, April 7, 1892, 1. New York, New Jersey, Massachusetts, and Kentucky reportedly were considering such actions. Ibid. See also *The American Sentinel*, April 14, 1892, 119; Handy, *Undermined Establishment*, 72–76; Foster, *Moral Reconstruction*, 101–102.

80. *Washington Post*, April 7, 1892, 1; April 8, 1892, 1; April 9, 1892, 1; "Progress of Religious Legislation at Washington," *American Sentinel*, April 14, 1892, 119; ibid., April 21, 1892, 123.

81. "Sunday and the World's Fair," *The Truth Seeker*, April 16, 1892, 244

82. Quoted in Stokes, *Church and State*, 159–160; *Washington Post*, April 8, 1892, 1; "The Week in Washington," *National Tribune*, May 12, 1892, 7.

83. "Shall We Obey God's Commandment? Opinions of Senators and Representatives in Congress," *The Independent*, Jan. 8, 1891, 1–5; "The World's Fair—Shall Its Gates Be Open Sunday?," ibid., Jan. 22, 1891, 4–5.

84. 23 Cong. Rec. 5941 (July 9, 1892), and 23 Cong. Rec. 6097 (July 13, 1892). Senator Hiscock: "I have favored the closure of the Fair on Sunday. I do not mean to say that I have not been influenced by the moral considerations involved, but I have been disposed to look at this question somewhat as a business one." Ibid., 6047. Senator Call: "I am not giving this vote because Sunday is a religious day, or prescribed by religion, but because it is a civil institution." Ibid., 6052.

85. Ibid., 6051.

86. "Another Congressional Hearing," *American Sentinel*, April 7, 1892, 124; Blakely, *American State Papers*, 370–377; "The Secular Union Wakes Up," *The Truth Seeker*, March 12, 1892, 166; "Sunday and the World's Fair," ibid., April 16, 1892, 244; "Sabbath Superstition," Ingersoll, *Works*, 12:369–375; Elizabeth Cady Stanton, "Sunday at the World's Fair," *North American Review* (Feb. 1892): 254–256; Stanton, "Shall the World's Fair Be Closed on Sunday?," *Freethinkers' Magazine* (May 1893): 167–174.

87. H.R. 9710, 23 Cong. Rec. 7064–7067 (Aug. 4, 1892); *Washington Post*, Aug. 6, 1892, 1; "Sunday Opening Still Demanded," *The Independent*, Nov. 24, 1892, 15; "Sunday Closing Hearing in Washington," ibid., Jan. 19, 1893, 15; J.H. Knowles, "Sunday Closing at the World's Fair," ibid., March 23, 1893, 13.

88. Foster, *Moral Reconstruction*, 105–106.

89. "The Fair on Sundays," *New York Times*, Jan. 11, 1893, 6; "Congress and the Sunday Opening of the Fair," *Christian Advocate*, Dec. 29, 1892, 863.

90. "The Government and the Fair," *The Sun*, May 13, 1893, 6; "May Be Open Next Sunday," *New York Times*, May 24, 1893, 1; John Henry Barrows, "The World's Fair and Sunday Opening," *Christian Union*, June 10, 1893, 1123. Low attendance on Sundays led the fair directors to close the gates for two Sundays in July, only to reopen it again. "Light Attendance at the Fair," *New York Times*, July 10, 1893, 2; "Fair to Close on Sundays," ibid., July 15, 1893, 2; "Sunday Open Again," ibid., July 29, 1893, 2.

91. Blakely, *American State Papers*, 375–377; United States v. World's Columbian Exposition, 56 Fed. 630 (N.D. Ill. 1893); World's Columbian Exposition v.

United States, 56 Fed. 654 (C.A. 7th 1893); "The Fair to Be a Sunday Fair," *The Independent*, June 22, 1893, 10, "World's Fair Notes," *The Truth Seeker*, June 10, 1893, 360: "Fair Open, But Visitors Few," *New York Times*, July 31, 1893, 2.

92. John Henry Barrows, *The World's Parliament of Religions* (Chicago: Parliament Publishing, 1893); David F. Burg, *Chicago's White City of 1893* (Lexington: University of Kentucky Press, 1976).

93. Sohn, *The Man Who Hated Women*, 3–7; "The World's Fair Columbian Exposition," *Scientific American*, Sept. 9, 1893, 169.

94. Sohn, *The Man Who Hated Women*, 11–12; Werbel, *Lust on Trial*, 239; Broun and Leech, *Anthony Comstock*, 225–228; "Trouble on the Midway," *New York Times*, Aug. 6, 1893, 2.

95. Sohn, *The Man Who Hated Women*, 181–184; "No More Midway Dancing," *New York Times*, Dec. 7, 1893, 3.

96. Sohn, *The Man Who Hated Women*, 168–176. See *The Truth Seeker*, Jan. 11, 1890, 20 (listing Craddock as holding both positions); Leigh Eric Schmidt, *Heaven's Bride: The Unprintable Life of Ida C. Craddock, American Mystic, Scholar, Sexologist, Martyr, and Madwoman* (New York: Basic Books, 2010).

97. Sohn, *The Man Who Hated Women*, 3–5; Silberman, "The Perfect Storm," 338.

98. Sohn, *The Man Who Hated Women*, 176–179, 193–197; Silberman, "The Perfect Storm," 338–341; Shirley J. Burton, "Obscene, Lewd, and Lascivious: Ida Craddock and the Criminally Obscene Women of Chicago, 1873–1913," *Michigan Historical Review* 19 (Spring 1993): 1–16; "Observations," *The Truth Seeker*, Dec. 16, 1893, 793; Broun and Leech, *Anthony Comstock*, 211.

99. Burton, "Obscene, Lewd, and Lascivious," 6–7; Sohn, *The Man Who Hated Women*, 207–210.

100. "Mrs. Craddock Sentenced," *New York Times*, March 18, 1902, 7; Sohn, *The Man Who Hated Women*, 212–215, 228–231; Silberman, "The Perfect Storm," 342; Burton, "Obscene, Lewd, and Lascivious," 7; Broun and Leech, *Anthony Comstock*, 211–212.

101. "Escapes Jail by Death," *The Sun*, Oct. 18, 1902, 16; "Priestess of Yoga a Suicide," *The World*, Oct. 17, 1902, 3; "Chose Death before Prison," *New York Times*, Oct. 18, 1902, 2; Sohn, *The Man Who Hated Women*, 235–239; Broun and Leech, *Anthony Comstock*, 212; Bates, *Weeder in the Garden of the Lord*, 190–191.

102. Editorial, "Ida Craddock and Anthony Comstock," *Medico-Legal Journal* 20 (1902): 429–433.

103. Bates, *Weeder in the Garden of the Lord*, 191; "Mr. Comstock Denounced," *New York Times*, Dec. 8, 1902, 2; "Attacks Anthony Comstock," ibid., Oct. 29, 1902, 16.

104. 23 Stat. at Large 332, Chap. 164 (Feb. 26, 1885); United States v. Church of the Holy Trinity, 36 F. 303 (C.C.S.D.N.Y. 1888). Justice David J. Brewer's opinion in Church of the Holy Trinity is examined in detail in Green, *The Second Disestablishment*, 364–383, and in Steven K. Green, "Justice David Josiah Brewer and the 'Christian Nation' Maxim," *Albany Law Review* 63 (1999): 427–476.

See also Linda Przybyszewski, "Judicial Conservatism and Protestant Faith: The Case of Justice David J. Brewer," *Journal of American History* 91 (2004): 1–2, and Linda Przybyszewski, "The Religion of a Jurist: Justice David J. Brewer and the Christian Nation," *Journal of Supreme Court History* 25 (2000): 228–242; Lynford Lardner, "The Constitutional Doctrines of Justice David Josiah Brewer" (unpublished PhD dissertation, Princeton University, 1938).

105. Rector of Holy Trinity Church v. United States, at 463, 465. "The common understanding of the terms 'laborer' and 'laborers' does not include preaching and preachers, and it is to be assumed that words and phrases are used in their ordinary meaning." Ibid., 463.

106. Ibid., 465–472. "[N]o purpose of action against religion can be imputed to any legislation, state or national, because this is a religious people. This is historically true. From the discovery of this continent to the present hour, there is a single voice making this affirmation." Ibid., 465.

107. Linda Przybyszewski, "Judicial Conservatism and Protestant Faith: The Case of Justice David J. Brewer," in *Great Christian Jurists in American History*, ed. Daniel L. Dreisbach and Mark David Hall (New York: Cambridge University Press, 2019), 194.

108. Rector of Holy Trinity Church v. United States, at 465–471.

109. See Brief of the Plaintiff in Error, 4; Church of the Holy Trinity, 36 F. at 304. In one place in the opinion, Brewer quoted the First Amendment, but solely to demonstrate that the Constitution acknowledges religion. Rector of Holy Trinity Church v. United States, at 470.

110. Ibid., 465–470, 471. The opinion does note that the statute's restriction would be equally invalid against a contract to employ a Catholic priest or a Jewish rabbi. Ibid., 472.

111. David J. Brewer, "Personal Character as a Responsibility of Citizenship," *Yale Law Journal* 10 (April 1901): 229–235; David J. Brewer, "What I Have Gained from Bible Teaching," *Congregationalist and Christian World*, Dec. 3, 1904, 813. Brewer prayed for a day when "[w]e shall not be wrangling about definitions of the Trinity. . . . We shall cease striving to solve the mysteries of the Incarnation, defining the limits of the human and the divine in the one being." David J. Brewer, *The Twentieth Century from Another Viewpoint* (New York: Fleming H. Revell, Co.,1899), 35–36, 38–39, 44, 54.

112. David J. Brewer, "Women in the Professions," *The Delineator* (May 1906), 877; David J. Brewer, "Address to the Congregationalist Club of Rhode Island," n.d., box 6, folder 205, Brewer Family Papers, Yale Library. See also David J. Brewer, "Address on Women's Changed Relations to Life and Security, delivered to Women of Vasser College, Washington, DC," n.d., ibid., box 5, folder 202; David J. Brewer, "Address on Woman's Suffrage," n.d., ibid., box 5, folder 203.

113. Brewer, *The Twentieth Century from Another Viewpoint*, 50–51.

114. Ibid., 50. "Do not misunderstand me as decrying all legislation, as intimating that the state must stand indifferent to matters of vice and has no duty of protection

against its temptations. . . . Society may by statute and ordinance guard itself against the temptations and evil influences which fill these abodes of vice. But that is a minor matter. No man is reformed by a statute— made good by an ordinance. The Master taught a more excellent way." Ibid., 50–51. See also David J. Brewer, "Washburn College Address," June 16, 1883, *Topeka Daily Capital*, June 17, 1883, 5.

115. David J. Brewer, "Address at the Dedication of the New Building at the Normal School," *Emporia Gazette*, June 25, 1880, n.p.; Scrapbook II, 29, Brewer Family Papers, Yale Library.

116. David J. Brewer, *American Citizenship* (New York: Charles Scribner's Sons, 1902); David J. Brewer, *The United States a Christian Nation* (Philadelphia: John C. Winston, 1905). A similar discussion is contained in "Address to First Congregational Church," Dec. 15, 1905, Brewer Family Papers, Yale Library.

117. Brewer, *American Citizenship*, 22–23; Brewer, *A Christian Nation*, 84–85. Christian cultures were superior because they stood for "purity in the home," "business honesty and integrity," "liberty and the rights of man," "education," "the great charities and benevolences," "peace," and "temperance." Ibid., 58–64. See also David J. Brewer, "Why Do I Believe in Foreign Missions?," *American Board of Commissioners for Foreign Missions* 8 (April 1905), 7; David J. Brewer, "The Nations Safeguard," *Proceedings of the New York State Bar Association*, 16th Annual Meeting (1893), 38.

118. Brewer, "Why Do I Believe in Foreign Missions?," 7; David J. Brewer, "Jubilee Anniversary: An Address Delivered to the 50th Meeting of the American Missionary Association," Oct. 21, 1896, 8; Brewer, *American Citizenship*, 43; Brewer, *A Christian Nation*, 69.

119. Brewer, *American Citizenship*, 22; Brewer, *A Christian Nation*, 54.

120. See Lyman Abbott, "Can a Nation Have a Religion?," *The Century* (Dec. 1890): 275–281. "It is not necessary for the nation to establish a form of worship, or to proclaim its adherence to a system of theology, or to give support to a church or churches, in order to be profoundly and deeply religious." Ibid., 281.

121. Commissioners of Wyandotte County v. First Presbyterian Church of Wyandotte, 1 P. 109, 112 (Kan. 1883).

122. Brewer, *A Christian Nation*, 55–56, 61.

123. Brewer, *American Citizenship*, 21–22; David J. Brewer, "The Supreme Court Not a Sabbath-Breaking Body," *Congregationalist*, May 9, 1895, 730 (disputing NRA criticisms about the Court's reputed activities on Sundays).

124. "Trinity's Rector Not a Laborer," *Washington Post*, March 1, 1892, 2; "Pastors Are Not Laborers," *New York Times*, March 1, 1892, 9; "E. Walpole Warren, An Alien," ibid., April 12, 1892, 6; "Important Supreme Court Decisions," *The Independent*, March 10, 1892, 11; "Law: Religion in America," *Christian Advocate*, May 5, 1892, 302.

125. *Pearl of Days*, May 7, 1892, reprinted in *The American Sentinel*, May 19, 1892, 155; *The Christian Statesman*, May 7, 1892, reprinted in Blakely, *American State*

Papers, 508; "The Supreme Court Decision," *The Christian Statesman*, Nov. 19, 1892, in ibid., 509–513; J. M. Foster, *Christ the King* (Boston: James H. Earle, Pub., 1894), 256.

126. "The Secular Union Wakes Up," *The Truth Seeker*, March 12, 1892, 166; *The Jewish Tribune*, n.d. (post 1905?), Brewer Family Papers, Yale Library; "The Supreme Court and a National Religion," *American Sentinel*, April 14, 1892, 114–115; "Christianity and the Nation," ibid., April 7, 1892, 108–109; "The Christian Religion Not a Part of the Common Law of the Land," ibid., April 21, 1892, 125; "The United States Not a Christian Nation," ibid., July 7, 1892, 221–222; "A Judicial Profession of Christianity for the Nation," ibid., June 16, 1892, 187–188.

127. "Congressional Hearings," *American Sentinel*, April 2, 1892, 123; "Progress of Religious Legislation at Washington," ibid., April 14, 1892, 119.

128. 26 Cong. Rec.1374, 1430 (January 25, 1894): "We the people of the United States, devoutly acknowledging the supreme authority and just government of Almighty God in all the affairs of men and nations, grateful to Him for our civil and religious liberty, and encouraged by the assurances of His Word to invoke His guidance as a Christian nation, according to His appointed was, through Jesus Christ, in order to form a more perfect union . . . ." The introduction of various petitions can be found at 26 Cong. Rec. 1974–3247.

129. "Hearings before the House Committee on the Judiciary on H. Res 28, Proposing an Amendment to the Constitution of the United States" (March 11, 1896), 3, 5, 20, 23, 32.

130. Ibid., 5. Other specific references to Holy Trinity are found at pages 21 and 42.

131. Ibid., 11–18, 21–23, 38.

132. Abbott, "Can a Nation Have a Religion?," 275; "Jesus Christ in the Constitution," *The Independent*, March 26, 1896, 10–11; "God in the Constitution," *Washington Post*, March 12, 1896, 4.

133. Sanford H. Cobb, *The Rise of Religious Liberty in America* (New York: Cooper Square, 1902), 524–525, 527; Green, *Second Disestablishment*, 380–383.

134. Bates, *Weeder in the Garden of the Lord*, 174; Anthony Comstock, "Vampire Literature," *North American Review* (Aug. 1891): 160–171.

135. "A Case for Mr. Comstock," *Literary World*, March 7, 1885, 78; "Mr. Comstock and 'The Arabian Nights,'" *The Critic*, April 4, 1885, 161.

136. Comstock, *Traps for the Young*, 168–169.

137. "A Case for Mr. Comstock," *Literary World*, March 7, 1885, 78.

138. Webel, *Lust on Trial*, 190–203; People v. Muller, 96 N.Y. 408, 411 (1884); "The Fine Arts: Art Notes," *The Critic*, Nov. 19, 1887, 263; "Comstock's Latest Raid," *The Evening World*, Nov. 12, 1887, 1; "Mr. Comstock's Work," *New York Times*, Nov. 13, 1887, 3; Nicola Beisel, "Morals versus Art: Censorship, the Politics of Interpretation, and the Victorian Nude," *American Sociological Review* 58 (April 1993): 145–162.

139. "The Comstock Nuisance," *New York Times*, Nov. 16, 1887, 4; "Mr. Comstock's Crusade," ibid., Nov. 17, 1887, 9; Frederick Keppel, "Impure Pictures and Impure Minds," ibid., Nov. 19, 1887, 3; "Comstock's Crusade on Art," *The Sun*, March 13, 1887, 14; *Life*, Dec. 29, 1887, 374; "My Note Book," *The Art Amateur* (Jan. 1888), 28.

140. Webel, *Lust on Trial*, 192–193; "Our Art Censor," *The Evening Telegraph*, Nov. 16, 1887, 1; "Comstock's Application Denied," *New York Times*, Nov. 20, 1887, 9.

141. "A Question of Obscenity," *The World*, March 24, 1888, 1; "Against the Knoedlers," *New York Tribune*, March 4, 1888, 2; "Mr. Knoedler Pleads Guilty and Is Fined," ibid., March 27, 1888, 2; "The Knoedler Case," *New York Times*, March 24, 1888, 8.

142. "A Question of Obscenity," *The World*, March 24, 1888, 1; "Mr. Comstock's Censorship," *New York Times*, March 24, 1888, 4; Webel, *Lust on Trial*, 201–202.

143. "Society for the Suppression of Vice," *New York Evangelist*, Feb. 9, 1888, 2; "Anthony Comstock on Art," *New York Times*, Dec. 20, 1887, 1; Comstock, "Vampire Literature," 165.

144. Anthony Comstock, *Morals versus Art* (New York: J.S. Ogilvie & Co., 1887), 11–12; Webel, *Lust on Trial*, 197–200.

145. "My Note Book," *The Art Amateur*, March 1888, 81; "Comstock at Princeton," *New York Times*, March 31, 1888, 1.

146. Anthony Comstock, "Vampire Literature," *North American Review* (Aug. 1891): 160–171; Anthony Comstock, *The Independent*, March 14, 1889, 2.

147. "Comstock Not Yet Enlightened," *New York Times*, May 26, 1894, 5; "Comstock Overruled," ibid., June 22, 1894, 9; "Where Is Comstock," ibid., March 29, 1895, 4; "Comstock," ibid., Nov. 21, 1895, 4; "A Shock to Sir Anthony: His Moral Sensibilities Overcome by a Brooklyn Advertisement," ibid., Dec. 28, 1895, 8.

148. "George Bernard Shaw," *New York Times*, Sept. 21, 1905, 8; "Bernard Shaw Resents Action of Librarian," ibid., Sept. 26, 1905, 1; "Who's Bernard Shaw? Asks Mr. Comstock," ibid., Sept. 28, 1905, 9; "Shaw and Comstock," Sept. 29, 1905, 8; "Comstock at It Again," ibid., Oct 25, 1905, 1; "Comstock vs. Shaw Again," ibid., Oct. 26, 1905, 8; "Daly to Make a Fight to Give Shaw's Play," ibid., Nov. 2, 1905, 9; "Comstockery," ibid., Dec. 12, 1895, 4; Broun and Leech, *Anthony Comstock*, 229–235; Bates, *Weeder in the Garden*, 192–194.

149. "Art Students League Raided by Comstock," *New York Times*, Aug. 3, 1906, 1; Amy Werbel, "The Crime of the Nude: Anthony Comstock, the Art Students League of New York, and the Origins of Modern American Obscenity," *Winterthur Portfolio* 48 (Winter 2014): 249–282; Werbel, *Lust on Trial*, 268–272.

150. Werbel, *Lust on Trial*, 273; "Art Students Jeer at Comstock's Raid," *New York Times*, Aug. 4, 1906, 7; "Views of Comstock's Act," ibid., Aug. 4, 1906, 7; "Art Students Angry," *New York Tribune*, Aug. 4, 1906, 1;

151. "Comstock Battles with Art," *The Sun*, Oct. 15, 1906, 4; "Comstock Shouts in Court," ibid., Oct. 31, 1906, 7; "Comstock Again Has a Brick Day in Court," *New York Times*, Oct. 31, 1906, 7; "Comstock Ready to Drop Case," *New York Tribune*, Dec. 30, 1906, 10; "Comstock Still Inspector," ibid., Dec. 30, 1906, 10; "Comstock Lets Up in Art Students' Case," *The World*, Dec. 31, 1906, 5; Werbel, *Lust on Trial*, 278–279; Werbel, "Crime of the Nude," 272–273.

152. Emma Goldman, "The Hypocrisy of Puritanism," in *Anarchism and Other Essays* (New York: Mother Earth, 1910), 175–176; "The Consolidated Picture," *Mother Earth* (July 1906), in Peter Glassgold, *Anarchy! An Anthology of Emma Goldman's Mother Earth* (Washington, DC: Counterpoint, 2001), 230–232; "Anthony B. Comstock's Adventures" (Sept. 1906), ibid., 233–234; "Recent Adventures of St. Anthony" (Feb. 1907), ibid., 235–236.

153. "Press Agent, Says Comstock," *New York Times*, Jan. 27, 1910, 16; "Comstock Heckled at Labor Temple," ibid., Nov. 2, 1910, 8; "Emma Goldman Arrested," ibid., Feb. 12, 1916, 18; Emma Goldman, "The Philosophy of Atheism," in *Anarchy*, 88–93; Sohn, *The Man Who Hated Women*, 254–258; Martha Soloman, *Emma Goldman* (Boston: Twayne, 1987), 27–28.

154. Margaret Sanger, "Contraceptives or Abortion," in *Woman and the New Race* (New York: Blue Ribbon Books, 1920), 122, 129; Karen Weingarten, "The Inadvertent Alliance of Anthony Comstock and Margaret Sanger: Abortion, Freedom, and Class in Modern America," *Feminist Formations* (Summer 2010): 42–59.

155. "'Woman Rebel' Barred from Use in Mails," *The Sun*, April 4, 1914, 1; "Post Office Defied by 'Woman Rebel,'" ibid., April 14, 1914, 3; "The 'Woman Rebel' Is Indicted," ibid., Aug. 26, 1914, 7; Margaret Sanger, *An Autobiography* (New York: W.W. Norton, 1938), 110–116, 119–121; Sohn, *The Man Who Hated Women*, 269–270.

156. Sanger, *An Autobiography*, 176–177, 182; "A Sign of the Times," *New York Tribune*, May 30, 1915, 10; "Trial Sought by Mrs. Sanger," ibid., Aug. 24, 1914, 14; "Sanger Prefers Prison to Fine," ibid., Sept. 11, 1915, 14; "To Fight in Court for Birth Control," *New York Times*, Sept. 5, 1915, 8; "Disorder in Court as Sanger Is Fined," ibid., Sept. 11, 1915, 7; Sohn, *The Man Who Hated Women*, 272–273.

157. "Anthony Comstock Seriously Ill," *New York Times*, Sept. 19, 1915, 15; "Anthony Comstock Dies in His Crusade," ibid., Sept. 22, 1915, 1, 6; "Anthony Comstock's Service," ibid., Sept. 23, 1915, 12. See also "The Most Spectacular Modern Crusader," *Washington Herald*, Oct. 10, 1915, 1.

158. "Anthony Comstock," *Detroit Times*, Sept. 24, 1915, 1; Walter Hurt, "An Apostle of Obscenity Passes," *The Menace*, Oct. 2, 1915, 1; "Anthony Comstock, Vice Fighter, Dead, *The Sum*, Sept. 22, 1915, 1.

Conclusion

By the turn of the twentieth century, the combatants in the battle over whether America was a Christian nation—and thus over freethought, censorship, sexual freedom (free love), and women's rights—were exhausted. Anthony Comstock had become an object of rebuke and ridicule long before his death in 1915. The moralizing efforts of the NRA and ASU had encountered greater resistance from business and commercial interests that increasingly saw the reformers' actions as hindering economic development. With the death of Frances Willard in 1898, the WCTU stepped back from her "do everything" platform, concentrating its efforts on temperance activity.[1] On the other side, Robert Ingersoll's death in 1899 accelerated the already declining influence of the freethought movement. With Elizabeth Cady Stanton's death in 1902, the fledgling feminist movement lost its most indefatigable leader, one who believed that achieving women's equality necessitated both religious and sexual freedom. The women's suffrage movement, deprived of Stanton and then Susan B. Anthony in 1906, continued with its more cautious approach, one that did not require the denunciation of either marriage or religion. And Margaret Sanger would distance herself from her earlier radicalism as she concentrated on garnering wider acceptance of family planning and contraceptive use.[2]

Yet freethought, as an intellectual force and popular movement, was not quite on its deathbed. The American Secular Union, *The Truth Seeker* and *Free Thought Magazine*, and a hodgepodge of local, unaffiliated groups carried on the tradition. But freethought would never replicate its "golden age" after the death of Robert Ingersoll. Several factors contributed to the decline of the movement after 1900.[3]

One was something that had bedeviled freethought for decades—the inability of its leaders to put aside their quibbles and create a united, intellectually cohesive critique of organized religion. Freethinkers were a contrarian bunch who liked to disagree, often about small and insignificant matters.[4] Many of the articles that appeared in *The Truth Seeker* throughout this period fluctuated between laborious and petty critiques of religion, but provided little of intellectual substance. Freethought was chiefly a negative enterprise, exposing the errors and hypocrisy of religion but rarely advancing a comprehensive alternative to it. *The Independent* dismissed freethinkers as "loud-tongued, profane infidels" and malcontents—"[a] more ignorant set of cranks it would be difficult to find." And as the *New York Times* reported about an 1883 freethought convention, the group's platform advocated "the disproof, destruction, and removal of all errors of theological dogmas, together with all the[ir] attendant evils." This, opined the *Times*, "does not commend itself to many minds of grandeur," nor could it be "regarded as productive or useful." Despite Robert Ingersoll's and Elizabeth Cady Stanton's occasional promotion of a "religion of humanity," freethought offered little in the way of a positive alternative to religion. Aside from their differences in style, little of substance separated Ingersoll's witty critiques of religion from Bennett's caustic ones. As *The Independent* put it, "[f]rom the witty, blackguarding lecturer Ingersoll down to the dirty jailbird, D.M. Bennett, there is not to be found in the whole lot of [freethinkers] anything beyond the most superficial scholarship. It is all pretentious and conceited ignorance."[5]

Another explanation for the stagnation if not decline of the freethought movement was its inability to find an affable spokesperson to replace Robert Ingersoll. Ingersoll's death on July 21, 1899, garnered national attention. Most obituaries praised Ingersoll for his wit and oratorical skills, despite his unyielding commitment to freethought; as the *New York Times* remarked, "[s]o far as is known, the eloquent opponent of Christianity died unshaken in his agnosticism."[6] Religious journals were less forgiving, of course, with the *Baptist Courier* declaring that Ingersoll "was not only an unbeliever, but he was an open, aggressive enemy of the revealed religion of the Bible. He was the most pronounced agnostic, or, as he was most popularly known, infidel, of his generation. . . . No man in America had managed to advertise himself better than he and in a more objectionable way."[7] Commentators also declared that Ingersoll's crusade on behalf of freethought had been ineffectual. Ingersoll's "influence was [] largely that of a rhetorician rather than as a leader and inspirer of men," declared one commentator, while another added that "his influence as a denouncer of religion was with the ignorant rather than with the intelligent."[8] Although few lecturers had attracted larger or more applauding audiences, noted yet another commentator, "probably no man of commensurate power has had less real influence on the religious and ethical thought of America. . . . Nothing that Mr. Ingersoll has said or written has had any serious effect to lessen Christian faith."[9] Whether accurate or not, commentators roundly saw the "age of infidels" as coming to an end with the Great Agnostic's death.

By the early twentieth century, the public image of freethought had also changed. No longer was it led by people who emerged from the liberal Protestant or post-Transcendental tradition. Now, the public faces of freethought—which was increasingly styled as "atheism"—were the likes of Emma Goldman, Michael Mockus, and the Haymarket Square defendants: recent immigrants who willingly associated their heterodoxy with political and social radicalism. For Goldman, there was no light between her atheism and her advocacy of anarchism, labor reform, and sexual freedom.[10] In her 1916 essay in *Mother Earth*, "The Philosophy of Atheism," Goldman castigated "the absolutism of theism [with] its pernicious effects on humanity." The "philosophy of Atheism," she asserted, "expresses the expansion and growth of the human mind."[11] While dedicated freethinkers—atheists and agnostics— wistfully concurred with Goldman, their numbers were declining. According to one historian of the movement, whereas the American Secular Union boasted between forty and fifty thousand members in 1900, "ten years later it lapsed into a state of impotence from which it never recovered." After 1910, *The Truth Seeker* no longer carried notices of any meetings of the organization. "With the disappearance of the better-known personalities went the secular society itself."[12]

Instead, by then, critics increasingly associated freethought with socialism and social anarchism, if not its political version. That the most recognizable freethinkers following Ingersoll's death were Goldman, Clarence Darrow, H.L. Mencken, and Roger Baldwin (the founder of the ACLU), all of whom advocated for free speech rights for political extremists while denouncing religion. This only served to further undermine the legitimacy of the movement. For example, Darrow, a self-professed agnostic, eagerly attacked the "absurdities of the Bible" at the same time that he represented socialists (including Eugene V. Debbs), anarchists, and labor extremists in court. Mencken, the journalist and critic, went a step beyond Ingersoll to characterize religious faith as a sickness—"a chronic infection"—or a mental illness. "A man full of faith is simply one who has lost (or never had) the capacity for clear and realistic thought. He is not a mere ass; he is actually ill." Such views did not appeal to a wide audience. Popular reaction to political extremism during World War I and the subsequent Red Scare of the 1920s also damaged freethought.[13]

A final reason for the decline in organized freethought is that it lost much of its relevance. By the early twentieth century, many of the causes that freethinkers embraced and believed were inhibited by organized religion—scientific inquiry, evolution, greater artistic and intellectual freedom, and social reform—were gaining ground on their own. While many freethinkers had promoted these causes, they believed that "the fountainhead of all freedom was Freethought; that it was the only road to social progress." But greater social and economic progress, as well as a growing secularity, was occurring regardless of militant freethought. A related factor was that liberal Protestantism was able to adapt and reconcile itself with the various social, scientific, and theological challenges it faced, something that both Henry Ward Beecher and Lyman Abbott had predicted. The rise of the Social Gospel and Modernism allowed liberal Protestants and the descendants of the Free Religion Association to remain within liberal theism. Freethinkers "failed to consider they were living in an age when sectarian concentration had given way to secular diffusion." As historian Martin Marty observed, "[n]ow it was difficult to determine what to oppose."[14]

The negative image of freethought, agnosticism, and atheism persisted throughout most of the twentieth century. A handful of writers and scholars openly embraced unbelief—Mencken, John Dewey, Bertrand Russell, Carl Van Doren, and Walter Kaufman, among others—but their audience was chiefly among the educated classes. In 1927, a group of professors and students at the University of Chicago founded the Humanist Fellowship, reorganizing in 1941 as the American Humanist Association.[15] During the second Red Scare, following World War II, people eagerly embraced the idea that America was "one nation under God" while they decried "godless Communism," thus giving atheism a further black eye. Not all atheists were Communists, but all Communists were atheists, critics claimed, so the association stuck.[16] And when the US Supreme Court entered the fray in mid-century by mandating the secularity of government functions and the separation of church and state, it did not help matters that the plaintiff in the first religion-in-the-schools case,

Vashti McCollum, was an avowed freethinker. McCollum's public heterodoxy, though, paled next to that of Madalyn Murray (later Murray O'Hair), a plaintiff in the Court's 1963 decision striking down prayer and Bible readings in the public schools. Murray was an abrasive and unapologetic atheist (and a former Communist) who inherited Emma Goldman's moniker as "The Most Hated Woman in America." Murray O'Hair would go on to found the American Atheists Association, which was mired in controversy throughout her leadership, culminating in her eventual assassination by former employees.[17]

Writing at mid-century, religious sociologist Will Herberg declared the attraction of infidelity to be over. "Through the nineteenth century," Herberg wrote in 1955, "America knew the militant secularist, the atheist or 'freethinker,' as a familiar figure in cultural life, along with considerably larger numbers of 'agnostics' . . . . These still exist, of course, but their ranks are dwindling and they are becoming more and more inconspicuous." By contrast, members of the "present generation" sought a sense of "religious belonging"; they "can hardly understand the vast excitement stirred up in their day by the 'atheists' and 'iconoclasts' who vied for public attention less than a half century ago, or imagine the brash militancy of the 'rationalist' movements and publications now almost all extinct." Herberg, of course, had his own agenda of demonstrating the vibrant nature of an ecumenical American religious landscape. Still, he expressed the then prevailing attitude about the novelty of freethought. "The old-time 'village atheist' is a thing of the past." "[N]ot to identify oneself and be identified as either a Protestant, a Catholic, or a Jew is somehow not to be an American."[18]

In the late twentieth century, the nation's freethought community would replicate its earlier mistakes by splintering into several competing groups: American Atheists, American Humanist Association, the Council for Secular Humanism, and the Freedom From Religion Foundation, alongside Felix Adler's Ethical Culture Society. Yet Herberg may have spoken too soon about unbelief being a "thing of the past." While it may be inaccurate to speak today of an influential freethought *movement*, studies in the early twenty-first century indicate that a significant percentage of Americans (29%) identify as nonreligious or "nones."[19] The nation's composition of Protestants is below fifty percent for the first time since in its history. *The Truth Seeker* magazine continues publishing to this day, as does the Council for Secular Humanism's *Free Inquiry* magazine. Possibly Robert Ingersoll was on to something, after all.[20]

Anthony Comstock's Legacy

Anthony Comstock's name and his legacy as a moral crusader also fell on hard times. As discussed, Heywood Broun's and Margaret Leech's 1927 biography of Comstock, *Anthony Comstock, Roundsman of the Lord*, painted a picture of an insecure, sexually repressed, and publicity-seeking man whose notoriety far exceeded his intelligence and skills.[21] More recent studies of Comstock and his crusade have been even less flattering—Comstock was a religious fanatic, a delusional, self-appointed agent of God, and a misogynist to boot, *namely* "The Man Who Hated Women."[22] But Comstock, if anything, was a fighter, as Charles G. Trumbull's 1913 fawning biography declared. Possibly that characteristic allowed remnants of Comstock's crusade to outlive him.[23]

Prosecutors continued to use the Comstock Act's prohibition on mailing obscenity well into the twentieth century. Comstock's open-ended definition of obscenity—lewd and lascivious (sexually explicit) material that had the tendency to corrupt morals—remained the standard, derived from the 1868 British case of *Regina v. Hicklin*, which Comstock regularly cited: material that tends "to deprave and corrupt those whose minds are open to such immoral influences." Employing that standard, by the time of Comstock's death in 1915, forty-three states and the District of Columbia had statutes outlawing "lewd, obscene or indecent writings" and other materials "designed to corrupt the morals of youth." The book *Lady Chatterley's Lover* was held to be obscene, whereas James Joyce's *Ulysses* escaped the same fate thanks to heroic efforts of prominent judges Agustus Hand and Learned Hand (cousins).[24]

By mid-century, the *Hicklin* standard had come under increasing criticism from judges, scholars, and civil libertarians, leading Professor Louis Henkin to assert that "[p]rivate morals . . . and what 'corrupts' them . . . are not in the realm of reason and cannot be judged by standards of reasonableness; they ought not, perhaps, to be in the domain of government."[25] Finally, in 1957, the Supreme Court in its first modern consideration of obscenity statutes, rejected the *Hicklin* test as being both overbroad and indefinite (*Roth v. United States*). Yet the *Roth* decision was a limited victory for freedom of expression, with the Court declaring that obscenity "deals with sex in a manner appealing to prurient interest," and then dropping in a footnote that defined "prurient" in Comstockian terms: material "having a tendency to excite lustful thoughts" or "having itching, morbid, or lascivious longings."[26] Sixteen years later the Supreme Court modified that standard by defining obscenity as material which, taken as a whole, "appeals to the prurient interest . . . or depicts or describes, in a patently offensive way, sexual conduct" (*Miller v. California*). Although the *Miller* test, which remains the standard for obscenity to this day, improved on Comstock's subjective definition by considering the material "as a whole" and whether it "lacks serious literary, artistic, political, or scientific value," it continues to reflect Comstockian influences by reaffirming the concept of pruriency (inviting "lustful thoughts") and in applying local "community standards" for determining what is prurient, and therefore obscene. As recently as January 2025, officials at the Fort Worth, Texas, Modern Art Museum—acting at the behest of a county judge and local religious conservatives—removed four photographs from an exhibit by celebrated photographer Sally Mann that depict her young children naked. Even though the same photographs had been displayed in museums and exhibits for over thirty years, the local sheriff launched an investigation as to whether they are "lewd" and thus obscene. Somewhere, Anthony Comstock must be smiling.[27]

The long arm of the Comstock Act regulating access to contraceptives and abortion also extended for many years. By 1920, nineteen states had outlawed access to and information about abortion and contraceptives, with another twelve prohibiting "articles and instruments of immoral use or purpose," with several statutes employing terms like "self-pollution" and "self-abuse." Tellingly, in true Comstockian form, ten states listed their prohibitions on abortion/contraceptives and obscenity within the same statute, and even more did so in successive statutes. As an example, an Indiana law outlawed within the same sentence the sale or possession of "any obscene, lewd, indecent or lascivious book, pamphlet, . . . picture . . . photo . . . [or] instrument or article [for] indecent or immoral use or instrument or article for procuring abortion." A handful of statutes contained exceptions related to medical training, though not expressly including medical textbooks and thus leaving the legality of those in doubt. The conflation of birth control with obscenity remained common long after Comstock's death.[28]

In 1965, however, the US Supreme Court used a newly found "right to privacy" to strike down a Connecticut law making it a crime to "use any drug, medicinal article or instrument for the purpose of preventing conception." Even though the state's brief in the case tied the law's 1879 origins directly to the Comstock Act, none of the six opinions in *Griswold v. Connecticut* mentioned the Act or opined on whether the Court's decision nullified it.

The decision, however, made that portion of the Act regulating contraceptives unenforceable.[29] Eight years later, in *Roe v. Wade*, the high court declared that states could not outlaw abortion entirely and could regulate it only in limited circumstances. Again, none of the Court opinions cited to the Comstock Act, even though, as in *Griswold*, the state's brief in *Roe* cited the Comstock Act as authority for Texas's anti-abortion law. Once again, the Comstock Act appeared to be a dead letter.[30]

But, to borrow a phrase from Justice Antonin Scalia, just "[l]ike some ghoul in a late-night horror movie that repeatedly sits up in its grave and shuffles abroad, after being repeatedly killed and buried," the Comstock Act was not dead.[31] In 2022, after years of challenges to *Roe*, a Supreme Court majority reversed itself, holding that the Constitution does not recognize a right to an abortion. Rather, the conservative majority ruled in *Dobbs v. Jackson Women's Health Organization*, the ability to regulate access to an abortion, or to forbid it outright, rests with states pursuant to their plenary authority to legislate on matters regarding public health and welfare.[32]

In addition to representing a monumental shift in precedent regarding reproductive rights, the *Dobbs* decision opened the door for conservative state legislatures to enact substantial, if not total, restrictions on access to abortion, which twenty states did almost immediately. A handful of state legislatures went a step further, seeking to ban abortifacients in the form of prescription drugs that produce what are termed "medical abortions," including forbidding access to the drugs via telemedicine and through the mail. For instance, in May 2024, the Louisiana legislature enacted a law that reclassifies two common prescription drugs used to terminate a pregnancy—mifepristone and misoprostol—as controlled substances, thus criminalizing their possession or use. Finally, some laws have gone so far as to restrict people from traveling to other states to access surgical abortions or to assist someone in doing so.[33]

In 2024, the US Supreme Court heard arguments in an appeal from a lower court order enjoining the US Food and Drug Administration's approval of mifepristone, the most common drug used in medical abortions that may be sent through the mail. (Mifepristone's use had become increasingly common, accounting for approximately 50% of US abortions in 2020.[34]) The Comstock Act played a prominent role in the briefing and arguments before the Court. In their brief, the challengers, a group of doctors opposed to abortion, cited to the Comstock Act in three places, identifying it by its name. They argued that the FDA's approval of the drug and its distribution through the mail violated the Act's prohibition on shipping "any drug . . . designed, adapted, or intended for producing abortion."[35] Whereas the challengers' references to the Comstock Act were pro forma, briefs of supportive friends of the court praised the law, even when acknowledging its less than stellar reputation.[36] Two of the Court's more conservative members, Justices Clarence Thomas and Samuel Alito, referred to the Comstock Act favorably in their questioning, with Justice Thomas bluntly challenging the attorney representing mifepristone's manufacturer that "mailing your product and advertising it would violate the Comstock Act."[37] The possibility of breathing new life into the Comstock Act caused a public outrage in the press, with the *Washington Post* calling on Congress to repeal the Act.[38] Conservative advocacy groups such as the Heritage Foundation, on the other hand, praised the Act, though their analysis generally ignored Comstock's religious agenda, which had been so central to its enforcement. Regardless of one's perspective about the issue, Americans were refamiliarizing themselves with Anthony Comstock after more than one hundred years.[39]

The Christian Nation Debate

In a related vein, journalists, scholars, and progressive groups have documented the resurgence of a Christian nationalist movement in the early twenty-first century. The idea that America was a Christian nation was relatively widespread in the late nineteenth century, though what exactly people meant by it was always fuzzy. Despite Justice Brewer's bold declarations, few people— including Justice Brewer himself—were interested in taking that idea to its logical conclusions by enacting legislation to legally enforce Christian doctrine. Thus, efforts to enact a national Sabbath law and national school prayer law—the two Blair bills—failed to gain traction, as did a national divorce law. Because late nineteenth-century culture was already imbued with a strong Protestant ethos, many people believed additional laws were unnecessary. But people had also raised concerns about the ineffectiveness (and hypocrisy) of enacting such laws.[40]

Since the 1960s, however, religious and political conservatives have decried the growing secularism of American culture. A small but influential number of evangelical writers began to resurrect the idea of America as a Christian nation.[41] The Reagan-era "Religious Right" became a home for people espousing versions of Christian nationalism, with the movement advocating a "return" to Christian moral values through such mechanisms as restoring prayer and Bible reading in the public schools or restricting abortion access and protections for the LGBTQ+ community. That impulse gained momentum in the new century in response to ongoing cultural shifts that distressed religious conservatives: declining church membership, increased immigration, a breakdown in traditional gender roles, acceptance of gay marriage and LGBTQ+ rights, and the growth of online pornography. As scholars and journalists have documented, the Christian nationalism impulse of the twenty-first century is more militant and reactionary than its antecedents, as demonstrated by the January 6, 2021, insurrection at the US Capitol, which had strong Christian nationalist elements. One manifestation of this new form of Christian nationalism—besides restricting reproductive rights, as discussed above—has been renewed efforts to censor information that is not obscene but challenges older moral visions of human and family relationships and long-accepted renditions of the nation's history. So religious conservatives have sought, with some degree of success, to ban books in libraries and teaching materials in public schools that discuss evolutionary theory, sex education, LGBTQ+ rights, and so-called critical race theory. Efforts to reinstate prayer and Bible reading in the public schools persist. And the high court has upheld the government's ability to use religious rhetoric and symbolism—for example, legislative prayer, crosses, Ten Commandments monuments—even if that use reflects a distinctly Christian perspective. The political and legal campaign to guarantee America's Christian nationhood has not subsided.[42]

The Comstock Act and the religious impulses behind it were not quite dead after all, as much as freethinkers might have wished otherwise. The persistence of this impulse as it relates to censorship and the contraction of reproductive and LGBTQ+ rights should invite us to examine our past so as not to repeat our earlier mistakes.

NOTES

1. Epstein, *The Politics of Domesticity,* 145,
2. See Linda Gordon, *Woman's Body, Woman's Right: A Social History of Birth Control in America* (New York: Grossman, 1976), 221, 228; Joan M. Jensen, "The Evolution of Margaret Sanger's Family Limitation Pamphlet, 1914–1921," *Signs* 6 (Sept. 1981): 548–567.

3. D.S. Phelan, "The Limitations of Freethinking," *North American Review* (Sept. 1883): 287–295; Jacoby, *Freethinkers*, 262–263.

4. Warren, *American Freethought*, 228.

5. "The New University," *The Independent*, Aug. 31, 1882, 16–17; "The Rochester Freethinkers," *New York Times*, Sept. 3, 1883, 4; Marty, *The Infidel*, 179–185.

6. "Robert G. Ingersoll Dead," *New York Times*, July 22, 1899, 3. "Chronicling America," the Library of Congress's online database, lists approximately one thousand newspaper stories about Ingersoll's death within the first three months.

7. *The Baptist Courier*, July 27, 1899, 1.

8. Edward M. Chapman, "Robert G. Ingersoll, Theologian," *The Forum* (Sept. 1912): 339–353; *The Independent*, July 27, 1899, 2035–2036; "Mourned in Washington," *Washington Evening Times*, July 22, 1899, 2.

9. "Robert G. Ingersoll," *Outlook*, July 29, 1899, 696–698.

10. Jacoby, *Freethinkers*, 233; Solomon, *Emma Goldman*, 52–54.

11. Emma Goldman, "The Philosophy of Atheism," in *Anarchy*, 88–93.

12. Warren, *American Freethought*, 175; Jacoby, *Freethinkers*, 263.

13. Jacoby, *Freethinkers*, 227–246; Clarence Darrow, "Why I Am an Agnostic," and "Absurdities of the Bible," in *The Essential Words and Writings of Clarence Darrow*, ed. Edward J. Larson and Jack Marshall (New York: The Modern Library, 2007), 18–21, 84–88; H.L. Mencken, *Prejudices, Third Series* (New York: Alfred A. Knopf, 1922), 267–268; Mencken, *Prejudices, Fourth Series* (New York: Alfred A. Knopf, 1924), 65–76. See also H.L. Mencken, *Treatise on the Gods* (New York: Alfred A. Knopf, 1930).

14. Warren, *American Freethought*, 228–229; Marty, *The Infidel*, 143–144, 170–176, 179–180; Hutchinson, *The Modernist Impulse*, 111–184.

15. S.T. Joshi, *Atheism: A Reader* (Amherst, NY: Prometheus Books, 2000), 60–65, 87–94, 209–215, 216–226, 250–259; John Dewey, *A Common Faith* (New Haven, CT: Yale University Press, 1932); https://americanhumanist.org/about/our-history/.

16. Jacoby, *Freethinkers*, 308–313; Kevin M. Kruse, *One Nation under God: How Corporate America Invented Christian America* (New York: Basic Books, 2015), 106–107.

17. McCollum v. Board of Education, 333 U.S. 203 (1948); Vashti McCollum, *One Woman's Fight* (Garden City, NY: Doubleday, 1951), 9–11 (McCollum preferred to call herself a humanist rather than an atheist); Curlett v. Murray, 374 U.S. 203 (1963); Green, *The Third Disestablishment*, 134–135, 274–275; Jacoby, *Freethinkers*, 313–314; Bryan F. La Beau, *The Atheist: Madalyn Murray O'Hair* (New York: New York University Press, 2003), 1, 307–321; https://www.mysanantonio.com/news/local/article/true-crime-SA-kidnapping-murder-Madalyn-OHair-11017782.php.

18. Will Herberg, *Protestant—Catholic—Jew* (New York: Anchor Books, 1955, 1960), 46–47, 257–260.

19. https://www.pewresearch.org/religious-landscape-study/.

20. Martin E. Marty, *Varieties of Unbelief* (New York: Holt, Reinhart, and Winston, 1964). See *The Truth Seeker*, https://thetruthseeker.net/; https://secularhuman ism.org/.

21. Broun and Leech, *Anthony Comstock*.

22. Sohn, *The Man Who Hated Women*; Werbel, *Lust on Trial*; Bates, *Weeder in the Garden of the Lord*.

23. Trumbull, *Anthony Comstock*.

24. Regina v. Hicklin, L.R. 3 Q.B. 360, 371 (1868); Knowles v. United States, 170 F. 409 (8th Cir., 1909); Commonwealth v. DeLacey, 271 Mass. 327 (1930); Commonwealth v. Isenstadt, 318 Mass. 543 (1945); United States v. One Book called "Ulysses," 72 F.2d. 705 (2nd Cir. 1934); J.C. Ruppenthal, "Criminal Statutes on Birth Control," *Journal of the American Institute of Criminal Law and Criminology* 10 (1919): 48–61; Leo M. Alpert, "Judicial Censorship of Obscene Literature," *Harvard Law Review* 52 (1938): 40–76.

25. Alpert, "Judicial Censorship of Obscene Literature"; Harry Klavern Jr., "The Metaphysics of the Law of Obscenity," *Supreme Court Review* (1960): 1–45; Louis Henkin, "Morals and the Constitution: The Sin of Obscenity," *Columbia Law Review* 63 (1963): 391, 407; Andrew Koppelman, "Does Obscenity Cause Moral Harm?," *Columbia Law Review* 105 (2005): 1635–1679.

26. Roth v. United States, 354 U.S. 476, 487, n.20 (1957).

27. Miller v. California, 413 U.S. 15, 24 (1973); Koppelman, "Does Obscenity Cause Moral Harm?," 1639–1641; https://fortworthreport.org/2025/01/09/photos-removed-from-fort-worth-museum-as-police-investigate-child-pornography-alle gations-2/; https://theconversation.com/seizure-of-sally-manns-photographs-in-texas-revives-old-debates-about-obscenity-and-freedom-of-expression-247 321?utm.

28. Ruppenthal, "Criminal Statutes on Birth Control," 52–61.

29. Griswold v. Connecticut, 381 U.S. 479 (1965), Brief for Appellee, 7, 14.

30. Roe v. Wade, 410 U.S. 113 (1973), Brief of Appellee, 55–56.

31. Lamb's Chapel v. Center Moriches Free Union School District, 508 U.S. 389, 398 (1993) (Scalia, J., dissenting).

32. Dobbs v. Jackson Women's Health Organization, 597 U.S. 215 (2022).

33. https://www.guttmacher.org/2023/12/state-policy-trends-2023-first-full-year-roe-fell-tumultuous-year-abortion-and-other; https://reproductiverights.org/maps/state/texas/. See Yellowhammer Fund v. Marshall, 2025 WL 959948 (M.D. Ala. March 31, 2025), holding that the State of Alabama cannot criminally prosecute people for traveling out-of-state to secure an abortion in another state.

34. https://www.guttmacher.org/article/2022/02/medication-abortion-now-accou nts-more-half-all-us-abortions.

35. See Respondents' Brief in Opposition to Petition for Certiorari, in U.S. Food and Drug Administration v. Alliance for Hippocratic Medicine, nos. 23–235, 23–236, 3, 8, 49.

36. See Amicus Brief of Ethics and Policy Center, in Support of Respondents, nos. 23–235, 23–236, 6; Amicus Brief for Former US Attorney General Edwin Meese, in Support of Respondents, nos. 23–235, 23–236, 17–29; Brief of Amicus Curiae Women Injured by Abortion, in Support of Respondents, nos. 23–235, 23–236, 28; Brief of Amicus Curiae Heartbeat International, in Support of Respondents, nos. 23–235, 23–236, 20.

37. "Supreme Court Abortion Case Brings 19th Century Chastity Law to the Forefront," CNN, March 29, 2024, at https://www.cnn.com/2024/03/29/polit ics/comstock-act-alito-thomas-abortion/index.html. On June 13, 2024, in FDA v. Alliance for Hippocratic Medicine, no. 23–235, the Court held that the plaintiff doctors lacked standing (i.e., a particularized injury) that enabled them to bring the lawsuit, and it dismissed the case. The question about the authority of the Comstock Act remained alive for another legal challenge.

38. "The 150-Year-Old Comstock Act Could Transform the Abortion Debate," *The Smithsonian*, June 15, 2023, at https://www.smithsonianmag.com/history/ comstock-act-transform-abortion-debate-180982363/; Editorial, "Repeal the Comstock Act Before the GOP Tries Using It to Ban Abortion," *Washington Post*, April 2, 2024, at https://www.washingtonpost.com/opinions/2024/04/ 02/comstock-act-abortion-trump-alito-thomas/; "Why Anti-Abortion Groups Are Citing the Ideas of a 19th-Century 'Vice Reformer,'" NPR, April 18, 2023, at https://www.npr.org/2023/04/18/1170371877/abortion-pill-mifeprist one-judge-comstock; Gillian Frank, "Resurrection of 'Comstock Laws' Would Threaten Access to Abortifacients—But Even That Fear Misses the Bigger Picture," *Religion Dispatches*, April 16, 2024, https://religiondispatches.org/ resurrection-of-comstock-laws-would-threaten-access-to-abortifacients-but-even-that-fear-misses-bigger-picture/?utm_source=email&utm_campaign= weekly.

39. https://www.heritage.org/life/report/the-justice-department-wrong-federal-law-does-prohibit-mailing-abortion-drugs. The Heritage Foundation's *Project 2025, Mandate for Leadership*, expressly calls for renewed enforcement of the Comstock Act on page 562 of the report; see https://static.project2025.org/ 2025_MandateForLeadership_FULL.pdf; Steven K. Green, "What a Turn-of-the-Century Anti-Abortion and Contraception Crusader Reveals about GOP Efforts to Ban Abortion Pills by Mail," *Religion Dispatches*, Aug. 2, 2022, https:// religiondispatches.org/what-a-turn-of-the-century-anti-abortion-and-contra ception-crusader-reveals-about-gop-efforts-to-ban-abortion-pills-by-mail/.

40. See discussion in chapter 6, supra.

41. See Julie J. Ingersoll, *Building God's Kingdom: Inside the World of Christian Reconstruction* (New York: Oxford University Press, 2015);

42. Andrew L. Whitehead and Samuel L. Perry, *Taking America Back for God: Christian Nationalism in the United States* (New York: Oxford University Press, 2020); David Rosen, "Banned in America!," *Church and State* (Jan. 2024): 6–10; "Christian Nationalism Rising," ibid. (Dec. 2023): 4–9; Town of Greece

v. Galloway, 572 U.S. 575 (2014); American Legion v. American Humanist Association, 588 U.S. 29 (2019); Van Orden v. Perry. 545 U.S. 677 (2005); Caroline Mala Corbin, "The Supreme Court's Facilitation of White Christian Nationalism," *Alabama Law Review* 71 (2020): 834–866; Steven K. Green, "The Legal Ramifications of Christian Nationalism," *Roger Williams University Law Review* 26 (2021): 430–494.

Index

For the benefit of digital users, indexed terms that span two pages (e.g., 52–53) may, on occasion, appear on only one of those pages.